Backstage in the Novel

Winner of the Walker Cowen Memorial Prize
for an outstanding work of scholarship
in eighteenth-century studies

Backstage in the Novel
Frances Burney and the Theater Arts

Francesca Saggini

Translated by Laura Kopp

University of Virginia Press

Charlottesville and London

University of Virginia Press

Printed in the United States of America on acid-free paper

First published 2012

1 3 5 7 9 8 6 4 2

Library of Congress Cataloging-in-Publication Data
Saggini, Francesca.
[Messinscena dell'identita. English]
Backstage in the novel : Frances Burney and the theater arts / Francesca Saggini ;
translated by Laura Kopp.
p. cm.
Includes bibliographical references and index.
ISBN 978-0-8139-3254-5 (cloth : alk. paper) — ISBN 978-0-8139-3264-4 (e-book)
1. Burney, Fanny, 1752–1840—Criticism and interpretation. 2. English fiction—
18th century—History and criticism. 3. Performing arts in literature.
4. Theater in literature. I. Title.
PR3316.A4Z7713 2012
823'.6—dc23

2011045975

For Mirella

Lady Smatter. I love criticism passionately, though it is really laborious Work, for it obliges me to read with a vast deal of attention. I declare I am sometimes so immensely fatigued with the toil of studying for faults and objections, that I am ready to fling all my Books behind the Fire.

—Frances Burney, *The Witlings*

Contents

Acknowledgments

Writing a book is like undertaking a long journey through a changing landscape. Progress brings a distillation of experiences, memories, questions, and research—leading both inward and outward. Writing this book, through all of the various shapes it assumed as I traveled from one stage to the next, reached one turn after another, and shifted from viewpoint to viewpoint, has taken me almost fifteen years. It is the result of a complex process of inquiry and research that led from an analysis of the eighteenth-century novel to that of the multilayered contexts in which the novel is situated, and from the apparent bi-dimensionality of the written page to the multiple perspectives and codes of the performed text. Along the way, I paused at a succession of rest stops, engaging with the dimensions of performativity, of textual pragmatics, of urban studies, of iconography, and, finally, of the many forms and manifestations of culture, including popular culture and, especially, those counter-canonical cultural forms that have not been assimilated into canonical discourse or that have been repressed by it.

I would like to express my heartfelt thanks to those institutions that have generously given this study their direct support, moral and financial, through its various seasons and mutations. In 2005, the Accademia Nazionale dei Lincei graciously awarded its "Mario di Nola" prize for the best Italian work of literary, philosophical, and historical scholarship to the original shorter Italian version of this book, *La messinscena dell'identità. Teatro e teatralità nel romanzo inglese del Settecento.* Among the members of the Accademia dei Lincei, I cannot but recall with the highest esteem Arnaldo Pizzorusso, renowned *dix-huitiémiste,* and Marcello Pagnini, the late and greatly missed master scholar of literature. My respectful thanks also to the University of Virginia Press, and particularly to the patrons of the Walker Cowen Memorial Prize, who in 2005 took on the challenge of selecting for this prestigious international award an obscure book published in Italy, giving it the chance to begin a second life in a new, more polished form and a different language. The University of Virginia Press has given me a safe haven in difficult times, and for this I express my thanks to Penelope Kaiserlian and Angie Hogan, with deepest appreciation for their patience and understanding.

I would also like to thank the Università degli Studi della Tuscia and Gaetano Platania, then the dean of the Facoltà di Lingue e Letterature Straniere di Viterbo, for granting me a short leave of absence during which I completed the revision of two central chapters of this book.

For her impeccable contribution as translator, adviser, and friend, and for her solid interactive feedback on all of Burney's various facets, my deep thanks to Laura Kopp. Without her linguistic wizardry and editorial expertise this manuscript would never have come to fruition, in this or another form. If her magic wand has not made every error disappear, the fault is entirely my own. Finally, I thank the global community of the Burney Society, and particularly Peter Sabor, whose meticulous scholarship allowed me to open the secret door to Frances Burney, dramatist, as long ago as 1995.

Backstage in the Novel: Frances Burney and the Theater Arts is the result of a complex process of revision and updating of *La messinscena dell'identità.* Two early versions of brief portions of this study—worded differently, significantly shorter, and making less extensive arguments—appeared as "Miss Ellis and the Actress: For a Theatrical Reading of *The Wanderer,*" in *A Celebration of Frances Burney,* edited by Lorna Clark (Newcastle: Cambridge Scholar Publishing, 2007), and as "Teaching *Evelina* as a Dramatic Text," in *Teaching British Women Playwrights of the Restoration and Eighteenth Century,* edited by Bonnie Nelson and Catherine Burroughs (New York: MLA Press, 2010).

My debts to my family are too numerous to list, here or elsewhere, especially to loved ones who are no longer with us. The same holds for my teachers, who over the course of twenty years, from Florence to Pescara and from Viterbo to Glasgow, must have discovered to their chagrin how very difficult it is to transmit even the most consolidated knowledge if the vessel into which it is decanted is flawed.

Having reached the end of a journey in which the human element has been no less important than the research, my most affectionate thoughts turn, for her lucidity, her sincere affection, and her inexhaustible capacity for communicating her passion for study to others, to my mentor—and, I have the honor to say, my friend—Mirella Billi. Many years ago, when I was her doctoral student, Mirella gave me a priceless pearl of advice, which I have treasured ever since: "The context, Saggini, the context!" It is therefore to Mirella and her fateful prescription that I dedicate this work with the deepest gratitude.

Abbreviations

CP	*The Complete Plays of Frances Burney*
DL	*The Diaries and Letters of Madame D'Arblay*
ED	*The Early Diary of Frances Burney, 1768–1778*
EJL	*The Early Journals and Letters of Fanny Burney*
JL	*The Journals and Letters of Fanny Burney (Madame D'Arblay), 1791–1840*

Backstage in the Novel

Introduction
A Wide Angle on the Muses

In Britain, the novel emerged as a new genre in the context of sweeping social, political, and economic changes that also had a strong impact on the theater. But whereas the theater of the Restoration has been the subject of informed historical studies focusing on its ideological, social, and even sexual components, the theater of the eighteenth century has received only recent attention and less systematic treatment. Still a secondary field of research, its restrictive confines remain the preserve of relatively few specialists. This is particularly the case where the theater's close ties to the novel are concerned. Here, the full range and complexity of a once dense transtextual layering have become so imperceptible as to take on the quality of an ever more elusive haunting.[1]

Viewed from a synchronic perspective, however, the affinities between the eighteenth-century novel and the theater, whether on cultural, social, or economic grounds, become immediately apparent. The genres shared the same audience and were bound by a thick web of intertextual references—some explicit, others covert—that today can be grasped only by readers (and spectators) equipped with a high level of literary competence but that were readily identified and understood at the time. Novels contained frequent references to plays, as is attested by the various overt or implicit references to the drama in *Tom Jones, The Female Quixote, The Vicar of Wakefield,* and many other novels. However, the theater was just as indebted to the novel. In discussing one of his most famous comedies, *The Jealous Wife,* the successful midcentury playwright George Colman expressed his debt to Fielding this way: "The Use that has been made in this comedy of *Fielding's* admirable Novel of *Tom Jones,* must be obvious to the most ordinary reader."[2] Colman himself evoked the inextricable commingling of—and experimentation with—the rapidly evolving genres of the novel, the romance, and the drama in the title of the printed version of his farce *Polly Honeycombe* (Drury Lane, 1760), a light satire against novel reading. The subtitle he gave to the publication is an allusive hybrid, entirely symptomatic of the current context: *Polly Honeycombe: A Dramatick Novel of One Act.*

If we next turn our attention from the mixing of genres, modes, and media to the issue of reception, the first thing to note is the well-known fact that eighteenth-century audiences identified with the characters and situations in plays—and later, in novels—often developing strong attachments to particular protagonists. This high degree of involvement and appreciation was expressed, for example, in the subgenre of literary Quixotism, whose many variants, from Charlotte Lennox's Arabella (*The Female Quixote* [1752]) to Jane Austen's Catherine Morland (*Northanger Abbey* [published in 1818]), to mention only the most famous, continued to flourish well beyond the turn of the next century. Sympathetic participation reflected an economy of appropriation that worked simultaneously on the levels of identification, critique, and possession. While the new affective aesthetics that came into vogue during the century (in the wake of Adam Smith's influential theory of the sympathizing imagination in *The Theory of Moral Sentiments* [1759]) allowed readers to recognize themselves in fictional characters and respond deeply to them, the same readers would also debate the merits of the characters' conduct "as if they had been living friends"—in J. E. Austen-Leigh's famous phrase—and would articulate their preferences in ways that revealed their sensibility and moral refinement or exposed their lack of such qualities.[3] Furthermore, in a society that had witnessed a spectacular rise in conspicuous consumption, the book (and the theatrical performance via its metonymy, the admission ticket) took on all of the attributes of an indispensable material possession, the necessary complement to a fully rounded social—and, to a lesser extent, cultural—life that could be bought, owned, read (or attended), and circulated.

As readers exchanged opinions, theories, and anxieties about the events shaping their favorite literary characters' lives, the characters in novels reproduced this intense self-reflexive circulation: they compared themselves to characters in plays and turned to them for comfort and guidance, even appropriating them by writing detailed critiques and reviews that reflected the aesthetics of the time. This fascinating transtextual dialogue can be seen as a genuine meta-literary "embedding" fraught with gender, class, and social implications.[4] Pamela, for example, compiles an impeccable notebook on the theater, recording her reflections as an exemplary newcomer to society, and Samuel Richardson, who was always attuned to the market's tastes, apparently considered publishing the notebook as an independent volume. Similarly, the histrionic Lovelace repeatedly compares his captive Clarissa's situation to that of Nicholas Rowe's betrayed Calista, while Sophia Western's reflections on her own situation lead her to empathize deeply with the fate of the unfortunate Isabella, the heroine of a late-seventeenth-century pathetic tragedy: "Poor Sophia, alone and melancholy, sat reading a tragedy. It was *The Fatal Marriage,* and she was now come to that part where the poor distressed Isabella disposes of her wedding ring. Here the book dropped from her hand, and a shower of tears ran down into her bosom."[5]

I would thus concur with Robert Noyes, who has devoted two meticulous studies to unearthing evidence of the theater in the early novel, that this lively meta-literary dialogue between texts and between characters reveals "the interrelation of the arts in the nexus of a culture which was more highly unified than that of today. It was an age when the arts of fiction and drama were closely allied and mutually influential. Novels and dramas reflected the same literary fashions . . . and both made use of the same kind of characters."[6]

In my view, however, an analysis of the interaction between the theater and the novel in the eighteenth century needs to move beyond identifying the many intertextual links between the genres and compiling lists of the mnestic traces inscribed in the hypertexts, or secondary texts.[7] Such an approach, no matter how learned or intriguing, often yields little more than an interesting compilation of quotations, allusions, and borrowings and cannot fully illuminate the complex cultural dynamics at work in a given period. The mapping of textual traces can instead serve as the starting point for a metatextual and intersemiotic investigation into the eighteenth-century novel, an interdisciplinary critical approach most useful, in the case of this study, when closely tied to an analysis of literary praxis and of the forms of the novel, especially in light of the theories of reception and of the role of the reader that underpinned eighteenth-century cultural consumption. Textual comparison and cultural contextualization are therefore the first step toward the main objective I have in view here: that of examining how the novel renders the dramatic text into narrative through what we might call a transmodal adaptation of seventeenth- and eighteenth-century plays. This kind of close analysis can provide a more comprehensive mapping of the extensive transtextual discourse of the hypertexts.[8]

For the novel and the play did share similar formal and structural features. Many novels had the same basic structure as contemporary comedies, their protagonists a pair of young lovers kept apart by an assortment of familial or financial obstacles that were invariably resolved in the happy ending. Assured of this habitual and comforting denouement, audience members, like the nobleman from Madrid in Colman's *Polly Honeycombe,* could awaken from their hearty slumbers in the theater's boxes, trusting to the formulaic inevitability of the comic *fabula:* "How now? Gentlemen! What? Is it OVER then? Are the Actors MARRIED?"[9] The plot device of lost, forged, or intercepted letters, so frequent in eighteenth-century novels, is equally common in the century's plays, as are fortuitous reunions with long-lost parents who reappear providentially to bless the concluding nuptials. From a formal standpoint, finally, eighteenth-century novels make extensive use of dialogue, and their diegetic progression tends to coincide with the progression of the narrative, demonstrating how close the novel's diegesis is to the direct mimesis of the drama.

On the level of narrative discourse, a close semiotic analysis of several textual passages allows me to show how the physical description of characters is just as significant: not only their facial expressions and body posture (or kinesics) but also their spatial (or proxemic) relations are always specified, and dialogue is often accompanied by paralinguistic notation such as dashes and exclamation marks. Toward the end of the eighteenth century, furthermore, especially in relation to the rhetoric of the passions staged by the Gothic, novels devote much more space to the description of emotions and powerful feelings. The characters' affective reactions, as expressed through their movements and gestures, are carefully noted in the text, now recoded as an outright semiotic score through which the author directs—one might even say arranges as a *mise en scène*—the reader's "mental" visualization of them.

Finally, where communications networks and textual pragmatics are concerned, it should be noted that the social context of theatrical reception was re-created in the common practice of reading novels aloud in the family circle or at social gatherings. This thoroughly performative activity in a domestic or private setting—which hinged on imaginative evocation and on the current of sentimental empathy running among reader, audience, and fictional characters—had taken on a new resonance by the end of the eighteenth century, with the Romantic resurgence of closet drama. At this time, some of the greatest contemporary actors (among them Sarah Siddons) began to offer enthralling and impassioned dramatic readings both in prose and in verse, often for public rather than private consumption.[10] The link between oratory, acting, and reading for an audience had been evident and entirely intentional from the start, as I suggest in chapters 2 and 3, in relation to the reading aloud of excerpts from Frances Burney's fiction and drama. As these episodes show, during domestic reading sessions the reader imitated the rhetorical and performance conventions employed by actors on stage. Like actors, readers presented themselves to their (arguably playgoing) audiences as embodiments of a multiple sign system composed of emotive, linguistic, gestural, and rhetorical signs. As a result, even a reading within a select coterie was invested with a public, ideological function. This was all the more the case in play reading, exemplified in chapter 3 by Charles Burney's reading of Frances's play *The Witlings* (1779). This authoritative, and in many ways paradigmatic, instance of a *pater legens* reminds us that even when novel and play reading took place in a purely domestic context, it nevertheless showed all of the characteristics of a performance. The skillful Shakespearean reading offered by Henry Crawford in Austen's *Mansfield Park* should therefore be understood as the sign and symptom par excellence of a widespread performative practice shared by the Burney family, as well. It can thus be argued that the eighteenth-century novel was a hybrid genre, an intersemiotic form with strong dramatic characteristics, in which narrative mimesis is often coupled with (and just as often replaced by) theatrical display.

It is also true that this interplay of influences and intersections between distinct arts and codes was not unidirectional and instead involved a complex two-way dialogue. We must not forget that the Licensing Act of 1737 and the onset of preventive censorship affected the careers of many authors, redefining and redirecting their efforts away from the theater. This was true of Eliza Haywood and, later, of Henry Fielding, whose last stage productions—the notorious satires *Pasquin* and *The Historical Register,* performed at the Little Theatre in the Haymarket in 1737—contributed to irritating the sensibilities of Prime Minister Robert Walpole and his colleagues. Other authors, such as Samuel Johnson and Tobias Smollett, were similarly affected by censorship and were forced to turn from the stage to the page.[11] We thus find that in recent amendments to the literary canon, the disputed title of "first novel" is often awarded to one or the other of two works by Aphra Behn, who was primarily a playwright: *Oroonoko* (1688), one of her final works, and the slightly earlier *Love-Letters between a Nobleman and His Sister* (ca. 1684).[12] If, therefore, we can say that in the course of the eighteenth century the novel was increasingly becoming more theatrical, then due to the wide circulation of plays in print, the drama itself sought a corresponding "textualization." To quote Marcello Pagnini, "The 'written text' becomes 'spoken text,' and the 'spoken text' becomes part of the 'stage text.'"[13]

In light of these underlying contextual premises, I aim to examine the work of Frances Burney (1742–1840) by activating two methodological lines of inquiry. The first consists of establishing an open dialogue that I would call "holistic" and "plural" (in the Barthesian sense) with a number of eighteenth-century literary-cultural formations.[14] These I read—or, better, reread—anti-hierarchically and as correlated rather than discrete. As a direct consequence, the wide angle of cultural reassessment inevitably comes to focus on the figure of the reader, as well. In the second line of inquiry, I therefore turn to the emblematic case of Frances Burney, a highly versatile and successful author, but also—and this is crucial to my critical approach—an avid reader who kept abreast of the latest publications, as her many autobiographical writings attest. Burney is precisely the kind of subject, simultaneously critical and authorial, whom I would not hesitate to define (in a phrase from our contemporary critical lexicon) as a "transitive user" of the texts she read. In her engagement with literary texts, forms, and models, and in her active reworking of these into her novels and plays, Burney takes on the status of a writerly reader, a reader who is active and in control, equipped with a productive mode of using the text.[15]

The next and final step is to bring this theoretical and methodological approach to bear on textual practice. In my reading, the kind of creative consumption that Burney stages in her double, overlapping roles of reader-author and author-reader requires that we project the cultural material she produced (the novel, the drama) onto the source texts of which she offers a dynamic re-actualization. In terms of an archaeology of the text, this means that the study of a writer in relation to the broad spectrum of the arts with which her work enters into open dialogue prompts a creative recovery of what lies sub-textually *in potentia* from underneath what is textually *in actu.* Retracing the explicit and implicit transtextuality of a text—and of an entire literary corpus—in this way can thus actualize (or, rather restore) to a text and to a macro-text the "semantic potential," in Marco de Marinis's words, that historiography and the politics of the canon often have muffled and suppressed.[16] In sum, this study of Burney's work across the arts aims to restore to the author's whole corpus (drama, fiction, and nonfiction prose) that depth—perhaps that three-dimensionality—that characterized it originally but that has been obscured through the decades by successive waves of fiction-oriented critical discourse.

Two closely related developments have prompted me to examine the work of Frances Burney within this co-textual framework linking eighteenth-century drama and the novel. The publication in 1995 of Burney's *Complete Plays,* four comedies and four tragedies—among which only *Edwy and Elgiva* was performed once during the author's lifetime—has sparked great interest in the dramatic works of an author long considered primarily a successful novelist and diarist.[17] Margaret Anne Doody's pioneering recognition of Burney as a playwright has thus borne fruit and has also recently been endorsed by the authoritative *Cambridge Companion to Frances Burney,* a critical collection that, besides providing the usual introduction to the novels, offers the general reader for the first time a substantial chapter on "Burney as Dramatist."[18] One might say, therefore, that this increased interest in the comedies and tragedies written by Burney between 1779 and 1802 has opened a new phase in the process of reappraising the author's opus that began as long ago as 1832 with the publication of the *Memoirs of Doctor Burney,* followed in 1842 by the letters and journals edited by Charlotte Barrett and, more than a century later, by the massive edition of the *Journals and Letters* compiled by Joyce Hemlow and her colleagues.

The publication of Burney's complete comedies and tragedies thus serves as the springboard for this study, which aims to show how the author, faced with her father's unwavering disapproval, and strongly discouraged from writing for the stage, opted instead to theatricalize her novels indirectly, by operating a transmodalization of Restoration and Georgian drama.

Chapter 1 discusses the eighteenth-century context for Frances Burney's work, paying close attention to the relation between the still emergent—literally, *novel*—genre of the novel and the drama, which had long been consolidated by tradition. This moment of transition, one of the most controversial and significant turning points in the history of English literature, has been the subject of intense interdisciplinary debate for more than half a century, and it continues to engage scholars and critics from a wide range of theoretical and critical perspectives.[19]

The chapter offers an overview of the changes undergone by serious drama and by comedy in the late seventeenth century and early eighteenth century to identify the thematic and formal elements that the novel borrowed from the stage and that it would then adapt and modify to its own ends.[20] The shift from heroic to affective tragedy and later to domestic drama, on one hand, and that from comedy of manners to moral comedy, on the other, reveal how tragedy and comedy were both transformed by middle-class morality, with its emphasis on the private lives of ordinary people; on virtue; and on the expression of emotion, particularly pathos. From a pragmatic standpoint, the dominant feeling solicited from audiences ceased to be admiration; spectators instead were expected to feel sympathy and an affective identification with the characters on stage.

This overview of the development of the theater shows how playwrights sought to provide a cultural response to the sweeping material and ideological changes that had overtaken British society at this time. The drama, and later the novel, offered distinct but analogous solutions to the new challenge of representing the intimate details of everyday human experience. Situated midway between the solemn heroism and the flippant satire of Restoration theater, the new types of characters that appeared on stage were endowed with a psychological complexity that required revising, if not jettisoning, the rules of neoclassical universalism. The new quest for psychological verisimilitude that was to characterize modern culture—an epistemic shift that, with ever greater subtlety and variety, would accompany the novel's entire history—is signaled by the emergence of the novel, a new form of representation that privileged personal moral action over public action and that focused on the inner lives of characters, their internal debates, and their motivations for acting.

Building on the discussion in chapter 1 of the relation between the theater and the rise of the novel in the early eighteenth century, the chapters that follow trace this relationship in the work of Frances Burney, focusing especially on the years from 1778 to 1782, which coincided with the early phase of her career and the remarkable success of her novels *Evelina; or, The History of a Young Lady's Entrance into the World* and *Cecilia; or, Memoirs of an Heiress.* Through close semiotic analysis, intertextual comparison, and cultural contextualization, chapters 2–5 aim to retrieve the extensive metatextual discourse in Burney's novels, allowing the theater *within* the novels to reemerge at the surface.

Chapter 2 analyzes the formal and transtextual connections linking *Evelina* with its contemporary theatrical context. After noting the structural similarity between the plot of the novel and that of comedies of the time, I consider whether this similarity also operates on a transtextual level. In particular, I focus on the novel's dramatic denouement, analyzing Evelina's reunion with her father, Belmont, in light of the acting techniques promoted by David Garrick. I explain how the English Roscius's interpretation of Shakespeare's King Lear can be considered the implicit intertextual model for the scene in the novel—the climactic moment to which Evelina's entire history has tended from the very first page and a moment rich with epistemic implications.

Chapter 3 is devoted to *The Witlings,* composed by Burney in the wake of *Evelina*'s success and with the encouragement of the playwrights Richard Sheridan and Arthur Murphy. The comedy was never performed because of the unwavering opposition put up by Charles Burney, who seems to have shared the strong anti-theatrical prejudice that characterized the century as a whole. Although *The Witlings* was never staged during the author's lifetime, my analysis shows that the comedy is fully viable as a dramatic text, especially in its handling of stage action and dialogue. Analyzing one of Burney's plays allows me to verify that the dramatic elements present in the novels are due to Burney's thorough familiarity with the formal requirements of writing for the stage.

The suppression of *The Witlings* seems to have had a strong impact on the theme of Burney's second novel, *Cecilia,* discussed in chapter 4. Set in London's high society, the novel has a greater topographical scope and a larger cast of characters than *Evelina.* Its contextual references are broader, as well, shifting from the scale of the theatrical, which dominated the first novel, to that of the spectacular. After identifying Burney's dramatic models for the novel (comedies and early examples of bourgeois tragedy, as is signaled at the intertextual level by many references to playwrights such as Richard Sheridan, Susannah Centlivre, Nicholas Rowe, and Thomas Otway), the chapter goes on to examine the phenomenon of urban and civic spectacularity in Georgian London. We thus find that the novel's dominant textual isotopies of *inversion* and *artifice* are reflected thematically and formally in the period's taste for the counterfeit, for theatrical illusions, and for spectacular effects. I conclude my analysis of *Cecilia* by discussing three aspects of this widespread taste for the artificial that serve as paradigmatic examples of the overarching textual isotopy of the fictitious: the inversion of domesticity that transforms the refuge of the home into a social prison; the aesthetic inversion of Vauxhall, which reverses the order of nature to create a constructed and dramatized theatrical space; and the masquerade attended by Cecilia—predicated on falsehood, masking, and disguise—that puts the artificiality of eighteenth-century society on display and thus exemplifies what I would call the degree zero of the fictitious in the novel.[21]

Chapter 5, finally, addresses the discourse of madness in an illustrative selection of Burney's works. After contextualizing madness, particularly in relation to the climate of anxiety and social malaise associated with the political implications of the mental illness of George III, I discuss this isotopy's epistemic significance for eighteenth-century literature and culture and for two of Burney's novels in particular, *Cecilia* and *The Wanderer* (1814), which seem indebted—albeit in diverging ways—to she-tragedy as filtered through end-of-the-century Gothic.

A final note on late-Georgian generic hierarchies is in order here, given the mixing and cross-pollination of genres, forms, and characters that my theatrical rereading of Burney's macro-text brings back to the surface. As her reworking of the spectacular scenic effects of the Gothic suggests, Burney can be considered a typical reader-spectator, not least because of her ability to move anti-hierarchically between the high and low cultural forms that intersected and counterbalanced each other on the Georgian stage. When Burney introduces carnivalesque and grotesque characters derived from the tradition of physical comedy and comic buffoonery such as Madame Duval, Captain Mirvan, or Morrice into a "high"—sentimental or dramatic—plot in *Evelina* or *Cecilia,* she demonstrates her familiarity with the "low" forms of entertainment associated with harlequinades and the broad comedy of afterpieces and other such unrefined stage acts popular in her time. In terms of market strategy, Burney's combination of comedy of language and intrigue with farce shows that she is fully capable of exploiting the perhaps less "noble," but certainly wide, appeal of the crowd-pleasing entertainments supplied by the unlicensed actor-managers and *farceurs* who operated beyond the monopolistic pale of the Theatres Royal. One might say, then, that Burney produces an ideal *narrative* theatrical bill in her novels, equipping them with main- and afterpieces. For the lighter fare, she creates amusing sketches and lazzi that she inserts into the narrative in safe, homeopathic doses; elsewhere, she adroitly intersperses into the text numerous references to the celebrities and tutelary deities of Georgian theater, from Garrick to Sheridan by way, inevitably, of Shakespeare. Once again, we see how intertextual comparison and a rereading that encompasses the entire spectrum of the dramatic arts provides an anti-hierarchical and historically informed view of the cultural contexts in which Burney's corpus can be situated.[22]

An appendix closes the volume that provides a comprehensive index to the theatrical and musical performances, as well as the actors, mentioned in Burney's writings between 1768 and 1804, offering a detailed reconstruction of the cultural contexts in which she was working and to which her works refer explicitly. As these records show, Burney's knowledge of the theater is fully representative of the tastes and genres of the time. Knowing what performances she attended or wrote about can therefore give us a better understanding of the complex transtextual connections inscribed in her works, allowing us to reestablish through objective means the metatextual framework, and what I would call the latent archaeology, of Burney's macro-text—that is, its three-dimensionality.

One of the greatest contributions of feminist criticism has been to activate a thorough revision of the literary canon. The ideological and critical value of this project is especially apparent where Frances Burney is concerned: only recently published in wide-circulation paperback editions and now the subject of extensive critical surveys such as the *Cambridge Companion,* her works are available to more readers than ever before. Julia Epstein, one of the most perceptive Burney scholars, has written that the critic's task is to "convert Burney from the status of 'minor' writer to that of 'major' writer." She continues, "But those terms—major and minor—lean on issues of canonization and the politics of literary course reading lists. . . . I have tried to approach Burney's *prose writings* as a vantage point from which to ask certain questions about the representation of women in late Eighteenth-century fiction and about the interpretations one woman's writings have received."[23] It seems to me, however, that Epstein's project can be fully realized only by addressing the complete works of the author, illuminating the inter- and intratextual connections within Burney's entire macro-text—that is, not only her prose writings but also the complete range of her narrative and dramatic works. These, I argue, should be also considered in the full complexity of their interrelations, both explicit and implicit, with the contemporary dramatic and stage arts, across the whole spectrum of licensed and unlicensed theater.

The conclusion I have reached at the end of my journey across and around Frances Burney and Georgian England's theater arts is that the task of rewriting, reevaluating, and revising must by its nature be comprehensive, holistic, and plural; otherwise, as one of her closest literary advisers remarked to Burney, writing becomes a "dance with fetters on."[24] In her lifetime, Burney worked under the constraint of familial and social ties that hindered the full expression of her talent. It is paradoxical that those fetters should so long have hampered the critical reception of her work, as well.

ONE

In the Beginning

New things to come, and old to pass away.

—John Dryden, *The Latter Part of the Third Book of Lucretius, against the Fear of Death. De Rerum Naturae* (1685)

Upon the restoration of the Stuart monarchy, the Puritan ban against theaters was lifted immediately. A strong supporter of both public and private theatrical entertainments, Charles II issued patents to William Davenant and Thomas Killigrew to stage productions in the capital, granting their theaters direct royal patronage and protection. From its inception, therefore, Restoration theater was closely tied to the Court and reflected its core values.

In tragedy, it was heroic drama that most fully expressed the chivalric ideology favored by the Court. Strictly bound by the rules of classical drama, heroic tragedy provided a mimetic representation of noble characters engaged in noble actions and was highly artificial both in theme and style. Its protagonists were heroic military leaders, valiant characters whose actions, set in remote times and exotic locations, were unrealistic and detached from the present. Plots usually concluded with the euphoric union of Love and Honor, always assumed to be mutually dependent rather than antithetical. The traditional heroic protagonist—indomitable in battle and admirable in conduct—could rely on a stable hierarchy of values and was seldom faced with difficult choices as he made his way toward the happy resolution envisaged by the chivalric-epic code. Among the literary models for heroic drama were Elizabethan hero-plays, courtly romances, French neoclassical tragedy, Italian opera, and, of course, Renaissance epic poetry, especially Ariosto. Indeed, according to Dryden, Ariosto's theme—"le donne, i cavalier, l'arme e gli amori"—set the standard for the entire genre.[1] The overarching cultural model instead was Platonic: the heroic protagonist of Restoration drama is an ideal being, a model of perfection to be imitated, superior to contingent reality. This made for somewhat static characters lacking in psychological development or pronounced tragic qualities; the hero was supposed to inspire the audience's admiration for his noble spirit and martial prowess. Furthermore, dramatic conventions imposed a rigid structure on the genre, which inevitably concluded with the requisite happy ending, confining the tragic elements of the play to the first four acts.

But from the very first productions by William Davenant, such as *The Siege of Rhodes* (Rutland House, 1656), and by Roger Boyle, Earl of Orrery (*Mustapha* [1665], as well as *Henry the Fifth* [1664]), heroic tragedy was seldom formally pure and coherent and often featured a tormenting dilemma or a tragic choice between Love and Honor that exposed the fragility of the heroic moral code. As Paolo Bertinetti remarks, "Heroic tragedy offered an image of the upper ranks of society that corresponded to their desired self-representation. . . . But it was only an image, an illusion belonging to a world that had ceased to exist by the time of the Restoration, when in the span of a few short years harsh realities intervened to belie the rhetoric of an aristocracy unable to discharge its role as guide to the nation."[2]

The best early example of the mixed heroic, which integrates pathetic elements into the pure heroic, is provided by the work of the greatest dramatist and critic of the time, John Dryden (1631–1700), in whose plays one can clearly discern the emergence of opposing tensions. In Dryden the heroic mode comes up against, and mixes with, its counter-mode, exposing the breakdown of the heroic and foreshadowing the formal changes that would lead to pathetic tragedy. The Herculean hero (such as Montezuma in *The Indian Queen,* by Dryden and Sir Robert Howard [1664]) yields the stage to a divided and tormented protagonist, whose sphere of action is increasingly private rather than public and political. Laura Brown has pointed out, for example, that frustrated love is the real theme of the play that epitomizes Dryden's heroic drama, *The Conquest of Granada* (staged from December 1670 to January 1671 and printed in 1672).[3] A similar theme resurfaces a few years later in *Aureng-Zebe* (1676), built on the manifestly pathetic contrast between the innocent and persecuted Indamora and the blind but blameless Aureng-Zebe. As Dr. Johnson acutely observed many years later, the tragedy is characterized by an unprecedented generic mixture: "The personages [in the play] are imperial; but the dialogue is often domestick, and therefore susceptible of sentiments accommodated to familiar incidents."[4] As Aureng-Zebe lucidly describes his predicament:

Strong Virtue, like strong Nature, struggles still:
Exerts itself, and then throws off the ill.
I to a Son's and Lover's praise aspire:
And must fulfil the parts which both require. (*Aureng-Zebe,* 1.461–64)

A similar transformation can be clearly discerned in the plays of another great heroic dramatist writing at this time, Nathaniel Lee (1652–1692), whose masterpiece *The Rival Queens; or, The Death of Alexander the Great* (1677), in spite of the fulsome style and pompous diction typical of aristocratic drama ("Death, Hell, and Furies! you have sunk my Glory; / O I am all a blot, which Seas of tears, / And my hearts bloud, can never wash away," declaims the emperor at the end of act 4), would come to epitomize impassioned love:

Alexander. Ha! Villains, are they mortal?—what, retire!
Raise your dash'd Spirits from the Earth, and say,
Say she shall live, and I will make you Kings.
Give me this one, this poor, this only life,
And I will pardon you for all the wounds
Which your Arts widen, all Diseases, Deaths,
Which your Damn'd Drugs throw through the ling'ring world.
(*The Rival Queens,* 5)

Alexander's tormented love for his wife Statira, whom he fatally betrays for Roxana (both a seductive femme fatale and a sincerely love-struck woman), shifts the focus of the tragedy from Alexander's public role as heroic leader to his private role as unfaithful but passionate husband. It is hardly surprising therefore that audiences should come to associate Alexander, as suffering lover rather than bloodthirsty tyrant, with Shakespeare's Romeo, the unhappy lover par excellence, a point illustrated by one of the anonymous letters in the novel *The Correspondents* (1775): "Romeo and Alexander became my heroes. I was pleased with alternate sighs and storming; and the most extravagant scenes of the most extravagant tragedies appeared to me the noblest and most delightful."[5] In Lee's play, admiration gives way to pity, and the emperor's antiheroic choice (whose fatal consequences are already represented at an epitextual level as more important than his political triumphs) calls for the audience's empathetic identification.

We can note with Ian Watt here that in Greek tragedy, as in "the other literary forms which preceded the novel, . . . [t]he circumstance of public theatrical performance, the nobility of the hero and the exceptional horror of his fate" strongly curtailed the possibility of empathetic identification and, hence, of their cathartic power for the spectator.[6] The transformations undergone by tragedy in the second half of the seventeenth century instead brought to the fore precisely those elements that encouraged this kind of identification, elements that would be fully developed in the novel.

Almost from its inception as a form, heroic tragedy already harbored within it the formal features that would characterize the subsequent mode of affective, or pathetic, tragedy, which emerged in the 1670s and 1680s. At this time, the epistemic shift described earlier was being reflected in corresponding thematic and formal changes in the drama, and moments of pathos became more frequent, soliciting the audience's pity rather than admiration. The decline of the heroic thus went hand in hand with the rise of the sentimental, and playwrights began to write scenes and dramatic situations whose main end was to provoke an affective reaction in the audience. Tragedies featured a succession of pathetic tableaux that employed the new magniloquent and declamatory recitative style, much used in the next century, as well.[7] Scenes with a strong emotional impact, which served as "visual summaries of events" and of feelings,[8] gradually gained in importance. By the end of the eighteenth century, emotional display had become one of the hypograms, or semantic nuclei, of the Gothic, itself a truly intersemiotic mode connected to the theater by a thick web of contaminations, adaptations, and transmodalizations. Ann Radcliffe's work is exemplary in this respect: while the villains in her novels are strongly indebted to Elizabethan theater, the scenes of terror and tension on which Radcliffe's Gothic was predicated became a rich source of inspiration for the sensational plays of her contemporaries, among them James Boaden, who was particularly skillful in adapting her work.[9]

An early indication of tragedy's shift away from Honor and toward Love is found in the doubts expressed by Dryden in the preface to his masterpiece, *All for Love; or, The World Well Lost* (staged at the Theatre Royal in December 1677 and printed in 1678). While overtly disavowing any intention to dwell on the pathetic, Dryden simultaneously asserts its emergence and reveals the novelty of its irruption onto the stage: "The greatest error in the contrivance seems to be in the person of Octavia, for, though I might use the privilege of a poet to introduce her into Alexandria, yet I had not enough considered that the compassion she moved to herself and children was destructive to that which I reserved for Antony and Cleopatra, whose mutual love, being founded upon vice, must lessen the favour of the audience to them, when virtue and innocence were oppressed by it."[10]

The breakdown of the heroic love–honor dyad entailed the eclipse of honor and the ascendancy of love, and the play's subtitle, *The World Well-Lost,* makes this clear while simultaneously foreshadowing both the fatal choice that Antony and Cleopatra will make and the ultimate resolution of their (apparent rather than real) dilemma. As Brown explains, "*All for Love* includes a residual heroic dimension, superimposed upon the 'real' pathetic definition of the protagonists' character and plight."[11]

The supremacy of Love over Honor, of private passion over reasons of state and public duty, inevitably leads to a dysphoric resolution—death and catastrophe. Dryden's Antony is caught between two incompatible moral (and temporal) dimensions: his glorious heroic past—experienced only as a lingering memory, incapable of summoning him into action—and the present eclipse of that power. Antony is portrayed as the passive victim of his fate, determined less by the aristocratic or martial qualities expected of him than by his unfortunate situation. Cleopatra herself is no longer Shakespeare's seductive and majestic queen, the embodiment of Beauty and Eros, and has become "a wife, a silly, harmless household dove,/Fond without art, and kind without deceit" (*All for Love,* 4.92–93). The encounter between Antony's lover and his wife, Octavia (a new scene interpolated by Dryden), is a good indication of the altered climate of the time; its bourgeois overtones anticipate the early-eighteenth-century themes of marriage, jealousy, and adultery, soon to become staples of the Georgian novel.

Cleopatra prevails over Octavia because of her greater suffering in love and because her situation is more pitiful. As Antony puts it to the other characters on stage, although the question is actually meant for the audience: "Pity pleads for Octavia,/But does it not plead more for Cleopatra?" (*All for Love,* 3.339–40). This prototypical contrast between the loving woman and her rival would be taken up by eighteenth-century novelists, among them Fielding, whose Mrs. Slipslop vies for Joseph Andrews's attentions in an overt and parodic allusion to Dryden's play: "At last finding Joseph unmoveable, [Mrs. Slipslop] flung herself into the chaise, casting a look at Fanny as she went, not unlike that which Cleopatra gives Octavia in the play."[12]

The disjunction between Love and Honor, and the resulting breakdown of the chivalric heroic code, accentuated the importance of the innocence and vulnerability of the protagonist. Female protagonists became more common, in a definitive break with the heroic associated, after 1660, with the arrival of female actresses on the stage. They were typically innocent and virtuous victims whose troubles were placed at the center of the narrative. This focus on the private signals a deep epistemological shift made manifest in the narrowing of the gap between the literary work and the reality it imitated. Realistic and domestic settings were now privileged, and characters were selected for the ordinary and everyday quality of their stories rather than for their high or heroic status, as the rules of classical decorum demanded.

Pathetic tragedy thus effected a dialectical overturning of the ancient tragic conventions based on decorum and the representation of heroic characters who were perfectly virtuous and superior to real men and women. The social status of tragic characters was permanently dissociated from their moral status, and nobility of rank was recoded as noble moral propensity, potentially within reach of anyone, independent of birth.[13]

The new rules of decorum entailed a thorough reconfiguring of the dialectical relation between content and form, affecting not only emplotment, but also characterization and diction, while the centrality of the ordinary individual that was to be a mainstay of the novel in the next century was already becoming apparent. As Isabella, in Thomas Southerne's *The Fatal Marriage; or, The Innocent Adultery* (Drury Lane, 1694), states:

> The Beggar and the King,
> With equal steps, tread forward to their end:
> Tho' they appear of different natures now;
> Not of the same days work of Providence;
> They meet at last: the reconciling Grave
> Swallows Distinction first, that made us Foes,
> Then all alike lie down in peace together. (*The Fatal Marriage,* 2.2–7)

Similar sentiments are expressed in the dedication to *The London Merchant; or, The History of George Barnwell* (Drury Lane, 1731) by George Lillo, who explicitly asserts the moral and educational responsibility of the playwright and plots the course for this new kind of bourgeois tragedy:

> If princes, etc., were alone liable to misfortune arising from vice or weakness in themselves or others, there would be good reason for confining the characters in tragedy to those of superior rank; but, since the contrary is evident, nothing can be more reasonable than to proportion the remedy to the disease. . . . I have attempted, indeed, to enlarge the province of the graver kind of poetry. . . . Plays founded on moral tales in private life may be of admirable use, by carrying conviction to the mind with such irresistible force as to engage all the

> faculties and powers of the soul in the cause of virtue, by stifling vice in its first principles.[14]

Moral tragedy's ultimate goal is to elicit the audience's pity, awaken its emotions, and dwell poignantly on the pathetic to bind spectators to the characters through compassion and sensibility. This is made explicit in Rowe's dedication to *The Fair Penitent:* "I hope that there may be something so moving in the misfortunes and distress of the play as may be not altogether unworthy of your Grace's pity. This is one of the main designs of tragedy, and to excite this generous pity in the greatest minds may pass for some kind of success in this way of writing."[15]

It seems clear that what increasingly determined both the content and the form of serious drama in the late seventeenth century was the spectator's emotional response. The new model of the world being designed at this time relied heavily on character types who were invariably represented as innocent and persecuted to increase the emotional involvement of the audience. Moral action replaced heroic action, compassion replaced admiration, and the first outlines began to take shape of the epochal shift leading to the eighteenth-century emergence of the moral interiority of the individual—and the new formal constraints it brought with it. Late-seventeenth-century pathetic tragedy thus put an end to the affective assumptions of heroic tragedy and foreshadowed the themes and formal features of eighteenth-century bourgeois drama.

The emphasis on pity over horror (or terror) and the greater importance assigned to the expression of emotion led to changes in the choice of subjects and to the development of tragic didacticism. After 1680, Horace's criterion of the *dulce et utile*—the pleasure and instruction offered by poetic justice—and Aristotle's criterion of catharsis, which aroused the purifying emotions of pity and terror, were supplemented by the pathetic, now seen as crucial to the education of theatergoers and readers. The preface to Samuel Richardson's *Clarissa* is explicit: "[Some gentlemen] were of opinion that in all works of this, and of the dramatic kind, *story* or *amusement* should be considered as little more than the vehicle to the more necessary *instruction.*"[16] The expression of sentiment, its verbal utterance, and its physical manifestation were indissolubly linked and dependent on the morality of a character: "Mirth and Joy give but single and transitory Sensations; but Sorrow and Compassion are compounded of two, sometimes more; of Pity for the Distress, a generous Wish to relieve it, and, in some Cases, an honest

Indignation, against the Author of it. These Sentiments sink deeper in our Hearts, and consequently dwell longer in our Minds."[17]

Tragic catharsis privileged the emotional response of the spectator, for whom pity and terror themselves became a source of pleasure—that is, of *pleasurable fear*:[18]

> Otway was peculiarly happy in a full and unrivalled possession of the true Pathos; in his two plays of Venice Preserved and the Orphan, the audience are never left to a state of indifference, but tied down by a succession of interesting strokes to a most feeling, sympathetic attention; his versification is the most unaffected and natural for dialogue of any we know; but the whole of his reputation should rest upon the two pieces we have mentioned; . . . it seems to have been a settled maxim of Otway, to show the most unfavourable pictures of human life, yet, by a kind of bewitching power, he annexes pity to the distress of such characters as should rather fall under contempt.[19]

At the end of the eighteenth century, the moralizing and didactic aspect of a work, hitherto embodied in the hero whose perfection solicited the public's admiration, underwent a displacement. Instruction now lay in the expression of emotion as well as in the exemplary status of the hero or heroine. Sentiment became the dominant element in the process of cultural production and consumption and acquired an autonomous formative function, enabling the moral refinement of the characters on stage and, through their means, of the spectators who could identify with them.

The epistemic shifts described thus far also involved a reappraisal of the concept of poetic justice, which had been closely linked to literature's perceived moral function. At the start of the century, Joseph Addison drew attention to the fact that Aristotle's theory of tragedy envisaged no such concept, and he argued that its employment produced a lack of verisimilitude and correspondence to everyday life, making it impossible, furthermore, to give free rein to the feelings of pity and terror: "We find that Good and Evil happen alike to all Men on this Side of the Grave; and as the principal Design of Tragedy is to raise Commiseration and Terror in the Minds of the Audience, we shall defeat this great End, if we can always make Virtue and Innocence happy and successful. . . . Terror and Commiseration leave such a serious Composure of Thought, as is much more lasting and delightful than any little transient Starts of Joy and Satisfaction."[20] In contrast, critics such as John Dennis (*The Usefulness of the Stage to Religion* [1698] and *The Causes of the Decay and Defects of Dramatick Poetry* [ca. 1725]), and later Samuel Johnson, maintained that a moment of final retribution was essential. Perhaps the most famous example of this view is Johnson's preface to Nahum Tate's *Lear,* which echoes the aesthetic stance taken by Dennis in *Remarks upon Cato* (1713): "A play in which the wicked prosper, and the virtuous miscarry, may doubtless be good, because it is a just representation of the common events of human life: but since all reasonable beings naturally love justice, I cannot easily be persuaded, that the observation of justice makes a play worse; or, that if other excellencies are equal, the audience will not always rise better pleased from the final triumph of persecuted virtue."[21]

By the mid-Georgian period, this change in cultural sensibility led to a critique of certain types of pathetic tragedy, to which moral comedy was increasingly preferred. The latter would later serve as the basis for the novel, in which vice is punished and virtue triumphs. The new conceptual model of the world required a happy ending for the just and the good, who would invariably overcome the obstacles that the comedic framework placed in their way. As the wrongly persecuted Mrs. Heartfree assures us, "PROVIDENCE WILL, SOONER OR LATER, PROCURE THE FELICITY OF THE VIRTUOUS AND INNOCENT,"[22] a conviction on which a few years earlier Richardson had built his immensely successful *Pamela.*

Relying on the pathetic to awaken the emotions of audiences involved further changes, closely linked to the emergence of the female actress on stage. By the 1680s, the suffering, innocent heroine had become the emotional center not only of tragic drama but of other forms, as well. An *annus mirabilis* in this respect was 1680, when in the course of only a few months a number of works were published or staged in a wide variety of genres, from the *Poems* of John Wilmot, Earl of Rochester, to comedies by Aphra Behn (*The Feign'd Curtizans*) and Thomas Shadwell (*The Woman-Captain*), tragedies by Dryden and Lee (*Troilus and Cressida, Caesar Borgia,* and *The Princess of Cleve*), and, of course, Thomas Otway's *The Orphan.* This overlapping and intersection of literary modes testifies to the widespread shift away from the heroic warrior of Davenant's, Orrery's, and to some extent Dryden's aristocratic tragedies in favor of the ill-fated female protagonist of she-tragedy, with Otway's Monimia serving as the dramatic model for generations of writers. Richardson himself would adapt this type of female heroine in what was to become the most famous domestic drama of the century, *Clarissa,* a novel also indebted to George Lillo's *Marina* (Covent Garden, 1738), Rowe's *The Fair Penitent,* and Charles Johnson's *Caelia; or, The Perjur'd Lover* (Drury Lane, 1732).[23] In 1772, the *Theatrical Review* described *The Orphan* in glowing terms that reveal the extent of the cultural shift:

"The fable is familiar and domestic, and the Poet has expressed himself with amazing energy, both in the Language and the Sentiments, at the same time that the Incidents are strongly affecting, and the Catastrophy truly distressful; his Talent of writing to the Heart . . . has perhaps, never been excelled by any of our *English* tragic Writers."[24]

The transformations undergone by serious drama of the late seventeenth century reflect the emergence of a new construction of femininity, submissive and passive, that was fast gaining ground in English culture. As the eighteenth century progressed, the devoted daughter (Euphrasia in *The Grecian Daughter,* by Arthur Murphy [1772]), the affectionate and passionate wife (the majestic Zara in William Congreve's *The Mourning Bride* [Lincoln's Inn Fields Theatre, 1697], or the unfortunate, faithful Belvidera in *Venice Preserv'd* by Thomas Otway [1682]), and the tender and long-suffering mother (Isabella in Southerne's *The Fatal Marriage,* based on Aphra Behn's *The History of the Nun* [1688]) became recurrent and highly codified figures, so popular as to radically transform the contemporary theatrical canon. As we shall see, this transformation affected not only serious drama but also comedy.

Central to this development was the pragmatic function served by citation, and particularly by theatrical reference. For example, in *Clarissa,* which intersects with the drama in countless ways, Lovelace plans to employ Rowe's affective tragedy in hopes that Belvidera's pathetic misadventures will act on Clarissa with that same "force of example" lamented by Johnson in his famous essay in *Rambler* no. 4: "The woes of others so well represented, as those of Belvidera particularly will be, must I hope unlock and open my charmer's heart."[25] Juliet, Ophelia, Desdemona, Cordelia, and Perdita, the great female roles of the eighteenth century, now supplemented by new characters such as Indiana and Belvidera, served as models of femininity that were assimilated, reinterpreted, and recast in many contemporary novels, largely due to the visually enthralling interpretations of the greatest female tragic actresses of the century, from Susannah Maria Cibber (1714–66) to Sarah Siddons (1755–1831). Exemplary among these novels is Frances Burney's first, *Evelina* (1778), which features not only the figure of the faithful and injured wife but also those of the loving but persecuted daughter and the insensitive and negligent husband.

The new evaluative criteria governing affective tragedy, and—after 1730—bourgeois drama, centered on the exaltation of suffering virtue, while a play's pragmatic function lay in the audience's sympathy, according to an affective model that involved "the sympathetic identification between the pitying audience and the beset protagonist."[26] Even before the eighteenth century, the success of a play was thus determined by its pathemic aspects, as in the case of *Ibrahim, the Thirteenth Emperor of the Turks* by Mary Pix (Drury Lane, 1696), which garnered praise insofar as "the Distress of Morena never fail'd to bring Tears into the Eyes of the Audience; which few Plays, if any since *Otway*'s have done; and yet, which is the true End of Tragedy."[27]

There is a clear link here to the conduct literature of the time, on which so much eighteenth-century novel writing, whether by men or by women, was based and that recommended passive virtue to women, considered defenseless and naturally incapable of controlling either the events sweeping them along or their own emotional responses to them. In the theater this construction of femininity found expression in innumerable scenes of madness, fevered ramblings, and delirium, such as the scenes following the violence done to the innocent Monimia by Polydore in *The Orphan:*

> *Monimia.* Well,—
> Let mischiefs multiply! Let every hour
> Of my loath'd life yield me increase of horror!
> Oh let the Sun to these unhappy eyes
> Ne'er shine again, but be eclips'd for ever!
> May every thing I look on seem a prodigy,
> To fill my Soul with terrors; till I quite
> Forget I ever had Humanity,
> And grow a Curser of the works of Nature! (*The Orphan,* 4)

Novels contained not only mad scenes, but also other displays of the heroine's extreme sensibility, which served as visual symptoms of her emotional responsiveness and vulnerability and spoke to her moral refinement. The protagonists of novels were seized by fainting fits, swoons, palpitations, and tears, as illustrated not only by the behavior of Pamela Andrews, Harriet Byron, and Amelia Booth, but also by the convulsed reactions of eighteenth-century men of feeling such as David Simple (in Sarah Fielding's *The Adventures of David Simple* [1744]) and Harley (in Henry Mackenzie's *The Man of Feeling* [1771]), who is often captured with a "look of the most frantic wildness" (*The Man of Feeling,* chap. 34). These men not only witnessed, but just as often produced, cathartic showers of tears, as in this instance in *The Man of Feeling:*

> His daughter was now prostrate at his feet. "Strike, said she, strike here a wretch, whose misery cannot end but with that death she deserves."

> Her hair had fallen on her shoulders! her look had the horrid calmness of out-breathed despair! Her father would have spoken; his lip quivered, his cheek grew pale! his eyes lost the lightning of their fury! there was a reproach in them, but with a mingling of pity! He turned them up to heaven,—then on his daughter.—He laid his left hand on his heart—the sword dropped from his right—he burst into tears.[28]

As the private sphere began to dominate the stage—in sharp contrast with the classical tragic tradition's emphasis on the public realm—the subject matter of plays became domesticated, and even figures of power were portrayed as private individuals. Seventeenth-century affective tragedy, and later moral drama, precipitated the demise of the heroic standard, while the "simple domesticity" that had emerged as the new thematic focus celebrated less the choice between Love and Honor (or Empire) than "the elimination of empire altogether."[29]

In *The Orphan,* this shift is still in its early stages, and the domestic realm is kept separate from the dramatic events affecting Monimia, Castalio, and Polydore by a formal division into acts. The young men's father, Acasto, has relinquished military glory without regret, and his past serves merely as an antiheroic backdrop to the first part of the tragedy, without being part of it. In *Venice Preserv'd; or, A Plot Discovered* (1682), the political sphere does have a bearing on the plot: the conspiracy against the Senate has repercussions on the relationship between the rash and weak Jaffeir and his wife. Belvidera, who pressures her husband into betraying his comrades to save the lives of innocent mothers and children. Jaffeir's and Belvidera's fate is determined by that of the political conspiracy insofar as he has impulsively promised to stab his wife should the conspiracy fail, in an oath of undying fealty to the cause of the rebels.

Jaffeir's tragic dilemma thus transfers onto the private level of sentiment the heroic choice between Love and Honor, recoding it into a choice between retaining his wife's love and respect, on one hand, and fulfilling his pledge, on the other. Jaffeir ultimately perjures himself for love of his wife, for whom he shows an extreme and obsessive devotion:

> *Jaffeir.* Remember, remember him who after all
> The sacred bonds of oaths and holier friendship,
> In fond compassion to a woman's tears
> Forgot his manhood, virtue, truth, and honour,
> To sacrifice the bosom that reliev'd him. (*Venice Preserv'd,* 4.1.15–19)

Belvidera herself is an innocent victim, sacrificed first to the ambition of her father, Senator Priuli (who would have been assassinated by her husband, had he honored his pledge), and later to her husband's honor. Her fate is inevitable: motivated by an admirable but mistaken generosity, the prey of forces over which she has no control, she is driven to madness and dies:

> *Belvidera.* Then hear me too, just heaven,
> Pour down your curses on this wretched head
> With never-ceasing vengeance; let despair,
> Danger or infamy, nay, all surround me;
> Starve me with wantings, let my eyes ne'er see
> A sight of comfort, nor my heart know peace,
> But dash my days with sorrows, nights with horrors
> Wild as my own thoughts now, and let loose fury
> To make me mad enough for what I lose,
> If I must lose him; if I must, I will not. (*Venice Preserv'd,* 5.2)

In the final scene of the tragedy, the emotion solicited from the audience has gone beyond terror, as Belvidera's heart-rending delirium upstages even the terrifying apparition of Jaffeir's and Pierre's ghosts. Her pathetic ravings close the play: "My love! my dear! my blessing! help me! help me!/They have hold of me, and drag me to the bottom!/Nay—now they pull so hard—farewell."

A good example of the gradual shift from heroic public subjects to private histories—often involving a combination of both—is provided by the cycle of plays that John Banks devoted to outstanding episodes in the history of England. For his protagonists, he chose heroines that fit the historical theme: ill-fated female rulers and noblewomen. But Banks disconnected his queens from their public roles, distancing them from factional political struggle to describe the private sufferings of Anne Boleyn, Mary Queen of Scots, and Lady Jane Grey, the heroines, respectively, of *Vertue Betray'd; or, Anna Bullen* (1682), *The Island Queens; or, The Death of Mary, Queen of Scotland* (1684), and *The Innocent Usurper; or, The Death of the Lady Jane Grey* (ca. 1694). The domestication of history attempted by Banks led directly to the emphasis on familial passions of bourgeois drama (it is no accident that the virtuous Anne Boleyn's misfortunes in love, especially her forced marriage, reappear as a background to *Clarissa*).[30] But Banks's historical dramas soon gave way to more realistic and middle-class productions that drew on folkloric forms such as historical ballads (Nicholas Rowe's *Jane Shore*), sensational pamphlets (George Lillo's *Fatal Curiosity* [Haymarket Theatre, 1736]), and popular tales, as is the case of the story of George Barnwell told by *The London Merchant,* another drama by Lillo whose prologue states: "A London 'prentice ruin'd, is our theme,/Drawn from the fam'd old song that bears his name."[31]

Political tragedies, meanwhile, increasingly took the form of she-tragedies (e.g., *Jane Shore* [1714] and *Lady Jane Gray* [1715], both by Rowe), an intermediate dramatic form between affective tragedy and the domestic bourgeois drama, eminently emotive in tone and anti-aristocratic in content, and predicated on the flawless virtue of an unfortunate heroine. (We see a very early anticipation of the form in Otway.) The crux of the historical drama *Tamerlane* by Nicholas Rowe (1701) is the love story between Moneses and Arpasia, whose death scene—later one of Sarah Siddons's set pieces—provoked the deepest empathy and horror in audiences: "In the last act, when by order of the tyrant, her lover Moneses is strangled before her face, she worked herself up to such a pitch of agony, and gave such terrible reality to the few convulsive words she tried to utter, as she sank a lifeless heap before her murderer, that the audience remained in a hush of astonishment, as if awe-struck."[32] Even classical tragedy was adapted to blend traditional heroic elements with the sentimental, as in the case of Joseph Addison's *Cato* (Drury Lane, 1713), which has two sentimental subplots (Juba's love for Cato's daughter Marcia and the rivalry between Cato's sons, Portius and Marcus, for Lucia's love). Although the play is convoluted and hardly passionate, it was nevertheless highly thought of by eighteenth-century novelists.

The domestication of historical drama that followed the breakdown of the Restoration's heroic ethos prepared the way for, and was formally contiguous with, the birth of bourgeois tragedy in a domestic setting. Audiences pitied and identified with the ordinary characters and private histories in these tragedies, which clearly anticipate the novel.[33] Central to this shift was the importance assigned to the inner worth of the individual, the ideological and formal linchpin of the narrative. Humble characters thus became the subjects of tragic actions that had previously been the exclusive preserve of exceptional individuals. Evolved directly from the innocent victims of pathetic tragedy, these characters were exemplary, and in their portrayal psychological verisimilitude was rejected in favor of didactic necessity. They were cast as types, simple characters whose perfect innocence and virtue was reflected in their names, straightforward poetic signs rich with social, and often symbolic, connotations, such as Lillo's Thorowgood and Trueman, or, in the novel, Fielding's Allworthy, Abraham Adams, and Heartfree.

The appeal to sentiment and to the inner worth of the individual was far more marked than in pathetic tragedy, where characterization was bound by the rules of classical decorum. Although invoking universally shared moral standards, the ideological thrust of bourgeois tragedy was thoroughly middle class, based on principles of women's chastity, conjugal faithfulness, benevolence, commerce, charity, and civic responsibility:

If, in the Conduct of these Scenes, you find
Some Characters in lower Life design'd;
Poets, like Painters, Light oppose to Shade,
Or all their Colours languid prove, and dead.

He wou'd his humble Sentiments impart,
In Words that flow directly from the Heart;
To lofty Numbers he has no Pretence,
Who makes his Characters talk common Sense.[34]

Stylistically, as we are reminded by this extract from Theophilus Cibber's prologue to *Caelia* (the domestic tragedy in prose that, as we have seen, was one of the theatrical models for *Clarissa*), the triumph of mercantile ideology led to the rejection of poetic meter (primarily heroic couplets, but also free verse), which was replaced by prose, a change that went hand in hand with the emergence of formal realism in the novel.[35] The implications of this change appear most fully in the narrative technique perfected some years later by Richardson, considered by Watt "a reflection of a much larger change in outlook—the transition from the objective, social and public orientation of the classical world to the subjective, individualist and private orientation of the life and literature of the last two hundred years."[36]

The definitive shift from domestic to specifically bourgeois subjects was announced in the preface to Lillo's *The London Merchant,* a play whose characters in the middle station of life could well have stepped out of the pages of a novel by Defoe. Lillo sketches a lineage of models that explicitly links the affective tragedy of the 1670s and 1680s to the new form now gaining ground:

The Tragic Muse, sublime, delights to show
Princes distrest and scenes of royal woe;
In awful pomp, majestic, to relate

The fall of nations or some hero's fate, . . .
    In ev'ry former age and foreign tongue
With native grandeur thus the goddess sung.
Upon our stage, indeed, with wish'd success,
You've sometimes seen her in a humbler dress—
Great only in distress. When she complains
In Southerne's, Rowe's, or Otway's moving strains,
The brilliant drops that fall from each bright eye
The absent pomp with brighter gems supply.
Forgive us then, if we attempt to show,
In artless strains, a tale of private woe.
A London 'prentice ruin'd, is our theme,
Drawn from the fam'd old song that bears his name.
We hope your taste is not so high to scorn
A moral tale, esteem'd ere you were born;
Which for a century of rolling years,
Has fill'd a thousand thousand eyes with tears.[37]

The subtitle of the play, *The History of George Barnwell,* is a clear indication of how close the drama has come to the novel: on an architextual level, tragedy is no longer considered mimesis of action through verse and prose but, rather, *history,* or narrative, in line with a compositional practice shared with the major novelists of the time, who variously define their works as *adventures, authentick memoirs,* and, indeed, often as *histories* (as in the titles of novels by Manley, Defoe, Richardson, and Fielding). Heroic tragic action is replaced by a narrative of "domestic misery," as one of Lillo's characters fittingly terms it (*The London Merchant,* 5.2), which has already shed most of the elements of *acted* narrative and has transformed into *narrated* narrative.

The central scene of the tragedy, in which Barnwell is persuaded to murder his uncle by the calculating Millwood—a crucial episode marking his ruin and foreshadowing his execution at the hand of justice—takes place entirely off-stage and is related to us only after the fact by means of a dialogue between servants. This "sad relation" (*The London Merchant,* 3.2) has lost its theatrical function (we might call it *dramatic narrative,* in Richardson's phrase): language and action are disjoined, temporally separated. The episode has an expository quality and is carried forward through typically diegetic interrogative formulas, such as, "But how did Barnwell behave?," "But then Millwood?," and "What said he?" (*The London Merchant,* 3.2).

Lillo even anticipates the use of the epistolary expedient (*The London

Merchant, 3.1)—later one of the most frequently used devices in novels—through which Barnwell explains his disappearance. And the false but moving account of Millwood's troubled youth is a true novelistic *mise en abyme* that invests the entire story with meta-narrative implications:

> *Lucy.* Why, you must know, my lady here was only a child; but her parents, dying while she was young, left her and her fortune (no inconsiderable one, I assure you) to the care of a gentleman who has a good estate of his own. . . . All things went on as one could wish till, some time ago, his wife dying, he fell violently in love with his charge, and would fain have married her. Now, the man is neither old nor ugly, but a good, personable sort of man; but I don't know how it was, she could never endure him. In short, her ill usage so provoked him, that he brought in an account of his executorship, wherein he makes her debtor to him. (*The London Merchant,* 2.2)

The London Merchant is governed by a new domestic poetics whose realism is based on the ascendancy achieved by middle-class morality. The use of pathos, which comes to a climax in act V, in the scenes between the repentant Barnwell, his friend Trueman, and the loving Maria,[38] is thus primarily didactic and serves as a unifying element designed to appeal to the greatest number of spectators. Justifying his attempt to "enlarge the province of the graver kind of poetry," Lillo explains: "Plays founded on moral tales in private life may be of admirable use by carrying conviction to the mind with such irresistible *force* as to engage all the faculties and powers of the soul in the cause of virtue, by stifling vice in its first principle."[39] Lillo's didactic intent foreshadows that of the eighteenth-century novel, in which a single individual's story is always a vehicle for the universal and exemplary. Indeed, the playwright's axiom according to which "the more extensively useful the moral of any tragedy is, the more excellent that piece must be of its kind" does fit Richardson's didactic philosophy closely.[40] According to Richardson, the novel's objective is "to *divert* and *entertain,* and at the same time to *instruct* and *improve* the minds of the YOUTHS of *both sexes;* . . . to inculcate *religion* and *morality* . . . ; to paint VICE in its proper colours, to make it *deservedly odious,*"[41] since "*story* and *amusement* should be considered as little more than the vehicle to the more necessary *instruction.*"[42]

An analysis of the changes undergone by Restoration and Augustan serious drama reveals a deep epistemological shift: tragic narratives came to reflect with ever greater accuracy the actual experience of large segments of the public through a process that was occurring simultaneously in comedy. The testing of virtue and the exemplary morality of the tragic protagonist were the product of a code of moral values that could be shared and easily assimilated by the spectators, who could note with pleasure and gratification the resemblance—on both moral and aesthetic grounds—between the events on stage and those in the real world. The spectators' emotional response, their compassion and identification with the characters on stage, were the prerequisite for, and the direct consequence of, the formal realism that was emerging as the eighteenth century progressed and that was to be perfected by the novel, as is evident in *Clarissa,* perhaps the most famous example of domestic tragedy of the time.

Eighteenth-century realism, whether in the theater or in the novel, centered on the description of the familiar detail and on conveying the experience of the individual by means of a simple middling style. It became the form best suited to representing interiority, the psychological and emotional states, the thoughts and moral values of characters. Print, the new communications technology for modern urban culture, thus came to replace performance and oral narrative as the best means for reproducing the intimate and private dimension of human experience. Brown's qualification is relevant here: "The novel is distinguishable from the drama not as a unique repository of fictional realism in the eighteenth century, but rather as the genre that finds the most successful means of representing a fundamentally realist form."[43] It is no accident that Johnson's midcentury praise for *The Fair Penitent* also applies perfectly to most eighteenth-century novels: "There is scarcely any work of any poet at once so interesting by the fable, and so delightful by the language. The story is domestick, and therefore easily received by the imagination, and assimilated to common life."[44]

Between the seventeenth century and the eighteenth century, serious drama underwent sweeping formal and thematic changes that, as we have seen, were linked to a new way to model the world conceptually. As the heroic ethos gave way to bourgeois moral values, highly placed heroes were supplanted by characters of a middling sort, and the educational function of affect was supplied no longer by pity and terror but by the pathetic. These changes had their counterpart in comedy, as well.

In the broadest cultural terms, comedy replicated the transformation of tragedy, with the social satire of the Restoration giving way to early Georgian moral comedy. The shift was due to a new interest in moral theories and theories of human behavior based on what has been called "the culture of sensibility."[45] The new kind of comedy that grew out of it, its contents purified and its tone moralizing, valued moral action over public concerns, privileging benevolence and human charity over the worldliness, the moral vacuity, and the uninhibited manners typical of plays set in courtly and urban environments. The emergence of sentimentality in the theater broadened the scope of comedy, which began to embrace new social phenomena and to describe new kinds of emotional experiences that were also becoming central to the bourgeois novel.

The several subgenres of Restoration comedy (referred to variously as comedies of manners, social satires, Spanish comedies,[46] or comedies of romantic intrigue, depending on the formal or thematic aspects emphasized) were commonly set in London's high society and shared a quasi-documentary (and thus self-referential) description of specific worldly gathering places, customs, characters, and manners. The incidents, the conflicts, and the language of the characters were drawn from contemporary genteel society, making the dramatic context clearly identifiable—another label used for such plays is "genteel comedy." The relations between characters were conveyed overtly, through their social interaction, and were dominated by economic concerns. The characters are easily identifiable social stereotypes, lacking in psychological depth and largely subservient to the satirical ends of the plays.

On the pragmatic level, the relationship between audience and characters on stage was based on separation and lack of empathy; spectators would judge characters by their actions and subject them to criticism. The discrepancy between the manners and assumptions of society, on one hand, and a playwright's assessment of them, on the other, was crucial to the development of satire, and playwrights were under no necessity to present the situations on-stage, or their final resolutions, as acceptable. Rather, they could operate in implicit opposition to the conventions governing what Congreve called "the way of the world."

As we have seen, in the changes affecting late-seventeenth-century serious drama, the inclusion of pathetic elements foreshadowed the dissolution of the heroic ideal. Although it was a fairly incoherent genre from the start, a similar process took place in social satire, as is revealed by the gradual shift in the 1670s from pure comedy of intrigue (examples are John Dryden's *The Wild Gallant* [Theatre Royal, 1663]; George Etherege's *She Would If She Could* [Lincoln's Inn Fields Theatre, 1668]; or William Wycherley's *Love in a Wood* [Drury Lane, 1671]) to comedy characterized by the increasing importance of moral judgment, accompanied by an incipient critique of social hypocrisy.

The detachment of moral action from social action characterizing this first phase of late-seventeenth-century comedy is apparent in Etherege's *The Man of Mode* (Dorset Garden, 1676) and even more so in William Wycherley's *The Plain-Dealer* (Drury Lane, 1676), which introduced a new type of character onto the stage. Wycherley juxtaposes the subplot centered on Freeman—willing to marry the quarrelsome but wealthy Widow Blackacre to gain access to her property—with the plot revolving around Manly, whom the list of dramatis personae describes as "of an honest, surly, nice humor." Manly represents a new type: he is idealistic and entirely disconnected from the amoral world surrounding him and thus can serve as a vehicle for the author's critique of the hypocrisy and conventions of the time, as the prologue, "Spoken by the Plain-Dealer," announces:

> Plain-dealing is, you'll say, quite out of fashion;
> You'll hate it here, as in a Dedication.
> And your fair Neighbors, in a Limning Poet,
> No more than in a Painter will allow it.[47]

Aphra Behn's *The Rover* (published in 1677), similarly casts the intrigue plot concerning Hellena and Florinda as background to the sentimental doubts of the courtesan Angellica, torn between her sincere love for Willmore and economic necessity, a state of affairs her maidservant laments:

> *Moretta.* Now my curse go with you! Is all our project fallen to this? To love the only enemy of our trade? Nay, to love such a shameroon; a very beggar; nay, a pirate beggar, whose business is to rifle and be gone; a no-purchase, no-pay tatterdemalion, and English picaroon; a rogue that fights for daily drink, and takes a pride in being loyally lousy? Oh, I could curse now, if I durst. This is the fate of most whores. (*The Rover,* 2.2)

In the decades immediately following the Restoration, significant new changes were being introduced. In Behn's play we can already note one of the fundamental thematic developments of Restoration comedy: plots based on financial concerns, with their laws of entail, contracts, and matrimonial clauses, were replaced by plots involving an affective choice, as financial and legal codes were supplanted by the sentimental.

As discussed earlier, serious drama of the early eighteenth century was transformed by the emergence of the mercantile class and of the moral principles associated with it (benevolence, humanitarianism, Christian paternalism). The important changes that ensued were closely linked to the rise of realism and led to the consolidation of domestic bourgeois drama. A similar trajectory occurred in comedy, where the social critique typical of the satire on manners was first coupled with, and later substituted by, the exaltation of the inner virtue of the individual. As a result, although audiences still recognized the values represented by the traditional comedy of manners, by the end of the century (and already before the publication of Jeremy Collier's treatise *A Short View on the Immorality and Profaneness of the English Stage* [1698]) they no longer shared the moral order it represented; nor did they identify with it. Female spectators in particular were increasingly demanding a greater correspondence, both in tragedy and in comedy, between the reigning moral code and that represented on-stage, requesting the inclusion of a didactic element previously absent from pure comedy of manners, a concern voiced by Congreve's *Amendments of Mr. Collier's False and Imperfect Citations* (1698):

> After the Action of the Play is over, and the Delight of the Representation at an end; there is generally Care taken, that the Moral of the whole shall be summ'd up, and deliver'd to the Audience, in the very last and concluding Lines of the Poem. The Intention of this is, that the Delight of the Representation may not so strongly possess the Minds of the audience, as to make them forget or oversee the Instruction: It is the last thing said, that it may make the last Impression; and it is always comprehended in a few Lines, and put into Rhyme, that it may be easy and engaging to the Memory.[48]

The reformation of the theater precipitated by Collier's campaign necessarily affected the position of playwrights, as well. In contrast to the earlier comic tradition, the playwright's role was now considered integral to the general reformation of manners of eighteenth-century English society, a development that was linked to the feminization and moralization of culture simultaneously becoming evident in the novel. The result was a mixed comedy marked by compromise: while retaining most of the stock characters and situations of the comedy of manners, playwrights eliminated its racier scenes and corrosive humor and appended to their plays the sort of irreprehensible conclusion that later critics have often considered forced.

The biting, unforgiving satire of the comedy of manners thus gave way to a new kind of comedy characterized by greater tolerance of human imperfections. The figure of the brilliant, cynical, and disenchanted Restoration wit was replaced by the early-eighteenth-century "amiable humorist" and then by the kindly and cheerful characters of sentimental comedy, who can wisely smile with—rather than at—their fellow humans, without evading their responsibilities toward society.[49] Pitiless laughter, bawdy jests, and brilliant repartee were by now equated with dissipation and lack of moral responsibility. As Steele put it in the epilogue to *The Lying Lover* (Theatre Royal, Drury Lane, 1703):

Our too advent'rous Author soar'd to Night
Above the little Praise, Mirth to excite,
And chose with Pity to chastise Delight.
For Laughter's a distorted Passion, born
Of sudden self Esteem, and sudden Scorn;
Which, when 'tis o'er, the Men in Pleasure wise,
Both him that mov'd it, and themselves despise,
While generous Pity of a painted Woe
Makes us our selves both more approve, and know.[50]

Satire was invariably and necessarily directed against one's fellow human beings and revealed an egocentric pleasure in one's own linguistic and associative skills that testified to a deplorable hardness of heart.

The formal proximity between this sort of comedy and contemporary bourgeois tragedy—and later, the novel—is clear. It is demonstrated in particular by Samuel Richardson's *The History of Sir Charles Grandison* (1753–54), an epistolary condemnation less of the libertine spirit (criticized by means of the dissolute rake Sir Hargave Pollexfen and the uninhibited father of the hero himself, both put to shame and redeemed by the matchless hero) than of the dueling wit of the Restoration "gay couple," represented here by Lord and Lady G., whose love is repeatedly put to the test by the use, and abuse, of wit.[51] Without realizing that she is "jest[ing] away her own happiness,"[52] the brilliant Lady G. is in fact steadily alienating the affections of her tolerant husband: "Humour and raillery are very difficult things to rein in: They are very curvetting like a prancing horse; and they will often throw the rider who depends more upon his skills in managing them, than he has reason to do."[53] The triumph of the new kind of moral sociability represented by *Grandison,* and later by Richardson's direct descendant, Jane Austen,[54] relied on the contrast between the eccentricity of the wit who typified the comedy of manners and the "urbanized laughter" of Georgian society,[55] which condemned those who did not assimilate quickly to an irreparable social isolation.

But this moralizing process also radically transformed comedy's protagonists. The amoral libertine of Restoration theater was abandoned in favor of the exemplary lover. If, on one hand, what was emerging was the idea of an affective union based on free choice (or, in Lawrence Stone's classic phrase, companionate marriage),[56] on the other, what was being registered was a growing ambivalence about the figure of the rake, the true protagonist of the mid- to late-seventeenth-century sexual comedies. Dominated by voluptuousness and sexual passion, his "life is governed by the rhythms of courtship, seduction, conquest, and abandonment," as is the case for Wycherley's Dorimant and Horner, who clearly show the influence of the Earl of Rochester's libertine philosophy.[57] As a result of the radical change in sexual mores that took place in the course of the century (in no small part due to the societies for the reformation of manners), the rake began to lose his characteristic disenchanted amorality and either mended his ways, undergoing a personal reformation that reflected, on the private micro-level, the broader reformation of society, or else was transformed into a fundamentally decent and generous scapegrace, the forefather of a numerous literary progeny from Tom Jones to Charles Surface. Only later, as a result of further changes (of which the most important are perhaps due to the influence of de Sade), would the figure take on the negative moral traits of the Gothic novel's ambiguous and morally corrupt antihero.

These transformations are already evident in *The Squire of Alsatia,* a work staged by Thomas Shadwell in 1688 that foreshadows eighteenth-century exemplary comedy. A didactic tale with moralistic overtones, its protagonist, Belfond Junior, is a type of reformed rake, an irresponsible youth endowed with filial piety who anticipates Fielding's Tom Jones in several ways: he is "given to Women, and now and then to good fellowship; . . . a man of Honour and of excellent disposition and temper."[58] Shadwell also included a benevolent avuncular figure in the play, Sir Edward Belfond, a merchant "possessed with all Gentlemanlike qualities," among them "great humanity and gentleness and compassion towards mankind." This type will also recur in the next century—one need only recall Sir Oliver Surface in *The School for Scandal* (Drury Lane, 1777) or Sir Hugh Tyrold in Frances Burney's *Camilla; or, A Picture of Youth (1796).* Finally, Shadwell even includes the seduction of a young woman, Lucia, whose ensuing misfortunes cast pathetic shadows over the comic romp.

The reformation of Shadwell's Belfond is distinctly of its time. According to the prevailing philosophical ideas, arrogance and meanness could be corrected only by appealing to the individual's natural propensity to goodness. The new religious concept of a benevolent deity, to whom we are brought closer by our virtuous actions and feelings, paid tribute to the innate goodness of human beings. Instead of representing the unscrupulous intrigues of the rakes, the theater thus turned to representing the consequences of involuntary errors—always rectifiable and, indeed, always rectified—in which the rash but honest protagonists of eighteenth-century moral comedy became invariably entangled. Aimwell, the main character in George Farquhar's comedy *The Beaux' Stratagem* (Haymarket Theatre, 1707), already shows the features of this new type of exemplary lover, "a character somewhere between the traditional reformed rake and the future exemplary lover of sentimental comedy."[59] Even his Jonsonian-style humoral name has lost the gallant connotations it would have had in the social satire of a few decades earlier and now reflects the moral virtue of the individual in a way that will later be taken up by Fielding.

The emphasis placed on moral action over social action at the end of the century was accompanied by a revaluation of affective ties. Marriage was no longer dictated by crude financial interests or by brutish sexual instincts. Rather, it was the result of a conscious choice that was resisted—until, of course, the last act—by the usual blocking characters: the cantankerous parents or relatives derived from Greek Old Comedy and the Latin tradition.

The new form adopted by moral comedy also has bearing on the historically determined representation of marriage, which became one of the central themes developed by authors. The marriage described in *Love's Last Shift; or, A Fool in Fashion* (Drury Lane, 1696) by the playwright and poet laureate Colley Cibber, often considered the first English sentimental comedy, is a good example on the formal level of the transitional comedy that intervened between Restoration social satire and early Georgian moral comedy. While retaining the characteristic vitality of the older comedy of manners, *Love's Last Shift* envisions the triumph of moral virtue thanks to the ultimate reformation of the cynical protagonist, Loveless, who brings to mind Richardson's Lovelace not only by homophony but also through their similar conduct. Loveless's "change of heart" at the end of the comedy, followed by the celebration of a final (and improbable) reconciliation with his wife, is due to the constancy and exemplary fidelity displayed throughout the first four acts by the injured Amanda, repeatedly deceived by her enterprising husband:

Amanda. Then let me strike you nearer, deeper yet:—But arm your Mind with gentle Pity first, or I am lost for ever.

Loveless. I am all Pity, all Faith, Expectation, and confused Amazement: Be kind, be quick, and ease my wonder.

Amanda. Look on me well: Revive your dead Remembrance: And oh! for Pity's sake (*kneels*) hate me not for loving long, faithfully forgive this innocent Attempt of a despairing Passion, and I shall die in quiet. (*Love's Last Shift,* 5.2.144–51)

A few years later, *The Careless Husband* (Drury Lane, 1704) similarly represents the libertine Sir Charles Easy being conquered by the generous selflessness of his wife, Lady Easy. In a celebrated scene, Lady Easy discovers her husband asleep in compromising proximity to the maid, and after unexpectedly berating herself, she lovingly lays a handkerchief over his head to prevent his catching cold:

The Scene Opens, and Discovers Sir Charles without his Periwig, and Edging by him, both asleep in two Easy Chairs.

Then Enter Lady Easy, who Starts and Trembles some time, unable to speak.

Lady Easy. Ha!
Protect me Virtue! Patience! Reason!
Teach me to bear this killing Sight, or let
Me think my dreaming Senses are Deceiv'd!
For sure a Sight like This might raise the Arm
Of Duty, even to the Breast of Love! At least
I'll throw this Vizor of my Patience off:
Now wake him in his Guilt,
And Bare-fac'd Front him with my Wrongs.
I'll talk to him till he blushes, nay, till he—
—Frowns on me, perhaps,—and then
I'm lost again—The Ease of a Few Tears
Is all that's left to me—
And Duty too forbids me to insult; . . .
Ha! Bare-headed, and in so sound a Sleep!
Who knows, while thus Expos'd to th' unwholesome Air
But Heav'n offended may o'ertake his Crime,
And, in some languishing Distemper, leave him
A severe Example of its violated Laws—

> Forbid it Mercy, and forbid it Love.
> This may prevent it.
>
> [*Takes her Steinkirk from her Neck, and lays it gently over his Head.*]
>
> And if he shou'd wake offended at my too Busy Care, let my heart-breaking Patience, Duty, and my Fond Affection plead my Pardon. (*The Careless Husband,* 5.5.1–29)

The greater attention paid to marital relations in the drama was due to the same change in sexual mores that the novel was exploring at this time, particularly in its focus on courtship, although the novel was able to analyze it far more systematically and thoroughly: "The stage, in Western Europe at least, has never been able to go very far in the description of sexual behaviour, whereas in his novels Richardson was able to present much that in any other form would have been quite unacceptable to an audience whose public demeanour, at least, was very severely controlled by the intensified taboos of a Puritan morality."[60] This new attitude to love and marriage was "a historically significant development" that challenged the traditional hierarchy of the family.[61] As the concluding couplet of Wycherley's *The Gentleman Dancing-Master* (Dorset Gardens, 1673) puts it, "When Children marry, Parents shou'd obey,/ Since Love claims more Obedience far than they." Respect for the love choice of one's son or daughter became a sign replete with social and cultural implications. For example, the humanity of George Lillo's benevolent Thorowgood is confirmed by his willingness to be guided by Maria's choice of a husband:

> *Thorowgood.* I am daily solicited by men of the greatest rank and merit for leave to address you, but I have hitherto declined it, in hopes that by observation I should learn which way your inclination tends; for, as I know love to be essential to happiness in the marriage state, I had rather my approbation should confirm your choice than direct it. (*The London Merchant,* 1.1)

The greater value assigned to love over mere financial considerations is also voiced by Lucinda in Richard Steele's *The Conscious Lovers* (Drury Lane, 1722) when she likens her father's determination to choose her husband to a market transaction in which the physical person of the bride is bartered for goods and real estate. The critique is of course aimed at Restoration culture, represented in the comedy by the rich coxcomb Cimberton, who is more attracted by Lucinda's body and by her capacity to produce an heir than by her interiority and feelings:

> *Lucinda.* To love is a passion, 'tis a desire, and we must have no desires. Oh! I cannot endure the reflection! With what insensibility on my part, with what more than patience, have I been exposed and offered to some awkward booby or other in every county of Great Britain! . . . To be bartered for like the beasts of the fields, and that in such an instance as coming together to an entire familiarity and union of soul and body; oh! And this without being so much as well-wishers to each other, but for increase of fortune. (*The Conscious Lovers,* 3.1)

What was emerging in this altered social context was a new axiological order that had formal and thematic implications for comedy in general but that impinged particularly on the heroine's choice of a husband, which became the real focus of the action. Among the most frequently recurring situations in plays was the intermarriage between merchant and aristocratic families, a theme that reflected the reality of the time (Watt describes the phenomenon as "hypergamy," applying it in particular to women marrying into a higher status) and that would be developed by playwrights and novelist throughout the century, from Steele in *The Conscious Lovers* to Frances Burney in *Cecilia* (1782).[62]

From a formal standpoint, the centrality of the sentimental plot had definite structural implications: the resolution of the lovers' difficulties always coincided with the conclusion of the play, whose generically determined comedic character often required a final wedding that reasserted familial as well as social ties and rewarded the (often regained) virtue of the protagonists.

The formal changes affecting comedy between the seventeenth century and the eighteenth century were not only far-reaching but also historically inflected, operating a dialectical reassessment of classical comic conventions. As middle-class morality gained ground, the same rejection of aristocratic values occurred in comedy as had earlier taken place in pathetic tragedy: privileging moral criteria over social and class considerations brought about the demise of the older satirical stereotypes and thus a rejection of the high–low, tragic–comic distinctions belonging to the classical hierarchy of genres. The three distinctive characteristics of ancient comedy, or *comédie basse*—"low" characters, happy endings, and an emphasis on laughter—were replaced by the new conventions and decorum of *comédie haute,* whose main characters had a higher social status, while the primary function of a play was to provide instruction and a moral. This made it possible to adapt serious moral histories to comedy.

In a reversion to ancient norms, broadly comic roles were now assigned to servants, comic types who would eventually migrate to the novel, especially the Gothic novel. In the latter, the protagonists' terror is often kept in check or exorcised by the comic relief provided by servants, thus reassuring readers of the overt fictionality of the tale and allowing them to take pleasure in its predetermined actantial structure.[63] But laughter was also dissociated from comedy by being relegated to quasi-farcical subgenres such as pantomime, comic opera, and harlequinades, which were scheduled separately from the main entertainment, usually as afterpieces, when the lower admission price brought a poorer (and presumably less refined) audience to the theater. These amusements could be performed only in theaters without a royal patent and were thus subject to the varying commercial and legal fortunes of such theaters.

The value now being placed on good, honest, and idealistic characters had direct formal repercussions on plays. Dramatists created far more situations in which the hero could show his benevolence or his assistants could contrive ways to resolve the young lover's problems or compensate for his shortcomings, thus displaying an exemplary disinterestedness while providing extensive admonitory sermons. The traditional comic situation based on the criticism of vice was replaced by scenes displaying this new concept of goodness; lengthy edifying lectures and moralizing speeches took the place of satire or the lighthearted romp, and the more overtly farcical elements were rejected in favor of sentimentalism.

Amid all of the instruction were numerous love scenes and scenes of conflict, as well, in which the young protagonists rationally and reasonably discussed their affection for each other (thus showing the "consciousness" advocated by Steele) or confronted characters who opposed them. Open, displays of affection were conveyed through a range of codified gestures and expressions, and as a sign that the Georgian theater (as well as the novel) was responding to the cultural valuation of feeling at this time, emphasis was laid on the positive effects that displays of feeling had on others.

Prior to the revolutionary period, when an anti-aristocratic trend led to new formal and thematic changes, the ancient comedic device of mistaken or exchanged identities was recoded and frequently employed to ratify middle-class ideology. The moment in which the heroine's true identity was revealed thus served to restore her to her proper—that is, higher—rank, allowing her to marry a representative of the status quo, the scion of an aristocratic, or at least wealthy, family:

> *Sealand.* O my child! How are our sorrows past o'erpaid by such a meeting! Though I have lost so many years of soft paternal dalliance with thee, yet, in one day to find thee thus, and thus bestow thee in such perfect happiness, is ample, ample reparation! (*The Conscious Lovers,* 5.3)

The dialectical transformation of generic conventions thus also impinged on the representation of relations between classes, particularly relations between the merchant class and the aristocracy, and some critics consider this to be the most significant change effected by Augustan comedy.[64] The influence of historical and economic changes, as well as altered moral attitudes, contributed to converting the traditional contempt with which the figure of the merchant was regarded in Restoration comedy (where he was usually portrayed as the deceived and derided "cit") into a more benign characterization that had an educational and moral value rather than a comic one. Plays began to include an increasing number of scenes in which proud representatives of British mercantile fortunes challenged, as equals, arrogant and often impoverished members of the aristocracy:

> *Myrtle.* I must tell you, Cousin, this is the first merchant that has married into our house.
> *Lucinda.* (*aside*) Deuce on 'em! Am I a merchant because my father is?
> *Myrtle.* But is he directly a trader this time?
> *Cymberton.* There's no hiding the disgrace, Sir; he trades to all parts of the world.
> *Myrtle.* We never had one of our family before who descended from persons that did anything.
> *Cimberton.* Sir, since it is a girl that they have, I am, for the honour of my family, willing to take it in again, and to sink her into our name, and no harm done. (*The Conscious Lovers,* 5.1)

Watt attributes this power for change to Richardson, as well, whose novels are built on the premise that social status is entirely independent of, and often inversely proportional to, morality: "*Pamela* . . . represents the first complete confluence of two previously opposed traditions in fiction; it combines 'high' and 'low' motives, and, even more important, it portrays the conflict between the two."[65] As in Shaftesbury's moral system, virtue is the great leveler of humankind.

By the start of the eighteenth century, therefore, comedy had rejected the more farcical elements that had characterized it previously (later mourned by Oliver Goldsmith in his famous *Essay on the Theatre; or, a Comparison between Laughing and Sentimental Comedy* [1773]) and was moving ever closer to the pathos of tragedy, to its exemplary characters and its persecution of virtuous innocence, and to the heavy didacticism of affective tragedy. William Congreve testifies to this shift in his dedication to *The Way of the World* (Lincoln's Inn Fields Theatre, 1700), a comedy that in many ways foreshadows the formal transformations to come and thus, as one might expect, would be appreciated most by later generations of spectators. In his reply to Collier's attack on the theater, Congreve states: "Those characters which are meant to be ridiculed in most of our comedies are of fools so gross that, in my humble opinion, they should rather disturb than divert the well-natured and reflecting part of the audience; they are rather objects of charity than contempt; and, instead of moving our mirth, they ought very often to excite our compassion."[66] According to Congreve, the ability to distinguish a "Witwould" from a "Truewit" requires discrimination.[67] The audience must be able to rise above the unremitting brilliance offered by strings of witticisms, rejecting it in favor of a more complex dramatic characterization based on moral values previously ignored by the satirical comic tradition.

Early-eighteenth-century theater was thus marked by a complex dialectical relationship—made up of advances, retreats, and compromises—with the social, political, economic, and cultural forces that were gaining strength between William of Orange's rise to the throne (1689) and the death of Queen Anne (1714). It was these forces that determined the drama's evolution and, subsequently, the transmodal adaptations that would lead to the new form of representation dominating the century: the novel.

The plays of Richard Steele (ca. 1672–1729), the most influential critic, journalist, and playwright of the first decades of the eighteenth century, are an excellent example of comedy's radical transformation at the turn of the century. After campaigning for the moral reformation of manners in the pages of the *Tatler*,[68] Steele turned his attention to the practical application of the moral instruction he had thus far offered only theoretically, identifying in the comic genre a "didactic instrument appropriate to castigate bad manners and to celebrate virtue."[69]

A corollary to this radical transformation followed: characters would have to embody new axiological values. *The Christian Hero* (1701), Steele's first experiment in prose (and note here the explicit subtitle, *An Argument Proving That No Principles but Those of Religion Are Sufficient to Make a Great*

Man), has already moved away from the classical representation of "persons who are worse . . . than the present generation,"[70] and seeks rather to be a genuine moral treatise, exalting the virtues of benevolence, compassion, and forgiveness, and thus anticipating many of the moral imperatives later adopted by Georgian novelists. It comes as no surprise therefore to find it among Richardson's models for *Grandison,* whose eponymous hero is defined as "the Example of a Man acting uniformly well thro' a Variety of trying Scenes. . . . A Man of Religion and Virtue . . . happy in himself and a Blessing to others."[71]

On a structural level, the most significant changes Steele introduced into the basic pattern of Restoration comedy were the addition of pathetic subplots and the inclusion of exemplary characters who claim the audience's admiration, thus violating neoclassical rules. He defended these alterations in the preface to *The Conscious Lovers*, a play that has been called "the final, mature expression of [Steele's] reformist efforts in the drama":[72]

> The case of the father and daughter (Indiana) [is] esteemed by some people no subject of comedy; but I cannot be of their mind; for anything that has its foundation in happiness and success must be allowed to be the object of comedy, and sure it must be an improvement of it to introduce a joy too exquisite for laughter. . . . I must therefore contend that the tears which were shed on that occasion flowed from reason and good sense. . . . To be apt to give way to the impressions of humanity is the excellence of a right disposition and the natural working of a well-turned spirit.[73]

Steele's poetics here was evidently influenced by Collier's criticism of the seventeenth-century satirical tradition, which Steele evoked in the prologue to distance himself from it:

> No more let ribaldry, with licence writ,
> Usurp the name of eloquence and wit;
> No more let lawless farce uncensur'd go,
> The lewd dull gleanings of a Smithfield show.
> 'Tis yours with breeding to refine the age,
> To chasten wit, and moralize the stage.
> Ye modest, wise and good, ye fair, ye brave,
> To-night the champion of your virtues save;
> Redeem from long contempt the comic name,
> And judge politely for your country's fame.[74]

In *The Conscious Lovers,* inner virtue (primarily a feminine attribute) triumphs over crude mercenary concerns in a celebration of true love that is free from external constraints and based on reason, integrity, and plain honesty. "How laudable is Love, when born of Virtue!" (*The Conscious Lovers,* 5.3) exclaims the reformed Mr. Sealand at the end of the play, before he embraces the devoted Bevil and his long-lost Indiana. The moralizing and didactic intent, now at the center of the comic plot, is asserted explicitly, and Steele takes pains to emphasize the moral thrust of Bevil's impeccable behavior: "I [do not] make any difficulty to acknowledge that the whole was writ for the sake of the scene of the fourth act, wherein Mr. Bevil evades the quarrel with his friend, and hope it may have some effect upon the Goths and Vandals that frequent the theatres, or a more polite audience may supply their absence."[75] The play's attack on dueling dramatizes one of the most important campaigns for the reformation of manners waged by the evangelical societies early in the century.[76] It, too, was inspired by a pamphlet by Jeremy Collier unambiguously entitled *Of Duelling* (1698), and it illustrates Steele's departure from pure comedy to emphasize the exemplary and the sentimental. We see again here how the theater provided a cultural response to—and often anticipated—the great moral changes that were reshaping English society. These calls for reform would later be echoed by Richardson, whose "man of sensibility," Grandison, is an exemplary guardian of the welfare of the defenseless and the unfortunate and who refuses a duel with the libertine Sir Hargrave in a crucial episode of the first volume of the novel. A comparison between Steele's and Richardson's language illustrates the development of the theme:

> *Myrtle.* Dear Bevil, your friendly conduct has convinced me there is nothing manly but what is conducted by reason and agreeable to the practice of virtue and justice. And yet how many have been sacrificed to that idol, the unreasonable opinion of men! Nay, they are so ridiculous, in it, that they often use their swords against each other with dissembled anger and real fear. (*The Conscious Lovers,* 4.1)

Richardson's baronet expresses himself similarly: "I will not meet any man, Mr. Reeves, as a duellist. . . . I live not to the world: I live to myself; to the monitor within me. . . . Where is the magnanimity of a man that cannot get above the vulgar breath? . . . A man who defies his fellow-creature into the field, in a private quarrel, must first defy his God; and what are his *hopes,* but to be a murderer?—To do an irreparable injury to the innocent family and dependants of the murdered?"[77]

As a result of Steele's moral emphasis in *The Conscious Lovers,* the purely comic elements of the genre were relegated to the subplot featuring the lovers' faithful servants. Here we still find the traditional intrigues and disguises of ancient comedy, albeit employed solely to smooth the way for the union of the two virtuous protagonists. The main plot, instead, was ennobled by references to classic authors such as Heliodorus, Plautus, and Terence, with Terence filtered through Cibber, who collaborated with Steele on parts of the play and who was himself the author of a number of early sentimental comedies, as we have seen.[78]

The main marriage plot—the crux of the story at which all of its episodes converge—employs the traditional device of hindering the lovers' union to create a series of situations that allow the characters to display their benevolence, respect for others, and magnanimity. It is left to the servants to take the initiative and contrive to bring the lovers together, since the lovers would not dare act for fear of wounding the delicate feelings of their parents and friends. As the faithful Humphrey states: "Well, though this father and son live as well together as possible, yet their fear of giving each other pain is attended with constant mutual uneasiness" (*The Conscious Lovers,* 1.1). Similarly, after having fruitlessly "[laid] such fair occasions in [Bevil's] way that it will be impossible to avoid an explanation," Indiana herself can do no more than acknowledge the impenetrable reserve of the young man, which she fears is due to a mortifying indifference: "I protest, I begin to fear he is wholly disinterested in what he does for me" (*The Conscious Lovers,* 3.1).

The plot of *The Conscious Lovers,* the archetypal early-eighteenth-century sentimental comedy, is thus driven—or hindered—by the reticence, delicacy, and hyper-sensibility governing the characters' sentimental behavior. The traditional complications of courtship are turned into the exclusive focus of the plot and are so de-contextualized that they risk imploding and jeopardizing the ultimate happiness of the protagonists. But the code of conduct advocated by Steele has fruitful implications that will be explored throughout the century by many authors, from Richardson in *Grandison* to Hugh Kelly in *False Delicacy* (Drury Lane, 1768) and Frances Burney, who makes it one of the central symbolic themes of her novel *Camilla.*

The developments described thus far worked together to ensure that there was strong historical continuity not only between heroic drama and bourgeois tragedy, but also between social satire and moral comedy and, later, between both these genres and the novel. What emerges clearly from this picture is a common process of change involving the rejection of aristocratic ideals and the affirmation of domesticity, of the pathetic, and of the moral interiority of the individual, together with a new focus on personal experience, often conveyed by means of a love story. Crucial to all of these was the audience's identification (and sympathy) with the ordinary characters and events represented on-stage, as well as with the moral values advocated by playwrights, which were increasingly expected to reflect the moral order that was transforming society outside the theater's walls. It thus seems that between 1730 and 1740 the changes that would lead directly from the drama to the rise of the novel were already in place, thanks also to the "individualist and innovating reorientation" of English culture at this time.[79]

Brown has argued that the novel emerged out of the inability of serious and comic drama alike to represent not only the full range of individual experience, but also the emotional development of characters and their interactions with society: by their very nature, even when they are not merely passive victims, the virtuous protagonists of the drama cannot take action; nor can they engage fully with their social context. According to Brown, furthermore, the drama was unable to match the novel's ability to give expression to bourgeois ideology. Her argument is convincing, especially in light of the strong thematic and formal continuity that links the two genres, and that accounts for the eighteenth-century novel's distinctly transtextual character. I would therefore concur with Brown that not only the theater, but also the eighteenth-century novel, are "the products of their historical time in respect to the shapes of the stories that they attempt to tell." But it is no less true that both genres are even more the product of literary convention, "of their generic past, which dictates the specific ways in which those stories can be told,"[80] as well as of a wide array of forces connected to the radical ideological shift that characterized the period as a whole, including the moralizing campaigns associated with the emergence of the culture of sensibility, the entrenchment of preventive censorship and of the dual monopoly of the theater, and the triumph of moral action and didacticism.

Early Georgian theater experimented with many forms (tragicomedy, ballad opera, burlettas, pantomime) that worked against the dominant trend towards didacticism and classicism. But experiments in prose were no less fertile, ranging from autobiographical narrative to cautionary tales, from Christian fiction to journalism. It is in this context that the novel was able to overcome the formal impasse to which the emphasis on moral action had led the drama. Central to the novel was the psychological complexity (or internal verisimilitude) of its characters, which could embrace not only the perfect virtue of the typical pathetic heroine—as it does in Richardson's novels—but also the contrast between the innocent protagonist and his or her surrounding world (or social verisimilitude), as is the case for Fielding's characters or Burney's heroines, whose integrity is always contrasted with the imperfections of others.

The product of decisive historical forces and of changes in literary convention and form, the novel was able to move beyond the boundaries of the older genre, exploring themes and situations that had already undergone as much formal and linguistic change as the drama would allow. As a new genre, its beginnings dovetail exactly with the endpoint reached by the theater of the Restoration.

TWO

"In the Novel Way, There Is No Danger" Transmodal Adaptations and Transtextuality in *Evelina*

Therefore I think I am most safe—& know I am most easy—in resting a quiet spectator.

—Frances Burney, *Early Journals and Letters,* 28 October 1779

Frances Burney's literary career was framed by two episodes that can be considered emblematic both of her poetics and of her life. In 1767, at fifteen, she destroyed all of her manuscripts in a bonfire, afraid that her father would discover she had been writing; sixty-four years later, as she prepared to write her father's biography, she burned a substantial portion of his manuscript materials, which had been entrusted to her after his death.

Outwardly identical, but of opposite significance, the two episodes reveal much about Burney's complex attitude toward writing and professional authorship. Women's writing in the eighteenth century was subject to ideological constraints that required careful acts of negotiation within an intricate network of personal and social relationships. In Burney's case, these ideological constraints were reflected in her relationship with her father, Charles, the renowned musicologist, critic, and man of letters. Understanding how Burney constructed her relationship with her father is therefore crucial to understanding how she negotiated her position not only within the family but also within the patriarchal structure that impinged on all women's writing.

Although Charles Burney came from a humble background, his remarkable musical talent led to his employment, at seventeen, in the household of Fulke Greville, a wealthy aristocrat who was glad to secure the services and companionship of a promising young music master endowed with "mind and cultivation, as well as finger and ear."[1] At Wilbury House, their country estate, the Grevilles held a salon frequented by the most elegant and refined members of the beau monde, some of whom became Charles Burney's lifelong friends. Samuel Crisp, for example, later became so close to the Burney family that he earned the nickname "Daddy Crisp."

In 1749, Charles Burney left his position with Greville to marry Esther Sleepe, and in the next few years he gradually worked his way into London society, becoming one of the best-paid music masters in the city. His remarkable musical abilities and indefatigable work habits led to a doctorate from Oxford University in 1769, and his rising professional standing—and well-chosen friendships—allowed him to turn his London home into a highly sought-after musical salon. The Burney children reaped the benefits of this lively cultural environment, often enjoying the company of prominent public figures and artists, among them David Garrick and Joshua Reynolds.

As the ambitious Charles Burney was well aware, it was his literary aspirations that held the key to his social advancement. No matter how highly paid, the position of a music master remained socially and financially subordinate; the status of a critic and man of letters was far more respectable and prestigious, and Burney began to build his reputation by publishing two successful musical travel accounts, *The Present State of Music in France and Italy* (1771) and *The Present State of Music in Germany, the Netherlands, and the United Provinces* (1773). Both works were praised by critics, including Samuel Johnson. His next publication was a four-volume magnum opus, *A General History of Music from the Earliest Ages to the Present Period* (1776–89), for which he is still remembered today.[2]

Charles Burney did not effect this refashioning of his identity alone. After his first wife's death in 1762, he was assisted by his second wife, Elizabeth Allen, whom he had married in 1764, and by his children—especially his daughters—who felt the deepest respect and admiration for him. After his first-born, Esther, married in 1770, the arduous task of transcribing his voluminous manuscripts and preparing them for the press fell to Frances, whose role as amanuensis created a strong bond of mutual dependence between father and daughter. It was at this time, and in her father's shadow, that Frances Burney began to nurture a desire to write.

It is no accident that Frances Burney's literary career was symbolically bounded by the two bonfires mentioned at the start of this chapter. They can be said to represent opposite, but crucial, moments in her lifelong dialogue with her father. Throughout Frances Burney's life as a writer, Dr. Burney remained her main (although often implicit) interlocutor. The influence he exerted both on her work and on her life was so strong as to have convinced

Margaret Anne Doody, one of Frances Burney's most sensitive biographers, to turn her straightforward literary biography (tracing the "deep connection between the life and the writings") into a "psychobiography." As Doody admitted, "In my study of Frances Burney's life and works I have become, though almost unwillingly, increasingly impressed by the vital importance to her—both in her life and in her writings—of her relationship with her father."[3]

Charles Burney's approval or opposition affected his daughter's writing directly, and he seems to have evaluated each of her works in light of its potential effect on his own public image. Given these familial constraints, Frances Burney's work can be seen as a long journey toward self-definition, a quest for an autonomous authorial and professional identity. As we shall see, the theater played a crucial role in this complicated quest, shaping the way Burney expressed, repressed, and ultimately camouflaged her poetic voice.

The story of the bonfire that marked the beginning of Frances Burney's literary career was told long after the fact in the complex dedication to her father that opens *The Wanderer* (1814), her last novel.[4] Alternating between the stance of a diligent daughter and that of an independent author, Burney takes her father and herself back nearly half a century to 13 June 1767, when she consigned to the flames everything she had composed for her own amusement thus far. Among the manuscripts was a short novel, *The History of Caroline Evelyn,* the urtext for *Evelina; or, The History of a Young Lady's Entrance into the World,* the novel that a few years later would make her famous. Described as "Elegies, Odes, Plays, Songs, Stories, Farces—nay Tragedies and Epic Poems,"[5] the burned manuscripts diverged widely in genre, encompassing not only narrative prose but also drama and poetry and reveal the broad range of Burney's earliest literary experiments.

In the dedication to Dr. Burney, Frances Burney recalls how she was driven to this self-punishing act by the shame she would have felt had he discovered her literary inclinations:

> So early was I impressed myself with ideas that fastened degradation to this class of composition, that at the age of adolescence, I *struggled against the propensity* which, even in childhood, even from the moment I could hold a pen, had *impelled* me into its toils; and on my fifteenth birth-day, I made *so resolute a conquest over an inclination at which I blushed,* and that I had always kept secret, that I committed to

> the flames whatever, up to that moment, I had committed to paper. And so enormous was the pile, that I thought it prudent to consume it in the garden.
>
> You, dear Sir, knew nothing of its extinction, for you had never known of its existence. Our darling Susanna, to whom alone I had ever ventured to read its contents, alone witnessed the conflagration; and—well I remember!—wept, with tender partiality, over the *imaginary ashes* of Caroline Evelyn, the mother of Evelina.
>
> The *passion,* however, though resisted, was not annihilated: my bureau was cleared; but my head was not emptied; and, *in defiance of every self-effort, Evelina struggled herself into life. . . .*
>
> [T]hen, even in the season of youth, *I felt ashamed* of appearing to be a votary to a species of writing that you, Sir, liberal as I knew you to be, I thought condemned. (*The Wanderer,* 8–9; emphasis added)

Burney's account of her first literary efforts openly describes the extent to which Charles Burney's opinion influenced and constrained her, inducing her even long after the fact to write a literary manifesto. The first remarkable thing about the author's confession is how she explains her creative process: by overtly disavowing any desire for self-assertion, the process of composition becomes depersonalized, almost automatized, a creative parthenogenesis that "def[ies] every self-effort." The psychological difficulty of accepting her own assertive drive is indicated by the "blush" of shame produced by her awareness of her father's likely opposition. And here a second motif of Burney's bonfire of the vanities emerges: burning one's self, erasing and annulling it (as we shall see, "nobody" is a recurring term—both explicitly and implicitly—in Burney's work) appears to be the only possible response to the repressive will of the father.[6]

The third motif of the autobiographical reconstruction Frances Burney addresses to her father emerges out of the axiological intersection between paternal authoritativeness and literary authority, or biological creator and fictional creature; between a parent and his abject and unspeakable "monstrous progeny."[7] Not only does Charles Burney come between Frances and her work ("a species of writing that you . . . I thought condemned"), but the imaginary ashes of Caroline Evelyn, whose death gives rise to the events narrated in *Evelina* (1778), are mixed in with the real ashes produced by the bonfire of the manuscripts.

This remarkable imbrication of the author figure (Burney), the novel written by her (*The History of Caroline Evelyn*), and the heroine of the same novel (Caroline Evelyn) becomes clearer when we compare the dedication's retrospective reconstruction in *The Wanderer* with the dedication "To ———" at the beginning of *Evelina,* her first novel. Before *Evelina,* Burney had written extensive journals and diaries to be read by her sister Susanna and Samuel Crisp, but for the first time she now chose to move beyond the private and para-literary genre of journal writing to seek publication and a broader audience.

After a lengthy and unnerving process of negotiation with the printer Lowndes, partly delegated to her brother Charles due to gender constraints, *Evelina* was finally published as an anonymous work. Burney's timidity even drove her to alter her handwriting, since it could easily have been recognized as the hand that transcribed Dr. Burney's manuscripts. This timidity speaks to a self-imposed desire for anonymity shared by many female authors of the time and is easier to explain if we recall that Burney had referred to her first work as "a mere frolic, to see how a production of my own would figure in that Author like form" (*EJL,* 3:32). The need to justify, pre-emptively define, and recommend her work is evident in the volume's peritextual apparatus, aimed at three different audiences, implicit and explicit. The volume opens with a dedicatory poem addressed to her famous father, "To ———," followed by a dedicatory letter to the critics of the *Monthly Review* and the *Critical Review.* Only after this double *captatio benevolentiae* do we come to the real preface.[8] The progressive broadening of the field of addressees reveals the implicit connection linking the dominant authority within the family—the father—to the culture at large: the literary critics and, beyond them, the reading public.

Burney's composite prefatory material insistently downplays both her authorial persona and the value of her literary work. But this exercise in humility is ultimately undercut in the dedicatory poem addressed to her father ("Oh author of my being"), whose contempt for—or, at least, disapproval of—his daughter's novel experiment is taken for granted. The central stanzas of the poem, in particular, are highly suggestive of the tension between the literary authority Burney is seeking and the authority of the father she is addressing:

> Could my *weak* pow'rs thy *num'rous virtues* trace,
> By filial love each fear should be repress'd;
> The *blush* of Incapacity I'd chase,
> And stand, recorder of thy worth, confess'd:

But since my niggard stars that gift refuse,
Concealment is the only boon I claim;
Obscure be *still* the unsuccessful Muse,
Who cannot raise, but would not sink, thy fame.
(*Evelina,* 3; emphasis added)

This apparently straightforward dedication introducing the (implicit and explicit) author and the work is, however, open to a reading that bypasses its overtly apologetic intent. The textual palimpsest concealed in the dedication emerges in the fourth stanza,[9] where praise of the father ("thy num'rous virtues," "thy worth") appears to verge on the ironic, turning into a mock dedication. The author's feeble voice ("weak pow'rs")—previously suppressed out of fear of paternal disapproval but now freely expressed under the protective cover of anonymity—anticipates a future in which the incognito now eagerly sought might be discarded. For the time being, however, the work Burney is presenting is described as so mediocre that were her name to be known, the revelation would risk sullying her father's fame. It is therefore best that her identity remain, for the moment, concealed.

If we set aside the flattering rhetoric of filial piety, Burney's language sounds doubly assertive. On one hand, she asserts her will to continue to write, cloaked in the anonymity that guarantees her independence from Dr. Burney's criticism and control. On the other hand, the refusal to link her own work to her father's name allows her to claim full social and poetic autonomy while declining to contribute any further to her father's fame. Anonymity thus becomes not only a protective device and a means to enable expression, but also an ingenious strategy to distance herself from the cumbersome fatherly figure who stands between the author and her work.

The decision to present her novel in a "concealed" and "obscure" manner thus served to free Frances Burney from the ties and limitations that defined her social identity as a daughter. Constructing an anonymous voice, independent of the family context that defined her, the author freed herself of the code of silence, passivity, and submission through which the eighteenth century's dominant ideology governed women's lives, relegating them to their salvific role as silent auditors of masculine discourse.[10]

The freedom granted her by anonymity and the rejection of the protection available to her through her surname—a crucial social sign whose lack, and recovery, in fact constitute the symbolic crux of the novel—are further stressed in the appeal to the critics of the *Monthly Review* and the *Critical*

Review (*Evelina,* 4–6), addressed pointedly as "Authors." Here, Burney's apparently deferential authorial persona presents her work to the critics as a "frivolous amusement," the fruit of a "few idle hours" (*Evelina,* 4), the amateurish pastime of a dilettante who is emphatically not a "hackneyed writer," or, worse, "a half-starv'd garretter" (*Evelina,* 5).[11]

Introduced as "without name, without recommendation," the book is entrusted to the "protection" and the "patronage" of the critics in a clever reactivation of the patrilineal pact that the reiterated rejection of her father's name had instead persisted in violating:[12]

> Without name, without recommendation, and unknown alike to success and disgrace, to whom can I so properly apply for patronage, as to those who publicly profess themselves Inspectors of all literary performances?
>
> The extensive plan of your critical observations,—which, not confined to works of utility or ingenuity, is equally open to those of frivolous amusements,—and yet worse than frivolous dullness,—encourages me to seek for your protection, since,—perhaps for my sins!—it entitles me to your annotations. (*Evelina,* 4)

Burney concludes her appeal with a self-censoring gesture: "*Here let me rest,*—and snatch myself, while yet I am able, from the fascination of EGOTISM—a monster who has more votaries than ever did homage to the most popular deity of antiquity" (*Evelina,* 6).

This tension between the need for submission and for recognition, between silence and expression, central to Burney's poetics, comes to a head semantically with the stress on the term "egotism," while the appositive "monster" carries a further connotation linked to its etymological origins: *monstrum* is an "extraordinary, prodigious, marvelous exemplum" (from the Latin *monstrare* [to show] and *monere* [to admonish]). Thus, egotism not only makes the author monstrous and locates her outside the norm, but by removing the veil of privacy, it transforms her into a "strange sight," a "prodigy," and, by extension, a marvelous spectacle, capable of arousing admiration or fear.[13]

Burney would soon bitterly regret the violation of privacy that resulted from her book's appearance on the market, as is apparent in a journal entry where her references to herself as poetic subject are linked to the commercial circulation of the object she has produced: "I have an exceeding odd sensation, when I consider that it is in the power of any & every body to read what I so carefully hoarded even from my best Friends, till this last month or two,—& that a Work which was so lately Lodged, in all privacy, in my Bureau, may now be seen by every Butcher & Baker, cobbler & Tinker, throughout the three Kingdoms, for the small tribute of 3 pence" (*EJL,* 3:5). Burney's description of her sense of profanation and exposure exhibits two main features of the epistolary genre: private life is made public through publication, and simultaneously the text—the paper metonym for the author's body and zone of intimacy, as hypostatized by Burney's literary model, Samuel Richardson—becomes eroticized by being intercepted, handled, and scrutinized both by fictional readers and by real ones. This exposure is intensified by the economy of the book market: as the book is sold or exchanged in the theater of Bell's circulating library, the circulation of printed type also commodifies the human type—*Evelina* and Burney both pay the price for their respective "entrance into the world."

The volume's preface completes *Evelina*'s presentation. Here Burney projects her aspiration to literary authority within the cultural context of the time. After again stressing the need to preserve her anonymity, motivated by the "peculiar situation of the editor" (*Evelina,* 7), the author suggests a contextualization of her work that reads like a full-blown poetic manifesto:

> To avoid what is common, without adopting what is unnatural, must limit the ambition of the vulgar herd of authors: however zealous, therefore, my veneration of the great writers I have mentioned, however I may feel enlightened by the knowledge of Johnson, charmed with the eloquence of Rousseau, softened by the pathetic powers of Richardson, and exhilarated by the wit of Fielding, and humour of Smollett, I yet presume not to attempt pursuing the same ground which they have tracked; whence, though they may have cleared the weeds, they have also culled the flowers, and though they have rendered the path plain, they have left it barren. (*Evelina,* 8–9)

Burney therefore presents her work "*with a very singular mixture of* timidity and confidence" (*Evelina,* 7),[14] seeking recognition and legitimation within the context of the masculine tradition of novel writing that preceded her. In spite of the early self-deprecating references to famous novelists of the time (she describes herself as a "humble Novelist," her gender masked by masculine adjectives: "his brethren of the quill," "his fate" [*Evelina,* 7]), Burney mentions Rousseau, Richardson, Fielding, and Smollett only to distance herself from them and to create her own literary antecedents. If the reference to the tradition of novel writing serves implicitly to insert Burney in the canon, and to confer authoritativeness on her, at the same time it contains an invitation to the implied reader to recognize and appreciate the difference, and hence the originality, of the book he or she is about to read.

> She would give him his choice whether he would
> know whom she was, or see her face.
>
> —William Congreve, *Incognita* (1692)

Burney's ambitious juxtaposition of her work with that of the literary giants of the past in *Evelina*'s preface turned out to have been fully justified: the "Year [that] was ushered in by a grand & most important Event . . . the first publication of the ingenious, learned, & most profound Miss Burney" (*EJL*, 3:1), as she mockingly described it, saw the novel reach four editions in quick succession. There were many reasons for this extraordinary achievement. In the preface, the author had briefly described the narrative formula that would ensure the astonishing success of the novel, which related the adventures of the ingenuous and virtuous young heroine as she made her way onto the brilliant London social scene:

> To draw characters from nature, though not from life, and to mark the manners of the times, is the attempted plan of the following letters. For this purpose, a young female, educated in the most secluded retirement, makes, at the age of seventeen, her first appearance upon the great and busy stage of life; with a virtuous mind, a cultivated understanding, and a feeling heart, her ignorance of the forms, and inexperience in the manners, of the world, occasion all the little incidents which these volumes record, and which form the natural progression of the life of a young woman of obscure birth, but conspicuous beauty, for the six months after her *Entrance into the world.* (*Evelina*, 7–8)

Two plot lines intertwine and overlap in the novel, producing a narrative whose episodes are connected by relations of cause and effect. The primary mover of the plot is Evelina's quest for recognition. Although she is the legitimate daughter of Sir John Belmont and Caroline Evelyn, her father inexplicably fails to acknowledge her at birth. This lack of paternal recognition is concretized by Evelina's lack of a proper surname—the name Anville, chosen by her guardian as a fictional social sign, is merely an anagram, a simple contrivance that reflects the young woman's social vulnerability.[15]

Intertwined with the quest for social recognition associated with acquiring the surname Belmont is the second main strand of the narrative, the love story between Evelina and Lord Orville. By disclosing his love for Evelina before she has been claimed by her father, Orville proves that he loves her for her many virtues ("[the] virtuous mind, [the] cultivated understanding, and [the] feeling heart" mentioned in the novel's preface, [*Evelina,* 7]) rather than for her family connections.

The novel's three-part structure reflects a story line built on suggestive symmetries and a series of events linked by relations of causality or probability, producing what the author called the "natural progression" (*Evelina,* 8) of the plot.[16] The first volume describes Evelina's London apprenticeship. Having left the protection of her guardian, Mr. Villars, and his home, Berry Hill, she is introduced to London's aristocratic society by a surrogate mother figure, her chaperone Mrs. Mirvan. In this first period spent in London, Evelina meets Lord Orville and—apparently by coincidence—Madame Duval, her maternal grandfather's widow, who now bears the surname of her second husband, a Frenchman, and who has long threatened to claim her rights over her granddaughter by taking her to Paris.

After an interlude set in the country, at Berry Hill, the first volume's adventures are followed in the second by a return to the capital, where Evelina, now accompanied by Madame Duval, is forced to associate with the latter's ill-mannered relations, the grotesque Branghtons, and becomes aware of the snares that make a young lady's entrance into society such a dangerous and critical rite of passage. At this time, she attends a number of social gatherings where she meets Lord Orville, who is evidently attracted by her ingenuousness and generosity. Orville observes Evelina as she moves through a hostile and insidious world whose rules she is imperfectly acquainted with, leading her to make repeated faux pas that, however, invariably demonstrate her innocence and simplicity.

In the last volume, Evelina's family difficulties are finally resolved. At the Bristol Hotwells, where she has accompanied Mrs. Selwyn, Orville asks for her hand in marriage. This first happy epilogue is followed—and socially sanctioned—by Sir John Belmont's long-awaited public acknowledgment of his daughter, which comes about as a result of the providential clearing up of a misunderstanding surrounding her birth. The happy conclusion of Evelina's social history (her legitimation by her father) thus coincides with the resolution of her personal history (her marriage with Orville), in a double dénouement that reasserts the values of sensibility and filial devotion while providing a solid foundation for the young woman's standing in society and for her own sense of her identity.

FIGURE 1. Characters' actantial roles in *Evelina*

Helpers		Opponents
	←	Madame Duval
Lady Howard		Captain Mirvan
Mr. Villars		Lady Louisa Larpent
Mrs. Mirvan		Lord Merton
Lord Orville		Sir Clement Willoughby
Macartney		Mr. Lovel
Mrs. Selwyn		The Branghtons
Mrs. Clinton		
	←	Sir John Belmont
		(Dame Green)
		(Polly Green)

Figure 1 shows how Evelina's relationships with the other characters in the novel can be grouped according to actantial criteria, based on whether the characters oppose or assist her quest for familial and social recognition. Dame Green (Evelina's nurse) and her daughter Polly Green are blocking characters only in part, since the nurse's exchange of newborns turns out to have been prompted by Caroline Evelyn's dying wish that her daughter be raised by Mr. Villars. Dame Green can thus truthfully plead, "[I] had no ill designs . . . as *Miss* [Evelina] would never be the worse for it" (*Evelina,* 416). Polly herself, presented to Belmont as his legitimate daughter and thus the unwitting cause of his considering Evelina an impostor, is cleared of all wrongdoing by the heroine in yet another display of her disinterestedness and humanity: "She is entitled to my kindest offices, and I shall always consider her as my sister" (*Evelina,* 417).

The double dénouement has the further effect of reversing the roles initially assigned to Sir John Belmont and Madame Duval, who were responsible, respectively, for Evelina's social isolation and for her social embarrassment. In the reversal, not only does Belmont solemnly acknowledge his daughter and organize her wedding, but Madame Duval makes Evelina her only heir (at the expense of her London relatives, the Branghtons), thus further ensuring her granddaughter's financial independence.

The novel's division into three distinct volumes replicates the stages in Evelina's development, as she frequents London's fashionable gatherings and completes her social education, learning how to negotiate high society's behavioral code and how to evaluate the actions and the true feelings of the characters she meets. Burney carefully describes the city and its endless attractions in a full-length portrait that takes in both the low-brow entertainments designed to satisfy the coarser cultural appetites of the "cits" and the more refined amusements favored by the beau monde ("the world" of the novel's subtitle), aptly summarized by George Colman in a comedy of the time:

> *Bon-Ton*'s a constant trade
> Of rout, *Festino,* Ball and Masquerade!
> 'Tis plays and puppet-shows; 'tis something new!
> 'Tis losing thousands ev'ry night at loo!
> Nature it thwarts, and contradicts all reason;
> 'Tis stiff French Stays, and fruit when out of season!
> A rose, when half a guinea is the price,
> A set of bays, scarce bigger than six mice;
> To visit friends you never wish to see;
> Marriage 'twixt those, who never can agree;
> Old dowagers, dressed, painted, patch'd, and curl'd;
> This is *Bon-Ton,* and this we call *the world!*[17]

The chronotopological structure of the novel also respects the story's subdivision into three distinct sections linked by the iteration of specular themes and episodes. The novel's topography is based on a clear-cut distinction between the ideal world of the country—the idyllic home of Evelina's childhood, positively associated with Nature—and the chaotic and seductive London world, on which Evelina gains a double perspective, first under the guidance of the attentive Mrs. Mirvan (in the first volume), and later under that of the ill-bred Madame Duval (in the second volume).[18] Her London experiences, and the inevitable misadventures that befall her in town, turn out to be essential to Evelina's development. Learning how to negotiate the social world to which she belongs by right is necessary to prepare her for the time when her identity will be defined by her new relationship with her father, Belmont, and her husband, Orville. The isolation in which she was brought up by Villars, and the retired and bucolic life of Berry Hill, are thus retrospectively seen to have contributed to her early social ostracism: "My father had no correspondent at Berry Hill, [and] the child [Polly Green] was instantly sent to France, where being brought up in *as much retirement as myself,* nothing but *accident* could discover the fraud" (*Evelina,* 416; emphasis added). The topological structure

FIGURE 2. Chronotopological structure in *Evelina*

	(*Evelina*, 1:1–24)	
Berry Hill	Howard Grove	London (Queen-Ann Street)
Villars	Lady Howard and *Mrs. Mirvan*	
	26 March–1 April	2–19 April
⟶	⟶	⟶
	(*Evelina*, 1:25–31, 2:1–9)	
		Mrs. Mirvan and Madame Duval
		20 April–5 June
	⟵	⟵
	(*Evelina*, 2:9–25)	
		London (Holborn)
		Madame Duval and the Branghtons
		6 June–8 July (approx.)
	⟶	⟶
	(*Evelina*, 2:26–30, 3:1–22)	
Bristol (Clifton)	Berry Hill	London (Holborn)
Mrs. Selwyn		*Madame Duval*
28 August–13 October	27 August	14 July (approx.)
⟵	⟵	⟵
	(*Evelina*, 3:23)	
Bristol	Berry Hill	
Lord Orville		
13 October		
⟶	⟶	

Note: The names of Evelina's chaperones are in italics. Their marked differences, and the order in which they succeed each other, contribute to the opposition–specularity motif that underlies the novel's plot.

of Evelina's movements in the course of the novel's three volumes, which is based on the classic city–country dichotomy typical of late seventeenth-century comedy,[19] reflects the novel's fairly rigorous chronological structure (see figure 2). The accelerating pace of events, whose entire duration Burney had noted in the preface to the novel ("the first six months after *[Evelina's] Entrance into the world*," [*Evelina*, 8]), suggests a subdivision of the story into two sections of unequal length, devoted respectively to the presentation of Evelina and the principal characters in her history (in volumes 1 and 2), and to the narrative of the private events leading to her recognition by her father and the ensuing resolution (volume 3). The letters written between 2 April and 8 July describe Evelina's new London acquaintances and the various public places she attends. Mrs. Mirvan (daughter of the aristocratic Lady Howard, and a surrogate mother figure for Evelina) and her home on elegant Queen-Ann Street are associated with the most fashionable and refined London gatherings, whereas Evelina's stay in Holborn, in the heart of the city, with the crude Madame Duval and her vulgar Snow Hill relatives introduces her to less refined diversions. We can thus draw an outline (figure 3) of the public places and theatrical sites frequented by the heroine with her two chaperones.[20]

The various worldly gatherings Evelina attends with Mrs. Mirvan and Madame Duval allow Burney to paint a realistic portrait of the many attractions of London society. The plays and elegant gathering places Evelina frequents with Mrs. Mirvan are specular counterparts to the diversions she attends with Madame Duval. In some cases, Evelina visits the same place twice, first in the aristocratic company of the Mirvans and then with the Branghtons, the family of vulgar upstarts related to Madame Duval. This

FIGURE 3. Public places and theatrical sites visited by Evelina

With Mrs. Mirvan	With Madame Duval
Drury Lane Theatre:	New Theatre, Haymarket:
1. Unidentified performance (Garrick)	*The Minor* and *The Commissary* (Foote)
2. *Love for Love* (Congreve)	
3. *King Lear* (Shakespeare–Garrick)	
Opera House	Opera House
Ranelagh Pleasure Grounds	Vauxhall
Pantheon	White-Conduit House
The Mall	Marylebone Gardens
Kensington Gardens	Kensington Gardens
The Ridotto	Long Rooms, Hampstead
Cox's Museum	
Fantoccini (puppet theater)	

happens at the Opera House, for example, and the juxtaposition of the two episodes provides much more than a comic interlude at the expense of the Branghtons. The mixing of classes in public spaces such as theaters and the opera—an extraordinary phenomenon at a time when the ideal of social equality had virtually no currency—reflected the sweeping economic changes associated with the pursuit of upward mobility and the business ethos that had emerged during the Restoration, and that was altering the landscape of Georgian society beyond recognition. The financial power wielded by Branghton, the wealthy widow Duval, and their like, had had an effect on the theater, as well, especially on the commissioning of plays and the cultural demand for them. Thus, in *Evelina,* two distinct but coexisting sets of spectators can attend performances specially designed for each. While a cultivated and literate audience enjoys William Congreve's comedy of manners or David Garrick's impassioned renditions of the Shakespearean repertory, a less refined audience can laugh at the farcical comedy offered by the self-styled English Aristophanes, Samuel Foote.

The choice of social gatherings Londoners attended hence was dictated by the rules of worldly decorum, linking each entertainment to a specific class. Thus, the gardens at Marylebone, described by a witness of the time as a gathering place for the "gentry, rather than the *haut ton,*"[21] are contrasted with those of Kensington, while Vauxhall is compared with Ranelagh, as in a farce of the time:

> *Lady Bab.* Oh! Fie! Lady Charlotte, you are quite indelicate. I am sorry for your taste.
>
> *Lady Charlotte.* Well, I say it again, I love Vaux Hall.
>
> *Lady Bab.* O' my stars! Why, there is nobody there but filthy Citizens.
>
> *Lady Charlotte.* We were in Hopes the raising of the Price would have kept them out, ha ha ha.
>
> *Lady Bab.* Ha, ha, ha. *Ranelow* for my money.[22]

In addition to London's public gathering places, Evelina goes to the famous Pump Room at Bristol Hotwells and to Bath, which was then undergoing rapid development at the hands of the architect John Wood, who created a new form of urban culture by providing a "grand Place for publick Assembly."[23]

The novel's juxtaposition of the legitimate theater associated with Garrick and the unpatented theatrical entertainments of Samuel Foote is therefore highly significant. Foote, whose farces caricatured famous public figures (including Garrick), was connected to popular theater and operated in environments, such as the Little Theatre in the Haymarket, where performances were staged without official sanction and at times, such as matinees, when the Theatres Royal were closed. *The Minor* (1760), the satire Evelina attends in Madame Duval's company, is a typical example of the kind of performance diametrically opposed to Garrick's productions both in technique and in theme. Foote's satire targeted the preacher George Whitefield and Methodism, the religious movement that appeared to reflect most closely the culture of sensibility emerging in the course of the century. It made a sensation by including the character of Mother Cole, "modelled on a real life bawd" converted to Methodism, who was represented "mouth[ing] Methodist pieces as she tries to sell the young hero one of the girls."[24] The contrast between Garrick and Foote had become newly topical just as Burney was writing *Evelina* in 1777, the year of Foote's death. The "English Aristophanes" had died only a few months after dramatically leaving the stage, and the simultaneous retirement of Garrick (he gave his last, much fêted performance at the end of the 1775–76 season) had once more drawn attention to the decades-old rivalry between the dramatists, an antagonism that now took center stage again thanks to this final professional coincidence.[25] The Garrick–Foote contrast is therefore richly significant. On one hand, it highlights the distinction between patented and unpatented theaters that would become ever more entrenched in the Georgian era and that was reflected in the opposition between Garrick's elevated acting style and the one-man shows staged by Foote, whose imitations "had [n]either the subtlety [n]or the finesse that David displayed";[26] on the other hand, it also reflects the historical opposition between the aristocratic values of the landed gentry—the Mirvans—and those of parvenus such as the Branghtons and Madame Duval, whose wealth and vulgar ostentation, linked to economic individualism and the emergence of the bourgeois merchant class, mimic, or even seem to parody, the social habits and tastes of the upper classes.

Evelina's vivid portrait of Georgian London's theater scene gives a sense of the variety of plays on offer, and the novel's theatrical references, shown in figure 4, span the range from contemporary to Restoration and Elizabethan drama. Clearly, the greatest number of plays by a single author are Shakespeare's (six out of a total of thirteen), and their importance to the economy of the novel is anticipated by the reiterated Shakespearean citations in the

FIGURE 4. Dramatic references in *Evelina*

Dedication "To the Authors of the Monthly and Critical Reviews"	Vol. 1	Vol. 2	Vol. 3
Macbeth Shakespeare (1606)	*The Suspicious Husband* Hoadley (1747)	*The Minor* Foote (1760)	*The Drummer* Addison (1716)
The Merchant of Venice (twice) Shakespeare (1596)	*Richard III* Shakespeare (1592–93)	*The Commissary* Foote (1765)	
	King Lear Shakespeare (1605)	*False Delicacy* Kelly (1768)	
	Twelfth Night Shakespeare (1623)		
	Love for Love Congreve (1695)		
	The Deuce Is in Him Colman (the Elder) (1763)		

prefatory letter to the critics of the *Monthly Review* and the *Critical Review* (*Evelina,* 4–6).[27] Shakespeare's fame had reached new heights in the eighteenth century, when he was considered an author of unmatched genius who presented a faithful mirror to nature.[28] Samuel Johnson had written extensively about his plays, and Garrick had contributed to raising his cultural status through his Stratford celebrations of the Bard in 1769. Frances Burney seems to have relied indirectly on Shakespeare to cast an aura of nobility over the novel she was submitting to the judgment of her audience and critics:

> As Magistrates of the press, and Censors for the public . . . to appeal to your MERCY, were to solicit your dishonour; and therefore,—though 'tis sweeter than frankincense,—more grateful to the senses than all the odorous perfumes of Arabia [*Macbeth*], and though

> It droppeth like the gentle rain from heaven
> Upon the place beneath,— [*The Merchant of Venice*]
>
> I court it not! . . . Your engagements are not to the supplicating author, but to the candid public, which will not fail to crave
>
> The penalty and forfeit of your bond. [*The Merchant of Venice*]
>
> (*Evelina,* 5)

This use of Shakespeare to endow the novel with the noblest of literary genealogies also anticipates the important role played by the performance of *King Lear,* which Evelina faithfully records in volume 1, letter 12 (*Evelina,* 42). I will return to this crucial episode later to discuss the formal and metatextual relations between the novel and its theatrical context.[29]

The topological and chronological division of the novel into five distinct sections subdivides the plot into three primary and two secondary moments that we can call, respectively, acts and entr'actes. During the acts, set in the city, the action proceeds according to a threefold forward movement (chronological, spatial, and narrative), while the entr'actes provide two brief interludes set in the country that release the tension built during the acts.

In the first act, Evelina makes her debut in London society, where her inexperience repeatedly causes her acute social embarrassment. At the various gatherings she attends she meets such members of high society as Lovel and Willoughby and the incomparable Lord Orville. Moreover, Lady Howard's solicitous concern sets in motion one of the two main plot lines of the novel: that of Belmont's long-overdue acknowledgment of Evelina's legitimacy.

Having unexpectedly run into the Frenchified Madame Duval, Evelina witnesses the frequent skirmishes between the latter and the patriotic Captain Mirvan, episodes that show all of the physicality of full-blown farce. At her first appearance, Madame Duval, "dresse[d] very gaily, paint[ed] very high," as the astonished heroine notes, immediately holds forth in a violent tirade against Mirvan who, having grabbed the woman unceremoniously by the arm, warns her: "Hark you, Mrs. Frog, you'd best hold your tongue, for I must make bold to tell you, if you don't, that I shall make no ceremony of tripping you out of the window" (*Evelina,* 57).[30]

The squabbles between Madame Duval and the captain continue in the first entr'acte, set in Howard Grove, where a crescendo of quips and taunts climaxes in the terrible punishment inflicted on her by Mirvan and Willoughby. Disguised as bandits, they assault her, leaving her bound and battered in a muddy ditch, to their great hilarity: "Her head-dress had fallen off; her linen was torn; her negligee had not a pin left in it; her petticoats she was obliged to hold on; her shoes were perpetually slipping off. She was covered with dirt, weeds, and filth, and her face was really horrible, for the pomatum and powder from her head, and the dust from the road, were quite *pasted* on the skin by her tears, which, with her rouge, made so frightful a mixture, that she hardly looked human" (*Evelina,* 165–66).[31]

Burney appears to have drawn on the theater for this image, as well, particularly Garrick's famous roles in drag. His impersonation of Lady Brute, for example, had been illustrated by Johann Zoffany in a painting (*Sir John Brute in the Lady in Disguise Scene;* see gallery) later made into a widely circulated print, and as a newspaper of the time reported, "When personating Lady Brute, you would swear [Garrick] had often attended the toilette, and there gleaned up the various airs of the fair sex. He is perfectly versed in the exercise of the fan, the lips, the adjustment of the tucker, and even the minutest conduct of the finger."[32]

In the second act, Evelina returns to London with Madame Duval. The new social embarrassments she is subjected to by her grandmother and the Branghtons, who now accompany the heroine in her social outings, form a foil to the pathetic story of Macartney, a poor Scotsman (Evelina's stepbrother, as it turns out) whose misfortunes arouse Evelina's pity, allowing her to display her tender sensibility. Meanwhile, further complications arise in Evelina's quest for legitimation, since Belmont categorically refuses to admit his paternity or even to meet her. These highly emotional episodes are occasions for Evelina's sensibility to shine forth, and they increase the narrative tension.

During the second entr'acte, set at Berry Hill, Evelina indirectly reveals her love for Orville to her friend Maria Mirvan. The development of the love-interest plot then comes to a climax in the third act, set in Bristol, where both main plot lines—family and love—are resolved. Belmont is reunited with Evelina in a dramatic scene that thrilled readers of the time, and Evelina and Orville are joined in marriage. During Evelina's stay with the aristocratic Mrs. Beaumont, she makes the acquaintance of the pretentious Lord Merton and Lady Louisa Larpent and suffers further social embarrassment at their hands. Meanwhile, Captain Mirvan again provides a comic counterpoint to the main plot by elegantly dressing up a monkey and presenting it to the fashionable Lovel as a mirror image of the fop. Enraged by the practical joke, Lovel is viciously bitten by the monkey.

The novel's organization into acts and interludes allows Burney to interweave four different types of dramatic action that alternate and displace

FIGURE 5. Theatrical structure of *Evelina,* by genre

Act	Entr'acte	Act	Entr'acte	Act
London	Howard Grove	London	Berry Hill	Bristol
Comedy of manners	Farce	Farce	Sentimental comedy	Sentimental comedy and domestic drama

each other: comedy of manners (Evelina's entrance into society), sentimental comedy (her courtship with Orville), domestic drama (Belmont's mysterious refusal to acknowledge her and her resulting misadventures), and farce (the violent physical comedy of the relationship between Madame Duval and Captain Mirvan). Each act and entr'acte is dominated by one of the four types of dramatic action (see figure 5). The first act, set in London, is dominated by comedy of manners, while the Howard Grove interlude is markedly farcical, as is the second act set in London. The second entr'acte at Berry Hill is dominated by sentimental comedy, and the last act at the resort resolves both the sentimental and domestic plot lines.

The novel therefore builds to a dramatic climax through a series of episodes linked not only by causal relationships, but also by a set of generic intersections and overlappings that create a balanced alternation of the tragic, the comic, and the farcical. This careful mixing of stage genres serves as a structural counterpart to the many theatrical references in the novel. Although *Evelina* remains resolutely within the bounds of the Aristotelian comedic model (with an opening situation that leads to obstacles and then to a reversal that is followed by the overcoming of the obstacles and the happy ending),[33] on the thematic level, the text seems to reflect perfectly the hybrid overlapping of forms that characterized the late-Georgian dramatic repertoire.

Evelina's extraordinary success (actually enhanced by Burney's insistence on anonymity, which produced a spate of hypothetical attributions), and the general consensus about its worth among both literary critics and ordinary readers, can be attributed to the effective narrative formula Burney devised. The novel's plot, made up of alternating comic, sentimental, and dramatic episodes, had a suitably edifying conclusion in full accordance with poetic justice. The author's deferential appeal to the critics of the *Monthly Review* and *Critical Review* had the desired effect: the novel was recommended as ideal reading for the entire family, and especially women, "[who] will weep and (what is not so commonly the effect of novels) will laugh and grow wiser, as they read."[34]

Undoubtedly, among the reasons for *Evelina*'s remarkable success was the narrative technique Burney selected. The heroine's personal and social history is told in the letters she writes to her guardian, Villars, to whom she reports in detail (nearly) all her adventures and encounters. Burney's choice of the epistolary technique was probably partly influenced by its popularity in the eighteenth century, but the decision is perhaps also due to her long apprenticeship as a diarist and compiler of detailed letter journals that can be said to constitute the first stage in her literary career.[35]

Burney's first diary was addressed to an imaginary "Miss Nobody" to whom she wrote in a colloquial style that reproduced the rhythms of ordinary speech, but from 1770 onward, she began to write to her sister Susanna and to Samuel Crisp, sending them notebooks filled with detailed accounts of events in a quasi-literary style made up of a "strangle medley of Thoughts and Facts" (*EJL*, 1:1). Having adopted real recipients for her journals and having thus placed them in circulation (those sent to Crisp were usually shared with the other residents of Chessington Hall), Burney began to pay closer attention to her style: the letters had to please and entertain—and might be subjected to criticism. In other words, they became a literary production.[36]

In a sense, then, *Evelina* can be considered the "longest journal letter" Burney had ever written,[37] and her use of the epistolary style should be seen as operating on two levels: as directly bearing on the characterization of the novel's heroine, but also as connected to Burney's own biography. The narrative is focused entirely on the character of Evelina; as the author of most of the novel's letters, she produces a strongly *voiced* narrative whose quasi-oral tone and emotional and expressive style is suited not only to the letter form but also to her main character traits: innocence, spontaneity, and naturalness.[38] No less important is the fact that, as a form, the letter is directed to (and composed for) a specific recipient. As such, it is a means of communication that is never impersonal; rather, it is eminently personal at both the composing and receiving ends. Evelina's devotion to her guardian Villars thus necessarily affects both the content and the form of her letters to him.

Evelina's descriptions of her feelings for Lord Orville, for example, are reserved for her friend Maria Mirvan, in a parallel correspondence to that with Villars, but rather more sentimental in tone and designedly more marginal. Evelina in fact admits to her guardian that she feels greater confidence in her young friend's understanding than in his severe judgment: "Will you forgive me, if I own that I *first* wrote an account of this transaction to Miss Mirvan?—and that I even thought of *concealing* it to you?" (*Evelina,* 290). For Evelina, Maria Mirvan is the "kind and sympathising bosom I might have ventured to have reposed every secret of my soul [in]" (*Evelina,* 283), the only correspondent to whom she can apparently freely express the hopes (and suffering) provoked by her love troubles: "Can you Maria forgive my gravity? but *I restrain it so much and so painfully* in the presence of Mr. Villars, that I know not how to deny myself the consolation of indulging it to you" (*Evelina,* 285; emphasis added). The epistolary exchange with Maria Mirvan is thus crucial to revealing to the reader how Evelina, far from being "ignoran[t] . . . and inexperience[d]" (*Evelina,* 7), is on the contrary fully aware of the ways and the uses of dissimulation.

The epistolary style is a highly sophisticated narrative technique that tends to mask its nature as literary construct. Its anti-rhetorical and paraliterary qualities place the author of an epistolary novel in a liminal position—that of the editor of someone else's letters—partly camouflaging her literary authority. As Julia Epstein reminds us, "Letters wear the mask of unelaborated vocal authenticity, of artifice forestalled, in their twin pretences to spontaneity and to not writing."[39] The letter thus satisfies the opposing needs for silence and expression that, as we have seen, are at the core of Frances Burney's poetics and of the permanently unresolved dialogical alternation that is its formal counterpart in her texts.

Toward the end of the novel's second volume, Evelina is disturbed by a letter apparently sent to her by Lord Orville. She had incautiously written to him to apologize for an incident involving Orville's carriage, which had been inappropriately borrowed in Evelina's name by the Branghtons. Evelina is perfectly aware that writing to a man is a reckless gesture and all too easy to misconstrue, but in her eagerness to preserve Orville's good opinion, she can think of no other means to exculpate herself.

By the next post, she receives a passionate answer signed Orville but in fact written by her equally ardent admirer, Sir Clement Willoughby. Not only does the letter absolve her completely for the incident; she is invited to take full advantage of the writer's devotion. Willoughby's letter is a perfect example of the power, and duplicity, of rhetorical artifice. The gentlemanly surface masks an unpardonable affront to Evelina's reputation, and were she to accept the letter as genuine, the moral integrity of Willoughby's rival, Orville, would be irremediably tarnished: "The correspondence *you have so sweetly commenced* I shall be proud of continuing" (*Evelina,* 286; emphasis added) are the words of ambiguous encouragement that open the letter, which closes with an invitation to complicity that could not be more explicit:

> In your next, I entreat you to acquaint me how long you shall remain in town. The servant whom I shall commission to call for the answer, has orders to ride post with it to me. My impatience for his arrival will be very great, though inferior to that with which I burn to tell you, in person, how much I am, my sweet girl,
>
> Your grateful admirer,
>
> ORVILLE (*Evelina,* 286–87)

Her admirer's flattering words assume Evelina's willingness not only to continue the clandestine correspondence but also to endanger her reputation by placing it at the mercy of the servant on whose discretion her honor now depends. The letter's intentions and insinuations become clear to the indignant Evelina, whose initial joyful discovery that "Orville" indeed loves her turns to dismay as she comes to understand that the answer she has received is unworthy of him. "Upon a second reading, I thought every word changed, it did not seem the same letter," she confesses to Maria Mirvan. "I could not find one sentence that I could look at without blushing: my astonishment was extreme, and it was succeeded by the utmost indignation" (*Evelina,* 287). She concludes, "I have a thousand times imagined that the whole study of his life, and whole purport of his reflections, tended solely to the good and the happiness of others:—but *I will talk,—write—think of him no more*" (*Evelina,* 292).

Evelina's language betrays Burney's indebtedness to Samuel Richardson's theories of epistolary composition: to write, to talk, and to think are three equivalent and interchangeable acts, inextricably linked to each other. Writing does no more than put on paper what one would express through speech. Lovelace, serving here as Richardson's spokesperson, had decreed that "*familiar writing* is but *talking,*" and the equivalence had become a hallmark of the epistolary genre.[40] Jane Austen, who experimented with the epistolary style in her first two novels, accepted the equivalence as well, as she jokingly confirms in a letter to her sister Cassandra: "I have now attained the true art of letter writing, which we are always told, is to express on paper exactly what one would say to the same person by word of mouth: I have been talking to you almost as fast as I could the whole of this letter."[41] In Richardson's novels, the letter is patently a metonymic representation of its author: for Mr. B., reading and possessing Pamela's journal is equivalent to possessing Pamela herself—or, rather, it is preliminary to possession.[42] Faithfully reproducing the innermost thoughts and feelings of the writer, Richardson's "to-the-moment" style emphasizes present-tense narrative and is predominantly mimetic; by employing parentheses and italics to render the character's words and actions simultaneously, he keeps the author's "directorial" presence in the background, suggesting a parallel with playwriting.[43] The correspondents' reactions, thoughts, and feelings are conveyed to the reader at the same time (and in the same way) that they appear in the mind, the heart, and out of the pen of the writer.

The extraordinary immediacy of Richardson's narrative technique in *Clarissa* is apparent in the famous letter 263, from Lovelace to Belford, in which Lovelace describes his attempts to interject while Clarissa is reproving him: "My dear—my love—I—I—I never—no never—lips trembling, limbs quaking, voice inward, hesitating, broken—Never surely did miscreant look so *like* a miscreant! While thus she proceeded, waving her snowy hand, with all the graces of moving oratory."[44] Besides evoking the emotions of the moment, the tender whisperings that Lovelace transcribes so faithfully for his friend Belford are the result of a careful visual reconstruction of the meeting between the libertine and his captive. The *lips–limbs* consonance that I would call "directorial" (a clever rhetorical construction that is clearly deliberate rather than involuntary) introduces a precise and unmistakably theatrical description of the writer's posture (his agitated body), voice (hushed, hesitant, "broken"), and guilty and distressed facial expression (with the significant detail of the trembling lips enclosed by dashes, in the real time conveyed by the present participle), which allows the reader to visualize Lovelace as he is speaking.[45]

This modulated intersection of theatrical codes—the precise description of gestures and expressions, the carefully judged language and rhetoric—recalls that of a play and can be linked to the instructions for interpreting the passions in many popular acting manuals of the time.[46] Before the reforms initiated by David Garrick after his debut on the London stage in 1741, actors relied on a multitude of catalogs of gestures, expressions, and movements on which they were encouraged to base their performance. Mirella Billi notes that "the actor becomes the focus of the semiotic registers that simultaneously 'signal' in a play; in order to exercise a conscious control over the various levels of the prescribed code, the actor cannot be guided by nature but rather by the methodical application of instructions, of *rules*."[47] Richardson was well acquainted with many of these acting manuals, partly because he had printed some himself, but also through his association with a group of literary and theatrical friends among whom were Colley Cibber, David Garrick, and Aaron Hill. Hill, perhaps Richardson's most trusted friend, was a writer, poet, and well-known connoisseur of the theater who had been editor of a theatrical periodical, *The Prompter* (1734–36). He had also written *An Essay on the Art of Acting* (1753), printed by Richardson, which rendered in prose his theatrical treatise in verse, *The Art of Acting* (1746).

According to Hill, an actor could not simply imitate a passion but had to become completely immersed in it until he felt that the passion arose from within, so that it might then flow outward naturally from the "impressive springs within his mind." "The *mov'd* actor moves—and passion shakes," Hill stated at the close of *The Art of Acting*, an idea he developed further in his prose treatise:

> First, the imagination must conceive a *strong idea* of the passion. Secondly, but that idea cannot *strongly* be conceived, without impressing its own form upon the muscles of the *face*. Thirdly, nor *can* the look be muscularly stamp'd, without communicating instantly the same impression, to the muscles of the body. Fourthly, the muscles of the body (braced, or slack, as the idea was an active or a passive one), must, in their natural, and not-to-be-avoided consequence, by impelling or retarding the flow of the animal spirits, transmit their own conceiv'd sensation, to the sound of the *voice*, and to the disposition of the *gesture*.[48]

Richardson's choice to draw on acting methods prior to Garrick's in describing his characters is also suggested by the phrase "moving oratory," applied to the intonation and articulation of Clarissa's speech. Sherburn reminds us how in a letter of 1756, Richardson complained to a correspondent "that ill health [kept] him away from the theatre *as well as* from hearing the debates in Parliament."[49] The juxtaposition is explained by the eighteenth-century custom of considering the art of oratory (as perfected by politicians and lawyers) a model for actors, as well. Thomas Betterton, in particular, the most famous English actor until 1710—and founder of an acting method that was not displaced until Garrick introduced his naturalistic style—considered the development of an actor's expressive capabilities essential. For Betterton, an actor's greatest gift, like a great orator's, was "a delivery dignified in the extreme,"[50] and Betterton's biographer, Charles Gildon, explicitly referred to this connection in the subtitle of his biography: *The Life of Mr. Thomas Betterton, the Late Eminent Tragedian. Wherein the Action and Utterance of the Stage, Bar, and Pulpit, Are Distinctly Consider'd* (1710).

The connection between writing "to the moment" and the dramatic mimesis that, as we have seen, is fundamental to *Clarissa* loses its centrality in Richardson's next novel, *The History of Sir Charles Grandison* (1753–54), in which the compression and descriptive immediacy of the letter are replaced by extended journal entries. In *Grandison,* philosophical dialogues and moral disquisitions go hand in hand with the meticulous dissection of characters' emotional states, and Richardson forgoes detailed descriptions of the movements of the characters, their expressions, or their gestures to emphasize their feelings, doubts, and moral quandaries. The interminable dissertations on the immorality of dueling (whose theatrical origins in Richard Steele's *The Conscious Lovers* are referred to explicitly but that are here deprived of their stage impact and dramatic pedigree),[51] the set pieces featuring Clementina della Porretta—the young Italian who loves, and is loved by, Grandison but who cannot marry him because of insurmountable religious differences—and the endless sentimental and moral embarrassments experienced by the heroine Harriet Byron, who knows of Grandison's prior attachment, all are signs of a work more indebted to midcentury moral treatises and courtesy books than to bourgeois drama. Detailed empathetic description of characters' emotions replaces their visual illustration, as the following extract shows, in which Grandison explains his moral dilemma to his confidant, Dr. Bartlett:

> But here, doctor, is the case, said I—Clementina is a woman with whom I had the honour of being acquainted before I knew Miss Byron: Clementina has infinite merits: She herself refused me not. . . . Till I had the happiness of knowing Miss Byron, I was determined to await either her [Clementina's] recovery or release. . . . While there is a possibility, tho' not a probability, of my being made the humble instrument of restoring an excellent woman . . . *ought* I to wish to engage the heart (were I able to succeed in my wishes) of the *equally*-excellent Miss Byron?[52]

Grandison was an unsuitable epistolary model for Frances Burney's first novel because its narrative technique would have required a detailed exposition of Evelina's every feeling and sentimental doubt regarding her troubled love story with Orville, whereas most of Evelina's letters are addressed to her elderly and austere guardian, Villars, a substitute father figure rather than a confidant.

Burney instead seems to approximate much more closely *Clarissa*'s mimetic equivalence between written exposition and physical expression, which work together to convey the feelings and passions of the characters. It is this external description of the gestures and movements of actors, according to a code of mimicry of the passions, that Burney selects as her method. Evelina's comment on the letter signed "Orville" is indicative in this respect: "If I find that the *eyes* of Lord Orville agree with his *pen,*—I shall then think, that of all mankind, the only virtuous individual resides at Berry Hill" (*Evelina,* 308).

The result of this method of composition is to convey a mental image of a scene that stimulates the reader's imagination, producing "pictures in depth of people, scenes and actions." In the case of *Clarissa,* the novel's already highly individualized characters are represented visually within scenes in which "people move, talk, and react."[53] As Clarissa herself complains to Anna Howe in terms that suggest a precise sequence drawn from the rules of stage acting, "You will always have me give you minute descriptions, nor suffer me to pass by the *air* and *manner* in which things are spoken that are to be taken notice of: rightly observing, that the air and manner often express more than the accompanying *words.*"[54]

Burney appears to adopt, with small variations, Richardson's visual narrative, a technique through which the author "encourage[s] the reader to see exactly what is going on."[55] When the description involves the inner states and emotional reactions of characters, their psychology is visualized through the two dimensions of speech. When a character is instead observed interacting with the world, the reader is allowed to follow the character into the three dimensions of representation, "not only to see him perceiving, but also to perceive the world with him."[56] In both cases, it is the perceptual abilities of the narrating character (and through her, of the reader) and her perspective on reality that become central. (Here we are reminded of the influence exercised in the eighteenth century by John Locke's *An Essay Concerning Human Understanding* [1690] and of Berkeley's *A Treatise Concerning the Principles of Human Knowledge* [1710])

Evelina's arrival at Clifton and her introduction to Mrs. Beaufort's aristocratic guests (*Evelina,* vol. 3, letter 3) is a perfect example of a purely external, physical description of embarrassment. It is an especially significant occasion because it is the first time Evelina meets Lord Orville's sister Lady

Louisa Larpent and her future husband, Lord Merton. This is therefore her first interaction with two important members of her future family circle. Both treat her with an indifference verging on insult, considering her no more than an orphan of obscure birth and lacking influential family connections. The encounter is therefore especially humiliating:

> In a few minutes Lady Louisa Larpent made her appearance. The same manners prevailed; for courtsying, with, "I hope you are well, Ma'am," to Mrs. Beaumont, she passed straight forward to her seat on the sofa, where, leaning her head on her hand, she cast her languishing eyes round the room, with a vacant stare. . . .
>
> Just then entered Lord Merton, stalking up to Mrs. Beaumont, to whom alone he bowed, he hoped he had not made her wait; and then advancing to Lady Louisa, said, in a careless manner, "How is your Ladyship this morning?" . . .
>
> In the midst of this trifling conversation Lord Orville made his appearance. . . . "Give me leave, Sister, to introduce Miss Anville to you."
>
> Lady Louisa, half-rising, said, very coldly, that she should be glad of the honour of knowing me; and then, abruptly turning to Lord Merton and Mr. Lovel, continued, in a half-whisper, her conversation.
>
> For my part, I had risen and courtsied, and now, feeling very foolish, I seated myself again; first I blushed at the unexpected politeness of Lord Orville, and immediately afterwards, at the contemptuous failure of it in his sister. . . .
>
> Lord Orville, I am sure, was hurt and displeased: he bit his lips, and turning from her, addressed himself wholly to me, till we were summoned to dinner. (*Evelina,* 316–18)

In describing the episode to Villars, Evelina focuses almost exclusively on externals. Her only comments on the embarrassing situation relate to the behavior of the other characters in the episode. Lady Louisa and Lord Orville turn their backs on each other, the former to signal her indifference and the latter to display protectiveness toward Evelina. The unconscious language of the body also betrays the disappointment and humiliation of the heroine, who literally performs her embarrassment at the rebuff by blushing twice without speaking. Evelina's comments are very brief but significant, retaining the sharp focus necessary to an epistolary account. As Ira Konigsberg notes, epistolary mimesis must make the reader "constantly aware of the heroine's voice as a dramatic presence. The focus is less on what has occurred and more on [the protagonist's] responses to the event; in other words, the drama is largely played out in the act of writing."[57]

Evelina first admits to feeling abashed by Lady Louisa's ill-concealed attempt to mortify her, but she then congratulates herself on Orville's show of solidarity ("Lord Orville, *I am sure,* was hurt and displeased"), and finally she notes with satisfaction the obvious respect with which he treats her, openly turning his back on his sister and "address[ing] himself wholly to me." Evelina's feelings and reactions are not described at length, and transpire—implicitly but unmistakably—from her own and the other characters' gestures and behaviors, as expressed by their proxemic relations and even their tone of voice, which bear the entire burden of description.[58] Burney's dramatic narrative thus achieves a heightened realism. The emphasis is not on reporting a sequence of events after the fact, which would dilute their impact, but on dramatizing details in a way that carries the reader into the fictional world of the novel. The overall effect of this technique is to transform the novel's drawing rooms and salons into a social stage.

Burney's epistolary technique is thoroughly mimetic: it selects, compresses, and transcribes in literary shorthand details of events, places, and characters, reproducing the quick shifts in characters' thoughts and conveying feelings and emotions by imitating the natural tones of conversation. The spontaneity of the epistolary utterance, according to Richardson's theory that "*familiar writing* is but *talking,*" is due to its direct engagement with the multidimensionality of enunciation, which in turn is conditioned by pragmatic relations and defined by paralinguistic conventions. The epistolary style thus appears to activate a transverse dramatization of narrative, emphasizing its transformation from written text to spoken text.

Burney seems to have been particularly interested in the letter's inherent potential for multidimensionality. Her extraordinary powers of recall allowed her to reproduce, even long after the fact, not only the tenor but also the actual words of conversations she had witnessed, and she always sought to re-create in her journal accounts the multiple levels of encoding that she recognized as peculiar to speech.[59] As she recalled many years later about her attendance at Warren Hastings's trial, "I came back so eagerly interested, that my memory was not more stored with the very words than my voice with all the intonations of all that had passed" (*DL,* 5:168–69).

We may now suggest a tentative classification of the many theatrical influences present in *Evelina.* These can be arranged according to three kinds of trans-textual relations that reflect the influence exercised on Burney by the theater both from a formal standpoint (the dramatization of narrative) and from a strictly textual standpoint. The transtextual relations fall into the following categories: formal; intertextual; and metatextual.[60]

FORMAL RELATION

For many episodes in the novel, the time of telling coincides with the time of the action, suggesting that such episodes are, in fact, constructed as scenes. Dialogue predominates, and the temporal axis is shifted to the present. Narration (particularly of characters' emotional and mental states) is replaced by ostension, or showing. The novel's scenes can thus be conceived of as a microsystem of intersecting codes, in which the characters' voices are not filtered through the first-person narrator,[61] but issue from them autonomously, as though from individuals on a mental stage (or *mise-en-scène*), each of whom is endowed with his or her own particular idiolect and body language.

This sort of dramatization is especially apparent in a number of episodes in volume 3 of the novel: Evelina's arrival at Clifton (*Evelina,* letter 3, discussed earlier); the conversations between Evelina and Lord Orville (*Evelina,* letters 11, 15); the explanation between Evelina and Sir Clement Willoughby (*Evelina,* letter 16); and, of course, Evelina's reunion with Sir John Belmont (*Evelina,* letters 17, 19), analyzed in detail later.

INTERTEXTUAL RELATION

An intertextual relation can be an overt reference to a specific play (e.g., the quotation from *Twelfth Night* in *Evelina,* vol. 1, letter 13, or the reference to Joseph Addison's *The Drummer* in *Evelina,* vol. 3, letter 15), but is more often an implicit reference. *Evelina* can usefully be conceived of as a novel situated at the center of a dense network of theatrical connections and thus requiring the literary competence of an ideal reader familiar with the theater of the time. Such a reader, for instance, would note that the climactic meeting between Evelina and Belmont seems intentionally to evoke the reunion between Indiana and Mr. Sealand in Richard Steele's *The Conscious Lovers* (Drury Lane, 1722), an extraordinarily successful moral comedy that was performed ninety-six times between 1747 and 1776.[62] The scene also closely resembles the meeting between Lucy and Mr. Wealthy in Foote's *The Minor.*

Where character portrayal is concerned, *Evelina*'s Captain Mirvan is identifiable as one of a host of seafarers who took over the English stage in popular mariner-themed melodramas such as Charles Dibdin's *Yo Yeah, or, The Friendly Tars,* staged at Sadler's Wells in 1777, just one year before the publication of *Evelina.*[63] From the standpoint of language, the theatrical sources for Madame Duval's Frenchified English, an idiolect Burney was to use again for Captain Aresby in *Cecilia,* are also easy to identify and range from Frenchlove, the prototype of a series of Francophile fops created by James Howard in *The English Monsieur* (Theatre Royal, 1663; published in 1674), to the servant Dufois in *The Comical Revenge; or, Love in a Tub* by George Etherege (1664) and on to Mr. de Paris in William Wycherley's farce, *The Gentleman Dancing-Master* (Dorset Garden, 1671) and the servant La Verde in *The Relapse* by John Vanbrugh (Drury Lane, 1696). All of these playwrights relied on the long-established technique of employing particular speech patterns for characterization. We cannot be certain that Burney knew these plays firsthand, although her knowledge of the stage was certainly vast. We do know that she was thoroughly familiar with George Colman's and David Garrick's *The Clandestine Marriage* (1766), and Madame Duval's English clearly draws on and revises Monsieur Canton's idiolect in that comedy.[64]

The figure of the fop had risen to prominence in the seventeenth century and was still ubiquitous on the eighteenth-century stage. Burney's fop, Mr. Lovel, is an obvious instance of typecasting: not only is his name assonant with Novel, William Wycherley's fop in *The Plain Dealer* (1676); it is the same name given to a number of fops throughout the seventeenth and eighteenth centuries, including Thomas Shadwell's young man of fashion in *The Sullen Lovers* (Lincoln's Inn Fields, 1668), and James Townley's wealthy Lovel in *High Life Below Stairs* (Drury Lane, 1759).

Sir Fopling Flutter, Sir Courtly Nice, Lord Froth, and Lord Foppington are only some of the fops created by the prolific playwrights of the Restoration.[65] Made famous at the start of the century by Colley Cibber, who played Sir Novelty Fashion in *Love's Last Shift* (1696) to such acclaim that he set a new trend in acting, fops were characterized by a taste for refined pleasures that reflected the growing love of luxury and of precious objects typical of the time. Their exquisite, feminine sensibility accorded well with contemporary epistemic changes, particularly the emergence of sentimentality and of end-of-the-century "mollifying elegance," and some of their qualities can be found in otherwise un-foppish characters, such as Lord Orville.[66] Evelina remarks on Lord Orville's moral qualities to her friend Miss Mirvan: "As a sister I loved him,—I could have entrusted him with every thought of my heart, had he deigned to wish my confidence; so steady did I think his honour, so *feminine* his delicacy, so amiable his nature" (*Evelina,* 292). The unaggressive sexuality of the fop was usually contrasted with the reckless debauchery and brutal virility of the rake, as in Burney's juxtaposition of Lovel with Willoughby and Captain Mirvan.

But as Susan Staves points out, in the course of the eighteenth century the fop gradually ceased to be an audience favorite and became an object of ridicule. Burney captures this shift nicely in her description of the violent prank involving a monkey that Captain Mirvan organizes at Lovel's expense. Presented with the monkey, "full dressed and extravagantly *à-la-mode,*" Mr. Lovel, "irritated beyond endurance, angrily demanded of the Captain what he meant? 'Mean?' cried the Captain, as soon as he was able to speak, 'why only to show you in your true colours.' Then rising, and pointing to the monkey, 'Why now, Ladies and Gentlemen, I'll be judged by you all!—Did you ever see any thing more like? Odds my life, if it was n't for the tail, you would n't know one from t'other'" (*Evelina,* 444).

According to Staves, "As the aristocracy lost power and self-confidence, not only did magnificence no longer seem an appropriate virtue, but men who were rich and not aristocratic increasingly were able to purchase the elements of magnificence, thus devaluing them as tokens of exclusivity. . . . It is, therefore, not surprising that the really amusing fops in the second half of the eighteenth century desert high comedy for the farces of Garrick and Foote."[67] The altered distribution of wealth went hand in hand with the emergence of a new social type, the uneducated nouveau riche who, despite his aspirations, had not yet succeeded in shedding his coarse tastes and idiom. An example is *Evelina*'s Mr. Smith, the "Holborn beau" whose "vulgar gentility" struck Dr. Johnson as particularly well observed (*ED,* 2:253). The contrast between the posturing Mr. Smith and the effortlessly elegant Sir Clement Willoughby provides another angle on the humiliations inflicted on the figure of the fop in the course of the century and would eventually relegate him to the status of a grotesque farcical character: "Yet I [Evelina] could almost have laughed, when I looked at Mr. Smith, who no sooner saw me addressed by Sir Clement, than, retreating aloof from the company, he seemed to lose at once all his happy self-sufficiency and conceit; looking now at the baronet, now at himself, surveying, with sorrowful eyes, his dress, struck with his air, his gestures, his easy gaiety; he gazed at him with envious admiration, and seemed himself, with conscious inferiority, to shrink to nothing" (*Evelina,* 225).

It may well be that Burney's ability to describe so precisely the change in taste that led to the fop's downfall was due not only to her inevitable awareness of the aesthetic and sexual implications of the altered cultural climate since the Restoration but also to her direct knowledge of the character's evolution from Restoration comedy through mid-eighteenth-century farce. In July 1771, Burney had played both Lady Easy and Lady Graveairs in her family's performance of Cibber's *The Careless Husband* (1704) and had thus become well acquainted with the character of Lord Foppington. Garrick's parodies of fops must have been equally familiar to her. In 1770, the Burney family had considered performing *Miss in Her Teens* (1747), a farce by Garrick, who had written the part of Fribble for himself.[68]

It seems plausible, then, that Burney was directly influenced by the contemporary theatrical repertoire in drawing the characters of Mr. Lovel and Mr. Smith in *Evelina,* and she would have relied on her readers' ability to grasp the pragmatics of the text, bringing their literary and theatrical competence to bear on the indirect references in the novel.

METATEXTUAL RELATION

This relation between a dramatic source text (a hypotext) and a narrative target text (or hypertext) is characterized by commentary. Knowledge of the source text is required to grasp the meaning of the hypertext, because the hypertext's metaphorical references would otherwise remain dormant. Thus, the metatextual dimension of a work can escape readers of later historical periods. The metatextual relation is dependent on a "model reader" whose competence and contextual knowledge are constantly solicited to set in motion his or her interpretation. This reader becomes the active consumer-producer of the narrative text.[69] An example of a metatextual relation in *Evelina* is the episode in letter 20 of volume 1 in which Evelina attends a performance of William Congreve's *Love for Love* (*Evelina,* 86–92). Evelina goes to the theater at Drury Lane with her chaperone, Mrs. Mirvan, her friend Maria, and Captain Mirvan. At the theater, they are joined by Sir Clement Willoughby, Mr. Lovel, and Lord Orville and settle into a side box. In the conversation preceding the play, Lovel anticipates the comedy's theme by raising the classic debate—and traditional art–nature opposition—about women's complexions, whose natural rosiness he doubts, insinuating that Evelina's rosy cheeks are the effect of cosmetics: "'But,' said Lord Orville, 'the difference of natural and artificial colour, seems to me very easily discerned; that of Nature is mottled, and varying; that of art, *set,* and *too* smooth'" (*Evelina,* 88). Lovel then extends the opposition between artifice and nature to that between the city (London) and the country (in Evelina's case, Berry Hill) and turns maliciously on the embarrassed Evelina:

"'The air we breathe here, however, Ma'am,' continued he, very conceitedly, 'though foreign to that you have been accustomed to, has not, I hope, been at variance with your health?'" (*Evelina,* 88). A clear set of oppositions is thus raised in the course of the conversation, pitting nature (associated with the country and natural color) against artifice (associated with the city and rouge), aligning Evelina with the former and Lovel with the latter.

The conversation ceases as the curtain rises; when it resumes, the subject shifts to Congreve's comedy, highlighting the metatextual relation between the play and the novel. We are first given Evelina's private opinion: "The play was Love for Love, and though it is fraught with wit and entertainment, I hope I shall never see it represented again; for it is so extremely indelicate,—to use the softest word I can—that Miss Mirvan and I were perpetually out of countenance, and could neither make any observations ourselves, nor venture to listen to those of others" (*Evelina,* 87). Willoughby feels no such timidity and encourages the others to comment freely. Mrs. Mirvan takes the standard Georgian moral view by politely condemning the licentiousness of the play, an example of the uninhibited satire on manners of the late seventeenth century: "Want of entertainment . . . is its least fault; but I own there are objections to it, which I should be glad to see removed" (*Evelina,* 89). Unlike his wife, Captain Mirvan is much amused by the comedy and openly praises it: "I'll maintain it's one of the best comedies in the language, and has more wit in one scene, than there is in all the new plays put together" (*Evelina,* 90), but he acknowledges that the ladies may have been less pleased with it: "I suppose it is not sentimental enough" (*Evelina,* 89).

This remark, together with the captain's allusion to "the new plays," signals Frances Burney's awareness of the contemporary debate pitting comedy of manners against sentimental comedy. The controversy had reached its climax a few years before *Evelina*'s composition with the publication of Oliver Goldsmith's "An Essay on the Theatre; or, A Comparison between Laughing and Sentimental Comedy" that appeared in 1773 in *Westminster Magazine.* The essay prepared the way for the first production of Goldsmith's *She Stoops to Conquer* by defending "laughing comedy" against the new sentimental comedy: "It depends upon the audience whether they will actually drive those poor merry creatures from the stage, or sit at a play as gloomy as at the tabernacle. It is not easy to recover an art when once lost; and it will be but a just punishment, that when, by our being too fastidious, we have banished humour from the stage, we should ourselves be deprived of the art of laughing."[70] It is no surprise that Burney should place Mirvan on the side of Goldsmith, who in his essay had accused the authors of sentimental comedies of being mere hacks without a spark of genius. "Those abilities that can hammer out a Novel, are fully sufficient for the production of a Sentimental Comedy," he had written. The attack was furthermore combined with criticism of the new genre of "tradesman's tragedy," also known as domestic drama, on which Burney had based the family plot in *Evelina.*[71]

Evelina's reservations about the play fulfill Lord Orville's expectations (and desires) perfectly. Indeed, instead of offering his own opinion of the play, Orville takes the ladies' point of view: "I could have ventured to answer for the Ladies . . . since I am sure this is not a play that can be honoured with their approbation" (*Evelina,* 89). This view echoes the attack against Restoration comedy in Jeremy Collier's *A Short View on the Immorality and Profaneness of the English Stage* (1698), which reflected a current of public opinion already dominant at the turn of the century. Thus. Burney's choice of *Love for Love* (first performed at Lincoln's Inn Fields in 1695) is apt. As a typical comedy of manners, it had been subjected, together with John Vanbrugh's *The Provok'd Wife* (Lincoln's Inn Fields, 1697), to Collier's harshest criticism. The criticism was to last well into the eighteenth century, and Samuel Johnson, as Burney certainly knew, had asserted that "it acknowledged with universal conviction that the perusal of [Congreve's] works will make no man better; and that their ultimate effect is to represent pleasure in alliance with vice, and to relax those obligations by which life ought to be regulated."[72]

The only character who does not comment directly on the comedy is Lovel, who claims he was too busy looking at—and being admired by—the audience to attend to the play: "'For my part,' said Mr. Lovel, 'I confess I seldom listen to the players: one has so much to do, in looking about, and finding out one's acquaintance, that, really one has no time to mind the stage. Pray,'—(most affectionately fixing his eyes upon a diamond ring on his little finger) 'pray—what was the play tonight?'" (*Evelina,* 89)

Burney's characters thus fall into three groups according to their aesthetic and moral views on Congreve's play: the three women, together with Lord Orville, form the disapproving majority; the foppish Lovel is alone in expressing (or feigning) indifference; and Willoughby and Captain Mirvan more or less heartily approve. The correctness of Evelina's moral response to the comedy is confirmed by Orville's agreement with it. Like Burney herself, her principal characters share the diffidence felt by Georgian audiences toward Restoration theater.[73]

FIGURE 6. Metatextual relations:
Character equivalence in Congreve's *Love for Love* and *Evelina*

Love for Love (hypotext)	*Evelina* (hypertext)
Mr. Ben	Captain Mirvan
Mr. Tattle	Lovel
Miss Prue	Evelina

Lovel's lack of interest in the comedy is revealed, however, to be a studied pose, associating him again with artifice. When Captain Mirvan pointedly asks him whether he had noticed the resemblance between himself and Mr. Tattle in the comedy, Lovel shows he has paid sufficient attention to the performance to caustically reply:

> "Pray, Sir, give me leave to ask,—what do *you* think of *one Mr. Ben,* who is also in the play?" . . . [Then] he turned very quick to me, and, in a sneering tone of voice said, "For my part, I was most struck with the *country* young lady, Miss Prue; pray what do *you* think of her, Ma'am?"
>
> "Indeed, Sir," cried I, very much provoked, "I think—that is, I do not think any thing about her." . . . I made no answer, for I thought his rudeness intolerable; but Sir Clement, with great warmth, said, "I am surprised that you can suppose such an object as Miss Prue would engage the attention of Miss Anville even for a moment."
>
> "O Sir," returned this fop, " 'tis the first character in the piece!—so well drawn,—so much the thing!—such true country-breeding,—such rural ignorance!—ha! ha! ha!—'tis most admirably hit off, 'pon honour!" (*Evelina,* 90–91)

Lovel's reply shows that Burney is intentionally drawing a parallel (see figure 6) between the characters in *Evelina* and those in Congreve's play.[74] The relation between hypotext and hypertext here is clear. In Congreve's comedy, Mr. Ben is a captain in the Navy, as is Captain Mirvan. Tattle is the fop, "vain and foolish, although capable of wit on occasion,"[75] who attempts to instruct the young and naive Miss Prue in the arts of feminine cunning. The famous instructions he proffers to the provincial young woman are a distillation of all of the artifices current in the culture of appearances to which he belongs:

> All well-bred Persons Lie. Besides, you are a Woman; you must never speak what you think; Your words must contradict your thoughts; but

> your Actions may contradict your words. So, if you can Love me, you must say no, but you must Love me too. If I tell you you are Handsome, you must deny, and say I flatter you. But you must think yourself more Charming than I speak you, and like me for the Beauty which you say you have as much as if I had it myself. If I ask you to Kiss me, you must be angry, but you must not refuse me. If I ask you for more, you must be more angry, but more complying; and as soon as ever I make you say you'll cry out, you must be sure you hold your tongue. (*Love for Love*, 2.2.663–76)

According to the rules of behavior set forth by Tattle, women must adhere to social conventions that do not reflect their real feelings. This construction of feminine discourse implies that a woman's refusal of a man's attentions is never sincere, as Evelina knows all too well, having experienced the importunities of Sir Clement Willoughby and Mr. Smith, among others.

The close link between the dramatic subtext (or hypotext) and the narrative situation (or hypertext) here is further signaled by Evelina's concluding words: "The curtain drew up, and our conversation ceased" (*Evelina*, 91). This exchange is actually interrupted by the beginning of the afterpiece rather than the play itself, but the diegetic placement of Evelina's remark suggests that the curtain has, in fact, risen on the characters of the novel itself, who have thus far merely been rehearsing the social comedy called *Evelina*.

> There are so many ways of communication independent of speech that silence is just one point in the ordinances of discretion.
>
> —Frances Burney, *Camilla*

The three types of transtextuality described earlier can also operate simultaneously, as illustrated in the second meeting between Evelina and her father in letter 9 of volume 3 (*Evelina*, 422–29), where the formal, intertextual, and metatextual links binding the novel to its theatrical context are all present. In her journal letter to Villars of 5 April in letter 12 of volume 1, Evelina briefly notes:

> Thursday night
>
> We are just returned from the play, which was King Lear, and has made me very sad. We did not see any body we knew.
>
> Well, adieu, it is too late to write more. (*Evelina*, 42)

Evelina's laconic journal entry is fitting, not only because of the play's tragic nature, but because its tale of an erring father who rejects his virtuous daughter resonates with her own story.

The performance attended by Evelina was one of the many productions of *King Lear* staged by David Garrick at Drury Lane between 1747 and 1776. Shakespeare's text had first been revised in 1681 by Nahum Tate, who had adapted it to the times by emphasizing its domestic qualities and thus turning it into a sentimental drama. It had been altered a second time in 1768 by Garrick himself, and throughout his long career Garrick performed the title role with immense success.[76] Burney's own accounts of seeing Garrick in *King Lear* are very close to Evelina's reaction to the play. In February 1773, Burney noted: "We had yesterday—I know not whether to say the *pain* or *pleasure,*—of seeing Mr. Garrick in the part of Lear. He was exquisitely Great—every idea I had of his talents, although I have ever idolized him, was exceeded" (*EJL,* 1:242). A few months later (most likely in May), she again expressed admiration for the actor after another performance: "We were at the Fund play last [night]. Garrick did King Lear—but too well!" (*EJL,* 1:265). The universal admiration audiences felt for Garrick's interpretation was mainly due to the period's fascination with the new style of acting he had developed, which employed a carefully calibrated expressive lexicon to represent the passions ("passion animated," as it was referred to at the time). Descriptions of Garrick's interpretation of Lear, in particular, emphasize the rapid succession and the intensity of his facial expressions. Operating as "functional signs," they anticipated the words spoken by the character, "His features at the same time telling what he was going to say before he uttered a word," as one spectator noted.[77]

The extraordinary intensity and natural quality of Garrick's acting style were especially apparent in the curse he utters against his daughter, introduced by the invocation, "Hear, Nature; Hear" (*King Lear,* 1.4) and followed by a masterfully modulated sequence of emotions. Figure 7 shows in detail how Garrick acted the scene. Audiences responded to Garrick's affecting interpretation by empathizing deeply with the characters, as James Fordyce wrote to Garrick himself about a performance he had attended: "[The most diversified and vehement sensations] possessed by turns all your frame, and appeared successively in every word, and yet more in every gesture, but most of all in every look and feature; presenting, I verily think, such a picture as the world never saw anywhere else."[78] Garrick's acting theory was the result of observation and analysis. It sought to represent the passions through a rational process based on the scientific study of their external symptoms

FIGURE 7. Garrick's interpretation of *King Lear*

You fall upon your *knees*, extend your *Arms*—clench your *Hands*— set your *Teeth*—and with a savage	Attitude (kneeling) Gesture (arms, hands)
Distraction in your *Look*—trembling in all your *Limbs*—and your *Eyes* pointed to Heaven . . . begin . . .	Expression (look)
with broken, inward, eager *Utterance*; from thence rising	Articulation
every line in *Loudness* and Rapidity of *Voice*, [and at last]	Intonation
bursting into *Tears*	Tears

Note: Garrick's interpretation of Lear, as witnessed by a spectator of the time, is in the left-hand column (quoted in Woods, *Garrick Claims the Stage*, 41; emphasis added). The right-hand column displays the semiotic analysis of the kinesic, proxemic, and paralinguistic conventions employed by Garrick. Garrick's interpretation of *Lear* is referred to in *Evelina*, vol. 1, letter 4.

and of the physical signs associated with them: emotions and passions were displayed somatically. By identifying physically with the characters he was playing, Garrick aimed to arouse the spectators' empathetic identification (or revulsion, depending on the role). The results were remarkable, as a female spectator attested: "My Friend fell in Love with you playing king Richard, but seeing you since in the Character of the Lying Valet—you looked so—*Shabby* (pardon me, Sir) that it cured her of her passion."[79]

A "sublime actor," as Diderot called him in *Paradoxe sur le comédien* (1769–78), Garrick abolished the distinction between the actor and the character he embodied. Spectators could not help but suspend their disbelief and be moved by his extraordinary evocation of reality, as was amusingly noted by the naive Partridge in *Tom Jones.*[80] One spectator described his sense of identification with Lear in tellingly physical terms: "Methinks I share in [Lear's] calamities, I feel the dark drifting rain, and the sharp tempest. His leaning against the side of the scene, panting for want of breath, as if exhausted, and his recollecting the feat . . . have more force, more strength, and more propriety of character, than I ever saw in any other actor."[81] It can be argued that Garrick's method for fascinating his audience and provoking their cathartic identification served as the model for Burney's description of the second meeting between Belmont and Evelina, in letter 19 of volume 3. The scene is the dramatic climax of the novel, a long-postponed encounter that holds the key to Evelina's future. As soon as Belmont has agreed to meet her, her legitimation is assured, allowing her to marry Orville and assume her proper place in society (*Evelina,* vol. 3, letter 23).

Burney adheres closely to the rules of classical tragedy here, stressing in particular the two moments of *peripeteia* (reversal of the situation) and *agnition* (recognition), creatively modified to suit her needs: the hero (in this case, Belmont) is made aware of his tragic error and acknowledges his daughter. Aristotle states that the moments of reversal and recognition are the turning points of a tragedy: "Reversal (Peripety) is . . . a change from one state of affairs to its exact opposite. . . . Recognition, as the word itself indicates, is a change from ignorance to knowledge. . . . The best form of recognition is that which is accompanied by a reversal."[82] According to Aristotle's *Poetics,* the meeting between Belmont and Evelina thus represents "the best form of recognition," since the heroine's social reinstatement is sanctioned not only by her recognition but also by her father's discovery of his error.

The meeting with Belmont takes place in a drawing room: Evelina enters, holding a letter written by her mother Caroline Evelyn on her deathbed, which she presses to her lips. The physical presence of the letter and the way it is constantly kept in the foreground are highly theatrical, but the letter is more than a stage prop and can be considered a third character in the scene, giving the reader the definitive proof both of Belmont's unconscious guilt and of the legality of his secret marriage to Caroline Evelyn. In the letter, Caroline assures Belmont of his paternity and begs him to care for his daughter while accusing him of having refused to avow their union publicly by destroying their marriage certificate and thus plunging Caroline into dishonor and ultimately causing her death. The letter thus functions as the novel's *ur-Brief:* written before all of the other letters, it is their indirect cause. It is the only remaining proof of the heroine's legitimacy, and it is precisely the attempt to convey Caroline Evelyn's last wishes to Belmont that gives rise to Evelina's story.

Once again, Burney relies on the rules of classical tragedy to elevate the moment of Evelina's acknowledgment by her father. The letter Evelina carries is the sign that persuades Belmont (in the kind of recognition Aristotle considers "least artistic"),[83] but the ultimate proof is Evelina's own face, which bears the indelible impression of her mother's features. Thus, memory cuts more deeply than the material proof of the letter, however symbolic. It is Belmont's memory that sanctions his recognition of his daughter, which is followed by the uncontrollable display of emotion prescribed by classical theories of tragedy, as reworked by Augustan dramatists. According to Aristotle, the third kind of recognition does indeed operate "through

FIGURE 8. Acting conventions in *Evelina* vol. 3, letter 19

I then *took* from my pocket-book her last letter, and, pressing it to my lips, with	Gesture (hand, lips)
a trembling hand, and still upon my *knees*,	Attitude (kneeling)
I *held it out* to him.	Gesture (hand)
Hastily *snatching* it from me, "Great Heaven!" cried he, "'tis her writing— Whence comes this?—who gave it you?—why had I it not sooner?" . . .	Gesture (hand)
He *went* from me to the window, where his	Movement
eyes were for some time rivetted upon the	Expression (eyes)
direction of the letter, though his *hand* shook so violently he could hardly hold	Gesture (hand)
it. Then, *bringing* it to me, "Open it," cried he, "for I cannot!" . . .	Movement/Gesture (hand)
[W]hen I had [*opened* the letter], he *took*	Gesture (hand)
it back, and *walked* hastily up and down the room, as if dreading to read it. . . . He then again went to the window . . . he	Movement
cast up his *eyes* with a look of	Expression (eyes)
desperation; the letter *fell* from his hand. . . . He continued some time fixed	Gesture
in this *melancholy* position; after which,	Attitude
casting himself with violence upon the ground, "Oh wretch," cried he, "unworthy life and light, in what dungeon canst thou hide thy head?"	Movement
I could restrain myself no longer; I *rose* and went to him; I did not dare speak, but	Movement
with pity and concern unutterable, I *wept* and hung over him. . . .	Tears (silence)
It was in vain I *attempted to speak*; horror and grief took from me all power of utterance. . . . "Come hither, Evelina: Gracious Heaven!"	(Silence)
looking earnestly at me, "never was likeness more striking!—the eye,—the face,—the form . . . Dear resemblance of thy murthered mother! . . . behold thy	Look
father *at thy feet*!—bending thus lowly to implore you would not hate him. . . ." "Oh rise, rise, my beloved father," cried	Movement
I, *attempting* to assist him. . . .	Gesture
Tears and sighs seemed to choak him!—and	Tears
waving his hand, he would have left me,—	Gesture (hand)

but, *clinging* to him . . . I kissed his hand on my *knees*;	Movement, Attitude (kneeling)
and then, with yet more *emotion*, he again blessed me, and *hurried* out of the room,—	Expression, Movement
leaving me almost drowned in *tears*. (*Evelina,* 426–29; emphasis added)	Tears

memory—i.e., a person's reaction upon seeing something. Thus in Dicaeogenes' *Cyprians,* the hero bursts into tears upon seeing the picture."[84]

Figure 8 offers a detailed look at how Burney constructs the scene. A semiotic analysis of the scene clarifies Burney's use of kinesic and proxemic elements to describe the emotions of the characters. Their kneeling positions are worth noting, in particular, given the importance of the figure of the father in the eighteenth century. By throwing himself at his daughter's feet, Belmont reverses the traditional family hierarchy and expresses the intensity of his shame. In turn, when Evelina kneels before him, she reestablishes the vertical patrilineal order, sealing her submission and forgiveness by kissing her father's hand. There is almost no trace of Burney's usual paralinguistic notations in the passage; she opts instead for an effective dramatic crescendo produced by the quickened succession and repetition of dialogue tags such as "cried he" to render the heightened pace of the dialogue. The technique curtails the narrator's presence severely, suggesting the unmediated, mimetic exchanges typical of the stage.

Although it may appear to be a mere exercise in emotionalism, the pathos of the scene stems directly from Evelina's situation and provides a dramatic, and cathartic, release for the reader. As Belmont weeps, overcome with tenderness and remorse, and Evelina weeps with joy at finally being accepted by her father, readers can share the fictional characters' emotion by shedding real tears.[85] This is where the inter-theatrical and interactive dimensions of the novel become especially apparent. Like those of Garrick's Lear, the frail old king overcome by pain and rage against his children, the tears at the end of *Evelina* are functional signs of the times, denoting an act of recognition, memory, and interpretation on the part of characters and readers alike.

THREE

Caliban's Mirror

The Witlings

> And this one thing I will venture to say, though against my Nature, because it has Vanity in it: That had the plays I have writ come forth under any Man's Name, and never known to have been mine, I appeal to all unbyased judges of Sense, if they had not said that Person had made as many good Comedies, as any one Man that has writ in our Age; but a Devil on't, the Woman damns the Poet.
>
> —Aphra Behn, preface to *The Luckey Chance* (1687)

Burney's first novel proved to be so popular that three reprints were issued in quick succession, followed by a pirate edition published in Ireland in 1779. After the first edition, Burney added the word "history" to the subtitle, changing it to *The History of a Young Lady's Entrance into the World.* The alteration was a tribute to established convention (Henry Fielding's *History of Tom Jones,* for example, or Samuel Richardson's *Clarissa,* subtitled *The History of a Young Lady*), but it also stressed the importance of verisimilitude to Burney's epistolary technique, as did the preface, in which Burney had followed tradition by representing herself as the "editor" of the correspondence.

Literary success marked a crucial turning point in Burney's life: within a few months her personal and social situation was completely transformed as she lost her cover of anonymity and her literary ambition was revealed for all to see. She was showered with praise from all sides, and her literary achievement reflected credit on the other members of the Burney family. Her celebrity, and the general consensus about the novel's worth, made it clear that her fear of her father's disapproval, which had once driven her to burn her juvenilia, was entirely unfounded.

Far from feeling ashamed or displeased about his daughter's literary aspirations, Dr. Burney found himself pleasantly caught up in the sudden celebrity that followed *Evelina*'s publication. He had worked tirelessly to establish his position as a man of letters, historian, and musicologist, and he immediately grasped that being the indirect beneficiary of Frances's achievement could only help consolidate his position. To the concerns voiced by his daughter Susanna, who had conspired with her sister in getting the novel published, Dr. Burney replied in benevolently encouraging terms, his social canniness surfacing through his pride: success required that the author's identity be revealed, and Frances "would not come to any discredit if she was known as the Authoress . . . no, indeed,—*just the reverse—'twould be a credit to her, to me and to you*" (*ED*, 2:248). Frances would therefore have to set aside the anxieties and desire for self-effacement expressed in the poetic dedication to her father that opened *Evelina:*

> *Concealment* is the only boon I claim;
> Obscure be still the unsuccessful Muse,
> Who cannot raise, but would not sink, *thy fame.*
> (*Evelina,* 3; emphasis added)

Achieving literary fame in her own right not only involved the loss of anonymity; it also meant that Burney lost the independence gained by dissociating herself from her father's name. Now that the public had witnessed her "weak pow'rs" proclaiming his "num'rous virtues," (*Evelina,* 3), Frances's success, and her public self, became her father's concern: "As the author discovered after *Evelina* was treated with more justice than she had ever dared to hope, paternal recognition had its disadvantages. . . . once she was publicly named as author . . . her father began to control her word."[1]

Susan Greenfield's observation points to the significant resemblance between the fictional events narrated in *Evelina* and the real ones experienced by its author, a resemblance that must have been apparent to Burney herself. In the novel's denouement, Evelina's difficulties are finally resolved when Belmont acknowledges her as his daughter, and this acknowledgment serves both as post facto justification and as proleptic reward for the social misadventures she had undergone. Paternal legitimation, however, requires a *bidirectional* acknowledgment: Belmont accepts Evelina as his long-lost daughter, but at the same time, Evelina must accept the authority of the father, activating a relationship of filial devotion with far-reaching implications, destined to control all of her actions. This is why Lord Orville's marriage proposal must first be sanctioned by Belmont, to the respect of whose will Evelina knows she is now indissolubly bound: "My Lord . . . you ask what I have no power to grant. This journey will deprive me of all right to act for myself" (*Evelina,* 393).

Similarly, the immediate consequence of *Evelina*'s success and of Charles Burney's acknowledgment of it was a strengthening of the ties binding Frances to her father, since her identity, previously concealed behind a "mantle of impenetrable obscurity" (preface to *Evelina,* 7), now became simply that of the famous daughter of the famous Dr. Burney. Even leaving Oedipal issues aside, it was to be expected that the family bonds that ultimately dominated Evelina's fictional life would sooner or later end up controlling Frances Burney's life, as well. As Beth Kowaleski-Wallace notes, "Literary daughters are special kinds of daughters, women who adapt themselves to a familial and a literary hierarchy."[2] It is hardly surprising therefore that Charles Burney should have taken it upon himself to supervise Frances's official introduction into society during a visit to Streatham Park, the country house of the Thrales and one of the most important cultural salons of the time. Hester Lynch Thrale (1741–1821) was a generous patron of Dr. Burney, who had first met the Thrales in 1776, when he was engaged to give music lessons to their eldest daughter, Queeney, and received an exorbitant £100 per lesson. Referred to as an "endless giver" by Dr. Burney in a panegyric he wrote for her, Hester Thrale had thus provided him with material support, as well as granted him invaluable access to her social network.[3] Dr. Burney's presentation of his famous daughter to the mistress of Streatham should therefore be seen as a crucial step in a strategy aimed at consolidating a social position that transcended that of a mere professional musician, however highly remunerated.

The visit to Streatham Park, on 27 July 1778, marked Frances Burney's formal entry onto a cultural scene frequented by the most prominent public figures of the time. Richard Brinsley Sheridan and Arthur Murphy were constant guests, as was Samuel Johnson, by far the most famous, admired, and respected man of letters of the century, who sought relief from his recurring attacks of hypochondria by enjoying the brilliant conversation of the Thrales' guests.[4] Burney also met Johnson's circle of influential friends, including Edmund Burke, James Boswell, and Sir Joshua Reynolds.

Frances Burney's first visit to Streatham immediately earned her the affection and esteem of Hester Thrale, and she remained her close friend and confidante until the death of her husband, Henry Thrale, in 1783.[5] Never having fully accepted her stepmother, Elizabeth Allen, Burney adopted Hester Thrale as a surrogate mother, and Streatham Park became her second home, an elegant and brilliant environment where she was accorded all the respect due to the author of a novel declared superior to the works of the masters of the time. Dr. Johnson in particular developed a strong affection for Frances Burney, whose wit and inventiveness he admired and with whom he could share those literary pastimes that helped him fend off depression: "I admire her for her observation, for her good sense, for her humour, for her discernment, for her manner of expressing them, and for all her writing talents" (*EJL,* 3:154). The three friends amused themselves by devising literary projects together. Mrs. Thrale and Burney briefly toyed with the idea of a "Weekly Paper" devoted to the visitors and events at Streatham, and Johnson himself suggested to Burney that they compose a comedy called *Streatham, A Farce,* whose characters would be based on the Thrales' guests.[6] Mrs. Thrale's humorous reaction to the suggestion anticipates the response that Burney would soon face in writing her own comedy: "O if she does!' cried Mrs. Thrale, if she *inserts* us in a *Coomedy* [*sic*]—we'll serve her trick for trick—she is a young Authoress, & very delicate,—say it will be hard if we can't frighten her into order'" (*EJL,* 3:111).

The teasing warning was warranted, although Hester Thrale was not aware of it at the time. Burney's presentation to the Thrales and to their brilliant circle had in fact coincided with the idea for a play on which Burney was working in secret. Readers of her novel had often remarked on the obvious and appealing similarity between some passages of *Evelina* and the text of a play; they had also noted that the novel's structure resembled that of a comedy. This indirect encouragement, which reached Burney insistently from all sides, soon turned into an open and irresistible invitation by the members of the Streatham circle to try her hand at playwriting. The witty men and women with whom she associated and the fashionable gatherings to which she was constantly invited became an ideal source of inspiration for Burney. She probably started working on the play in the summer of 1778 (significantly, her diaries hardly refer to it until 1779) and did not finish revising until 1780.

Hester Thrale was among the first to urge Burney to turn her talent to the stage. Their friendship was only a few weeks old when Burney was already noting in her journal that "she has sent me some very *serious advice* to write for the *Theatre,* as she says, I so naturally run into *conversations,* that Evelina absolutely and plainly points out that path to me" (*EJL,* 3:62). The inclination for dramatic writing that Burney had already shown in her earliest compositions, destroyed in the bonfire of 1767, was now warmly supported by Mrs. Thrale, who also advised that Dr. Johnson be directly involved in the project to ensure its success. "Ah! cried Mrs Thrale . . . how I wish You would hatch up a Comedy between you! . . . And then, she proceeded to give me her *serious advice* to actually set about one; she said it was her opinion I *ought* to do it . . . she stated the advantages attending Theatrical writing, & promised to *ensure* me success. . . . However, she has frequently *pressed* me to it since, nay, she declared to me *she should never be at rest till I did*" (*EJL,* 3:94). Mrs. Thrale was not alone in offering encouragement; a few months later (by which time Burney was presumably already writing the comedy), Richard Brinsley Sheridan expressed a more professional interest in Burney's play. In addition to being a successful playwright, Sheridan managed the Drury Lane Theatre, and his fame had recently reached new heights after the success in 1777 of *The School for Scandal.*

The meeting with Sheridan is reported in Burney's journal to her sister Susanna (11 January 1779), describing an evening that was "*perhaps* the most important of my life" (*EJL,* 3:225). After expressing his admiration for *Evelina,* "a most surprising book," Sheridan had addressed Sir Joshua Reynolds in an attempt to get Burney to reveal what she might be working on at the time:

> "Sir Joshua, I have been telling Miss Burney that she must not suffer her pen to lie idle;—*ought* she?"
>
> *Sir Joshua.* No, indeed, ought she not.
>
> *Mr. Sheridan.*—Do *you,* then, Sir Joshua, persuade her. But perhaps you *have* begun something? May we *ask?* . . .
>
> *Sir Joshua. Any* thing in the *Dialogue* way, I think, she *must* succeed in; & I am sure *invention* will not be wanting. . . . I am sure *I* think so; & I hope she *will.*
>
> I could only answer by *incredulous* exclamations.
>
> "Consider," continued Sir Joshua, you have already had all the applause & fame you *can* have given you in the *Clozet,*—but the Acclamation of a *Theatre* will be *new* to you."
>
> . . . I actually shook from head to foot! I felt myself already in Drury Lane, amidst the *Hub bub* of a first Night. . . .
>
> "Ay, cried Sir Joshua . . . And *you,* (to Mr. Sheridan,) would *take* anything of *Her's,*—would you not?—*Unsight unseen?*" . . .
>
> "*Yes;* answered Mr. Sheridan, with quickness,—& make her a Bow & my best Thanks into the Bargain!" (*EJL,* 3:234–35)[7]

It is likely that Sheridan's willingness to stage—"unsight, unseen"—any play Burney would have given him was due to its nearly certain attraction for the public, making it a good financial investment. As Dr. Burney remarked, the success of *Evelina* had in fact turned out to be "a *devilish good bargain*" (*ED*, 2:224) for her publisher, Lowndes (and only for Lowndes, since in spite of his substantial profits, he had refused to pay Burney more than the original £20 they had agreed on), and a comedy by the author of *Evelina* could well have been as successful as, if not more successful than, the novel.

The letter to Susanna concludes with a disclaimer, however. As she had done in *Evelina*'s prefatory material, Burney once again wished to conceal and repress her authorial assertiveness. Anonymity and the disavowal of professionalism had been strategies to contain and dissimulate her own desire for literary authority. Now it was the admiration and flattery of her new patrons that relieved her of direct responsibility in the matter. Had she decided to write for the theater, her ambition would have been excused—if not actually justified—by the strong pressure to which she had been subjected: "And now, my dear Susy,—if I *should* attempt the stage,—I think I may be fairly acquitted of presumption, & however I may fail,—That I was strongly pressed to *try* by Mrs. Thrale,—& by Mr. Sheridan,—the most successful & powerful of all Dramatic living Authors,—will abundantly excuse my temerity" (*EJL*, 3:236).

Burney's decision to write a comedy when she was at the apex of her literary and social celebrity following the success of *Evelina* and her introduction to the Streatham circle should be read in light of its consequences for her family, as well as for her social and personal life. Literary fame and the recognition of her talent not only by the public at large, but especially by the literary circle with whom she was increasingly spending her time, had placed her at the center of public attention and had allowed her to construct a new public persona. Her new role as a successful author forced her to measure her talent as a writer against the expectations of the reading public and against those (just as burdensome) of her father. In her early letters and journals, Burney's persona was still that of "the silent, observant Miss Fanny" (*JL*, 11:286)—as her eldest sister's suitor described her—a young girl reassuringly endowed with "sense, sensibility, and bashfulness" (*EJL*, 1:xv), "so meek, & so quiet" (*EJL*, 3:39). After the publication of *Evelina* and her friendship with the Thrales, she found herself heralded as a wit, a lively, sometimes sharp conversationalist who was expected to display her talents for observation and repartee in public.

Her new status as a brilliant literary lady made Burney aware that she could no longer avoid publicly acknowledging her will to write. Nor could she continue to cultivate her image as her father's retiring amanuensis, "so maidenly demure & prudish & shy" (*EJL,* 1:10). But writing for the theater would have entailed further exposing the authorial presence partly concealed by *Evelina*'s epistolary technique. The direct mimesis of the stage would have required permanently relinquishing the private sphere and adopting a new identity—that of a playwright—whose social connotations were largely negative.

In the eighteenth century, the figure of the female playwright was closely linked to that of the actress, and was considered no less morally questionable. The woman who decided to exhibit herself on stage chose to "sell her body," accepting a merchandising of the self that had been associated with prostitution for centuries by the patristic and Puritan traditions.[8] Like that of the actress, the scandal represented by the female playwright was due to the symbolic overthrowing of the walls of the closet, the domestic and private sphere that still enclosed female authors whose educational or religious novels were justified by their moral purpose. Writing for the stage meant exhibiting not only themselves but also their *poiesis* (*ποίησις*), their work, in an open declaration that writing was not a genteel pastime but a profession that should be rewarded financially.[9] The (economic) advantages "attending Theatrical writing," so readily mentioned to Burney by Hester Thrale, should therefore be considered in the context of the opposition between public and private, closet and stage, that had also been noted by Sir Joshua Reynolds in the conversation with Sheridan and Burney quoted earlier.

For an eighteenth-century woman, the choice to write for the theater was a decision that invested not only her social and professional status and her reputation, but even her sexual identity. The woman who defied the "Salic law of wit" by publicly presenting herself as a playwright was perceived as androgynous, a "hermaphrodite" (as a follower of the intransigent Italian critic Traiano Boccalini put it), whose work possessed "neither wit for a man, nor modesty enough for a woman."[10] By choosing to write plays rather than religious tracts, poetry, or novels, the female playwright thrust herself into the center of the public sphere, far removed from (or, indeed, in opposition to) the private and domestic sphere "natural" to her. "Shall we call that a honest trade, which makes a modest woman a *prodigy,* and which prompts us to despise those who follow it, unless we depend on a constant miracle?" asked Rousseau.[11] His rhetorical question plays on the biological and cultural connotations of the term "prodigy," evoking a gendered notion of the monstrous or unnatural. While the novel, a new genre that still lacked an established tradition, could be produced and consumed within the domestic space, the drama had always been a public genre and not only was associated with the dubious morality of actors but was also performed before an audience of clamoring spectators. The spectators' reaction to a play was not mediated by the act of reading. Rather, it was *im*mediate and often highly vocal: audiences launched a constant volley of comments at the stage, laughing in approval or whistling and jeering—behavior that lasted well beyond David Garrick's reforms. The theaters of the eighteenth century were rough, often aggressive places, the scene of frequent commotions and violent protests (e.g., against the increased price of tickets or the real or perceived slight directed by a performer against the audience) whose riotousness would be unthinkable for modern audiences.

In the eighteenth century, furthermore, as female playwrights became more common, a new paradigmatic connection had emerged next to the ancient one linking actress and prostitute: the female playwright, like the actress, offered her work for sale, and the scandal was made worse by the fact that she could earn more than a novelist. Were a play to succeed, she would be paid immediately after the third performance, and her earnings would increase with the number of performances. In addition, she could profit further by selling the rights to publication, a virtually obligatory step for a successful play, but one that would definitively reveal her identity as its author and therefore expose her to public notoriety for having actively sought literary fame.

In the letter describing her crucial meeting with Sheridan, Burney's desire and need to justify her decision to write for the stage are striking. Her feelings on the matter are better understood if one considers the cautionary letters she was receiving at this time from Samuel Crisp. Her correspondence with Crisp, carried on side by side with her journals to her sister Susanna, is an invaluable source for reconstructing the progress of the comedy's composition and for understanding and contextualizing the pressures she was subjected to as she worked on it.

The play was certainly well under way by the winter of 1778, as we know from the advice Burney received from Crisp, who in a letter written in November urged her to take advantage of the great success she had achieved, "turn[ing it] to some thing more solid than empty praise" before time would deprive her of the support of the influential Streatham circle:

> I do entirely acquit you of all wish or design of being known to the world as an author. I believe it is ever the case with writers of real merit and genius, on the appearance of their first productions: as their powers are finer and keener than other people's, so is their sensibility. . . . You will be convinced that a state of independence is the only basis on which to rest your future ease and comfort. You are now young, lively, gay. You please, and the world smiles upon you—this is your time. Years and wrinkles in the due season will succeed. You will no longer be the same Fanny of 1778, feasted, caressed, admired. . . . Let me only earnestly urge you to act vigorously (what I really believe is in your power) a distinguished part in the present [scene]. (*EJL*, 3:180)

Crisp also strongly recommended that Burney maintain absolute silence about the work in progress: "Lastly, if you do resolve to undertake anything of the nature your friends recommend, keep it (if possible) an impenetrable secret that you are even about such a work. Let it be all your own till it is finish'd intirely [*sic*] in your own Way—it will be time enough then to consult such friends as you think capable of Judging & Advising. If you suffer anyone to interfere till then, 'tis ten to one 'tis the worse for it—it won't be all of a piece" (*EJL*, 3:180). Crisp stressed the importance of Burney's creative independence even more strenuously in a letter of 19 January 1779: "I would not give a pin for the advice of the ablest Friend, who would not suffer me at last to follow *my own* Judgment, without resentment" (*EJL*, 3:239). It is ironic that only a few months later, the same friend who had so encouraged her would reverse his position and express his disapproval without doubting that Burney would unquestioningly obey his authority.

The apparently dispassionate suggestions Crisp offered while Burney was working on the play already harbored within them the anxiety he was to express more openly in a letter of 8 December. Here, his encouragement and praise is mixed with caution, and his recommendation to prudence is couched in terms that would affect Burney strongly:

> You would be Urg'd, strongly Urg'd, by your many Friends & Admirers, to undertake a Comedy.—I think You capable, highly Capable of it; but in the Attempt there are great difficulties in the way; some more particularly, & individually in the way of a Fanny than of most people—I will instantly name these, lest You should misapprehend. I need not to Observe to *You,* that in most of Our successful comedies, there are frequent lively Freedoms (& waggeries that cannot be called licentious, neither) that give a strange animation, & Vig[our] to the

> same, & of which, if it were to be depriv'd, it would lose wonderfully of its Salt, & Spirit—I mean *such* Freedoms as Ladies of the strictest Character would make no scruple, openly, to laugh at, but at the same time, especially if they were Prudes, (And You know You are one) perhaps would *shy* at being *known* to be the Authors of—Some Comic Characters would be deficient without strokes of this kind in Scenes, where Gay Men of the World are got together, they are natural and expected. (*EJL*, 3:187)

Crisp's anti-theatrical bias was fully consonant with the chastened theatrical repertoire of the 1770s—sentimental comedies, the newly popular historical dramas, and toned-down versions of some of the most spirited Restoration comedies.[12] But his warning also echoes the centuries-old prejudice against women who chose to link their reputations to the world of the theater, whether as actresses or as authors.

Crisp's words speak to a social phenomenon we might call an "economy" or "politics of spectacle" that was closely connected to the construction of the actor's social and sexual identity in the eighteenth century.[13] He presents Burney with the stark dichotomy current in the cultural imagination of the time that pitted the stage against the audience. According to this ideological hierarchy, the decision to link one's name to the world of the theater implied accepting one's subordination on moral, social, and financial grounds to the tastes and the will of the audience and entering willingly into a relationship built on the opposition between spectator and spectacle, subject and object of the gaze. The actor was considered a socially liminal, morally reprehensible, and sexually hybrid figure,[14] and Burney's willingness to link her name—and hence, the names of her closest friends and family—to the world of the theater was a choice that required careful consideration.

Burney did not act immediately on Crisp's cautionary advice. Torn between fear and determination, she wrote him a reply that shows her choice had already been made, although at the cost of much anxiety:

> Every word you have urged concerning the *salt & spirit* of gay unrestrained freedom in comedies, carries conviction along with it. . . . I would a thousand Times rather forfeit my character as a *Writer*, than risk ridicule and censure as a *Female*. I have never set my heart on Fame, & therefore I would not if I *could* purchase it at the expense of all my ideas of propriety. You who *know* me for a *Prude* will not be

> surprised, & hope not offended at this avowal,—For I should deceive you were I not to make it. If I should *try* it, I must ev'n take my chance,—& all my own expectations may be pretty easily answered! (*EJL*, 3:212)

Burney's intention—indeed, her need—to privilege the preservation of her respectability as a woman, even at the cost of compromising her recently acquired reputation as a successful author, is closely tied to the inevitable social consequences of her choice to write for the theater. As Crisp had remarked—and warned—successful comedies of the time contained a fair amount of sexual tension. A play, unlike a novel, could not mask such sexual overtones and would, instead, display them explicitly on stage. In *Evelina,* latent tensions of this sort had been safely contained.

The failed abduction of Evelina by Sir Clement Willoughby, for example, is a scene particularly charged with repressed undercurrents and sexual violence and illustrates perfectly the difference between the narrative mimesis reconstructed by a reader in the theater of his or her imagination and the deliberate visual representation provided by the stage. Coming out of the Opera House, Evelina accepts Willoughby's offer to take her home in his carriage. She does so to prevent Lord Orville from realizing that she has come to the Haymarket in the embarrassing company of Madame Duval and the Branghtons. Alone, without the protection of a chaperone, Evelina finds herself a prisoner in the baronet's carriage, in a part of London utterly unknown to her and in the power of a man whose attentions have become disturbingly obvious in the course of their brief ride:

> I let down the glass, and made a sudden effort to open the chariot-door myself, with a view of jumping into the street; but he caught hold of me, exclaiming, "For Heaven's sake, *what is the matter?*"
>
> "*I—I don't know,*" cried I (quite out of breath), "but I am sure the [coachman] goes wrong, and, if you will not speak to him, I am determined I will get out myself."
>
> "*You amaze me,*" answered he (still holding me), "*I cannot imagine what you apprehend.* Surely you can have no *doubts* of my honour?"
>
> He drew me towards him as he spoke. I was frightened dreadfully, and could hardly say, "*No, Sir, no,—none at all,*—only Mrs. Mirvan,—I think she will be uneasy."
>
> "*Whence this alarm,* my dearest angel?—*What can you fear?* my life is at your devotion, and can you, then, *doubt* my protection?"

> And so saying he passionately kissed my hand.
>
> Never, in my whole life, have I been so terrified. . . .
>
> Sir Clement, with great earnestness, endeavoured to appease and compose me; "If you do not intend *to murder me,*" cried I, "for mercy's sake, for pity's sake, let me go out!" (*Evelina,* 109–10; emphasis added)

The episode, described in a letter Evelina sends to her tutor, is clearly comparable to a scene in a play. The kinesic and proxemic relations of the two characters are accurately reported: "I made a sudden effort," "he caught hold of me," "(still holding me)"; and the dialogue is consistently accompanied by paralinguistic notation—"exclaiming," "(quite out of breath)," "could *hardly* say." The parenthetical notation is only the most obvious example of the many implicit stage directions in the passage. A semiotic reading of the episode suggests that Willoughby's physical aggression is a condensed version, on a visual level, of all the constraints, gendered obstacles, and social violence Evelina has to endure for most of the novel as a result of her uncertain familial status.

It is worth noting that Evelina is reporting her adventure to Villars, the upright and virtuous guardian whose judgment of her actions is always implicit in her letters. She is perfectly aware that the length of her stay in London depends on his will. This is why, when she implores Willoughby in the carriage, her appeal should be read as directed to Villars, as well, and indeed—in a broadening of the field of addressees—to the novel's ideal reader. Evelina must succeed in retaining her unsullied innocence even in this extremely unpleasant—even dangerous—situation, and even though she is aware of the sexual desire she has awakened in her escort. Were Willoughby to suspect Evelina's fear of being abducted, seduced, or even raped, she would immediately and permanently lose her ingenuousness and in the process would break the narrative pact between author and reader announced in the preface: Evelina must remain "ignoran[t] of the forms, and inexperience[d] in the manners" of worldly society (*Evelina,* 7). The only fear she is allowed to express is the fear of being *murdered,* a transparent recoding and sublimation of her sexual fear, but insofar as it expresses her terrible suspicion that she is about to become Willoughby's victim, it somehow succeeds in squaring the circle. Her frenzied calls for help are explained without necessarily implying her awareness of the erotic intentions of her kidnapper.

The broad scope for allusion and suggestion provided by the epistolary novel, where the conventional distinction between narrator and author is especially marked and where the various addressees of the letters filter the direct relationship with the reader, would no longer be available to Burney once she decided to write for the theater. Had it been performed on stage, a scene as emotionally intense as that of Evelina's failed abduction would necessarily have enacted openly the sexual tension that remains latent on the page of the novel. Burney was fully aware of this when she offered soothing moral reassurance to her mentor Crisp; she knew that writing for the stage was in itself reason enough to be considered one of "Virtue's female Foes,"[15] and that her only option was to choose a morally irreprehensible subject. As Crisp reminded her anxiously, "You have much to lose . . . because much you have gain'd" (*EJL,* 3:187). In particular, he said, "It appears to me extremely difficult, throughout a whole spirited Comedy to steer clear of those agreeable, frolicksome *jeux d'Esprit,* on the one hand; and languor & heaviness on the other—pray Observe, I only say *difficult* not *impracticable*—at least to your dexterity, & to that I leave it" (*EJL,* 3:189). Crisp concluded: "I will never allow You to sacrifice a *Grain* of female delicacy, for all the Wit of Congreve & Vanbrugh put together—the purchase would be too dear. . . . Do You remember about a Dozen Years ago, how You Used to dance Nancy Dawson on the Grass plot, with Your Cap on the Ground, & your long hair streaming down your Back, one shoe off, & throwing about your head like a mad thing?—now you are to dance Nancy Dawson with Fetters on—there is the difference" (*EJL,* 3:238–39).

The growing importance that the play had taken on for Burney is repeatedly stressed in her journal to Susanna in the winter of 1779. She confessed to being utterly absorbed by the comedy: "Journal I have kept none, nor had I any time for such sort of writing" (*EJL,* 3:236). With the summer came last-minute corrections, and even less time to write letters: "Very concise indeed must my Journal grow, for I have now hardly a moment in my *power* to give it" and "When the Copying my Play, & the Daily returning occurrences of every fresh Day, are considered, You will not wonder that I should find so little opportunity for scrawling Letters" (*EJL,* 3:333, 336).

In February 1779, besides Johnson, who continued to be encouraging, and Hester Thrale, who had become Burney's inseparable companion as she wrote her comedy, another influential figure expressed interest in the play. Arthur Murphy was a Shakespeare expert, a biographer, and a fairly well-known playwright whose tragedies and pleasant comedies were much appreciated by Burney. In 1777, the Burney family had staged their own private performance of *The Way to Keep Him* (1760), a brilliant comedy in which Frances had played Mrs. Lovemore (*EJL,* 2:237–44, 252–53).[16]

After meeting Murphy at Streatham, Burney wrote to Susanna describing the Irish author as "the man of all other *strangers* to me whom I most longed to see" (*EJL,* 3:243). Feigning ignorance about Burney's authorship of *Evelina,* Murphy had explained why he would recommend that the author of the novel attempt to write for the theater:

> "If I," said Mr. Murphy, looking very archly, "had written a certain Book,—a Book I won't name,—but a Book I have lately read,—I would *next* write a Comedy."
>
> "Good God," cried Mrs. Thrale, colouring with pleasure, "do *you* think so, too?"
>
> "Yes indeed; I thought so *while* I was reading it,—it struck me repeatedly. . . . *Comedy* is the *forte* of that Book,—I laughed over it most violently . . . and if the Author—I won't say *who* (all the Time looking *away* from *me*) will write a *Comedy,* I will most readily, & with great pleasure, give any advice or assistance in my power." (*EJL,* 3:245–46)

Soon after, Johnson convinced Burney to lay aside her reserve and take advantage of Murphy's willingness to help. Among Burney's various well-intentioned advisers, he was the only one in a position to offer concrete assistance, having both written and staged plays: "It would be well to make Murphy the last Judge, 'for *he* knows the stage,' [Johnson] said, '& I am quite ignorant of it'" (*EJL,* 3:251). Murphy's advice was to keep the project a secret while Burney was writing and to stage it as an anonymous work, except the prologue and epilogue, which would be provided by Johnson and Murphy, respectively, and would guarantee the work's success.

Burney finished the play on 4 May 1779, as she announced to Crisp in a letter of the same day (*EJL,* 3:261–63), and she immediately gave the first act to Murphy. Soon after, he joined Hester Thrale and Burney in Brighton, where he enthused about the dialogue and the characters: "He made me many very flattering speeches of his eagerness to go on with my Play,—to know what became of the several Characters,—& to what place I should next conduct them, assuring me that the first Act had run in his Head ever since he had read it" (*EJL,* 3:278). Then Murphy read the second act and again approved: "Murphy is quite charmed with [my] second act,—he says he is sure it will do, & *more* than do" (*EJL,* 3:286).

Throughout May and June 1779, Burney redrafted, corrected, and streamlined the play. Then she sent it to Chessington (on 30 June), where her two "Daddys" had organized a family reading of it. All of the comments Burney had received up to this point—whether from family or friends—had been positive, and the note she sent to her father with the play contained a fairly perfunctory appeal to her judges' "good nature & delicacy" (*EJL*, 3:342). Perhaps she felt no need to earnestly entreat for her home audience's favor: based on what she had experienced so far, her closest friends and relatives were unlikely to be very critical.

The only surviving manuscript of *The Witlings* is a fair copy now in the Berg Collection of the New York Public Library. The manuscript is made up of five small notebooks, one for each act, written in a firm, clear hand, with no corrections or erasures. The clearness of the handwriting and the precise pagination resemble those of a manuscript ready for use on-stage, suggesting Burney's eagerness to see it performed.[17]

The first page of the comedy gives the work's title, its genre, and the indirect formula Burney used to represent herself as its author:

The Witlings.
A Comedy
By a Sister of the Order. (*CP,* 1)

Burney's strategy of not placing her surname on the title page absolves her family of any direct involvement in the play, once again dissociating her own literary work from her father's image. The self-reflexive "Sister of the Order" has the further effect of including the author among the "witlings" in the comedy. Although very brief, the epitext of the comedy is thus highly significant: while the title does imply an attack against the coterie of wits who crowded the fashionable salons she had begun to frequent, by situating herself among the literary characters of her play, Burney takes some of the sting out of the satire.

The comedy has five acts, with one scene per act. The third act is the only one that can be divided into two scenes, a possibility signaled indirectly by the only scene change in the play. The main plot of the comedy concerns the troubled love story between the wealthy heiress Cecilia Stanley and Beaufort, Lady Smatter's nephew and heir. The serious plot involving the young lovers is linked to a subplot featuring the pretentious members of the "Esprit Party," a small circle of would-be literati headed by the conceited, and wealthy, Lady Smatter.

The curtain rises on Mrs. Wheedle's busy shop, where amid the merchandise on display and the general hubbub of orders being given several of the play's principal characters meet, including Beaufort and the misanthropic Censor. While Beaufort waits for his betrothed, his stepbrother Jack comes in, leaves, and eventually returns, having finally remembered to deliver Cecilia's message that she cannot keep her appointment with Beaufort.

At the start of act 2, we learn that Cecilia, who is staying with Lady Smatter, has been kept at home by her host, a woman overly fond of displaying her pretended erudition. They are joined by Beaufort's stepfather, Codger, and by the fashionable poetaster Dabler, Lady Smatter's protégé. Both are members of the Esprit Party, which is to meet that evening in Lady Smatter's library. Then Beaufort arrives, intent on discovering why Cecilia did not join him, and hears Jack's news that the banker Stipend, Cecilia's guardian and trustee of her fortune, has been bankrupted, losing all of his clients' money, including Cecilia's. No longer a wealthy heiress, Cecilia has suddenly become an unwanted guest. Lady Smatter tells her she must forget Beaufort and move to the country. But when Lady Smatter orders Beaufort to abandon his marriage plans, he states he cannot forsake Cecilia at such a crisis. His aunt then threatens to disinherit him and accuses Cecilia of wanting to marry him purely out of interest.

In act 3, Censor comes to Lady Smatter's to help Cecilia but finds she has left the house. Instead, he meets Beaufort, enraged by his aunt's behavior and ready to sever his ties with her and put an end to his financial dependence. Censor persuades him not to make an enemy of Lady Smatter and at the same time promises to find Cecilia and assure her that, although the situation might seem desperate, she has not been forsaken.

After a quick scene change, the action moves to Dabler's rooms. The poet is interrupted in his efforts at composition by his landlady, Mrs. Voluble, who is in the habit of breaking in on him on the slightest pretext to discover what he is writing. After requesting that no one be allowed into his rooms, Dabler leaves for the gathering of the Esprit Party. Mrs. Voluble immediately begins to rifle through his papers, but her search for new poems is interrupted by the arrival of Cecilia, who is seeking lodgings. Mrs. Voluble is uncertain how to help the now penniless Cecilia, and Cecilia's misfortunes are seemingly compounded by a message delivered by Censor, which convinces her that Beaufort has yielded to the threat of being disinherited and has abandoned her, leaving it up to Censor to make up an excuse.

Act 4 takes place in Lady Smatter's library, where a typically inconclusive gathering of the Esprit Party is under way. Every topic raised elicits a poetic outburst from Dabler, always keen to court admiration. The meeting is interrupted by Censor's arrival. He is swayed from his intention of pleading Beaufort's and Cecilia's case by his irritation at Lady Smatter's conceited displays of false erudition and the appalling poems declaimed by Dabler, whose sham inspiration is exposed in a poetry improvisation contest. Then Beaufort arrives and takes Censor to task for having left him waiting for news of Cecilia. Censor again advises patience, and Beaufort reacts by singing the praises of poverty and independence.

The final act opens on the supper that Mrs. Voluble and her son Bob are sharing with Mrs. Wheedle and a shop assistant. Cecilia comes in, anxious to know whether a letter has arrived on which her fate seems to depend. But no letter has been delivered, and to make things worse, Mrs. Voluble has advised Mrs. Wheedle to seize the moment to request payment of Cecilia's millinery bill. Since Cecilia cannot pay, Mrs. Wheedle suggests she seek employment as a companion to a wealthy lady about to go abroad.

Suddenly, loud knocking is heard at the door, and a "fine lady" is announced. In the general haste to make the parlor presentable, the table is overturned and the supper crashes onto the floor. The maid Jenny quickly sweeps the mess into a closet before Mrs. Sapient comes in. An ardent admirer of the poet, Mrs. Sapient has come to seek news of Dabler. Glad to show off her easy access to his writings, Mrs. Voluble invites Mrs. Sapient to follow her into the poet's apartment. But the premature breakup of the Esprit Party gathering brings Dabler home early, and he discovers that his poem is missing. Mrs. Voluble lays the blame on Mrs. Sapient, who has hastily hidden herself in the closet with the remains of the supper.

Beaufort arrives, ready to tell Cecilia that he has disobeyed his aunt and will marry her. He is followed by Lady Smatter, intent on preventing the young lovers' union. But with Jack's assistance, Censor has thought up a plan to force Lady Smatter's compliance: if she acts on her threat to disinherit Beaufort, London will be covered in lampoons about her. Meanwhile, Cecilia has received news of an unexpected improvement in her financial situation, and Censor offers the lovers a gift of £5,000. The comedy's epilogue therefore provides a threefold resolution: Lady Smatter relinquishes her plan to persecute Beaufort and Cecilia; the lovers clarify their misunderstanding; and their financial problems are resolved.

The turning point of the action comes in the middle of act 2 in an apparently casual way, when the "newshound" Jack happens to hear of Stipend's bankruptcy as he is rushing about London.[18] Although he knows about the banker's close ties with Cecilia, Jack seems indifferent to the grave implications of the news he is carrying:

> *Jack.* Well, if you will have it, you will! but I tell you before hand you will not like it. You know Stipend, the banker? . . .
> *Cecilia.* You terrify me to Death!—what would you say?
> *Beaufort.* No matter what,—Jack, I could murder you!
> *Jack.* There, now, I said how it would be! now would not any body suppose the man broke through my fault?
> *Cecilia.* Broke?—O Heaven, I am ruined! (*CP,* 2.445–46, 453–57)

The news of Stipend's failure affects Cecilia's social standing immediately. Instead of being a wealthy heiress, she has suddenly become a vulnerable young woman with no means of support. The personal implications of her plunge into poverty are revealed in the course of the next three acts, as her early relationships with those surrounding her are transformed. Figure 9 shows the other characters' actantial roles and the moment (in parentheses) that they are reversed. This outline reflects the characters' reactions to Cecilia's desperate situation, and these, in turn, govern the plot, whose final resolution depends largely on the eighteenth-century sentimental values of sympathy, generosity, and benevolence.

Jack, who at first reports Stipend's bankruptcy with no apparent emotion, by act 5 has become Censor's closest assistant, threatening to broadcast lampoons against Lady Smatter throughout London. Even Dabler, the modish poet whose first reaction to Cecilia's misfortune is to exploit it for his cloying poetry ("'Twill be the most pathetic thing I ever wrote! . . . I'll to Work while the subject is warm,—nobody will read it with dry Eyes!" [*CP,*

FIGURE 9. Characters' actantial roles in *The Witlings*

Helpers		Opponents
Beaufort	⟶	(Act 3)
(Act 5)	⟵	
(Act 5)	⟵	Jack
(Act 5)	⟵	Censor
(Act 5)	⟵	Dabler
Mrs. Voluble		
		Lady Smatter

2.496–99]), eventually agrees to help Censor by composing satirical verses against Lady Smatter:

> *Censor.* Speak out, man!—Tell Lady Smatter if she will not be a lost Woman to the Literary World, should she, in this trial of her magnanimity, disgrace it's expectations? Speak boldly!
>
> *Dabler.* Hem!—you,—you have Said, Sir,—just what I think. (*CP,* 5.852–55)

Censor's actantial function is also reversed by the end of the play, refuting the misanthropy implicit in his name—and made worse by a strong misogynist streak. In the first act, he had accused Cecilia of inconstancy and of making Beaufort wait: "And, pray, Sir,—if such a Question will not endanger a challenge,—what think you, by this Time, of the punctuality of your Mistress?" (*CP,* 1.405–7). Censor's function as a blocking character is further stressed in the course of acts 3 and 4. In act 3, his well-intentioned advice that Beaufort be patient ends up confirming Cecilia's worst fears that her lover has forsaken her, and in act 4, he fails in his intent to mediate between Lady Smatter and her nephew when his irritation at the pretentiousness of the Esprit Party leads him to waste time exposing their false erudition instead of pleading the lovers' case. In act 5, however, Censor's actantial function is reversed as he finally comes to Cecilia's aid by threatening Lady Smatter with exposure, and his final gift of £5,000 to the young couple confirms his status as deus ex machina.

The loss of her property also affects Cecilia's relationship with Beaufort, who is financially dependent on his aunt and thus forced to respect her despotic will if he wants to remain her only heir. Heeding Censor's advice, Beaufort does not immediately follow Cecilia when she leaves Lady Smatter's house, giving her the impression that he has abandoned her:

> *Cecilia.* Oh faithless Beaufort! lost, lost Cecilia!
>
> *Censor.* To sue for him,—Kneel for him,—
>
> *Cecilia.* Leave me, leave me, Mr. Censor!—I can hear no more.
>
> *Censor.* Nay, prithee, madam listen to his message.
>
> *Cecilia.* No, Sir, never! at such a Time as this, a message is an Insult! He must know I was easily to be found, or he would not have sent it, and, knowing that, whose was it to have sought me?—Go, go, hasten to your Friend,—tell him I heard all that it became me to hear, and that I understood him too well to hear more: tell him that

> I will save him and myself the disgrace of further explanation,—tell him, in short, that I renounce him for ever! (*CP,* 3.667–77)

In acts 3 and 4, the two lovers are kept apart while Censor carries messages between them. This separation, which leads to further misunderstandings and complications, finally ends in act 5, when Beaufort tells Cecilia that he has rebelled against his aunt's heartless order:

> *Beaufort.* . . . [I]f I have temporized, it has been less for my own Sake than for yours; but I have seen the vanity of my expectations,—I have disobeyed Lady Smatter,—I have set all consequences at defiance, and flown in the very face of ruin,—and now, will *you,* Cecilia (*Kneeling*), reject, disdain, and Spurn me?
>
> *Cecilia.* Oh Beaufort—is it possible I can have wronged you? (*CP,* 5.589–95)

In the last act, with the final resolution of the conflict between the lovers, Beaufort resumes his initial function as Cecilia's faithful suitor.

Among the women in the comedy, Mrs. Voluble appears to feel some sympathy for the penniless Cecilia and some desire to alleviate her sorrow: "Poor young lady!—I declare I don't know what to think of to entertain her" (*CP,* 3.755–56).[19] By contrast, as soon as she hears about the loss of Cecilia's fortune, Lady Smatter immediately turns her out of the house to prevent her marriage with Beaufort. Lady Smatter is the only character whose actantial function is not reversed in act 5. She accepts her nephew's marriage not because she has repented her previous conduct or because she has been reconciled with the young couple, but only out of fear that her name will be vilified. She thus ends up absorbing the full satirical thrust of the comedy through to the epilogue. The consequence is that the comedy's threefold resolution feels mechanical. Lady Smatter's consent to the marriage entails no acknowledgment of her error. As an antagonist, she remains unredeemed and fails to precipitate the moment of catharsis that current taste, inspired by Aristotelian aesthetics, demanded of comedy. As in classical tragedy, it was expected that the conclusion of a comedy contribute to purifying the spectators' emotions, turning laughter and ridicule to good purpose.

The actantial structure undergirds the plot of *The Witlings.* The play opens onto an idyllic situation in act 1 that is radically altered in act 2 by the

FIGURE 10. Chronotopological structure in *The Witlings*

Act	Place	Time
1	Shop (Mrs. Wheedle)	Morning
2	Drawing room (Lady Smatter)	Morning
3.1	Dressing room (Lady Smatter)	Evening
3.2	Dabler's apartment (Mrs. Voluble)	Evening
4	Library (Lady Smatter)	Evening
5	Parlor (Mrs. Voluble)	Late evening (supper)

loss of Cecilia's fortune, which in turn raises obstacles in the way of the couple's union. Only by overcoming the obstacles embodied by the blocking characters can the initial order be reestablished and redemption achieved in the last act—except that Lady Smatter's lack of contrition makes the moral reward less than satisfactory. Set in motion by a *catastrophe* (the loss of fortune) and concluding with a *peripeteia,* or reversal (the young lovers' reunion), the plot thus unfolds according to the rules of classical comedy as defined by Northrop Frye: a desire or a lack gives rise to the action, which is then blocked before being resolved. As the playwright Hugh Kelly observed in the preface to *The School for Wives* (Drury Lane, 1774), "The great business of comedy consisted in making difficulties for the purpose of removing them; in distressing poor young lovers; and in rendering a happy marriage the object of every catastrophe."[20]

It seems clear that throughout the play, Cecilia's social identity (she is first introduced as "a young Lady with a Fortune all in her own Hands" [*CP,* 1.72–73]) defines, circumscribes, and ultimately modifies her personal identity. The chronotopological structure of the play (outlined in figure 10) further emphasizes the importance and the implications of the theme of social identity. The three central acts, during which Cecilia and Beaufort are kept apart by Lady Smatter, are set in Lady Smatter's house, where she presides over her guests and wields her considerable influence. By contrast with this aristocratic setting, act 1 takes place in Mrs. Wheedle's shop, and act 5 takes place in the home of her friend Mrs. Voluble, who rents rooms to Dabler to make ends meet. Although this topological organization violates unity of place, it supplies a "low" frame to the lovers' story, reflecting the alternation between high and low, rich and poor, that is one of the main themes of the comedy. Mrs. Wheedle's millinery shop—the "news room" where Cecilia's impending marriage is first announced[21]—is thus contiguous to the home of Mrs. Voluble, who is always eager for news and gossip and who presides symbolically over the announcement of the partial recovery of Cecilia's fortune.

The contrast between the frame (acts 1 and 5) and the main body of the comedy (acts 2–4) activates the motif of specularity and intratextual reference that underlies the structure of the play. Had the play been performed, the scene changes would have involved elaborate sets and stage props in line with the design conventions of the time, which favored an increasingly technologized style of scenography. It is also worth noting that in this period the lighting on-stage had to compete with the wax candles illuminating the auditorium throughout the performance, a reason that many authors set their plays entirely indoors, particularly in domestic settings.[22]

The high–low opposition is indirectly emphasized by the characters' different relationships with the city of London. The main topological distinction is illustrated by Mrs. Wheedle, who teaches her shop assistants to attend to each client according to her provenance and status:

> *Mrs Wheedle.* Has any body been in yet?
> *Miss Jenny.* No, ma'am, nobody to Signify: only some people on foot. . . .
> *Miss Sally.* Am I to go on with this Cap, ma'am?
> *Mrs. Wheedle.* Yes, to be sure, and let it be sent with the other things to Mrs. Apeall in the Minories; it will do well enough for the City. (*CP,* 1.2–15)[23]

Originating in the late seventeenth century, the contrast that dominates the urban space in the comedy pits London's aristocratic neighborhoods against the city, the true nobility against the commercial classes who ape their manners. Indoors, it is reflected in the contrast between drawing room and library, on one hand, and shop and parlor on the other. Burney loosely follows the convention of resolving the conflict between bourgeoisie and aristocracy by marrying the heiress Cecilia, whose guardian is a banker, to Beaufort, nephew of the only aristocrat in the comedy.

The only character who physically crosses the social barriers separating the commercial and aristocratic sides of the city is Jack, Beaufort's stepbrother, who is constantly running from one end of the city to the other—from Hyde Park (*CP,* 1.351, 429, 2.520) to Fleet Street, Cornhill, and into the heart of the City (*CP,* 2.368–69, 371): "Jack is a character who Burney pointedly portrays as a late eighteenth-century descendant of the newshounds of the *Tatler* and the *Spectator,* figures whose frenzied ways of posting from one coffee-house to another, distributing the talk of the town, made them into human versions of the very newsletters they sought."[24] Jack's perpetual motion is crucial to the development of the plot. The news he hears as he dashes about town precipitates Cecilia's troubles, and at the end of the play he is made an instrument of Censor's threat to "drop Lampoons in every Coffee-house. . . . Send libels to every corner of the town" (*CP,* 5.832–36).

Chronologically, the play respects the classical unities by taking place during the very limited time frame of one day, a point Burney stresses particularly in the epilogue, when Beaufort celebrates the resolution of all his difficulties and the end of a trying day: "Allow me, Ladies, with all humility, to mediate, and to entreat that the calm of an Evening succeeding a Day So agitated with Storms, may be enjoyed without allay" (*CP,* 5.946–48). Mrs. Voluble also makes the point: "In all Families there will be some busy Days" (*CP,* 5.346). Mrs. Voluble's words place Burney's play firmly in the context of contemporary comic conventions (suffice it to recall Oliver Goldsmith's *She Stoops to Conquer* [Drury Lane, 1773], subtitled *The Mistakes of a Night*), and they will, of course, be echoed in the title of one of Burney's later comedies, *A Busy Day* (ca. 1801–1802).

Within this unified temporal framework, the events are distributed according to criteria of opposition/specularity (see figure 11), reflecting a formula already tested in *Evelina.* As the figure shows, besides the topological repetitions and oppositions underlying the comedy's structure, there are several recurring themes, among them especially that of a woman's reputation. Introduced at the start of the play and taken up again in the epilogue, it functions as an implicit hypogram of the text. In act 1, set in the millinery shop, various characters provide as many descriptions of Cecilia's social identity. Mrs. Wheedle's shop thus serves as a news clearinghouse in which the private becomes public. Here, Cecilia is constructed as Beaufort's flawless future wife (lines 12, 47, 72), as a rich orphaned heiress (lines 72–75), and as an inconstant and fickle young woman who takes pleasure in tormenting her lover by keeping him waiting (lines 405–407). In all of these cases, Cecilia's social identity is described, inscribed, and represented through the

FIGURE 11. Thematic specularities in *The Witlings*

Act	Female reputation	Private versus public life	Function of humor
1	Cecilia's reputation discussed		
2		Cecilia (private life) versus Lady Smatter (public life)	
4			Censor's "splenetic humor" prevents him from acting
5	Lady Smatter's reputation discussed		Censor's "splenetic humor" prevents Lady Smatter from acting

words of other characters. Cecilia does not define herself; she is defined by others.

A similar situation occurs in act 5 when Lady Smatter is cowed by Censor's threat of public exposure. As in the case of the protagonist, Cecilia, the reputation of the antagonist, Lady Smatter, is constructed in public, controlled and manipulated externally. Thus, although the two women's actantial roles are opposed, they are both subjected to the same ideological forces:

> *Censor.* . . . I have already shewn you my *power,* and you will find my *Courage* undaunted, and my *perseverance* indefatigable. If you any longer oppose the union of your nephew with Miss Stanley; I will destroy the whole peace of your life. . . . But if you relent,—I will burn all I have written, and forget all I have planned; Lampoons shall give place to panegyric, and libels, to Songs of Triumph; the liberality of your Soul, and the depth of your knowledge shall be recorded by the Muses, and echoed by the whole nation! (*CP,* 5.826–30, 843–48)

The threat of publicity—or, rather, of *publication*— dramatizes Lady Smatter's vulnerability to public opinion and to the power of those who, like

Censor, enforce gender constructions. The reputation of the bourgeois Cecilia is no less overly determined, in both gender and social terms, than that of the aristocratic Lady Smatter.

Burney conveys the powerlessness of women semiotically through her use of stage space. Cecilia's movements on the stage and off always depend on the presence of another character. In act 1, when Cecilia leaves Beaufort waiting in Mrs. Wheedle's shop, her apologies are belatedly delivered by Jack:

> *Jack.* O, it was all your aunt Smatter's fault,—somebody came in with the new Ranelagh Songs, so she stayed at Home to study them: and Miss Stanley bid me say *she was very sorry, but she could not come by herself.* (*CP,* 1.444–47; emphasis added)

The social conventions that controlled a young woman's movements, allowing her to go out only in the company of a chaperone, are represented by Cecilia's absence from the stage. She has not kept Beaufort waiting by design, as Censor had insinuated:

> *Cecilia.* Mr. Beaufort, I am quite ashamed to see You! yet the disappointment I occasioned you was as involuntary on my part, as it could possibly be disagreeable on yours. (*CP,* 2.53–55)

In the same way that Cecilia's social identity controls—or impedes—her movements off-stage, it also controls them on-stage. After her financial ruin, she is no longer able to act independently, and Burney illustrates Cecilia's new condition by showing how she must rely on Beaufort's physical assistance to move:

> *Cecilia.* Mr. Beaufort, let me pass—I can stand this no longer.
> *Beaufort.* Allow me to conduct you to your own Room; this torrent will else overpower you.
> *He leads* CECILIA *out.* (*CP,* 2.463–65)

Given Cecilia's dependence on others, the gravity of her situation is due precisely to the fact that she seems to have no one to turn to for help. This extreme social isolation is made explicit at the end of act 2 in her concluding monologue, when she remains alone on-stage.

The traditional education imparted to young women of the upper classes made them incapable of providing for themselves. As Lady Smatter cruelly points out, now that Cecilia has been reduced to poverty, the only way she could earn a living would be by marketing those accomplishments (such as sewing) that formed such a large part of women's education:

> *Lady Smatter.* She was brought up to nothing,—if she can make a Cap, 'tis as much as she can do,—and, in such a case, when a Girl is reduced to a Penny, what is to be done? (*CP,* 2.556–58)

Even before the loss of her fortune, the difference between the wealthy heiress Cecilia and Mrs. Wheedle's seamstresses (who in the opening scene are surrounded by "*Caps, Ribbons, Fans and Band Boxes*") is purely superficial. Within the framework of an emerging consumer society, the woman's condition remains one of dependence, now linked to a constructed public reputation, now to an equally constructed social identity, leaving women defenseless and dependent on external advice and guidance.

Faced with the sudden possibility of relieving her economic woes by entering the service of a lady about to go abroad, Cecilia is for the first time in a position to make an independent decision, but she is unable to do so: "Impossible! I must consult some friends ere I go at all" (*CP,* 5.516). The impossibility of her acting independently is again emphasized in the epilogue, when she passively accepts a return to Lady Smatter's house as soon as Lady Smatter has consented to the marriage: "Lady Smatter's returning favour will once more devote me to her Service" (*CP,* 5.886–87).

> It is with the spectator, in brief, that theatrical communication begins and ends.
>
> —Keir Elam, *The Semiotics of Theatre and Drama* (2002)

In a letter written in the winter of 1779, Samuel Crisp explained one of the reasons that prompted him to dissuade Burney from seeking success as a playwright. After stating, mistakenly, that even a writer of genius such as Henry Fielding "did by no means succeed in comedy,"[25] Crisp addressed the basic difference between a novel and a play:

> In these little entertaining, elegant Histories, the writer has his full Scope; as large a Range as he pleases to hunt in—to pick, cull, select, whatever he likes:—he takes his own time; he may be as minute as he pleases, & the more minute the better; provided, that Taste, a deep & penetrating knowledge of human Nature, & the World, accompany

> that minuteness.—When this is the Case, the very Soul, & all it's most secret recesses & workings, are develop'd, & laid as open to the View, as the blood Globules circulating in a frog's foot, when seen thro' a Microscope. . . . [In a comedy] every thing passes in Dialogue, all goes on rapidly;—Narration, & description, if not extremely Short, become intolerable.—The detail, which . . . is so delightful, on the *Stage* would bear down all patience,—*There* all must be compress'd into Quintessence—The Moment the Scene ceases to move on briskly, & business seems to hang, Sighs & Groans are the Consequence! Oh dreadful Sound!—in a Word, if the plot, the Story of the Comedy, does not open & unfold itself in the easy, natural unconstrain'd flow of the Dialogue; if that Dialogue does not go on with Spirit, Wit, Variety, Fun, Humour, Repartee &—& all in short into the Bargain—Serviteur!—Good bye—t'ye! (*EJL,* 3:189–90)

Crisp's description highlights the essential difference between a narrative text and the text of a play: the latter is composed of many overlapping textual levels in addition to that related to speech.[26] It therefore does not exhaust its communicative function in the act of reading; it is designed to be transformed into a stage text, and can be fully actualized only in performance, as a spoken structure for social consumption. This is why the language of the drama is necessarily performative, indexical, and hyper-codified. Theatrical spoken discourse cannot be dissociated from the movements of the actors, the relations between them on-stage, their rhetorical style, and the hyper-codification provided by makeup, costumes, and lighting.

Furthermore, in a play physical action is crucial, enabling the transformation of words into movement. As Alessandro Serpieri remarks, "The specificity of the theatrical consists in the organization of words *as* the movement of characters in relations of reciprocity to each other or with respect to objects or stage directions, according to deictic, ostensive, and spatial relations."[27] According to Serpieri, dramatic writing is an "altogether peculiar phenomenon":

> The linear word, or typographical word . . . has a tendency to become "square"; that is, it enters and moves through the three-dimensional space of the stage. . . . A theatrical text, no matter how great it may be, will always remain a pre-text for the stage. . . . A dramatic text is written in order to be performed, and to this end it contains, and has inscribed within its language, not only the stage directions, but

> also its full potential correlation with the specifically theatrical codes through which individual speech instances (the dialogue) are to be realized. And this potential . . . relates to intonation, mimicry, movements (kinesics), the physical distance between actors (proxemics), and finally—and no less crucially—to the implicit or explicit relationship that the character or characters, and the stage itself, always entertain with the audience.[28]

Thus, the stage text—or what we would now call the script—functions as a spoken structure that bridges the gap between the written text and the structure of performance. As Marcello Pagnini usefully summarizes, "The script is a particular structure . . . that fits within a macrostructure, in a *montage* together with all the other non-verbal structures pertaining to a staging. . . . Where in narrative we have description, in the theater we have ostension, or showing."[29] The text of *The Witlings* clearly lacks what Serpieri calls "three-dimensionality," which can be achieved only through the process of staging a play. Conciseness, successful characterization and pacing are not innate properties of a play. They are, rather, the result of practice and professional experience. Even a famous play such as Sheridan's *The Rivals* started out as a fiasco on opening night (17 January 1775). Rewritten and performed again on 28 January 1776, it eventually became, and remained, hugely successful.[30]

Burney had finished revising *The Witlings* by 30 July 1779, as we know from the note she sent with the manuscript to Chessington Hall, in which she apologizes for the length of the play. At this point, the text was what we might call a first reading version: "You [Crisp] will find it of an enormous length, though half as short again as the *original,* but you must advise me as to what parts to curtail" (*EJL,* 3:342). Burney here seems to be responding to Crisp's point about the need for a fast pace in comedy. The version sent to Chessington was probably still too reliant on the descriptive nuances and mimetic detail of a novel, in which narrated action takes precedence over performed action.[31] But an analysis of the first act of *The Witlings,* which Burney probably worked on more than the others—and which Arthur Murphy certainly appreciated—does show that she was aware of the need to connote the virtuality of the stage within the text. It is important to note, however, that the text we have of the play was never revised for performance; nor did it benefit from professional guidance or from the experience of rehearsal. It was never transformed from *fabula agenda* into *fabula acta.*[32]

Burney's directions for the play's opening scene, set in Mrs. Wheedle's millinery shop, clarify the exact location of the action, a professional environment very different from the domestic settings common to most comedies of the time:

> *Scene, a Milliner's Shop. A Counter is spread with Caps, Ribbons, Fans, and Band Boxes.* MISS JENNY *and several young women at Work.*[33]

The pragmatic context however is provided less by the set description (the only one in act 1) than by the characters' language, whose theatrical dimension is amplified through the repeated use of deictic expressions, linguistic signs that "gear the speech act to the dramatic context."[34] Mrs. Wheedle's scolding of one of her workers is immediately contextualized: "Why Miss Polly, for goodness' sake what are you doing?" (*CP,* 1.24–25). The rebuke conveys not only Mrs. Wheedle's gesture of irritation, but also Miss Polly's embarrassment and her prompt attempt to remedy her mistake.

When Mrs. Voluble comes into the shop, her entrance serves to further define the stage space, her words hyper-codified by implicit kinesic and proxemic directions:

> *Mrs. Wheedle.* Won't you take a Chair, Mrs. Voluble?
> *Mrs. Voluble.* Why yes, thank you, ma'am; but there are so many pretty little things to look at in your shop, that one does not know which way to turn oneself. I declare it's the greatest treat in the World to come to spend an Hour or two here in a morning; one sees so many fine things, and so many fine folks,—Lord, who are all these sweet things here for? (*CP,* 1.41–46)

Jack's entrance is also pragmatically contextualized. In his exchange with Mrs. Wheedle, the performance space is clearly marked through deixis:

> *Mrs. Wheedle* (*following him*). Sir would you not chuse to look at some Ruffles?
> *Jack.* O, ay,—have you anything new? what do you call these?
> *Mrs. Wheedle.* O pray, Sir, take care! they are so delicate they'll hardly bear to be touched.
> *Jack.* I don't like them at all! shew me some others.
> *Mrs. Wheedle.* Why, sir, only see! you have quite Spoilt this pair.
> *Jack.* Have I? well, then, you must put them up for me. But pray have you got no better?
> *Mrs. Wheedle.* I'll look some directly, Sir,—but, dear sir, pray don't put

your Switch upon those Caps! I hope you'll excuse me, Sir, but the set is all in all in these little tasty things. (*CP,* 1.352–63)

The first act is especially important because it is where Burney sets up the direct relationship between the play's characters and its action. The "high" plot featuring Beaufort and Cecilia is set in counterpoint to the subplot of the Esprit Party, and below that is the "lower" level of Mrs. Wheedle's shop and Mrs. Voluble's home. The comedy therefore operates on three distinct levels, each associated with a particular genre (see figure 12), according to a technique Burney had already used in *Evelina.* Several characters connect the levels to each other. Lady Smatter, the president of the Esprit Party (level 2), is also Beaufort's aunt, connecting her to the "high" plot of the love story. Like her, Codger simultaneously inhabits level 1 (as Beaufort's stepfather) and level 2 (as a member of the Esprit Party). In turn, the "lower" level 3 is connected to both of the others by functional and economic ties; thus Mrs. Voluble is Dabler's landlady and also takes in Cecilia as a lodger after she has left Lady Smatter's house:

Cecilia. I must beg you to hear me. . . . Mrs. Hobbins, who advised me to apply to you, said she believed you would be able to recommend me to some place where I can be properly accommodated till my affairs are settled. (*CP,* 3.466–70)

Similarly, Mrs. Wheedle does business both with Lady Smatter (level 2) and with Cecilia herself (level 1), whose wedding garments she has been preparing.

The levels are connected thematically, as well, primarily through the constant translation of private into public that takes place within the alternative

FIGURE 12. Genre and plot levels in *The Witlings*

	Plot (genre)	Participants
Level 1	Lovers (sentimental comedy)	Cecilia–Beaufort [Censor]
Level 2	Esprit Party (satire)	Lady Smatter and Mrs. Sapient Codger and Dabler
Level 3	World of Work (farce)	Mrs. Voluble and Miss Sally Mrs. Wheedle and Bob

Note: Censor's name is bracketed because, although he belongs to the sentimental comedy level, he is not one of the lovers.

sphere of eighteenth-century sociability. Mrs. Wheedle's artisanal workshop is a true manufactory of "gossip discourse," whereas Lady Smatter's Esprit Party produces and circulates "literary discourse," and the coffeehouses frequented by Jack and Censor are characterized by the circulation of "social discourse." Burney is careful to pinpoint how the various characters are distributed into their respective levels according to social rank. Mrs. Voluble, for example, does not know Lady Smatter personally, but when Cecilia arrives in search of lodgings, she politely inquires after the health of Lady Smatter's housekeeper and maid:

> *Mrs. Voluble.* I'm sure, ma'am, I've the greatest respect in the World for her Ladyship, though I have not the pleasure to know her; but I hear all about her from Mrs. Hobbins,—to be sure, ma'am, you know Mrs. Hobbins, my lady's House-keeper? . . . I hope, ma'am, all the rest of the Family's well? And Mrs. Simper, my lady's woman? (*CP,* 3.434–41)

The direct relationship between the action of the play and its characters is embodied by Jack, whose wanderings about town—as well as his forgetfulness—set the plot in motion. His primary function is to withhold and to communicate vital information, in turn. Instead of immediately giving Cecilia and Beaufort the news of the bankruptcy, for example, he builds suspense by procrastinating. Likewise, instead of delivering Cecilia's message to Beaufort, he leaves him waiting in Mrs. Wheedle's shop.

Jack's failure to convey information promptly is useful in other ways, as well: while Beaufort and Censor wait for Cecilia in the milliner's shop, Censor has the opportunity to introduce the other characters in the play to the audience and to describe their weaknesses. Burney follows the conventions of Restoration theater by giving her characters humoral or antiphrastic names whose symbolic and cultural connotations convey the dramatist's point of view and set up the audience's expectations. Censor describes the babbling Mrs. Voluble as a "Fool, a prating, intolerable Fool. She will consume more Words in an Hour than Ten Men in a Year" (*CP,* 1.156–59), while Lady Smatter is an "insufferable being" who thinks she is endowed with immense erudition but in reality does no more than provide "a display of Ignorance" (*CP,* 1.200, 203). Mrs. Sapient is censured because, although "more weak and superficial even than Lady Smatter, yet she has the same facility in giving herself credit for wisdom" (*CP,* 1.215–16). Where the Esprit ladies are concerned, name and speech are indissoluble; as characters, they function as autonomous poetic signs.

Of course, the all-disapproving, hypercritical Censor is himself determined by his name. Presented by Beaufort as a misanthrope dominated by "Splenetic Humour," he constantly "exert[s] that Spirit of railing which makes the whole happiness of [his] Life" (*CP,* 1.133, 136–37). It would, however, seem more appropriate to read his misanthropy as misogyny, since his chastisement of "the absurdities of [his] Fellow Creatures" (*CP,* 1.134–35) is mainly directed against women. His characterization of Mrs. Voluble, Mrs. Sapient, and Lady Smatter (later substantiated by their actions and language) thus takes up the theme of women's reputation and social identity, contributing to binding more closely the different levels of the comedy to each other.

Burney's decision to have the subplot of *The Witlings* revolve around the activities of a group of *femmes savantes* places the play at the center of the eighteenth-century debate about women's learning. Even leaving aside Molière (whose direct influence on Burney has not been conclusively proved, in spite of the fact that Crisp adduced it as a reason for suppressing *The Witlings*),[35] Burney had many English models to draw upon for her aspiring literary critics. On the stage, the *querelle* about women's education and its display in fashionable salons had been going on for decades, starting with Ben Jonson's Ladies Collegiates (in *Epicene; or, The Silent Woman* [Whitefriars, ca. 1609–10]), and ending with the conceited Mr. Dangle, "at the head of a band of critics" in Sheridan's *The Critic,* performed at Drury Lane in November 1779, a few months after Burney had finished *The Witlings.*[36]

The debate had begun in earnest at the end of the previous century with the publication of John Locke's influential treatise *Some Thoughts Concerning Education* (1693), closely followed by Mary Astell's response in *A Serious Proposal to the Ladies* (1694) and by a number of essays in the *Spectator* (e.g., Steele's "On the Education of Girls" in no. 66, 16 May 1711). By the late eighteenth century, it had given rise to its own literary subgenre: that of conduct books designed to instill virtue and the value of moral conduct in the minds of the young, especially young girls.[37] The long tradition of the eighteenth-century educational novel, from Daniel Defoe to Charlotte Lennox, is particularly significant in the literary landscape of the century due to its complex relationship with contemporary educational theory. The tradition stemmed from two schools of thought that were diametrically opposed but equally intent on improving women's education. The first recommended developing the same rational qualities in young women as were stressed in the education of boys, thus working against what Wollstonecraft would call "sexual character."[38] The second reflected an ideological construction of womanhood that tended to rely on repression to inculcate humility, whereby if a woman "happens to have any learning, she must keep it a profound secret, especially from the men."[39] Women's education, in this view, required stifling spontaneity and the desire to learn, while study (especially of traditionally masculine subjects such as classical languages) was regarded as an immoral encouragement to subvert the God-given gender hierarchy.[40]

In the course of the century, accusations of promiscuity and licentiousness had tarnished the reputation of female writers and, by extension, of all women who showed an inclination for learning. Typical examples are the misogynist poem by John Duncombe, *The Feminead; or, Female Genius* (1754) and the later attack against the prominent bas bleu Elizabeth Montagu published by Richard Cumberland in 1786. From the late 1770s on, though, this broad naturalized stereotype was challenged by the new model offered by the Enlightenment sociability of the Bluestocking Circle, which centered on the figures of the so-called Nine Living Muses of Great Britain (from the name of Richard Samuel's portrait of 1778; see gallery). The members of the mostly female Bluestocking Circle came from a variety of backgrounds and were determined to show that virtue and erudition were not necessarily opposed. The emphasis on virtue was key to gaining public acceptance of women who studied and wished to publish their work. Provided they respected the traditional injunctions about chastity and fidelity and did not forsake the Christian virtues and the domestic duties traditionally assigned to them, women could seek knowledge and not be blamed for it. A poem by Thomas Seward illustrates the new model that had emerged in the second half of the eighteenth century to challenge the repressive paradigm upheld by Duncombe. In "The Female Right to Literature, in a Letter to a Young Lady, from Florence" (1748), he described the ideal educated woman: "Her sprightly wit no forward pertness spoils; / No self-assuming air her judgment soils; / Still prone to learn, tho' capable to teach, / And lofty all her thoughts, *but humble all her speech.*"[41]

Clearly, some men of letters of the time favored the democratization of culture achieved by the bluestockings' literary salon, which for the first time granted women a public voice in a quasi-institutional setting where they could exercise their reason. It is less surprising that members of the Bluestocking Circle should themselves praise the cultivated, even erudite conversations and rational sociability that took place in the salons, as Hannah More does in her 1782 poem *The Bas-bleu; or, Conversation.* But, as noted earlier, other critics such as Richard Cumberland remained obdurate. In his lampoon against "Vanessa" (probably Mrs. Elizabeth Montagu), published in 1786 in the *Observer,* Cumberland mocked the overt theatricality of these fashionable gatherings, situated at a controversial intersection between performance art and *tableaux vivants.* In Cumberland's satire, Vanessa appears before her guests dressed in a flimsy petticoat embroidered with a motif of the ruins of Palmyra: "Vanessa in the centre of her own circle sits like a statue of the Athenian Minerva, incensed with the breath of philosophers, poets, painters, orators, and every votarist of art, science, or fine speaking."[42] In this masquerade of erudition, the display—or, rather, the exposure—of women's education has turned into the de-feminizing performance of a public identity, a self-conscious exhibition all the more dangerous because of its gender over-coding.

In spite of the satire, the ideological stance that gradually came to prevail in the course of the century allowed educated women a greater degree of assertive public expression than in the past. But it must be noted that the woman of learning could express her views only in a respectful and gender-appropriate way, humbly accepting her role as perpetual apprentice within a dominant masculine discourse that granted her access to knowledge. The desire to assert oneself publicly and to impose one's own view of the world was all too easily thought to violate feminine modesty, making the learned woman an object of curiosity, of ridicule, and even of contempt—a prodigy and a *monstrum* that challenged both nature and culture, forcing her constantly to negotiate her place within the patriarchal order.

In her study of eighteenth-century female playwrights, Jacqueline Pearson stresses how the learned woman remained a stock character on the English stage: "Although a key issue in contemporary writing about women is education, this is hardly reflected in the drama at all except in the conventional caricature of the pedantic female pretender to learning."[43] Frances Burney adapted these cultural stereotypes in her characterization of Lady Smatter and Mrs. Sapient. The first description of the cultural ambitions of the two aspiring critics is given in act 1 by Censor, who, as the misogynist spokesperson for the dominant discourse, describes them in the mocking terms of contemporary satires. He dismisses the literary competence of which Lady Smatter boasts:

> *Censor.* I hardly know a more insufferable Being, for having, unfortunately, just *tasted the Pierian Spring,* she has acquired *that little knowl-*

> *edge,* so dangerous to shallow understandings, which serves no other purpose than to stimulate a display of Ignorance. (*CP,* 1.201–203)

As Peter Sabor points out, the passage—and, in particular, the reference to the Pierian Spring associated with the Muses—is a reference to Alexander Pope's *An Essay on Criticism* (1711).[44] It also supplies a clue to the origins of the play's title, based on another passage of *An Essay:*

> Some have at first for *Wits,* then *Poets* past,
> Turn'd *Criticks* next, and prov'd plain *Fools* at last,
>
> . . . .
>
> Those half-learned *Witlings,* num'rous in our isle,
> As half-form'd insects on the banks of *Nile;*
> Unfinish'd things, one knows not what to call,
> Their generation is so *equivocal.*
> To tell 'em, wou'd a *hundred Tongues* require,
> or *one vain Wit's,* that might a hundred tire.[45] (lines 36–45)

In *An Essay on Criticism,* the world inhabited by the hybrid witlings is a parodic reductio ad absurdum of culture, a universe dominated by incompleteness and superficiality. In Burney's play, this sense of imperfection—implicit in Lady Smatter's name—is especially evident in the pointless literary gathering of the Esprit Party in act 4, where, as Margaret Anne Doody puts it, "The principles of clutter and anticlimax prevail. . . . [I]nterruption, incompleteness . . . [e]verything is retarded, deflected." That Burney's characters should "live comfortably in this world of bathos" makes the satire all the more stinging.[46]

The same paradoxical incompleteness is apparent in Censor's description of Mrs. Sapient, a witty parody of Locke's theory of the tabula rasa:

> *Censor.* [Mrs. Sapient] is more weak and superficial even than Lady Smatter, yet she has the same facility in giving herself credit for wisdom; for as Lady Smatter, from the shallowness of her knowledge, upon all subjects forms a *wrong* judgment, Mrs. Sapient, from extreme weakness of parts, is incapable of forming *any;* but, to compensate for that deficiency, she retails all the opinions she hears, and confidently utters them as her own. (*CP,* 1.215–22)

It is tempting to take the analogy with Lockean cognitive theory further, reading Mrs. Sapient's character as a parody of his definition of the understanding: "not much unlike a Closet wholly shut from light, with only some little openings left, to let in external visible Resemblances, or *Ideas* of things without."[47] In a brilliant rewriting of the traditional closet scene—here not a mere stage device but a metaphorically significant episode—Burney comments on Mrs. Sapient's habit of collecting fragments of others' knowledge by relegating her to the closet in which Mrs. Voluble has swept her broken crockery and the remains of her supper.[48]

Burney gives full rein to her satire on the witlings' superficial knowledge in her portraits of the poetaster Dabler and the ruthless Lady Smatter. The latter's false erudition—her inaccurate quotations, slips of the tongue, and malapropisms reminiscent of two plays well-known to Burney, Isaac Bickerstaffe's *The Doctor Last in His Chariot* (1769) and Sheridan's *The Rivals*—remains a target throughout the play, as befits her status as the only character who never reverses her actantial position toward Cecilia.[49] But Dabler offers Burney greater scope for criticizing not only the superficiality and fatuity of the witlings but also their sham sensibility. His casual plagiarism and haphazard versifying are an indictment of a mannerist and purely external sensibility from which sympathy and morality have been abstracted.[50] For Dabler, poetic composition consists of picking words to satisfy the requirements of rhyme, resulting in a mere associative play of signifiers, an empty and repetitive exercise that leaves Dabler—in a predicament worthy of Barthes—musing on the impossibility of creating something original or *jamais lu,* since he has already "written" all there is to write: "I protest I shall grow more and more sick of Books every Day, for I can never look into any, but I am sure of popping upon something of my own" (*CP,* 2.191–93).

The epigram Dabler recites for Lady Smatter's benefit can therefore be understood as a parodic ode to intertextuality that permanently eradicates any anxiety of influence:

> Ye gentle Gods, O hear me plead,
> And Kindly grant this little loan;
> Make me forget whate'er I read
> That what I write may be my own. (*CP,* 2.196–99)

Dabler's method of composing poems on sentimental subjects is also based on picking signifiers more or less at random. In the process, he forgoes what eighteenth-century aesthetics considered the primary purpose of literature—instruction:

> *Dabler. The pensive maid, with saddest sorrow sad,*—no, hang it, that won't do!—*saddest sad* will never do. With,—with—with *mildest,*—ay

> that's it! *The pensive maid with mildest sorrow sad,*—I should like now, to hear a man mend that line! (*CP,* 3.264–66)

There can be no sympathy between author and audience in such poetry—and, indeed, Lady Smatter and Dabler are incapable of sympathy and fellow feeling. When they hear of the financial disaster that has befallen Cecilia, their expressions of compassion are mere rhetorical formulae masking avarice and literary opportunism, as Burney's use of asides reveals:

> *Lady Smatter.* What an unexpected blow! Poor Miss Stanley!
> *Dabler.* 'Tis a shocking circumstance indeed. (*aside*) I think it will make a pretty good Elegy, though!
> *Lady Smatter.* I can't think what that poor Girl will do! for here is an End to our marrying her!
> *Dabler.* 'Tis very hard upon her indeed. (*aside*) 'Twill be the most pathetic thing I ever wrote! Ma'am, your Ladyship's most obedient. (*aside*) I'll Work while the subjict [*sic*] is warm, nobody will read it with dry Eyes! (*CP,* 3.491–99)

Read as an image of the literary society of the time, culled from Burney's own experience of fashionable salons, *The Witlings*—the realm of halfwits and their "miniscrips," as Mrs. Voluble calls them with a wonderful metonymy (*CP,* 1.274)—is a grotesque universe of intellectual deformity unexpectedly issued from the pen of an agreeable and successful novelist, a cruel Caliban's mirror in which aspiring men and women of letters would have been appalled to recognize their own reflection.

> Sir, the stage not answering my expectations, and the averseness of my Relations to it, has made me turn my genius another way.
>
> —Eliza Haywood (1720)

It was Charles Burney who carried the manuscript of *The Witlings* to Chessington Hall for the family reading. He also carried Frances's note of apology to "Daddy" Crisp for not being present herself: "but you seem so urgent, & my Father himself so desirous to Carry it to you, that I have given that plan up" (*EJL,* 3:342). Dr. Burney's and Crisp's anxieties about her theatrical project show how Burney's authorial persona was by now inextricably bound to her family context. Unlike *Evelina,* composed unbeknownst to Dr. Burney while she was transcribing his massive *History of Music, The Witlings* would have to bear the burden of the extraordinary success that had greeted Burney's first work and of the expectations it had inevitably raised both among the public and in Dr. Burney himself. In the space of only a few months, Frances Burney had conquered a place among the greatest authors of the time. Her first theatrical work would therefore be greeted with a degree of interest that must have worried Charles Burney greatly, and his earliest reactions to the play do indeed reveal his fear of the repercussions that a satire on London's pretentious literary circles might have on his daughter's reputation—and on his own.

The family reading at Chessington is described in an enlightening letter from Susanna. As in a real stage play, Charles Burney's reading sought to convey the intonation, expression, and pragmatic relations with the audience that the text required. Susanna summed up the result:

> *The Witlings*—"Good" s.^{d} Mr. Crisp—"Good—I like the Name" . . . the Milliners Scene & indeed all the first act diverted us *Extremely* all round—"It's *funny—funny* indeed" s.^{d} Mr. Crisp . . . the Second Act I think much improved, & its being more compressed than when I first heard it gives to the whole more *Zest*. . . . The 3^{d} is charming—and they all went off wth great Spirit. . . . *the fourth act was upon the whole that wch. seemed least to exhilarate or interest the audience,* tho' Charlotte laugh'd till she was almost black in the face at Codger's part, as I had done before her—The fifth was more generally felt—but to own the truth it did not meet all the advantages one could wish—*My Father's voice, sight, & lungs were tired . . . & being entirely unacquainted wth what was coming not withstanding all his good intentions, he did not always give the Expression you meant to be given.*
>
> For my own part the Serious part seem'd even to improve upon me by this 2^{d}. hearing, & made me for to cry in 2 or 3 places—I wish there was more of this Sort—and so does my Father—so, I believe, does Mr. Crisp—however their sentiments you are to hear fully from themselves.[51]

Ironically, Dr. Burney's family reading—a listless, tired performance increasingly lacking in the sympathy and enthusiasm that the cultural context of the time demanded of readings aloud—was to remain the only performance of the comedy for more than two centuries.[52] Because of Dr. Burney's obstinate disapproval, *The Witlings* was suppressed with no chance of appeal, and his displeasure can already be gleaned from Susanna's letter. The biting satire on the intellectual feebleness and behavioral idiosyncrasies of the Esprit Party in act 4 seem especially to have worried the doctor. After reading through the scene describing the literary circle's inane gathering, he had shown increasing signs of tiredness and dissatisfaction. As Susanna faithfully reported, his faltering performance had ruined the dramatic effect of the final act.

While Burney's sisters unreservedly enjoyed the absurdities of the characters in the play and "laugh'd till [they were] almost black in the face," Susanna notes that she, like their two "Daddys," would have liked Burney to have dwelled more on the sentimental plot of the lovers' woes. Their preference reflects the predilection of the time for pathetic situations, criticized a few years earlier by Oliver Goldsmith, who had ironically noted how the insertion of a few well-placed pathetic scenes would ensure a play's success: "It is only sufficient to raise the Characters a little, to deck out Hero with a Ribband, or give the Heroine a Title; then put in an Insipid Dialogue, without Character or Humour, into their mouths, give them mighty good hearts, very fine clothes, furnish a new sett [*sic*] of Scenes, make a Pathetic Scene or two, with a sprinkling of tender melancholy Conversation through the whole, and there is no doubt but all the Ladies will cry, and all the Gentlemen applaud."[53]

Following Susanna letter, written on or around 4 August 1779, there is a significant gap in the correspondence. We may surmise that Frances destroyed the letters exchanged immediately after the Chessington reading. It is clear from what followed, however, that Dr. Burney firmly enjoined her to give up the project. Two letters she wrote some days later to her father and to Crisp, both dated 13 August, can help us reconstruct why he did so and show how Frances reacted to the injunction.[54]

In her letter to her father, Frances specifies that she has consented to abandon the project purely in consideration of the potential damage to her father's reputation, now inextricably tied to her own:

> I am sure I speak from the bottom of a very honest Heart when I most solemnly declare that upon *your* Account any disgrace would mortify & afflict me *more* than upon my own,—for what ever appears with your *knowledge,* will be naturally supposed to have met with your *approbation,* & perhaps with your *assistance:*—& therefore, though all *particular* censure would fall where it *ought,* upon *me,*—yet any *general* censure of the *whole,* & the *Plan,* would cruelly, but certainly, involve *you* in it's severity.
>
> Of this I have been sensible from the moment my *Authorshipness*

> was discovered,—& therefore, from that moment, I am determined to have no *opinion* of my own in regard to what I should thenceforth part with out of my own Hands. (*EJL*, 3:346)

Burney then points out that her father's obdurate disapproval was entirely unexpected, since all of the signs she had received thus far had been favorable. Hester Thrale's disinterested approval and affectionate praise had been endorsed by "the repeated commendations & flattery of Mr. Murphy" (*EJL*, 3:347), an adviser who was perfectly cognizant of the tastes of the public and whose praise had given her the encouragement she needed to finish the comedy. Frances's letter also shows how *Evelina*'s success had contributed to transforming her into a professional author eager to retain the fame and success earned so unexpectedly: "I must be a far more egregious Witling than any of those I tried to draw to imagine you [Dr. Burney] could ever credit that I writ without some remote hope of success *now,* though I literally did when I composed Evelina" (*EJL*, 3:347). Although she accepts her father's decision, Burney defends the value of the labor she has put into the comedy and states her intention to start a new literary project immediately that will meet with his full approval. This assertion reveals how the general consensus by now had persuaded her to cease considering writing a "frivolous amusement," as she had described her work on *Evelina;*[55] writing, she now openly acknowledged, was the activity to which she would devote herself entirely: "The best way I can take of shewing that I have a true and just sense of the *spirit* of your condemnation, is not to sink, sulky and dejected, under it, but to exert myself to the utmost of my power in endeavours to produce something less reprehensible. And this shall be the way I will pursue . . . as soon as I have *read* myself into a forgetfulness of my old Dramatis persona,—lest I should produce something else as *Witless* as the last" (*EJL*, 3:347).

The letter Burney sent to Crisp contains her most uncompromising defense of the aborted theatrical project, expressed in affectionate but unambiguous terms: "The only bad thing in this affair,—is that I cannot take the comfort of my poor friend Dabler, by calling you a *crabbed fellow,*—because you write with almost more kindness than ever;—niether [*sic*] can I, (though I try hard) persuade myself that you have not *a grain of Taste in your whole composition*" (*EJL*, 3:349–50).

Lars Troide conjectures that Burney's replies to the now lost "hissing, groaning, catcalling Epistle" (*EJL*, 3:350) sent jointly by Dr. Burney and Crisp after the Chessington reading were followed by several other letters that are also now missing, either destroyed by Burney herself or lost (*EJL*, 3:351n.83). In these letters, Burney apparently stated her intention to revise *The Witlings* based on the criticism she had received. This is confirmed by a letter she received from Crisp on 29 August 1779 that reveals how important the project had become to her and how determined she was to produce another work as soon as possible. Crisp wrote: "I Observe what You say, that the pursuing *this project is the only Chance You have of bringing out any thing this Year—& that with hard fagging perhaps You might do that.* I agree with You, that for *this Year,* You say true—but, my dear Fanny, for God's sake, dont [*sic*] talk of *hard Fagging!* It was not *hard Fagging,* that produced such a Work as Evelina!" (*EJL*, 3:352). Crisp objected precisely to Burney's admission that her writing was not a casual pursuit but a causal one—the result of a creative effort consciously undertaken and requiring hard work. Like Johnson, who had cultivated the myth of her instinctive creativity, the irrepressible "true Sterling Genius" (*EJL*, 3:352) that had produced *Evelina*, Crisp preferred to think of her talent as a spontaneous overflowing rather than the fruit of a long literary apprenticeship now pursued with obstinate and thoroughly professional determination.[56]

Crisp's letter concludes with an invitation to abandon the theatrical arena once and for all and to take her proper place in the hierarchical order of literary composition—that is, to go back to writing those "little entertaining, elegant Histories, [in which] the writer has full Scope" (*EJL*, 3:189) and that from the start had seemed to him more suited to a woman's pen. His suggestion that she devote herself to a subject "of so general a Nature" furthermore would have preserved her from incurring the blame heaped on authors who "descend[ed] to the invidious, & cruel Practice of pointing out Individual Characters & holding them up to public ridicule" (*EJL*, 3:353).

It is still unclear exactly why Charles Burney and Samuel Crisp became convinced that the comedy was certain to fail. Crisp's language seems to support the hypothesis that *The Witlings* contained offensive—and unmistakable—references to influential figures of the time, particularly Elizabeth Montagu, the "Vanessa" mocked by Cumberland, who might have recognized herself in Lady Smatter. To be sure, like the president of the fictional Esprit Club, the queen of the bluestockings had adopted a nephew and made him her only heir, a coincidence that would have made it all too easy to read the satire on Lady Smatter's weaknesses and affectation as a harsh caricature of Mrs. Montagu.[57] The plausibility of this theory is apparently confirmed by Hester Thrale herself, who early on confided to Arthur Murphy that after reading the first two acts of the comedy she believed "that this rogue [Burney] mean[t] her for *Lady Smatter.*" In a later diary entry, Thrale states that Burney's two literary advisers had called for the suppression of the play because they feared irritating "the female Wits—a formidable Body."[58] This, however, is not positive proof. The fact that Hester Thrale herself was resorting to speculation seems, if anything, to suggest that Burney had relied on Aristotle's poetics in basing Lady Smatter's characterization on a common type rather than a particular individual. As Henry Fielding had stated in chapter 14 in volume 2 of *Joseph Andrews* (1742), "I describe not men, but manners; not an individual, but a species."

That Dr. Burney's disapproval had deeper roots and was due to reasons unrelated to passing concerns is confirmed by his muted but decided opposition not only to Frances's suggestion that she write a new play on a different subject for the next theatrical season, but also to all of her subsequent attempts—from 1789 to 1802—to stage the plays she had written. His censorship of *The Witlings* may indeed have been due partly to an awkward resemblance between the characters in the comedy and real people, but his long-term hostility must dissuade us from believing that Frances Burney's passion for playwriting was suppressed by a fatal combination of "ill advice and ill luck."[59] Perhaps, besides these, a deeper motive for Charles Burney was the strong anti-theatrical prejudice that characterized the century as a whole and that he shared.

Given Charles Burney's humble origins as the son of a musician, dancer, and painter, his hard-won position as a critic and man of letters was an extraordinary achievement. The doctorate from Oxford University and the literary fame that followed the publication of his writings on music had lifted him above the status of a music teacher.[60] But his background and profession—and his own father's early sexual irregularity—were not unlike those of actors and actresses and explain his lifelong preoccupation with preserving the new identity he had created for himself, along with the social standing that went with it.

Certainly, more than one reason must have prompted Charles Burney to oppose his daughter's theatrical efforts. Perhaps he feared that her reputation would be tarnished once she began frequenting the "green rooms" where men and women of the theater mixed freely. Her constant attendance at rehearsals and among actors would have been necessary to transform her text into a performable play, and although by the second half of the eighteenth century a number of female playwrights had achieved success without compromising their reputations (e.g., Hannah More), the taint of sexual license lingered.[61] The boundary separating the status of a woman who inhabited the public sphere from that of an outright *femme publique* was fragile and porous and therefore easily contaminating.

Besides these reasons of a general order, we can probably add more personal ones. Dr. Burney may have feared that a renewed family association with the stage would have lost him the social recognition he had worked so hard to gain and that remained precarious. His daughter's eagerness to enter the world of the theater, with its social misfits and outcasts, could well have felt like a return of the repressed that he—and the eighteenth-century anti-theatrical prejudice he embodied—had so strenuously fought to exorcise. After her unhappy experiment with *The Witlings,* Frances Burney's subsequent dramatic efforts would indeed turn into a "dance with Fetters on" (*EJL,* 3:238), as Crisp had predicted, and those fetters were made of the strongest family bonds.

Scene with Mr. Garrick as Sir John Brute and Mr. Vaughan, Mr. Hullet, Mr. Clough, Mr. Parsons, Mr. Watkins and Mr. Phillips as Watchmen in "The Provok'd Wife." (Also known as *Sir John Brute in The Lady in Disguise Scene.*) 1768. After Johan Joseph Zoffany. (Photograph © Victoria and Albert Museum, London)

"The Nine Living Muses of Great Britain." Foldout plate from *The Ladies New and Polite Pocket Memorandum-Book.* (By permission of the Folger Shakespeare Library)

Above, *Mrs. Siddons as Jane Shore in Rowe's "Jane Shore."* 1791. William Hamilton. (Photograph © Victoria and Albert Museum, London)

Opposite, *A View of the Tryal of Warren Hastings Esq.* 1789. After Edward Dayes. (© Trustees of the British Museum)

Lady Mary Catherine Thurlow, When Mary Bolton, as Ophelia in "Hamlet." 1813.

Mrs. Jordan in the Character of Hypolita. 1791. After John Hoppner.
(© Trustees of the British Museum)

Mr. Garrick as Jaffier and Mrs. Cibber as Belvidera in "Venice Preserv'd." 1764. After Johan Joseph Zoffany. (Photograph © Victoria and Albert Museum, London)

Portrait of Sarah Siddons as Euphrasia in *The Grecian Daughter.* 1782. After R. E. Pine. (Photograph © Victoria and Albert Museum, London)

Mrs. Siddons as Lady Macbeth. 1822. After George Henry Harlow.
(© Trustees of the British Museum)

FOUR

The Theater and the City

Cecilia

Let me counsel you to remember that a lady, whether so called from birth or only from fortune, should never degrade herself by being put on a level with writers and such sort of people.

—Frances Burney, *Cecilia*

Following the suppression of *The Witlings,* Charles Burney continued to caution his daughter against writing for the stage, encouraging her instead to return to novel writing: "For the stage, I w.^{d} have you very careful, & very perfect—that is, as far as your own Efforts, & the best advice you can get, can make you. In the Novel Way, there is no danger."[1] A few months after she received this letter, Burney was already complying with her father's wishes, announcing in the fall of 1779 to Samuel Crisp and Hester Thrale that she had begun a new literary project—"in the Novel Way." Burney spent two years working on the new novel, provisionally titled *Albinia;* it was finally published as *Cecilia* on 12 July 1782 to such acclaim that it remained the most outstanding literary phenomenon in England until the publication of Ann Radcliffe's *The Mysteries of Udolpho* in 1794.

According to Joyce Hemlow, the novel was "not a spontaneous but a forced production, written largely because Dr. Burney thought that the new author should seize and capitalize on the shining hour of her first success."[2] Hemlow emphasizes how Charles imposed his will, and his tastes, on Frances as she strenuously wrote and revised, subjecting her to emotional pressure that affected the novel's composition. My own view of her father's impact on *Cecilia,* however, has less to do with its pressurized composition—his injunctions that she write both quickly and prudently, as Frances complained to Susanna—than with the novel's transmodal quality. It was Charles Burney's role in suppressing her first play that led Frances to channel her gift for playwriting into the new novel.

With *Evelina,* Burney had served her literary apprenticeship, exploring the theatrical dimensions of Georgian society under the double cover of anonymous authorship and the novel's epistolary format. *Cecilia,* instead, was composed not in secret but under the watchful eyes of Samuel Crisp and Charles Burney. Frances's confidence as an author is apparent, her use of third-person narrative allowing for a stronger authorial presence than in her first novel. She also benefited from the comments sent to her by Hester Thrale, who received the novel in installments and described her reactions in a sort of "reading to the moment" that became an integral part of the process of composition.[3]

In *Cecilia,* the heroine inhabits a world that extends well beyond the precincts of fashionable London. As in *The Witlings,* the cast of characters in *Cecilia* spans the spectrum from high to low, and Cecilia moves both among the wealthy of the West End and among the humble residents of the dense warrens in the city of London. Working with a broader canvas, and with an expanded set of contextual references compared with her first novel, Burney thus shifts from *Evelina*'s focus on theatricality to the more ambitious scale of diffuse, pervasive spectacularity.[4]

Heavily indebted to *The Witlings, Cecilia* takes up many of the play's elements, transforming and adapting them to new ends. Burney toyed briefly with the idea of resurrecting *The Witlings* after Sheridan and Murphy urged her to do so in the winter of 1780. She considered thoroughly revising act 4 and planned to abolish the implausible financial resolution provided by Censor's gift of £5,000 to the protagonists. She also would have removed all traces of "the unlucky resemblance" between Lady Smatter and Mrs. Montagu, "our female pride of literature" (*DL,* 1:316). But after Crisp's polite reiteration of his disapproval of the comedy in late February (*DL,* 1:320–23), there is no further mention of *The Witlings* in Burney's correspondence; the next journal entry after Crisp's letter is dated 7 April 1780. At this time, Burney had been working on *Cecilia* for at least five months and it is certainly plausible that the early phases of the novel's composition went hand in hand with Burney's revision of her play.

If this is the case, then the concluding passage—later deleted—of her introduction to *Cecilia* can be read as an ironic comment on the suppression of the comedy orchestrated by Dr. Burney and Samuel Crisp: "As the fortunate editor of Evelina, I may sometimes, perhaps, admit a ray of that Hope which my first publication wholly obscured from me; yet it shines but faintly, if it shines at all, for I well know that the Success of one work is no security for the safety of another, since not only the annotations of the critics, but even the Approbation of the Friends of the First, frequently prove alike pirnicious [*sic*] to the second; the one by exciting Expectations unreasonable, the other by previously paving the way for severity of Judgement."[5] It could be argued that the "second" work Burney mentions here is not *Cecilia* but, more literally, *The Witlings.* If so, the "severity of Judgement" she refers to would signal the extent of the author's disappointment at her father's rejection of the play and would further confirm that as she started writing the novel, the comedy was never far from her mind. Margaret Anne Doody is therefore right in suggesting that "*Cecilia* is a 'wanted' novel (as we speak of a 'wanted' child), and incorporates at a very deep level the author's reaction not only to the suppression of *The Witlings,* but to what that suppression means."[6]

There are many traces of the suppressed play in *Cecilia.* Aside from bearing the same name, Cecilia Beverley undergoes similar trials to those suffered by the play's heroine. Both are wealthy heiresses who discover that their social identity places their personal identity in jeopardy. The London social world portrayed in both works is dominated by money and shaken by financial upheavals such as the bankruptcy of Cecilia's guardian in *The Witlings* and the ruinous extravagance that ultimately leads one of Cecilia Beverley's guardians to suicide. Wealth is the driving force behind both plots, altering or distorting the relationships between the heroines and the other characters.

The similarities between the novel and the play extend to the heroines' sentimental woes, since both are rejected by the aristocratic relatives of the men with whom they are in love. In *The Witlings,* Lady Smatter is opposed to the marriage because Cecilia has been financially ruined; in *Cecilia,* Mr. Delvile is adamantly against Miss Beverley's marrying his son because lineage is all important to him. As the only heir to the Beverley name and fortune, Cecilia must marry a man willing to relinquish his own name and take on hers, and Mr. Delvile's aristocratic pride recoils at such a condition. The dénouements of the two works are specular counterparts, as well. In *The Witlings,* Cecilia unexpectedly regains part of her wealth and thus can be joined to Beaufort in *Cecilia,* the heroine chooses to give up her fortune so her husband can retain his name.

Burney worked on the novel for two years, a period marred by illness and by the separation from her sister Susanna, who left home to marry the dashing Captain Molesworth Phillips. Frances felt this loss deeply, and her low spirits were made worse by the exhausting process of transcribing the novel in time for its almost simultaneous publication with the second volume of

Charles Burney's *A General History of Music from the Earliest Ages to the Present Period.* Dr. Burney had arranged for both works to be issued by his publisher, Payne and Cadell, and was looking forward to reaping the benefits of the combined publicity. Thomas Payne offered to pay Frances £250 for the novel, a much higher sum than she had received for *Evelina,* which had been poorly remunerated considering its great success. The agreement with Payne thus seemed to offer fair compensation and greater financial security. But to meet the publication deadline, Burney had to work at a pace that tested the limits of her endurance, and she could reveal her feelings about the pressure she was under only to Susanna.[7]

Once the novel was published, it became apparent that from a critical standpoint, Frances's efforts in these final months were to be fully rewarded. Her literary advisers were full of admiration, impressed by *Cecilia*'s more ambitious design and greater complexity compared with her first novel. Edward Gibbon and Edmund Burke, among other renowned figures, were unanimous in echoing Dr. Johnson's praise of the character portrayals in the novel. All of the requisites of eighteenth-century aesthetics—verisimilitude, morality, and instruction—were fulfilled in *Cecilia,* and, as Burke effused, life itself seemed to animate the image of society it reflected:[8] "MADAM,—. . . There are few—I believe I may say fairly there are none at all—that will not find themselves better informed concerning human nature, and their stock of observations enriched, by reading your *Cecilia.* They certainly will, let their experience in life and manners be what it may. The arrogance of age must submit to be taught by you" (*DL,* 2:92–93).

Ironically, the novel's extraordinary success reveals how poor a bargain Burney had made with her publisher. Her inexperience, and her father's imprudent advice, led her to sell the novel's rights to Payne. The greater part of the £250 she received for her two years of unremitting labor was invested by Dr. Burney in bonds that yielded a tiny allowance—"a well-secured annuity," as Crisp optimistically put it (*DL,* 2:99). As a result, she was no less financially dependent on her father than she had been before. But Crisp glowed nonetheless: "If she can coin gold at such a Rate, as to sit by a warm Fire, and in 3 or 4 months (for the real time she has stuck to it closely, putting it all together, will not amount to more, tho' there have been long Intervals, between) gain £250 by scribbling the Inventions of her own Brain—only putting down in black and white whatever comes in her own head, without labour drawing singly from her own Fountain, she need not want money."[9] Aside from dismissing the physical and psychological effects of months of literary composition off-hand, Crisp here portrays women's writing as inoffensive, modest scribbling, an amusing and pleasant pastime to while away the hours by the fireside. As Jane Austen would later comment, after all "it [was] only Cecilia, or Camilla, or Belinda."[10]

Unlike *Evelina,* which was written in secret and published anonymously, with Frances's brother Charles serving as front person, no mystery surrounded the authorship of *Cecilia.* Quite the reverse is true: Dr. Burney had arranged for the novel to come out shortly after the second volume of his *History of Music,* and Payne had astutely started advertising *Cecilia* several months in advance of publication. The family bond that Frances had earlier felt as an awkward encumbrance was now publicized by Dr. Burney, who was intent on making the most of the expected success of the novel.

Burney's wording of *Cecilia*'s title page reflects her unwillingness to disclose her surname:

CECILIA,
OR
MEMOIRS
OF AN
HEIRESS
BY
THE AUTHOR OF EVELINA (*Cecilia,* 1)

Burney was no less intent on preserving her anonymity when she published *Cecilia* than she had been in the case of *Evelina.* The motivation seems more straightforward, however. Modesty, and a sense of unworthiness—whether real or assumed—had been the reasons she alleged for publishing *Evelina* anonymously. Linked to these was the fear of causing offense to her father by tarnishing his name. But when she came to publish *Cecilia,* the overriding consideration seems to have been to dissociate her own identity as author from the family name, and the "Advertisement" affixed to the novel further stresses her independence by recalling the circumstances under which her first novel was published: "The indulgence shewn by the Public to EVELINA, which, *unpatronized, unaided and unowned,* past through Four Editions in a Year, has encouraged its Author to risk this SECOND attempt" (*Cecilia,* 3; emphasis added). Not only does Burney acknowledge that the authors of *Cecilia* and *Evelina* are one and the same; she also retrospectively disavows her role as mere "editor" of her first, epistolary, novel and so reconfigures it as the first stage of a literary career that is now well under way.

Cecilia's title page indirectly foreshadows a central theme of the novel: that of the family and its bearing on an individual's identity and freedom, an issue Burney had grappled with herself when she attempted to resist the suppression of *The Witlings*. The main plot line concerns the troubled romance between the orphaned heiress Cecilia Beverley and Mortimer Delvile, the last descendant of an ancient aristocratic family that, as was often the case in the mid-Georgian period, has become impoverished. Interwoven with the main plot is Cecilia's pursuit of social, affective, and personal independence. A clause in her uncle's will requires her to live with one of her three guardians until she reaches her majority. Lacking the guidance of parents or close relatives after the death of her uncle, the Dean, Cecilia learns that in England of the late eighteenth century, a wealthy young woman's freedom and autonomy are severely restricted. Indeed, her wealth reifies her, making her a target for unscrupulous adventurers.

The novel's highly complex plot follows a rigorous cause-and-effect order.[11] At the heart of the story is the insurmountable obstacle to Cecilia's marriage with Delvile produced by her uncle's will: to ensure the continued existence of the Beverley lineage, her future husband must take her name, or both will forfeit the Dean's fortune.[12] Since Delvile is the last male descendant of his ancient and illustrious family, such a marriage would put an end to his own lineage and cause a permanent rupture with his father. Burney introduces the problem on the first page of the novel, signaling how important it will be to the sentimental and social lives of her protagonists:

> Cecilia . . . had lately entered into the one-and-twentieth year of her age. Her ancestors had been rich farmers in the county of Suffolk, though her father, in whom a spirit of elegance had supplanted the rapacity of wealth, had spent his time as a private country gentleman, satisfied, without increasing his store, to live upon what he inherited from the labours of his predecessors. She had lost him from her early youth, and her mother had not long survived him. They had bequeathed to her £10,000 and consigned her to the Dean of —, her uncle. With this gentleman, in whom, by various contingencies, the accumulating possessions of a rising and prosperous family were centred, she had passed the last four years of her life; and a few weeks only had yet elapsed since his death, which, by depriving her of her last relation, made her an heiress to an estate of £3,000 per annum, with no other restriction than that of annexing her name, if she married, to the disposal of her hand and her riches. (*Cecilia,* 5–6)

The passage is carefully constructed, relaying information in the measured and efficient way typical of Burney's omniscient narrator. Throughout the novel, the narrator's diegetic task is to solicit the Ideal Reader's hermeneutic skills, inviting exploration beyond the apparently transparent surface of the narrative. Here, the chronological precision of the passage anticipates the structural importance of time in the novel. The Ideal Reader can easily glean that in a few months Cecilia will come of age and come into possession of her inheritance. Her identity, right from the start, is so bound up with her inheritance as to virtually coincide with it (in this brief passage, terms pertaining to the domain of money recur at least eleven times).[13] The reader can further deduce two important points: not only is Cecilia a young woman rather than a girl, as Evelina had been; she is also an accomplished young woman, having spent her formative years overseeing the household of a wealthy and respected member of society. On her arrival in London, therefore, she is already accustomed to formal social interactions and familiar with the upper classes' rules of etiquette: "Cecilia, though new to London . . . was yet no stranger to company; she had passed her time in retirement, but not in obscurity, since for some years past she had presided at the table of the Dean. . . . [His] parties had taught her to subdue her timid fears of total inexperience, and to repress the bashful feelings of shame-faced awkwardness; fears and feelings that rather call for compassion than admiration, and which, except in extreme youth, serve but to degrade the modesty they indicate" (*Cecilia,* 22–23). Readers familiar with established literary convention would immediately note that, unlike ingenues such as Evelina, who leave their innocent pastoral settings for the brilliant city, Cecilia is an adult capable of discrimination and of interpreting the world around her. Burney is here revising the classic model of the comedy of manners, moving away from the traditional opposition between country artlessness and city worldliness. She is also adapting for her own purposes—and her own time—the standard legal device used by Restoration comedy to hinder or enable the union of the so-called gay couple.

But the brief introductory passage tells us about Cecilia's past as well as about her current situation, and it proleptically sets the stage for her future financial and sentimental troubles. Despite her family's origins as wealthy farmers, Cecilia's status has risen as a result of her father's decision to live as a gentleman. The sole heiress of a £10,000 fortune from her parents (the relevance of the precise sum will increase as the novel progresses) and the beneficiary of a considerable yearly income from her uncle, her identity is reified from the start. The terms of the Dean's will do not allow her to

FIGURE 13. Chronotopological structure in *Cecilia*

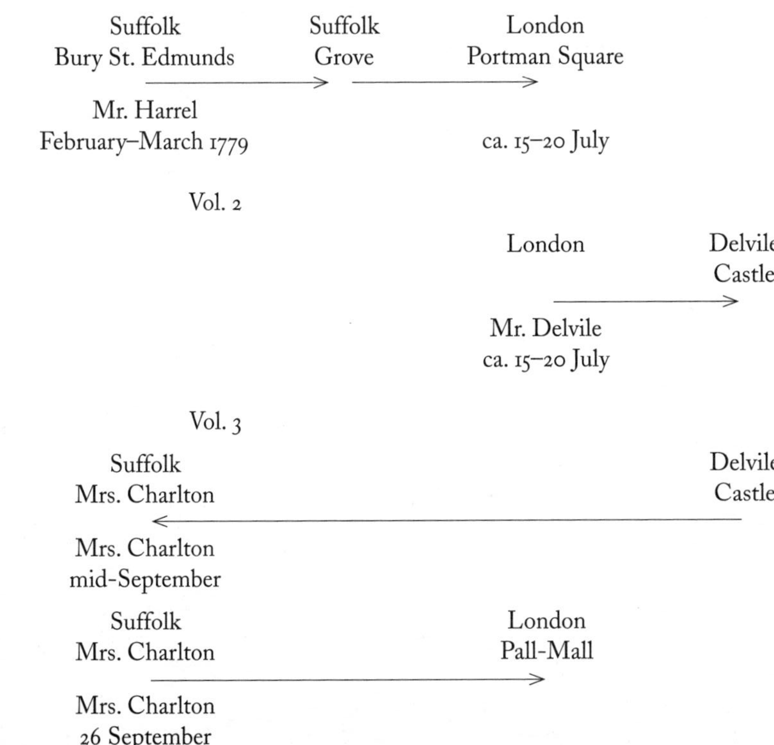

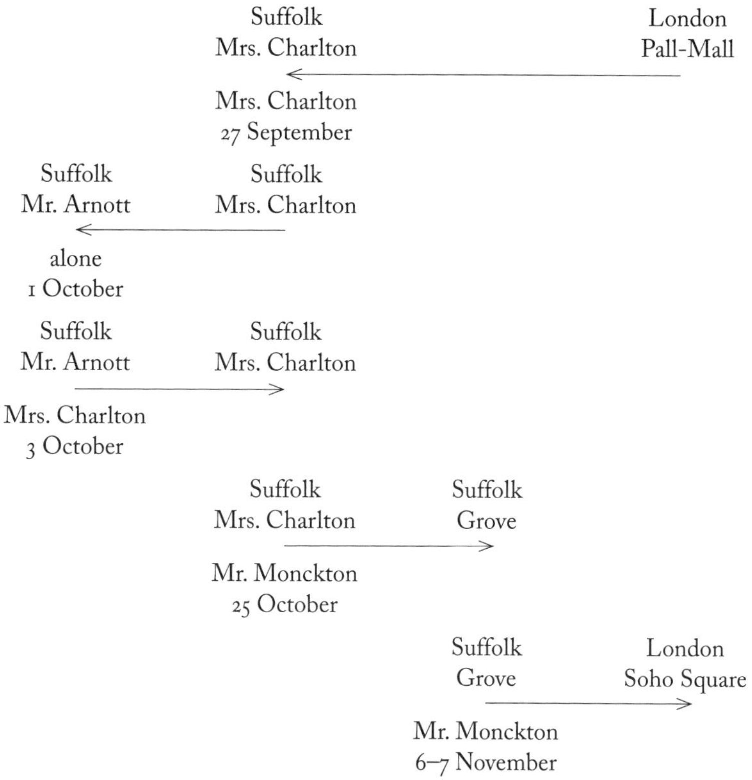

Suffolk
Mrs. Charlton ← London
Pall-Mall

Mrs. Charlton
27 September

Suffolk
Mr. Arnott ← Suffolk
Mrs. Charlton

alone
1 October

Suffolk
Mr. Arnott → Suffolk
Mrs. Charlton

Mrs. Charlton
3 October

Suffolk
Mrs. Charlton → Suffolk
Grove

Mr. Monckton
25 October

Suffolk
Grove → London
Soho Square

Mr. Monckton
6–7 November

(continued)

FIGURE 13. Chronotopological structure in *Cecilia, continued*

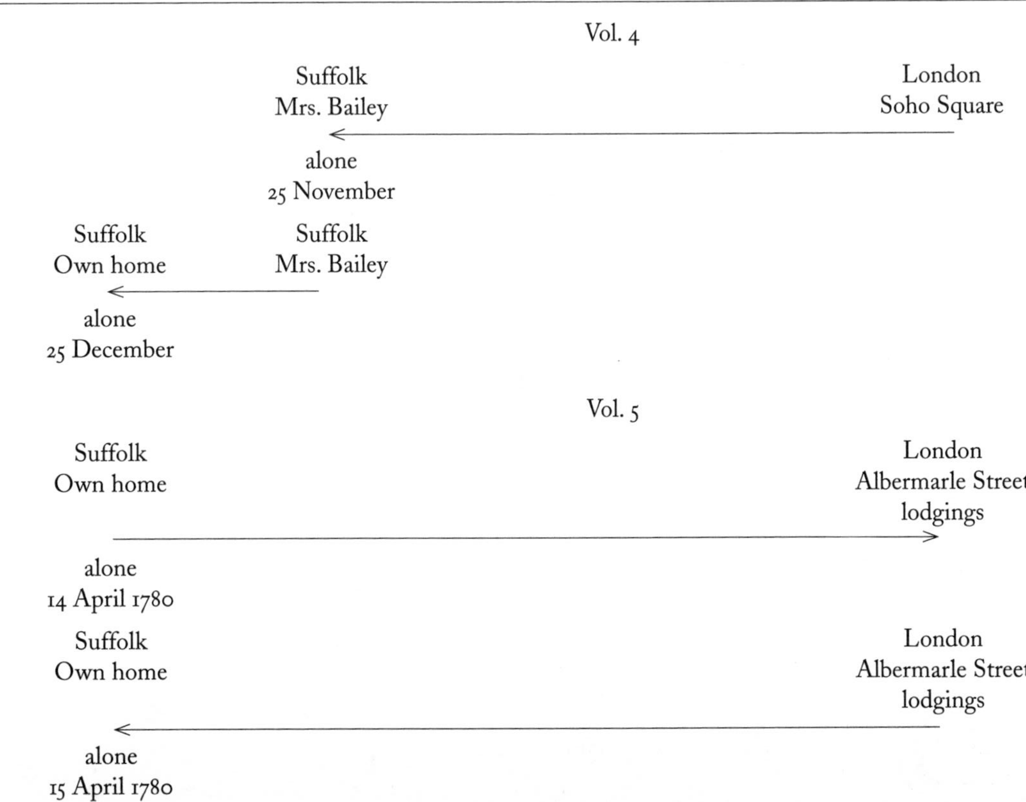

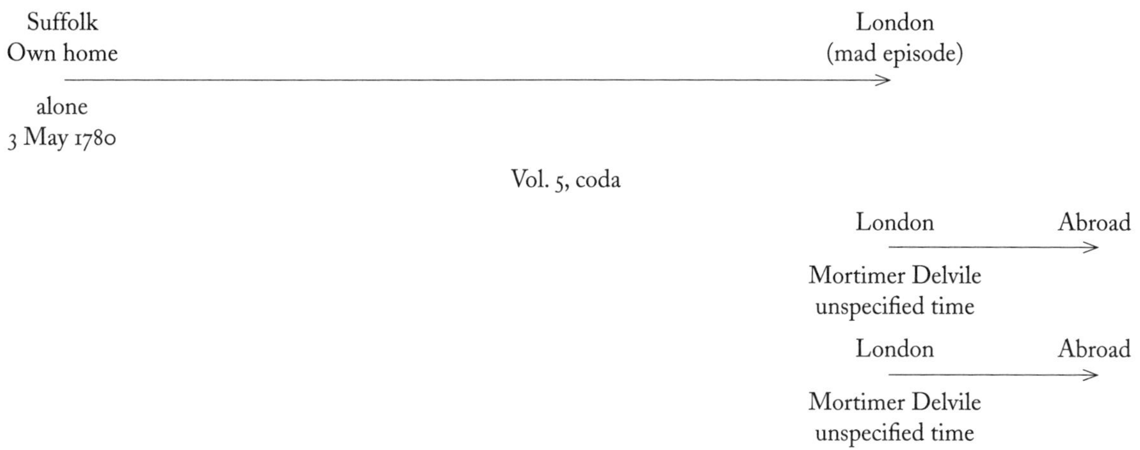

Suffolk
Own home
→
alone
3 May 1780

London
(mad episode)

Vol. 5, coda

London → Abroad
Mortimer Delvile
unspecified time

London → Abroad
Mortimer Delvile
unspecified time

benefit directly from her income; they allow her only to transfer it to her future husband, transforming her into a mere a conduit for the inheritance, "an object of transaction among men."[14] Far from benefiting her, her uncle's death has a negative impact on her individuality and independence, both of which are subject to the social and financial imperatives linked to preserving the family name. In this respect, Cecilia's situation is identical to that of Mortimer Delvile, whose father refuses to grant his consent to the marriage because the Delvile name must be preserved at all costs. In both cases, individual freedom and identity are compromised, if not crushed, because of the presence, or absence, of a social sign.

Structurally, the novel is composed of two parts: volumes 1–5 (containing books 1–6) and volumes 6–10 (containing books 7–12). Equal in length, they are set, respectively, in London and in Suffolk. But Burney rejects the clear-cut city–country opposition that had become traditional since the Restoration and instead chooses to trace Cecilia's frequent movements as a "fair traveller" (*Cecilia,* 5) between the city and the country. Cecilia's movements are represented in figure 13, as well as the guardian or host she stays with (or lack thereof). Figure 14 lists the various households in which Cecilia stays. The length and importance of Cecilia's stay with the Harrels is obvious, taking up exactly half of the books in the novel. It is during a masquerade at the Harrels' home in Portman Square that she first meets Mortimer Delvile, thus setting in motion the love plot. And it is Mr. Harrel's financial woes that bring into play the theme of Cecilia's independence, forcing her to resort to a moneylender and so compromise her future. In the company of the high-living Harrels, Cecilia attends the most fashionable gatherings in town and witnesses the profusion of spectacular events staged in the city (see figure 15). The increasing variety and complexity of such spectacles in the first five books of the novel marks a departure with respect to *Evelina*'s focus on the theatrical, for *Cecilia* moves well beyond the confines of the theater to explore the pervasiveness of the spectacular throughout society (see, for example, the trial of Warren Hastings depicted in the gallery). In *Cecilia,* theatrical events are significant not in themselves but only insofar as they provide a setting for the spectacularization of society. When Cecilia goes to the opera, there is no hermeneutically significant transtextual relationship between the work being performed and the text of the novel; on Cecilia's second visit to the Haymarket, for example, the narrator does not even mention which opera is being performed, and the reader's attention is directed instead to the seamless continuity between stage and audience, object and subject of the gaze, real and social actors. In emphasizing this

FIGURE 14. Cecilia's residences

Book (chapters)	Host or residence
1–5	Mr. Harrel
6	Mr. Delvile
7–8	Mrs. Charlton
9 (1–6)	Mr. Monckton
9 (7–11), 10	Cecilia's own home

FIGURE 15. Spectacular sites in *Cecilia*

Theater	Theatrical space	City
Opera House (Haymarket): *Artaserse* by Pietro Metastasio	Harrels' home: masquerade	Lord Belgrade's home: auction
Opera House (Haymarket)	Harrels' home: rout	Tyburn: mob
	Pantheon	
	Vauxhall	

continuity, Burney is describing a common feature not only of performances in Georgian London but also of eighteenth-century theatergoing in general. As we shall see, the lack of boundaries between stage and audience is closely linked to the novel's focus on acting as deception, artifice, and disguise.

Burney explicitly points out the continuity between stage and audience on Cecilia's first visit to the opera in a chapter titled "An Opera Rehearsal" by selecting a significant location for her characters within the space of the theater. Cecilia and Mrs. Harrel "secured themselves a box upon the stage" (*Cecilia,* 61). This was an especially prized position at the side of the stage, within a few feet of the performers. The audience seated elsewhere in the theater would be aware of the two women's presence beyond the proscenium arch—that is, beyond the recently introduced architectural element that framed the performance, ensuring that for the spectators, the scenes on the stage appeared removed from them, in a fictitious and isolated world of their own. The proscenium arch was thus designed to serve as an ontological boundary: by separating the audience from the fictional but verisimilar events taking place on stage, it contributed to the aesthetic and instructional function of art—the awakening of cathartic emotions. The barrier, however, was permeable. By placing themselves behind the arch, Cecilia, Mrs. Harrel, and the other spectators in the stage boxes are situated at the center of the audience's visual field, the only stable and unvarying visual element on a constantly shifting stage, where rapid set changes achieved the striking effects increasingly sought by eighteenth-century drama and opera. Inserted within the topography of the stage, these spectators not only shatter the illusion of the stage's autonomy; they become part of the performance, creating a confusion between audience and performance that troubled reformers such as David Garrick, who sought to abolish it, as did Luigi Riccoboni (known as Lelio) in Italy and France and Gotthold Lessing in Germany.[15]

In *Cecilia*'s spectacular world, the power hierarchy separating consumers and creators of spectacle is turned on its head. At the end of the *Artaserse* performance, the social performers take over the stage, displaying both the spectacular continuity between boxes and auditorium and that between the confined fictional world of the performance and the more complex fictitiousness of society:

> They all, therefore, marched upon the stage, their own party now being the only one that remained.
>
> "We shall make a triumphant entry here," cried Sir Robert Floyer; "the very tread of the stage half tempts me to turn actor."
>
> "You are a rare man," said Mr. Gosport, "if, at your time of life, that is a turn not *already* taken."
>
> "My time of life!" repeated he; "what do you mean by that? do you take me for an old man!"
>
> "No, Sir, but I take you to be past childhood, and consequently to have served your apprenticeship to the actors you have mixed with on the great stage of the world, and, for some years at least, to have set up for yourself."
>
> "Come," cried Morrice, "let's have a little spouting; 'twill make us warm."
>
> "Yes," said Sir Robert, "if we spout to an animating object. If Miss Beverley will be Juliet, I am Romeo at her service." (*Cecilia,* 68)

The references to *As You Like It* ("All the world's a stage") and to masquerade, artifice, and disguise frame Cecilia herself as spectacle. An alluring object in the masculine visual marketplace, she becomes a reified and fetishized body. (Sir Robert Floyer speaks of her as an "animating object.") She is transformed into a spectacular event by the perverse power of the probing gaze—a gaze that employs the epistemic codes of the eighteenth century to decipher its object's emotions.[16] On Cecilia's second visit to the opera, Sir Robert Floyer again subjects her to his gaze: "During the last dance [Cecilia] was discovered by Sir Robert Floyer, who sauntering down fop's alley, stationed himself by her side, and whenever the *figurante* relieved the principal dancers, turned his eyes from the stage to her face, as better worth his notice, and equally destined for his amusement" (*Cecilia,* 135).[17]

Early in the novel, Burney moves away from the theater to explore the pervasiveness of the spectacular throughout society. At the masquerade held by the Harrels at their house in Portman Square, a domestic technology of special effects is deployed to transform the house into a theatrical venue. Rather than merely replicating a stage set, however, the Harrels' home is filled with small-scale reproductions of the complex architectural structures that could be found in pleasure gardens and other places of entertainment frequented by fashionable Londoners. An "elegant awning" and temporary stairway leading to "a little gallery" hosting "a little orchestra" (*Cecilia,* 100) transform the domestic space into a miniaturized version of an urban entertainment venue. Often subdivided into separate moments—"concert," "ball," and "supper" (*Cecilia,* 321)—that duplicated the separation between the main piece and afterpieces in the theater, the domestic spectacularity of routs and masquerades such as that organized by the Harrels is just one example of the social spectacularity that pervaded the city, where the constant interplay of private and public gatherings accessible by "subscription ticket" suggests an ongoing performance on a vast metropolitan scale. Cecilia is surprised to discover that in London's capitalist society, the traditional invitation has become obsolete. Only those who possess an admission ticket are granted access to private receptions:

> Miss Larolles, turning suddenly to Cecilia, exclaimed . . . "Do you know Mr. Meadows says he shan't be well enough to go to Lady Nyland's assembly! . . . You shall be there, shan't you?"
>
> "No, ma'am, I have not the honour of being at all known to her ladyship."
>
> "O there's nothing in that," returned [Miss Larolles] . . . "she'll send you a ticket, and then you can go."
>
> "A ticket?" repeated Cecilia, "does Lady Nyland only admit her company with tickets?"
>
> "O lord," cried Miss Larolles, laughing immoderately, "don't you know what I mean? Why a ticket is only a visiting card, with a name upon it; but we all call them tickets now." (*Cecilia,* 23–24)

Just as the traditionally domestic space of the home has been transformed into the backdrop for a performance, so the city itself has been turned into an immense stage.[18] The novel's social gatherings are instances of the uninterrupted spectacle taking place in the city, and this extends to the auction held at the home of a bankrupt nobleman, a fashionable event for which the customary admission ticket is required.[19] Miss Larolles again instructs Cecilia: "All the world will be there; and we shall go with tickets, and you have no notion how it will be crowded" (*Cecilia,* 31).

Even the march of prisoners from Newgate to the Tyburn gallows becomes a choreographed urban scene, an immense procession designed to satiate the mob's hunger for ghoulish spectacle: "[Cecilia] had not proceeded far, before she saw a mob gathering, and the windows of almost all the houses filling with spectators. She desired her servant to enquire what this meant, and was informed that the people were assembling to see some malefactors pass by in their way to Tyburn. Alarmed at this intelligence from the fear of meeting the unhappy criminals, she hastily turned down the next street, but found that also filling with people who were running to the scene she was trying to avoid" (*Cecilia,* 176). One of the more disturbing and carnivalesque aspects of London life in the eighteenth century, this horrifying spectacle was an integral part of the ritual of execution. The eager and boisterous crowd gathering to witness the procession of carts carrying prisoners to the gallows (arguably similar to those employed in the Middle Ages to cross the city during such theatrical pageants as mystery plays) foreshadows the terrible Paris mob described some years later by Burke.[20] Enduring until the end of the century and beyond, the pervasive spectacularity that Burney explores in *Cecilia* turns the entire city and every aspect of its social and civic life into scenes of wonder, a phenomenon that caught the attention of William Wordsworth, as well:

At leisure let us view, from day to day,
As they present themselves, the Spectacles
Within doors, troops of wild Beasts, birds and beasts
Of every nature, from all climes conven'd;
And, next to these, those mimic sights that ape
The absolute presence of reality,
Expressing, as in mirror, sea and land,
And what earth is, and what she has to shew;
I do not here allude to subtlest craft,
By means refin'd attaining purest ends,

But imitation fondly made in plain
Confession of Man's weakness, and his loves.[21]

The first part of *Cecilia* introduces the heroine to London's fashionable gatherings and the genteel neighborhoods frequented by the beau monde, including the Harrels, the Delviles, and even the sober Mr. Monckton, a Suffolk friend of the Dean, on his visits to town. But the novel's urban landscape extends to the poorer quarters of the city, as well, where Cecilia does her charitable work. The topographic distribution of the characters' homes observes a strict urban decorum, each character inhabiting a space and location appropriate to his or her social status and aspirations. The miserly Briggs, one of Cecilia's guardians, fittingly lives in the heart of the city, whereas the city's commercial associations are precisely what young Belfield ruinously seeks to escape to climb the social ladder; he ends up living in a garret in Swallow Street. The destitute Hill family, exploited and ruined by Mr. Harrel, share a tiny lodging in Fetter Lane, one of the most crowded thoroughfares in London. Cecilia herself chooses lodgings in Albermarle Street in Mayfair when she visits the city incognito. In point of fact, *Cecilia*'s urban toponymy semanticizes the living conditions and life circumstances of the characters in the novel. Belfield's Swallow Street, for example, is perhaps the same Swallow Street that a contemporary description places in the midst of "a nest of dirty streets." It is "as crooked and devious as that bird's summer flight," reflecting almost literally Belfield's wavering progress up the social ladder.[22] Fetter Lane also had its distinct place in the urban imagination of the time due to its association with a chilling history of abuse and violence that had quickly become legendary. In the 1770s, the street had been the backdrop for the horrific persecution of two female apprentices who had nearly died after months of ill treatment by their mistress and her son.[23]

By juxtaposing the topological map of the novel with its chronological organization (see figure 13), we can see how carefully Burney linked each phase of her heroine's story to a specific place and time. Burney's precise timing of events in the novel starts with the specific information provided in the opening: "Cecilia . . . had lately entered into the one-and-twentieth year of her age" (*Cecilia,* 5). This precision has direct bearing on Cecilia's personal and social situation, linking the passage of time to her status as an heiress and, hence, to the importance of her choice of a husband. On attaining her majority, Cecilia will receive not only the £10,000 left her by her father but also the £3,000 yearly income provided by her uncle. Her uncle's inheritance is, however, compromised by the marriage clause, which will turn out to be an insurmountable obstacle to her happiness. Her father's fortune is ultimately illusory, as well, because it will gradually be eroded in the course of the novel by the repeated demands on it made by Cecilia's guardian, Mr. Harrel. An inveterate gambler, Harrel is being harassed by creditors and turns to his ward for help, pressuring her into borrowing immense sums from a moneylender. Since she has not yet come of age, her transactions with the moneylender are illegal: on turning twenty-one, she can simply refuse to pay. But she is scrupulous and does eventually honor her debt. Burney carefully notes the growing size of the debt Cecilia incurs as a result of Mr. Harrel's repeated, desperate pleas. All told, she ends up lending him £9,050, nearly the entirety of her paternal inheritance. Her generosity has dire consequences. Mortimer Delvile, unaware of the extent of Cecilia's financial assistance to Harrel, suggests that they can be married if she forgoes her uncle's inheritance and retains only her father's £10,000. This would allow him to retain his name and avoid being disowned by his own father: "At the proposal of parting with her uncle's fortune, which, desirable as it was, had as yet been only productive with her of misery, her heart, disinterested, and wholly careless of money, was prompt to accede at the condition; but at the mention of her paternal fortune, that fortune, of which, now, not the smallest vestige remained, horror seized all her faculties! she turned pale, she trembled, she involuntarily drew back her hand, and betrayed, by speechless agitation, the sudden agonies of her soul!" (*Cecilia,* 804)

The temporal dimension in *Cecilia* is therefore inseparable from the novel's treatment of money. Aligned with the novel's purely chronological timeline are two other temporal—and monetary—dimensions: that associated with Cecilia's charitable work, and that associated with debt. The time Cecilia devotes to her social responsibilities toward the poor is dictated by her own generous impulses and the advice of her philanthropic friend, Albany. The time relating to her finances is instead dictated by the inexorable passage of chronological time. The amount of Harrel's debt—and of Cecilia's own—increases exponentially as the weeks separating Cecilia from her majority go by. Having exhausted Cecilia's fortune and still facing ruin, Harrel is driven to suicide. He takes his own life during a final evening of diversion at Vauxhall, leaving his creditors a brief note: "*To be all paid to-night with a* BULLET" (*Cecilia,* 430).

Once she has come of age, Cecilia is no longer subject to the control of her three guardians and is free to accept Delvile's offer of marriage. But her twenty-first birthday, which should have brought her new personal, social, and financial independence, turns out to be only the prelude to further difficulties. Only two days after her birthday, Cecilia is to marry Delvile in London. Having finally resolved that his happiness is more important than preserving his relationship with his father, Delvile has arranged a secret ceremony, but just as the young couple are about to seal their vows, a mysterious female stranger cries out, interrupting the ceremony, and then precipitously leaves the church. As a turning point, the failed wedding foreshadows another ironic reversal in the last volume, when the Egglestons assert their rights over Cecilia's property and turn her out of the house she has been preparing to occupy on the grounds that she has forfeited her inheritance by marrying a man who refuses to take the Beverley name.

Burney carefully notes the chronological sequence of events in the novel. The letters Cecilia sends and receives are all dated,[24] and each chapter leading up to Cecilia's twenty-first birthday (books 1–7) is a microstructure in which Burney respects the unity of time. These chapters are often introduced by time markers such as "The Next Morning" or "The Next Day."[25] After Cecilia turns twenty-one, the chronological sequence is pinpointed so precisely that readers can follow the daily progress of events.[26] Cecilia moves back and forth between country and city at an increasingly frenetic pace until her marriage with Delvile finally takes place in chapter 11 of book 9. But the novel does not end here, and the tempo of the narrative changes in the last book, where the daily reporting of events gives way to the extended episode of Cecilia's madness. One third of this book's ten chapters are taken up by this dramatic episode, the climax of the novel. The paroxysm of tension is reached during Cecilia's increasingly bewildered and desperate search for her husband through London. Her wandering can be regarded as metaphorically retracing her progress throughout the novel. As she rushes from street to street, she passes sites familiar to the reader from the earlier volumes and finally collapses, exhausted, in a miserable pawnbroker's shop in one of the poorest neighborhoods of the city.

The moral, aesthetic, and epistemological aspects of the pervasive spectacularity that dominates *Cecilia*'s social world are brought to the surface of the text through what I would call an isotopy of inversion. References to artifice, deception, and duplicity are threaded throughout the text; illusion and performance appear to replace feeling and action. Cecilia's relationships with the other characters should thus be summarized in terms of inversion.

FIGURE 16. Characters' actantial roles in *Cecilia*

Helpers		Opponents
Mr. Monckton	⟶	
Lady Howard		Mr. Harrel
Mr. Villars		Mrs. Harrel
Henrietta Belfield		Sir Robert Floyer
Mrs. Charlton		Mr. Morrice
Dr. Lyster		Miss Bennett
Mr. Arnott		Mr. Briggs
		Mr. Delvile
	⟵	Mrs. Delvile
(Albany)		
(Mortimer Delvile)		

Note: Parentheses indicate characters who, despite their desire to help Cecilia out of love (Mortimer) or pity (Albany), instead cause her embarrassment or further difficulties.

It is the characters' sincerity or deceitfulness that determines their actantial roles (see figure 16).[27] But Cecilia herself is an atypical heroine. An heiress whose future husband must take her name, she is less the usual artless young lady than a "parodic man," as Doody aptly puts it.[28] The clause in the Dean's will can therefore be read as a legal device that operates another inversion by turning Cecilia into a mere channel for the preservation of her father's name. Furthermore, her immense wealth distorts her relationships with those surrounding her. Upon entering London's pleasure-seeking and extravagantly spendthrift social world, Cecilia soon realizes that her wealth makes her a magnet for those who see her only in light of the economic benefits they can reap from her friendship. In structural terms, therefore, the novel builds its analysis of London's spectacular society on a foundation of multiple instances of inversion. Burney signals their presence by repeatedly emphasizing the deceptiveness of appearances—that is, the pervasiveness of artifice throughout the society she describes.

That appearances are deceiving is immediately pointed out to Cecilia by her guardian Briggs, who has been entrusted with managing her fortune and protecting it from dowry hunters: "I'll give you some advice. Take care of sharpers; don't trust shoe-buckles, nothing but Bristol stones! *tricks in all things.* A fine gentleman sharp as another man. Never give your heart to a gold topped cane, nothing but brass gilt over. Cheats every where: fleece you in a year; won't leave you a groat . . . don't mind gold waistcoats; nothing but tinsel, all shew and no substance" (*Cecilia,* 95–96; emphasis added). "Tricks," a word much used by Briggs,[29] suggests the perverse inversion of appearances and reality that dominates London society. It applies not only to the marriage market but also to friendship. The most intimate affective ties also turn out to be a sham. Priscilla Harrel, for example, whom Cecilia had known since childhood and in whom she had expected to find a close friend, is too intent on performing her role as queen of a fashionable salon to devote any time to Cecilia or to pay any heed to her household's impending financial ruin. Mrs. Harrel's indifference and thoughtlessness strike Cecilia immediately, and she cannot mask her disappointment: "Ah Priscilla! . . . how little did I ever expect to see you so much a fine lady!" (*Cecilia,* 30).

The deepest level of duplicity—and the most damaging betrayal of Cecilia's trust—is reserved for Mr. Monckton, a neighbor and frequent associate of the Dean in Suffolk. Having made the mistake of marrying a jealous and ill-tempered noblewoman in hopes that her poor health would soon leave him a wealthy widower, Monckton exploits Cecilia's trust in him to influence her actions and opinions, with a view to marrying her after his wife's death. The reader learns about Monckton's true character and intentions long before Cecilia does. In the first pages of the first chapter, the omniscient narrator reveals that Monckton's friendship for Cecilia is far from disinterested: "He knew that the acquaintance of Cecilia was confined to a circle of *friends* of which he was himself the principal ornament, that she had rejected all the proposals of *marriage* which had hitherto been made to her, and, as he had sedulously watched her from the earliest years, he had reason to believe that her *heart* had escaped any dangerous impression. This being her situation, he had long looked upon her as *his future property*" (*Cecilia,* 9; emphasis added). Abruptly shifting from the sentimental register to the economic, Burney's rhetorical strategy here reveals the full extent of Cecilia's reification: her status as a subject is suddenly changed to that of an object.

The discovery of Monckton's treachery affects Cecilia deeply. This is a particularly striking instance of the inversion isotopy present throughout the novel, and Burney's description of Cecilia's reaction is heavily weighted with terms pertaining to the field of vision and perception, emphasizing the contrast between appearances and reality:

> Shocked and dismayed, [Cecilia] now *saw,* but *saw* with horror, the removal of all her doubts, and the explanation of all her difficulties, in the full and irrefragable *discovery* of the perfidy of her oldest friend and confidant. . . . The motive of such deep and accumulated *treachery* was next to be sought: nor was the search long; one only could have tempted him to schemes so hazardous and costly; and, unsuspicious as she was, she now *saw into* his whole design. . . . She considered, however, that the matter could not rest here: [Monckton] would demand an explanation, and perhaps, by his unparalleled address, could contrive *to seem* innocent, notwithstanding *appearances* were at present so much against him. [She expected], therefore, some *artifice,* and determined not to be *duped* by it. (*Cecilia,* 836–37; emphasis added)

On the level of the novel's structure, the revelation of Monckton's duplicity in the last volume reverses his actantial role and clarifies the roles of two other characters, Mr. Morrice and Miss Bennett, who on Monckton's orders had followed Cecilia on her way to her secret wedding with Delvile in London. It was Miss Bennett who had mysteriously cried out in church, putting a stop to the ceremony. The novel's emphasis on inversion therefore also encompasses the reversal of certain important characters' actantial roles. Like Monckton's, Mrs. Delvile's actantial role also changes in the course of the novel, but whereas in Monckton's case the reversal hinges on the deceptiveness of appearances, in the case of Mrs. Delvile it is substantive, and her change of heart about the young couple's marriage is revealed simultaneously to the reader and to the protagonists.

Convinced of her son's disinterested devotion to Cecilia, and mollified by Cecilia's affectionate respect for her, Mrs. Delvile ceases to oppose their marriage. But before she finally gives her consent in volume 5, a tense confrontation with the young couple occurs in volume 4, which gives Burney an opportunity to display her gifts for dramatic narrative. This conflict scene is the dramatic climax of book 7 (*Cecilia,* 671–81) and anticipates the quick succession of dramatic set pieces at the end of volume 5: Cecilia and Delvile's secret wedding (in chapter 11 of book 9), the discovery of Monckton's designs (in chapter 1 of book 10), the ensuing duel between Monckton and Delvile (in chapter 2 of book 10), and the arrival of the Egglestons (in chapter 3 of book 10), leading to Cecilia's journey to London and her madness (in chapters 5–8 of book 10).

Burney reveals the crucial importance of this episode in a letter to Samuel

Crisp, in which she refers to the chapter as "the scene for which I wrote the whole book, and so entirely does my plan hang upon it, that I must abide by its reception in the world, or put the whole behind the fire" (*DL,* 2:71). Her reference to the episode as a "scene" is telling and appropriate, given how the narration dovetails almost exactly with the diegetic sequence of events. Burney had employed this narrative technique in *Evelina,* where she had exploited the formal potential of the novel to approximate a theatrical text. This kind of textualization tends to do away with the time lapse between the narrated event and its transcription, implying "a diminution of the cognitive space between language and reality, as well as between reader and text."[30] The reader is brought closer to the text and experiences the event synchronically, much like a spectator watching a theatrical performance in real time.

Particularly suited to epistolary fiction, this technique had been employed by Richardson, whose novels' "spontaneous" writing and use of the present tense eliminated the temporal and cognitive distance separating the reader from the work. But unlike Richardson's novels, or *Evelina,* where the epistolary style allowed the unfiltered transcription of characters' conversations in the manner of dialogue in a play, *Cecilia* has an omniscient narrator whose constant presence makes the transition from the diegesis of a novel to the mimesis of drama far more complex. Burney has to limit significantly the presence of the narrator, whose role in the scene is confined to providing physical descriptions of the characters' emotions and of their gestures and movements. Instead of giving their thoughts or feelings, the narrator can give only external descriptions and so must translate emotions into mimic signs and virtual stage directions.

The narrator opens the episode by clarifying its setting, a parlor in Mrs. Charlton's house (*Cecilia,* 670) and by introducing the characters and carefully describing their pragmatic—kinesic and proxemic—relations to each other. Figure 17 reveals how closely Burney's technique resembles that used by Richardson in *Clarissa,* as described by Ira Konigsberg: "Attitudes, movements, spatial relationships, qualities of voice are so specified that the reader envisions the entire scene exactly as it would have occurred in real life."[31] Cecilia's silence is particularly expressive and semantically dense. Her inner turmoil is the result of conflicted emotions: on one hand, her awareness that she has accepted Delvile's marriage proposal despite his parents' opposition; on the other, a sense of wounded pride due to her equally strong conviction that her actions have been unimpeachable. Her emotions succeed each

FIGURE 17. Characters' formal, kinesic, and proxemic relations in *Cecilia*, 671

At length they were announced, and at length they entered the room.	Characters enter stage
Cecilia, with her utmost efforts for courage, could hardly stand to receive them.	Movement
They came in together, but Mrs. Delvile, advancing before her son, and endeavouring so to stand as to intercept his view of her, with the hope that in a	Movement
few instants *her emotion would be less visible*,	Expression: face, passions mimed
said, in the most soothing accents, "What honour Miss Beverley does us by permitting this visit! . . ."	Intonation
Cecilia courtsied; but depressed by the cruel task which awaited her,	Movement
had no power to speak;	Silence
and Mrs. Delvile, finding she still trembled, made her sit down, and drew a chair next to her.	Movement
(Cecilia, 671; emphasis added)	

other quickly, and it is this play of emotions rather than her words that strikes Mrs. Delvile most forcefully.

Mrs. Delvile has arranged the meeting to persuade the young couple to give up their plans to marry. Her intention is to appeal to Cecilia's moral scruples by stressing how her son's decision to marry her would lead to an irrevocable breach with his father. Before Cecilia can express her acceptance of this argument, Mortimer unexpectedly intervenes to oppose it, and the tension increases. The only argument that Mrs. Delvile can successfully bring to bear against him is the threat of his father's curses: "'The curses of my father!' repeated [Delvile], starting and shuddering. . . . 'O speak not such words!' . . . 'to disgrace her,—to be banished by you,—present not, I conjure you, such scenes to my imagination!.' . . . 'It shall not be!' cried he, in a transport of rage; 'cease, cease to distract me!—be content, madam,—you have conquered!'" (*Cecilia,* 676–77). Delvile's agitated tone of voice, and his hesitation, are represented typographically through the repeated use of dashes, while exclamation marks provide paralinguistic information about his delivery. The punctuation therefore gives implicit clues about Delvile's mode of articulation, but there are also explicit, directorial descriptions of his inflection. The narrator specifies that he quickly moves from "a tone of the deepest anguish" to "agonizing earnestness" and, ultimately, to "a transport of rage" (*Cecilia,* 676–77), reflecting his uncertain state of mind, now hopeful that he will ultimately convince his mother, now driven to distraction by her obstinate resistance.

Mortimer Delvile's reluctant submission to his mother's argument leads to the second part of the scene, in which outward descriptions of the characters' body language are particularly important. Delvile's first action is to assist the trembling Cecilia—a significant proxemic shift as he moves from his mother's side to Cecilia's and a visual counterpart to his wavering state of mind, torn between filial devotion and loyalty to his betrothed. As kinesic hyper-codification comes to mark the scene, Cecilia is gradually reduced to silence, overwhelmed by Mrs. Delvile's presence and the thought of Mortimer's father's disapproval. Thus, verbal ellipses, aphasic moments, and pregnant silences become more frequent. Verbal language is replaced by somatic ostension, and communication is increasingly entrusted to emotive mimesis: "But Delvile, penetrated and tortured, yet delighted at [Cecilia's] sensibility, broke from his mother, and seizing her hand, exclaimed, 'Oh Miss Beverley, if *you* are not happy—. . . That voice,—those looks,—' cried he, still holding her, 'they speak not serenity!" (*Cecilia,* 677).

Disturbed by Cecilia's renewed resolution to part from him, Delvile rushes out of the room, allowing her finally to show her despair openly. Once again, a silent gesture signals Cecilia's acquiescence to the older woman's will as she kisses Mrs. Delvile's hand: "But the heroism of Cecilia, in losing its object, lost its force; she sighed, *she could not speak,* tears gushed into her eyes, and kissing Mrs. Delvile's hand *with a look that shewed her inability to converse* with her, she hastened, though scarce able to support herself, away, with the intention of shutting herself up in her own apartment. But when she came into the hall, she started, and could proceed no further; for there she beheld Delvile, who in too great agony to be seen, had stopt to recover some composure before he quitted the house" (*Cecilia,* 678; emphasis added). The sight of Delvile, whose face and body betray his pain at the impending separation from Cecilia, makes her hesitate briefly before she summons the strength to take a few steps without replying to his agonized calls: "She shook her head, and made a motion with her hand to say no" (*Cecilia,* 678). Her hesitation is observed by Mrs. Delvile, who realizes that only the immediate separation of the couple will ensure their respect of the hard-won promise to part.

Cecilia's expressive silence, her faltering steps, and her symptomatic blushes demonstrate the power of the unconscious language of the body to communicate the emotions she cannot express verbally out of respect for Mrs. Delvile. The omniscient narrator does not describe Cecilia's anger or

FIGURE 18. Characters' formal, kinesic, and proxemic relations in *Cecilia,* 679–80

Mrs. Delvile now came to the parlour door,	Movement
and looked aghast at the situation in	
which she saw them: Cecilia again moved	Movement
on, and reached the stairs, but tottered,	Movement (tottering)
and was obliged to cling to the banisters. . . .	Gesture (clinging)
[T]urning from him, she walked again	Movement
towards the parlour, finding by her	
shaking frame, the impossibility of	
getting unaided up the stairs. . . .	
Cecilia . . . sinking into a chair, hid	Movement (sinking)
her face against Mrs. Delvile: but,	Attitude (hiding face),
reviving in a few moments, and blushing at	Blushing
the weakness she had betrayed, she raised	
her head . . . then arose, but her knees	Movement (rising, sitting)
trembled, and her head was giddy, and	
again seating herself, she forced a faint	
smile. . . .	Expression (smile)
"Can I bear this!" cried Delvile, "no, it	Articulation
shakes all my resolution!" . . .	
"Hot-headed young man!" interrupted Mrs.	Articulation
Delvile, with an air of haughty	Expression
displeasure. . . .	
Shame, and her own earnestness, now	
restored some strength to Cecilia, *who*	Mimed passion
read with terror in the looks of Mrs.	
Delvile the passions with which she was	
agitated, and instantly obeyed her by	
rising; but her son, who inherited a	Movement (rising)
portion of her own spirit, rushed between	Movement (rushing)
them both and the door . . . and snatching	Gesture (snatching hand)
the hand of Cecilia from his mother,	
exclaimed: "I cannot, I will not give her	Articulation
up! . . ."	
Grief and horror next to frenzy at a	
disappointment thus unexpected, and thus	
peremptory, rose in the face of Mrs.	Mimed passion
Delvile, who, striking her hand upon her	Gesture (hand)
forehead, cried, "My brain is on fire!"	Articulation
and rushed out of the room.	Movement (rushing)
Cecilia had now no difficulty to disengage	Gesture (disengaging)
herself from Delvile, who, shocked at the	
exclamation, and confounded by the sudden	
departure of his mother, hastened eagerly	
to pursue her: she had only flown into the	Movement (pursuing)

next parlour; but, upon following her thither, what was his dread and his alarm, when he saw here extended upon the floor, her face, hands, neck all covered with blood! (*Cecilia*, 679–80; emphasis added)	ostension

pain or Mrs. Delvile's distress at witnessing the young couple's brief encounter in the hall. The description of Mrs. Delvile's state of mind is followed by a meaningful diegetic break; the narrator merely registers the emotional turmoil impressed on her face. The body's emotive code takes the place of words, and Mrs. Delvile suddenly leaves the room uttering a single, terrifying exclamation. (For an analysis of the passage, see figure 18).

The climactic scene concludes with Mrs. Delvile's physical collapse due to a ruptured blood vessel. Having summoned help, Cecilia "glided hastily out of the room," pursued by Mortimer, who "followed her quick into the next parlour" (*Cecilia,* 681). The action moves to a different place, putting an end to the scene and to the chapter.

The scene Burney described as the climax of the novel thus concludes in a remarkably apt way, putting on display the materiality—the ostensive and demonstrative nature—of Mrs. Delvile's attitude of superiority. Her family pride, which causes her to plead so urgently for the importance of lineage and the ties of blood, produces an unsustainable tension that breaks, quite literally, leaving her covered in her own blood. Burney thus condenses the effects of the prolonged confrontation into a single iconic image. Exemplifying Dante's "law of contrappasso," or retaliation, this powerful image gives visual—indeed, almost plastic—expression to Mrs. Delvile's aristocratic prejudices.

Mrs. Delvile ceases to oppose the match after Delvile and Cecilia resolve to forgo the Dean's inheritance, ensuring that Delvile can retain his name. Her admiration for Cecilia's integrity and disinterestedness is matched by the affection Cecilia herself feels for her, and Mrs. Delvile's final scene with the young couple is tender: "Delvile's eyes were full, as he passionately exclaimed: 'This, this is the sight my heart has thus long desired! the wife of my choice taken to the bosom of the parent I revere! be yet but well, my beloved mother, and I will be thankful for every calamity that has led to so sweet a conclusion'" (*Cecilia,* 827). But in spite of Mrs. Delvile's best efforts to convince him, Mortimer's father's remains resolutely opposed to his son's marriage, leading to a permanent separation between husband and wife: "I [Mortimer] left not, however, your [Cecilia's] fame to a weak champion:

my mother defended it with all the spirit of truth, and all the confidence of similar virtue! yet they parted without conviction, and so mutually irritated with each other, that they agreed to meet no more" (*Cecilia,* 815).

The wedding ceremony celebrated two weeks later is therefore sanctioned only by Mrs. Delvile. Mortimer and Cecilia decide to defy Compton Delvile's will, rebelling against the authoritarian rule of the father and choosing instead to offer their devotion and respect to the mother. The fundamental epistemic—and generic—reversal operated by Burney's novel lies in this substitution.

> The difficulty of constructing an Epic or Dramatic Fable may appear from the bad success of very great writers who have attempted it.
>
> —James Beattie, "Essays: On Poetry and Music, as They Affect the Mind" (1776)

The epilogue describing the married couple's happiness despite the loss of Cecilia's inheritance did not satisfy Burney's closest literary advisers, or most of the novel's readers:

> The upright mind of Cecilia, her purity, her virtue, and the moderation of her wishes, gave to her in the warm affection of Lady Delvile, and the unremitting fondness of Mortimer, all the happiness human life seems capable of receiving:—yet human it was, and as such imperfect! she knew that, at times, the whole family must murmur at her loss of fortune, and at times she murmured herself to be thus portionless, tho' an HEIRESS. Rationally, however, she surveyed the world at large, and finding that of the few who had any happiness, there were none without some misery, she checked the rising sigh of repining mortality, and, grateful with general felicity, bore partial evil with chearfullest resignation. (*Cecilia,* 941)

As the careful balancing of the antithetical terms "heiress" and "portionless" and "chearfullest" and "resignation" shows, Burney stressed the theme of inversion, or reversal, through to the last page, and this emphasis was clearly incompatible with a conventional ending. Even in her draft of the novel, the author had rejected the customary happy resolution. Instead of devising some fortuitous event that would instantly grant the young couple not only married bliss but also wealth (such as Censor's unexpected gift in *The*

Witlings), she chose to avoid falling into the trap of writing a "whining end of a modern novel."[32] Her decision provoked many negative reactions. The critic for the *English Review*, for example, noted his disappointment while also praising the novel: "We shall conclude what we have to say on this excellent Novel with just hinting, that had the Eggleston family been represented as more worthy of their good fortune, or had a flaw in the Dean's will enabled Miss Beverley to enter again into possession of her estate, perhaps the conclusion would have left a more pleasing impression on the mind."[33]

Burney seems to have had two reasons to disregard her audience's expectations about poetic justice. Although classical dramatic theory required the traditional distribution of rewards and punishments in a conclusion, from an aesthetic standpoint the low-key ending seemed to fit best Burney's intention to respect verisimilitude. She replied to Burke's objections by asking, "When is life and nature completely happy or miserable?" (*DL*, 2:139) and wrote to Crisp a few months before the novel's publication that a "serious history" required an appropriate ending:

> With respect, however, to the great point of Cecilia's fortune, I have much to urge in my own defence, only now I can spare no time, and I must frankly confess I shall think I have rather written a farce than a serious history, if the whole is to end, like the hack Italian operas, with a jolly chorus that makes all parties good and all parties happy! . . . Besides, I think the book, in its present conclusion, somewhat original, for the hero and heroine are neither plunged in the depths of misery, nor exalted to UN*human* happiness, more according to real life, and less resembling every other book of fiction. . . . You find, my dear daddy, I am prepared to fight a good battle here; but I have thought the matter much over, and if I am made to give up this point, my whole plan is rendered abortive, and the last page in any novel in Mr. Noble's circulating library may serve for the last page of mine, since a marriage, a reconciliation, and some sudden expedient for great riches, concludes them all alike. (*DL*, 2:80–81)

Burney's second justification for her novel's conclusion relates to the drama. From a structural point of view, the protagonists' marriage without the inheritance suited the dramatic form that dominates the novel as a whole. Whereas *Evelina*'s plot appears to be organized along the lines of comedy, *Cecilia* contains tragic elements—derived particularly from sentimental tragedy and late eighteenth-century Gothic adaptations of she-tragedy—that could not coherently be made to fit an unequivocally happy ending.

Although the complicated sentimental and social history told in *Cecilia* is predominantly indebted to tragedy, there are other theatrical influences in the novel, as well. Like *Evelina, Cecilia* has a three-part structure and alternates comic, tragic, and farcical episodes. The intertextual references in the novel are often implicit and are not accessible to modern readers without the help of notes—we have seen this on an extraliterary level as well, in relation to the specific connotations of London's street names—but they would have been readily understood by Burney's contemporaries, who would have been able to note how the novel reflects the generically diverse, often hybrid, theatrical repertoire of the time.[34] And as required by neoclassical principles of decorum, the characters featured in the various episodes of the novel are suited to the genre of the episode, much as in Fielding's novels, where characters are equipped with a distinct idiolect, reflecting not only their personality but also their rank. In *Cecilia,* each social stratum is characterized by a specific style of speech, a high, or low, linguistic variety distinguishing the upper ranks from tradesmen, laborers, and the poor.

In the first part of the novel, set in London's high society, Cecilia makes the acquaintance of the fashionable set. Comedy of manners appears to dominate this section, where the characters thronging the brilliant gatherings of the beau monde have their own behavioral, syntactical, and rhetorical idiosyncrasies. The theatrical character typology is much like that of *Evelina,* ranging from the pleasure-seeking man about town to the army captain sporting a Frenchified vocabulary and the young lady of fashion given to hyperbolic expressions of displeasure.

But a good number of fashionable gathering places, such as Vauxhall or the Pantheon, included more mixed company: not only the aristocracy but also the wealthy middle classes who could purchase the inexpensive admission tickets and share in the amusements of the upper ranks. Here Cecilia encounters a number of "cits." Mr. Hobson, Mr. Simkins, and Cecilia's guardian Mr. Briggs, a wealthy merchant, are characterized by the "low" diction required by neoclassical theories of decorum. The contrast between their speech and the "high" diction of the aristocratic characters is exploited to comic effect. An example is this exchange between Briggs and the haughty Compton Delvile:

> Cecilia, earnest to have the business concluded, turned to Mr. Briggs, and said, "Sir, here is pen and ink: are you to write, or am I? or what is to be done?

> "No, no," said he, with a sneer, "give it 'other; all in our turn; don't come before his Grace the Right Honourable Mr. Vampus."
>
> "Before whom, Sir?" said Mr. Delvile, reddening.
>
> "Before my Lord Don Pedigree," answered Briggs, with a spiteful grin, "know him? eh? ever hear of such a person?" . . .
>
> "If your intention, Sir," cried Mr. Delvile, fiercely, "is only to insult me, I am prepared for what measures I shall take. I declined seeing you in my own house, that I might not be under the same restraint as when it was my unfortunate lot to meet you last." (*Cecilia,* 753)

Briggs's mockery of Mr. Delvile's aristocratic self-importance reflects a new eighteenth-century phenomenon that has been described as "the commercial middle classes' right to be represented, to become the *subject* of dramatic discourse, if not of politics."[35] Burney employs these contrasts and combinations among characters to create a comprehensive portrait of London society. She not only includes the various ranks of society in the novel but reproduces their codes of behavior, carefully describing the pragmatics of their interactions, as well as the gestural and linguistic registers they employ.

The contrast between the wealthy middle class and an impoverished aristocracy was a staple of British theater in the eighteenth century. Rich, honest merchants were typically represented as tussling with the sometimes disreputable aristocrats who were keen to marry their wealthy daughters to those merchants to set their own shaky finances to rights. Plays such as Susanna Centlivre's *A Bold Stroke for a Wife,* in which Feinwell plots to marry Anne Lovely, ward of the exchange broker Tradelove, and George Colman's *The English Merchant,* with its positive portrayal of the merchant Freeport (Colman's *The Man of Business,* like Centlivre's comedy, is referred to in *Cecilia* and is discussed later) are only two among innumerable sources Burney could draw on for inspiration. As John Loftis points out, the image of the merchant had undergone a process of social rehabilitation in the course of the century, reflecting a deep societal transformation as moneyed interests slowly gained ascendance over landed interests.[36] Cecilia's marriage to Mortimer Delvile reflects a change in perception that had begun in the late seventeenth century, when intermarriages between aristocrats and the middle classes were becoming common in the theater. In 1722, Steele's Mr. Sealand in *The Conscious Lovers* famously defended his fellow merchants: "We Merchants are a Species of Gentry, that have grown into the World this last Century, and are as honourable, and almost as useful, as you landed

Folk, that have always thought yourself [*sic*] so much above us" (*The Conscious Lovers,* 4.2).

Given the popularity of the figure of the merchant in contemporary theater, it is possible that Burney may have based Briggs's financial idiolect on that of the wealthy Mr. Sterling in Colman and Garrick's *The Clandestine Marriage* (Drury Lane, 1766). Like Cecilia's guardian, Sterling is presented in the play's opening as driven by a single passion: "Money . . . is the spring of all his actions, which nothing but the idea of acquiring nobility of magnificence can ever make him forgo—and these he thinks his money will purchase" (*The Clandestine Marriage,* 1.1).[37] Briggs constantly repeats certain idiomatic phrases characterized by a grammar so spare that it does away with conjunctions and even subjects, as though to reflect his own extreme thriftiness. His perpetual rude questions (such as "are warm?" to mean "are you rich enough?" [*Cecilia,* 118]) and his compulsive reduction of all human relations to financial transactions seem to have been adapted from Mr. Sterling's idiolect.[38] In appraising young Lovewell, a modest young suitor, Sterling states: "You're a good boy, to be sure—I have a great value for you—but can't think of you for a son-in-law.—There's no *stuff* in the case, no money, Lovewell! . . . Add one little round o to the sum total of your fortune, and that will be the finest thing you can say to me" (*The Clandestine Marriage,* 1.1). Sterling shows the same satisfaction in his wealth as Burney's Briggs, and the same contempt for the aristocracy: "Mind, now, how I'll entertain his lordship and Sir John.—We'll show your fellows at the other end of town how we live in the city.—They shall eat gold—and drink gold—and lie in gold.—Here cook! butler (*Calling*). What signifies your birth and education, and titles? Money, money, that's the stuff that makes the great man in this country" (*The Clandestine Marriage,* 1.1). The power shift that had shaken the city of London—and that Burney had first embodied in *Evelina*'s Branghton family—signaled the displacement of the weakened aristocracy in favor of the up-and-coming nouveaux riches.

Briggs's contempt for Delvile's aristocratic lineage (he refers to him disparagingly as a "Spanish Don Ferdinand" and "Don Vampus") seems closely related to Mr. Sealand's irreverent use of canine pedigrees to mock aristocratic lineage in *The Conscious Lovers:*[39]

> *Sir John Bevil.* Give me leave, however, Mr. Sealand, as we are upon a treaty for uniting our families, to mention only the business of an ancient house. Genealogy and descent are to be of some consideration in an affair of this sort.

Mr. Sealand. Genealogy and descent! Sir, there has been in our family a very large one. There was Galfried the father of Edward, the father of Ptolemy, the father of Crassus, the father of Earl Richard, the father of Henry the Marquis, the father of Duke John—

Sir Bevil. What, do you rave, Mr. Sealand?—all these great names in your family?

Mr. Sealand. These? Yes, Sir. I have heard my father name 'em all, and more.

Sir Bevil. Ay, Sir? and did he say that they were all in your family?

Mr. Sealand. Yes, Sir, he kept 'em all. He was the greatest cocker in England. He said Duke John won him many battles, and never lost one.

Sir Bevil. Oh, Sir, your servant! you are laughing at my laying any stress upon descent; but I must tell you, Sir, I never knew anyone, but he that wanted that advantage, turn it into ridicule.

Mr. Sealand. And I never knew anyone who had any better advantages put that into his account. (*The Conscious Lovers,* 4.2)[40]

Aside from providing comic relief, the squabbles between Briggs and Delvile bring to mind the interactions between the dramatic types called for by neoclassical aesthetic theories, thus endowing the characters with some measure of universality. But Burney also works with other, more physical genres of stage comedy in her novel and includes elements of farce, harlequinade, and pantomime. The exaggerated physicality of Mr. Morrice, for example, the eager lawyer Cecilia meets at Mr. Monckton's house, recalls the acrobatic feats popularized in English theaters by Harlequin and other Commedia dell'Arte characters who had been fixtures of the theater since the 1720s, when they performed in spectacular and remarkably successful afterpieces.

Pantomimes, which Richard Bevis has called "the quintessential Georgian entertainment,"[41] were introduced in England by the actors of the Comédie-Italienne after their success in France. In England, they created a hybrid form of mimed entertainment that relied on the gestural virtuosity of the actors. As Roberto Tessari reminds us, "Very effective productions . . . created a vogue for a new type of entertainment. Based on captivating magical-mythological plots, harlequinades would employ 'wonderful' stage effects . . . and included music and the occasional song. Above all, they were intended to highlight an art of acting that achieved its best effects through wordless *lazzi,* or gags."[42] Harlequinades quickly developed into an autochthonous art form thanks to promoters such as the pantomimist John Rich (1692–1761), whose immensely successful dance productions were staged first at Lincoln's Inn Fields, where he performed under the stage name Lun (in *The Necromancer; or, Harlequin Dr. Faustus* [1723] and *Harlequin Sorcerer* [1725]) and later at Covent Garden, where he served as artistic director from 1732 to 1761. Garrick himself was forced to respond to the craze and developed a number of pantomimes at Drury Lane featuring Henry Woodward (1714–77; known as "Lun, Jr."), one of the most popular actors of the time.[43]

Burney seems to be drawing on the mimed and choreographed sequences of harlequinades in her description of Morrice's overflowing, uncontainable physicality: "Not a word more said Mr. Morrice, but scampered out of the room. . . . [Cecilia] had hardly concluded [her relation] before again, and quite out of breath, [Morrice] made his appearance. 'I hope, Sir,' said Mr. Harrel, 'you have not given yourself the trouble of going to [Sir Robert's]?' 'No, Sir, it has given me nothing but pleasure; a run these cold mornings is the thing I like best.' . . . The matter was now settled in a few minutes, and having received his directions, and an invitation to dinner, Morrice danced off, with a heart yet lighter than his heels" (*Cecilia,* 49–51). Morrice's perpetual motion, as he dances and runs his way through the novel, is choreographed as a mumming performance by Burney: "Morrice . . . with a sudden spring which made the whole room shake, jumpt over [the sofa] into the vacant space" (*Cecilia,* 83). It is no accident that his name recalls that of the morris dancer, better known as "morricer."

Cecilia is introduced to the intricacies of London's fashionable world by two guides. The first, Mr. Gosport, is something of a classical *didascalus,* or teacher, but in the comic vein best suited to a satire on manners. He provides a taxonomy of Cecilia's new acquaintances, subdividing them according to their dominating passions:

> The TON misses, as they are called, who now infest the town, are in two divisions, the SUPERCILIOUS, and the VOLUBLE. The SUPERCILIOUS, like Miss Leeson, are silent, scornful, languid, and affected, and disdain all converse but with those of their own set: the VOLUBLE, like Miss Larolles, are flirting, communicative, restless, and familiar, and attack without the smallest ceremony, every one they think worthy of their notice. But this they have in common, that at home they think of nothing but dress, abroad of nothing but admiration, and that every where they hold in supreme contempt all but themselves. (*Cecilia,* 40)

Cecilia's other guide, whom she first meets at the Haymarket, is Albany, an elderly eccentric who roams the city trying to awaken the conscience of the upper ranks about the sufferings of the poor. Albany's originality is so pronounced that it verges on madness. He abruptly addresses those he meets, speaking to them like a preacher intent on reprimanding them for their indifference to the sufferings of others. He is the "plain dealer . . . often an outspoken critic of the tragic action" who performs the function of the chorus in ancient tragedy.[44] Burney suggests this dramatic lineage by having him "run into blank verse perpetually" (*Cecilia,* 291), in accordance with the stylistic conventions of eighteenth-century tragedy:[45] "At this moment the incognito [Albany], quitting the corner in which he had planted himself, came suddenly forward, and standing before the whole group, cast upon Cecilia a look of much compassion, and called out, 'Poor simple victim! hast thou already so many pursuers? yet seest not that thou art marked for sacrifice! yet knowest not that thou art destined for prey!'" (*Cecilia,* 68).

Given Albany's role as witness to tragedy, it is no accident that he should figure more prominently in the second part of the novel, from Harrel's suicide in chapter 13 of book 5 to Cecilia's madness episode in chapters 7–8 of book 10. The structure of this half of the novel builds to a crescendo, with one dramatic scene following another at an increasingly heightened pace. In the course of these episodes, Cecilia's tragic situation begins to close in on her, isolating her. The main tragic conflict to which she is subjected is that between honor and love, an opposition adapted from the heroic drama of Restoration theater and developed in the novel through further binaries (family obligation–sentiment, duty–love, lineage–wealth) that pertain to the family, morality, and society.[46] The underlying structure derived from Restoration tragedy also lends support to Burney's conclusion, allowing her to supply an ending whose verisimilitude fits the progress of the narrative.

Burney's adaptation of Restoration tragedy appears heavily indebted to the definition of domestic tragedy proposed by Nicholas Rowe in his influential prologue to *The Fair Penitent* (1703). As noted in chapter 1, this subgenre marked a transition from heroic tragedy's emphasis on eliciting the audience's admiration to a new emphasis on eliciting compassion for the "private Woes" of ordinary protagonists:

> Long has the Fate of Kings and Empires been
> The common Bus'ness of the Tragick Scene,
> As if Misfortune made the Throne her Seat,
> And none cou'd be unhappy but the Great. . . .

Stories like these with Wonder we may hear,
But far remote, and in a higher Sphere,
We ne'er can pity what we ne'er can share. . . .
Therefore an Humbler Theme our Author chose,
A melancholy Tale of private Woes:
No Princes here lost Royalty bemoan,
But you shall meet with Sorrows like your own; . . .

Let no nice Taste the Poet's Arts arraign,
If some frail vicious Characters he feign:
Who writes shou'd still let Nature be his Care,
Mix Shades with Lights, and not paint all things fair,
But shew you Men and Women as they are,
With Deference to the Fair he bid me say,
Few to Perfection ever found the Way.[47]

Instead of leading to a new independence, Cecilia's twenty-first birthday is the harbinger of catastrophe. The moment designated as the climax of the first half of the novel turns out to coincide with Cecilia's loss of her new home, then of her wealth, and finally, it seems, even of Delvile's affection in a dramatic buildup that vividly evokes her increasing isolation and impotence. Like the heroines of she-tragedy, in the final volume of the novel Cecilia undergoes an experience of extreme alienation that is patently Gothic in tone while approximating symbolically the physical violence associated with the *sparagmos,* or ritual death, of Greek tragedy. The young woman who wanders delirious through the streets of London has suffered a metaphorical dismemberment and a mutilation of her identity, marriage having deprived her both of her maiden name, Beverley, and—due to Compton Delvile's continued opposition to the marriage—of her full right to her husband's name, Delvile.

The chapters on Cecilia's madness lead directly into the novel's epilogue. Although Mrs. Delvile has acknowledged the marriage, Cecilia and Mortimer are constrained by their weak financial position, a reversal typical of the balancing intervention of *nemesis* (or divine retribution) in classical drama. The original imbalance that gave rise to the plot is righted: Cecilia gladly gives up the name that the Dean's will would have forced her to retain and bestow on her husband but at the cost of losing the material advantages associated with it. As we have seen, Burney's decision to give *Cecilia* this unusual ending ensures the structural coherence of the novel, allowing her to respect the classic structure of tragedy.[48] But Cecilia's personal experience of upheaval and dislocation also entails a shift in register as the novel moves away from the public sphere (symbolized by her uncle's will) to the private sphere of the family. Burney's strong emphasis on the domestic aspect of Cecilia's tragedy, and the careful attention given to her emotions and psychological turmoil thus seem to approximate most closely the architecture of Georgian bourgeois drama, which we can therefore consider the thematic and structural model for the novel.

The transtextual relations with contemporary theater that we find in *Cecilia* seem to confirm the relevance of high drama and even tragedy to the novel's overall structure. Intertextual references are threaded throughout the narrative; figure 19 also shows the frequency of references to plays, by genre. Two comedies listed in figure 19—*A Bold Stroke for a Wife* (1718) by Susanna Centlivre and *The Man of Business* (1774) by George Colman the Elder—are not cited within the body of the text but inspire the titles of two chapters in book 5: "A Bold Stroke" (chap. 7) and "A Man of Business" (chap. 12). In chapter 7, Mr. Harrel tries to convince Cecilia to accept Sir Robert Floyer's marriage proposal—an attempt to "compensate" Floyer for a substantial gambling debt. In chapter 12, Harrel tries to snub two creditors whom he encounters at Vauxhall. Mr. Hobson, the more aggressive of the two, refuses to submit to the snub and demands payment. A close thematic link thus seems to connect both comedies to the novel, particularly in regard to relations between merchants, or "cits," and the upper ranks of society. We can therefore consider Colman's and Centlivre's comedies to be the implicit hypotextual model for each of these chapters, and we may suppose that Burney was confident her readers would grasp the connection.

But figure 19 also shows that most references in *Cecilia* are to tragedies rather than to other genres (thirteen in a total of twenty-four), a clear sign of the structural importance of tragedy in the book. Particularly significant is the fact that references to *Hamlet* appear in each volume, suggesting that it can be considered an intertextual key to the novel: the repeated references seem to proleptically foreshadow Cecilia's episode of madness in the last volume, during which the state of impotence and isolation she has increasingly been reduced to reaches a dramatic climax. *Romeo and Juliet* also seems worth noting, because its tale of doomed love departs from the typical subject of classical tragedy (where the hero's undoing has political and social

FIGURE 19. Dramatic references in *Cecilia*

Genre (total references)	Vol. 1	Vol. 2	Vol. 3	Vol. 4	Vol. 5
Tragedies (11)	Shakespeare, *Hamlet* (1600)	Mason, *Elfrida* (1752)	Shakespeare, *Hamlet* (1600)	Shakespeare, *Hamlet* (1600)	Shakespeare, *Hamlet* (1600)
	Shakespeare, *King Lear* (1605)	Shakespeare, *Hamlet* (1600)	Kyd, *The Spanish Tragedy* (ca. 1580s)		Otway, *Venice Preserv'd* (1682)
			Shakespeare, *Macbeth* (1606)		
			Shakespeare, *Romeo and Juliet* (1594)		
Histories (2)	Shakespeare, 1 *Henry IV* (1597)				
	Shakespeare, 2 *Henry IV* (1597)				

Comedies (8)	Shakespeare, *The Merchant of Venice* (1596)	Vanbrugh and Cibber, *The Provok'd Husband* (1728)	Colman (the Elder), *The Man of Business* (1774)	Cibber, *The Lady's Last Stake* (1707)
			Centlivre, *A Bold Stroke for a Wife* (1718)	Shakespeare, *The Merchant of Venice* (1596) (twice)
				Shakespeare, *As You Like It* (ca. 1599, published 1623)
Operas and Afterpieces (3)	Metastasio, *Artaserse* (1730)	Smart, *An Epilogue Spoken by Mrs. Midnight's Daughter* (1753)	Addison, *Rosamond: An Opera* (1707)	

consequences) to take up the middling subject matter typical of the novel or of Rowe's domestic tragedies.

A particularly appropriate reference is that to Thomas Otway's *Venice Preserv'd* (1682), also in the last volume of the novel. Laura Brown has noted that the emergence of Restoration she-tragedy is particularly significant because these tragedies "portray a new kind of heroine, whose victimization provides the essential material of the plot."[49] Burney's reference to Otway in the final, crucial volume of her novel therefore signals her conscious choice to situate Cecilia's madness in relation to a genre that had attained canonical status. Furthermore, she-tragedy can be said to bridge the gap between heroic drama and the new bourgeois tragedy of George Lillo and Aaron Hill, something that *Cecilia* is also doing in the field of fiction. The novel thus seems linked both to the drama of the late seventeenth century (particularly in regard to its heroic opposition of honor versus love) and to contemporary plays featuring the commercial middle classes, whether in Georgian comedies (as the references to *The Conscious Lovers* and *The Clandestine Marriage* indicate) or in domestic tragedies.

Where comedy is concerned, Burney's reference to Cibber's *The Lady's Last Stake* (1707) has a direct thematic connection with the novel. The growing popularity of gambling in the seventeenth century and eighteenth century led to a subgenre of plays inspired directly by the movement for the reformation of manners, which had become very influential since the end of the seventeenth century. Cibber's play, like Edward Moore's *The Gamester* (1753) and the sentimental *The Note of Hand* (1774) by Richard Cumberland, provide a subtext for Burney's depiction of Harrel's compulsive gambling.[50] But the influence of contemporary comedy on Burney's novel is even more striking in the case of Centlivre's *A Bold Stroke for a Wife.* Although its intertextual relation with the novel (as the title of a chapter) is implicit, its plot bears a close relation with that of Cecilia. Centlivre's heroine, Anne Lovely, can marry Fainwell only if she gains the consent of all four of her guardians, each of whom is dominated by a particular passion (avarice, impertinence, hypocrisy, and pride). The similarity with *Cecilia,* in which Mr. Monckton can be considered a fourth, and distinctly self-interested, guardian is obvious.

Perhaps the strongest implicit intertextual link to a contemporary play, however, is to Sheridan's *The School for Scandal* (1777). Although it is never referred to explicitly in the novel, Burney certainly knew the comedy and briefly mentions it in a letter to her sister Susanna.[51] Her friendship with the playwright and his active encouragement at the time she was writing *The Witlings* make it very likely that Burney should have been influenced by the most successful comedy (together with Goldsmith's *She Stoops to Conquer*) of the decade leading up to *Cecilia*'s publication.

In Sheridan's comedy, the wealthy and elderly Sir Peter Teazle has married a young country girl who moves to London with him. In London, she transforms into a coquettish, pert lady of fashion, fond of amusement and, to all appearances, quite heartless. The play is clearly based on Wycherley's *The Country Wife,* picking up both its country–city opposition and the theme of the betrayal of a husband, although here the plot is foiled and turned against its architect. In explaining his marriage choice, Sir Peter states: "I chose with caution—a Girl bred wholly in the country, who never knew Luxury beyond one silk gown, nor Dissipation above the annual Gala of a Race Ball—yet now she plays her Part in all the extravagant Fopperies of the Fashion and the Town, with as ready a Grace as if she had never seen a Bush or a grass plot out of Grosvenor Square!" (*The School for Scandal,* 1.2.8–12). Burney's characterization of Priscilla Harrel seems particularly indebted to Sheridan's Lady Teazle. Both women are brought up in the country and adapt with extraordinary rapidity to London's giddy pleasures and love of consumption, attending all of the fashionable gatherings and enjoying the leisured pastimes of the upper classes.[52] Lady Teazle's reaction to her husband's complaints about her dissipation is indicative of the extent to which she has adopted the logic governing the social rituals of the fashionable world:

> *Lady Teazle.* My extravagance! I'm sure I'm not more extravagant than a woman of Fashion ought to be.
>
> *Lord Teazle.* No, no, madam, you shall throw away no more sums on such unmeaning Luxury. 'Slife! to spend as much to furnish your Dressing Room with Flow'rs in Winter, as would suffice to turn the Pantheon into a Green-house and give a Fête-Champêtre at Christmas. (*The School for Scandal,* 2.1.15–20)

Cecilia's remarks to Mrs. Harrel sound a similar note. Alarmed at the Harrels' excessive expenditures, she expresses her concern about their impending ruin:

> [Cecilia] began with hoping that the friendship in which they had so long lived would make her pardon the liberty she was going to take,

> and which nothing less than their former intimacy, joined to strong apprehensions for her future welfare, could authorise; "But oh Priscilla!" she continued, "with open eyes to see your danger, yet not warn you of it, would be a reserve treacherous in a friend, and cruel even in a fellow-creature."
>
> "What danger?" cried Mrs. Harrel, much alarmed, "do you think me ill? do I look consumptive?"
>
> "Yes, you are consumptive indeed!" said Cecilia, "but not, I hope, in your constitution."
>
> And then, with all the tenderness in her power, she came to the point, and conjured her without delay to retrench her expenses, and change her thoughtless way of life for one more considerate and domestic.
>
> Mrs. Harrel, with much simplicity, assured her *she did nothing but what every body else did,* and that it was quite impossible for her to *appear in the world* in any other manner. (*Cecilia,* 192–93)

Aside from addressing an issue of contemporary social relevance,[53] this passage's play on the word "consumption" again invokes the relation between appearances and reality that underlies the novel's structure. The double meaning of "consumption" is fully exploited in the passage. Mrs. Harrel mistakes Cecilia's concern as being about the state of her physical health rather than her financial (and, hence, moral) welfare, and she furthermore considers the question of her health purely in relation to her appearance ("do I *look* consumptive?"), revealing the superficiality of her attitude.

Mr. Harrel's character, similarly, seems to be partly drawn from that of the dissolute Charles Surface in *The School for Scandal,* whose addiction to gambling forces him to resort to moneylenders. Charles first appears onstage in the midst of an evening of revelry with his friends. Having sold his collection of family portraits to a rich moneylender (actually his own uncle, who dons the disguise to learn the true characters of his two nephews), Charles is scolded by his gambling companion Careless, who tells him that it is foolish to "squander . . . money on old Musty debts or any such Nonsense; for tradesmen, Charles, are the most Exorbitant Fellows" (*The School for Scandal,* 4.1.136–37). After sending some of the money to a poor relative, Charles follows Careless's advice and joins his friends at the gaming table, saying, "While I have, by Heaven, I'll give; so Damn your economy and now for hazard" (*The School for Scandal,* 4.1.169–72).

Harrel is a far less likeable character than Surface, but his situation is very similar. He is overwhelmed by gambling debts and harassed by the tradesmen he employs to make constant improvements to his home. The ostentation and love of opulence that lead to Harrel's ruin are made possible by an increasing temporal separation between the act of purchasing goods and the act of paying for them, a process of catastrophic deferral that *Cecilia* takes to its logical, melodramatic conclusion: Harrel's suicide at Vauxhall. Sheridan's comedy instead offers a more lighthearted version of this predicament, turning the looming threat of financial ruin on its head through ridicule and witty gossip:

> *Sir Benjamin.* . . . for my Part, I never believed [Charles] to be so utterly devoid of Principle as People say; and tho' he has lost all his Friends, I am told no-body is better spoken of by the Jews.
>
> *Crabtree.* That's true, egad, nephew. If the old Jewry was a ward, I believe Charles would be an alderman. . . .
>
> *Sir Benjamin.* Yet no man lives in greater Splendour: they tell me, when He entertains his friends he will sit down to dinner with a dozen of his own Securities; have a score Tradesmen waiting in the Ante-Chamber, and an Officer behind every Guest's Chair. (*The School for Scandal,* 1.1.307–18)

As the surname of Charles and Joseph Surface indicates, Sheridan's world is dominated by deceptive appearances. But the play ends with a happy reversal, or *peripeteia,* that shows how appearances can be deceiving in a positive sense, as well. Sir Oliver forgives Charles, who has reformed his ways and has turned out to be a better man than his reputation suggested. In *Cecilia,* instead, the bad advice and Machiavellian plots of "smooth-tongued hypocryte[s]" (*The School for Scandal,* 4.3.424) exert a greater influence on the lives of the characters. Falsehood is a fundamental textual hypogram in Burney's novel, a pervasive, structural signifying core. As we shall see, fabrications of all kinds abound in *Cecilia.* The fictitious is not only an aspect of social behavior; it also carries over into the realms of aesthetics and architecture (optical illusions, trompe l'oeil, fake ruins) and, ultimately, morality. Charles Surface's brother Joseph would fit very well in *Cecilia*'s world, as would Lady Sneerwell, who chides the hypocrite Joseph for almost forgetting that the social self he is accustomed to performing is not his real self: "O lud! you are going to be moral, and forget that you are among friends" (*The School for Scandal,* 1.1.104–105).

> In a Novel, a combination of incidents, entertaining in themselves, are made to form a whole; and an unnecessary circumstance becomes a blemish, by detaching from the simplicity which is requisite to exhibit that whole to advantage. Thus, as in dramatic works, those circumstances which do not tend, either to the illustration or the forwarding of the main story, or, which do not mark some character, or person in the drama, are to be esteemed unnecessary. Hence it appears that the legitimate Novel is a work much more difficult than the Romance, and justly deserves to be ranked with those dramatic pieces whose utility is generally allowed.
>
> —Thomas Holcroft, preface to *Alwyn; or, The Gentleman Comedian* (1780)

A few days before Harrel's suicide, Cecilia attempts to convey the extent of her moral confusion to Priscilla Harrel, finally giving vent to the doubts that have been tormenting her. Beset by the ever more pressing financial demands made on her by the Harrels, she has found herself forced to act against her judgment: "'Oh rise, Mrs. Harrel,' cried Cecilia, ashamed of her prostration . . . 'it is painful to me to refuse, but to comply for ever in defiance of my judgment—Oh Mrs. Harrel, I know no longer what is kind or what is cruel, nor have I known for some time past right from wrong, nor good from evil!'" (*Cecilia,* 396). Burney places this speech at the very center of the novel—in volume 3, book 5, chapter 11—and it epitomizes the structural inversion I have identified as the novel's governing textual isotopy. The inability to distinguish right from wrong in moral, social, and human terms is directly linked to the more general mechanism of social inversion operating in a society dominated by pervasive spectacularity. As the novel gradually broadens its frame of reference, both the private and the public components of this mechanism become apparent and can be analyzed in relation to domesticity, aesthetics, and the spectacular itself.

DOMESTIC INVERSION

A topological analysis of the novel allows us to trace the progress of Cecilia's domestic history in relation to inversion. Forced by the Dean's will to reside with one of her three guardians until she reaches her majority, Cecilia begins to search for a home that will give her the protection—and affection—she has lost by the death of her closest relatives. Her journey takes her from the country to the city, and from one residence to another, in a search that becomes increasingly frantic and that concludes with her headlong rush through the streets of London.

At each stage of this process, Cecilia learns that instead of granting her independence, her great wealth paradoxically subjects her to the socio-economic pressures exerted by a society dominated by materialism and consumption. Unable to act freely because of her guardians' control over her actions (and given the devious influence he exerts over her, the scheming Mr. Monckton should be considered a fourth guardian), she is also progressively deprived of the comfort of long-standing affective ties and of the secure refuge of a home. Indeed, the home quickly turns into a site of coercion and imprisonment. In the somber world of the novel, where all things are subject to inversion, the affections and friendship prized by eighteenth-century cultural theorists are replaced by the passion for money typical of an aggressively capitalist society.[54] Instead of finding asylum at a domestic fireside, Cecilia finds herself locked in a prison, a reversal that anticipates the function of the menacing castles and secret dungeons of Gothic literature and drama.

The term "asylum" can in fact serve as a crucial hermeneutic key to the world depicted in *Cecilia.* Burney constructs her critique of society through Cecilia's quest for a home, and the double connotation of "asylum" as a place of refuge or protection, on one hand, and a place of confinement (for the insane and other social outcasts), on the other, captures very well the effects of the cultural and economic transformation undergone by the institution of the family in the second half of the eighteenth century.[55] Ironically, the rise of the middle class and the entrenchment of a model of capitalism that favored the moneyed interests and encouraged conspicuous consumption increased women's dependence on the protection provided by the family. In a society already experiencing the first signs of class conflict, the financial vulnerability of women—due to their ill-conceived education and a legal system that regarded wives as appendages of their husbands—was bound to translate into sexual vulnerability, as well. In the course of the eighteenth century, the forms of repression, regulation, and increasingly hierarchical organization affecting the family unit—and gender relations in general—went hand in hand with a shift in values that reconfigured as economic and financial transactions what had hitherto been considered the moral and ethical qualities of the individual. The language of family relationships was itself affected by the rise in consumption and the burgeoning market economy: a woman's relationship with her family was expressed through verbs such as "to own" and "to belong," revealing how the epistemic transformations of the period were slanted toward reification, possession, and exchange.[56]

Cecilia's story begins with a departure that upsets an equilibrium: the death of the Dean forces her to move to London, where she chooses to stay with the Harrels because her early friendship with Priscilla Harrel leads her to expect that she will find a new family unit that can satisfy her affectively. Instead, she discovers that her childhood friend is married to a spendthrift and has herself become hardened by her new life. Very soon, Mrs. Harrel's friendship is revealed to be a hollow pretext for exploitation. The Harrels' extravagance turns Cecilia into a hostage, to be used, or exchanged, to repay Harrel's gambling debts. She becomes his last resort for obtaining financial credit once he has completely ruined his reputation at the gaming table and exhausted his moral credit. Cecilia's presence in the company of the Harrels is enough, at first, to achieve this end:

> "But if we do not *all* go," said Mr. Harrel, "we do almost nothing: you are known to live with us, and your appearance at this critical time is important to our credit. If this misfortune gets wind, the consequence is that every dirty tradesman in town to whom I owe a shilling, will be forming the same cursed combination those scoundrels formed this morning, of coming in a body, and waiting for their money, or else bringing an execution into my house. The only way to silence the report is by putting a good face upon the matter at once, and showing ourselves to the world as if nothing had happened." (*Cecilia,* 273)

Only the superficial, artificial appearance of domestic harmony (the equivalent of a moral masquerade, or a trompe l'oeil of financial solvency) can save Harrel's reputation and his credit.

Harrel's recklessness causes Cecilia such serious financial problems that she reluctantly seeks shelter with her other two guardians, first Briggs, the "cit" whose miserliness makes his house an unacceptable parody of a home—in fact, its domestic and affective reductio ad absurdum[57]—and then Compton Delvile, whose aristocratic pride makes him recoil from assisting his bourgeois ward. The fact that Harrel, Briggs, and Delvile are all equally incapable of taking care of Cecilia makes them morally and functionally interchangeable, specular images of each other. Although they appear to embody different vices (extravagance, avarice, pride), they all share a quality of excess and the same actantial function, wielding their power to hinder Cecilia's progress.[58]

The interchangeable quality of Cecilia's guardians is expressed materially through their homes, which can be said to occupy interchangeable positions on the paradigmatic axis of domestic spaces in the novel. The Harrels' lavish home, which turns out to be a gilded prison, is replaced by its specular opposite, Briggs's claustrophobic and dingy dwelling: "He then led her upstairs, and took her to a room entirely dark, and so close for want of air that she could hardly breathe in it. She retreated to the landing-place till he had opened the shutters, and then saw an apartment the most forlorn she had ever beheld, containing no other furniture than the rugged stuff bed, two worn-out rush-bottomed chairs, an old wooden box, and a bit of a broken glass which was fastened to the wall by two bent nails" (*Cecilia,* 372). Briggs's miserliness and his crude materialism are expressed in the squalid room he has selected for Cecilia, but the room's function is the same as that of the Harrels' luxurious house, standing in for any place of confinement designed to curb women's independence.

Briggs's metaphorical prison foreshadows the real fortified structure of the Delviles' decaying castle, an austere building accessed by a drawbridge, making it worthy of use as "a gaol for the county" (*Cecilia,* 505). The Delviles' feudal splendor has been eclipsed not only by the financial reversals of previous generations but especially by the inexorable forces of time and history. The isolated, crenellated ramparts are genuine, but the anachronistic bulwark they enclose resembles nothing more than one of those pasteboard castles used as stage sets, a "gothic ugly old place," impressive and unreal, as though "paint[ed] for an opera scene" (*Cecilia,* 506–7).[59]

In the final volume of the novel, Cecilia is finally able to move into a home of her own. Her newfound domestic stability reflects the much anticipated resolution of her sentimental woes after her marriage to Delvile. But it does not last. No sooner is she settled than another upheaval forces her to leave when the Eggleston family claims possession of the home she has forfeited—together with the Dean's inheritance—by marrying Delvile.[60] Cecilia goes to London, where she plans to join Delvile, but the constant emotional strain and the psychological and social violence she has experienced lead to a mental breakdown that soon turns into outright insanity. Her final refuge is a miserable pawnshop where her delirious state so alarms the owners, who fear she might die before they can obtain a reward, that they decide to post a notice in the *Daily Advertiser,* a widely circulated daily listing notices of all kinds.[61]

According to Donna Andrew, the nature of many of the advertisements placed in eighteenth-century periodical literature remains fairly obscure. "Especially under-studied are those which communicated information," such as "advertisements which sought marriage partners, which begged for charitable assistance, or which enquired about lost pets and stolen animals."[62] The implicit intertextual positioning of the advertisement about Cecilia does, however, allow us to reconstruct the subtext that must have been obvious to contemporary readers. The advertisement placed by Mr. Wyers concludes: "Whoever she belongs to is desired to send after her immediately" (*Cecilia,* 901). Wyers, Cecilia's last temporary guardian, is a pawnbroker; his pragmatic notice strips Cecilia of all residual human attributes and reveals her for what she has been all along: an article on the London market. An impersonal extension of the language of economics, devoid of all deceptive, and now useless, affective connotations, Wyers's advertisement can be read as the ultimate and most explicit expression of the reification Cecilia has been subjected to throughout the novel.

AESTHETIC INVERSION

In one of Samuel Crisp's letters to Burney in which he described his reactions to the novel, we find the first comment on what we might call the spectacular, ostensive quality of the chapter 13 (in book 5 of volume 3), later given the ironic title "A Solution." It is worth looking closely at this episode because it illustrates the social aspect of the mechanism of inversion that undergirds the novel's emphasis on the spectacular. The chapter is in the middle of the novel and is set in Vauxhall Gardens, where Mr. Harrel, having once again lost an exorbitant sum during a final night at the gaming table, decides to put an end to his life. Crisp writes:

> I think nothing struck me more forcibly than the Foxhall scene; it is finely—it is powerfully imagined; it is a noble piece of mortality! the variety—the contrast of the different characters quite new and unhackneyed, and yet perfectly in nature; and the dreadful catastrophe that concludes the whole make it a masterpiece. What a subject for that astonishing lad, Edward, to make a finished drawing, and Bartolozzi a print of! The scene of the Foxhall illuminated—the mangled, bleeding body carried along—the throngs of spectators crowding after, filled with various expressions of horror, wonder, eager curiosity, and inquiry; and many other particulars, which the perusal of the passage itself, and his genius, would suggest. (*DL,* 2:69–70)[63]

Structurally, the episode's position at the center of the novel serves to highlight its importance, as does its relationship to the narrative as a whole. Harrel's suicide marks the conclusion of the first section of the novel set in

London; it also spells the definitive loss of Cecilia's inheritance from her father, and thus prevents her from accepting Delvile's first offer of marriage. Thematically, it epitomizes the isotopy of inversion, particularly in relation to the artificial and the spectacular.

Located on the south bank of the Thames, Vauxhall's relatively low admission fee (1 shilling) made it attractive to a broad cross-section of London's population. Richard Altick notes that "the gardens throughout most of the century attracted a clientele notable—indeed, virtually unique in its time—for its democratic spread. Nobility, sometimes even royalty, mingled in perfect amity with commoners, eventually including those as low in the social scale as servants and ordinary soldiers."[64] Like other public gathering places such as the theaters and Ranelagh Gardens, Vauxhall was a microcosm of London's society at the end of the eighteenth century.[65] The condensed, miniaturized version of society found in the gardens was made possible by its design, as Altick explains:

> Open from 5 PM onward during the Summer months, Vauxhall offered a diversity of delights: straight unbroken lines of trees and gravel paths to invite the stroller, triumphal arches, semicircular colonnades and domed pavilions, artificial ruins, statuary, open-air tea shops and restaurants, platforms for *concerts d'été,* and thousands of lamps and lanterns, which after nightfall transformed the grounds. . . . No other London showplace accommodated as many activities—promenading, flirting, dining, drinking, listening to music, admiring vistas, pictures, and statuary—and no other one figures as often in literary record, from Smollett, Goldsmith, and Fanny Burney all the way to Thackeray.[66]

Hydraulic engineering, artificial lighting effects, tricks of perspective, and topiary art transformed the gardens into an artistic spectacle that embodied the contemporary taste for stage effects, optical illusions, and artifice, all according to the rules of what we might call "natural stagecraft." Carefully tended plants, avenues, squares, theaters, halls, arches, pillars, niches, galleries: Vauxhall's relationship with London was dialectical, its plasticity replicating and extending the city architecturally. Nature in the gardens was modified, designed, constructed, and corrected to emphasize the triumph of the fictitious. Among the most famous stage effects in the gardens were the trompe l'oeil paintings by Francis Hayman, a renowned scene painter and illustrator who had relied on David Garrick's advice for his Shakespeare frescoes in the Prince of Wales Pavilion. The paintings helped turn the space into an approximation of a stage set where visitors could feel like performers in a fashionable play. The aesthetic fictitiousness of the gardens thus seems to mirror the fictitiousness and artifice that dominated London society.[67] Every evening, at suppertime, thousands of oil lamps were lighted simultaneously at the sound of a whistle, turning the gardens into a triumphal display of special effects and making them a favorite source of nighttime entertainment for Londoners.

A number of attractions in the gardens were designed to take the taste for artifice and illusion to new, astounding heights. The most famous was the artificial cascade visible at the end of the long perspective formed by one of the main avenues. Every evening at nine o'clock, a bell would announce the start of the spectacle, the mechanism was set in motion, and the waterfall would appear to start flowing. In reality, "The illusion of falling water was evidently produced by strips of tin shimmering in the light of concealed lamps."[68] The excitement and anticipation elicited by the cascade's nightly performance is described in Evelina in terms that foreshadow the dramatic Vauxhall episode in *Cecilia:* "As we were walking about the orchestra, I heard the bell ring, and, in a moment, Mr. Smith, flying up to me, caught my hand. . . . At last, however, I insisted about stopping; 'Stopping, Ma'am!' cried he, 'why, we must run, or we shall lose the cascade!' And then again, he hurried me away, mixing with a crowd of people, all running with so much velocity, that I could not imagine what had raised such an alarm" (*Evelina,* 217).

At the center of the gardens was the orchestra, surrounded by about fifty supper boxes where Londoners could dine among their friends. All around them were the trees and luxuriant vegetation of the "Grove," as the central area was called. The term "grove" appears frequently in Burney's work. In *Evelina,* Lady Howard's country home is called Howard Grove, and the Grove is the name of Mr. Monckton's home in Sussex. In the economy of the pleasure garden, the toponym "grove" suggests a counterfeit countryside, as befits the artificial ideology of the *rus in urbe,* or country in the city, typical of Georgian garden squares.[69] It thus seems to encapsulate the art of illusion dominating Vauxhall, which was not only designed entirely in accordance with human taste but was also so transformed by the activities that took place in it as to become a sort of interactive social stage as well as a reductio ad absurdum of London life. The constructed artifice of Vauxhall Gardens would thus appear to be an inverted version of the "green world" of the pastoral, or of comedy's country idyll.[70]

Burney had already employed Vauxhall for an episode in *Evelina*—in letter 15 of volume 2— where the heroine accompanies Madame Duval and the Branghtons to the gardens. While she is looking for Molly and Polly Branghton in one of the "dark walks" leading off the main avenue (*Evelina,* 218), Evelina is mistaken for a prostitute by a group of young swells who unceremoniously grab her by the arm. Sir Clement Willoughby arrives just in time to rescue her, but he, too, seems so influenced by her isolated situation in the shadowy walk as to forget himself and behave with some impudence. When they rejoin her group, Evelina is forced to undergo the humiliation of introducing the baronet to her ill-bred companions. Having first met her in the company of the elegant Mrs. Mirvan, Willoughby now sees her in a context of social vulnerability: not only has she just been mistaken for a prostitute, but her family connections turn out to be far from genteel. The change in her contextual relations triggers a mechanism of comic inversion as Sir Willoughby's attitude toward her shifts: "[Willoughby] seems disposed to think that the alteration in my companions authorizes an alteration in his manners. It is true, he has always treated me with uncommon freedom, but never before with so disrespectful an abruptness. This observation, which he has given me cause to make, of his *changing with the tide,* has sunk him more in my opinion, than any other part of his conduct" (*Evelina,* 225). As on previous occasions, Evelina's social context causes her embarrassment, and in spite of the comic treatment, we can already see the (female) body being mistaken for an object of sexual commerce—a point that in *Cecilia* broadens into an analysis of the process of social reification.

Having arranged to leave for the continent to escape his creditors, Mr. Harrel asks his wife and Cecilia to accompany him to Vauxhall for a final evening of entertainment. Cecilia is immediately struck by the inappropriateness of staging such a light-hearted "parting scene" (*Cecilia,* 398), given the gravity of the Harrels' situation. She is against going and is convinced that her guardian intends to put on an illusory performance, an antiphrastic masquerade of happiness. Indeed, at Vauxhall Harrel dons "the mask of levity" (*Cecilia,* 399) and settles into one of the supper boxes, much as an actor would enter the stage, ordering a lavish meal to which he invites, among others, the two creditors he has just met by chance in the gardens and Sir Robert Floyer, also met by chance. Instead of being sobered by his impending departure (and by the prospect of a permanent separation from his wife, who has chosen to remain in England), Harrel is in euphoric high spirits. As one toast succeeds another, he creates a spectacular self-representation, displaying an alarming lack of concern about his personal tragedy: "Mr. Harrel then began to sing, and in so noisy and riotous a manner, that nobody approached the box without stopping to *stare* at him; and those who were new to such *scenes,* not contented with merely *looking in,* stationed themselves at some distance before it, *to observe* what was passing, and *to contemplate* with envy and admiration *an appearance* of mirth and enjoyment which they attributed to happiness and pleasure!" (*Cecilia,* 412; emphasis added).

At the height of this artfully staged euphoria, Harrel suddenly embraces his wife and then rushes off before anyone can stop him. Soon after, the report of a pistol is heard, followed by frenzied calls for help. Immediately realizing what must have happened, Cecilia joins the crowd running to the spot and discovers with horror that, instead of hurrying to the carriage bound for Dover, Mr. Harrel had rushed "off stage" to commit suicide. The narrator does not describe Harrel in the act of taking his own life and leaves it up to the imagination of the readers to reconstruct the event, in keeping with the norms of classical tragedy, where violence was never represented on-stage.[71] The narrator instead describes the reactions of the characters at the scene: "And then, eager to see [her orders] executed herself, [Cecilia] ran, fearless of being alone, and without thought of being lost, towards the fatal spot whither the crowd guided her. She could not, indeed, have been more secure from insult and molestation if surrounded by twenty guards; for the scene of desperation and horror which many had witnessed, *and of which all had heard the signal,* engrossed the universal attention, and took, even from the most idle and licentious, all spirit for gallantry and amusement" (*Cecilia,* 415; emphasis added). The onlookers' morbid curiosity makes them forget everything but the appalling spectacle, a "special effect" that, much like the cascade, had been announced by a startling sound signal.

At the center of the gathered onlookers, Cecilia is shocked to see the lifeless body of her guardian, who had been assisted in his last moments by a stranger and a waiter. "'A waiter!' cried Cecilia, reproachfully looking at Sir Robert, 'and was there no friend who for the few poor moments that remained had patience to support him!'" (*Cecilia,* 417). In the artificial world of Vauxhall, the corpse of Mr. Harrel appears to be a final, grotesque example of those mechanical marvels and automata that astounded Londoners daily. Now the visitors have come to gape at yet another astonishing spectacle, this time announced not by a whistle or a bell but by a single, dramatic gun shot.

SPECTACULAR INVERSION

Chapter 3 of book 2, titled "A Masquerade," describes the masked ball held by the Harrels at their Portman Square home; it provides the best illustration of what I have been calling the pervasive spectacularity that dominates

Cecilia's social world. The masquerade marks an important stage in Cecilia's education in London in the first section of the novel (books 1–5), and like the other urban amusements Burney describes, it relates to the city both on a thematic and on a structural level. Thematically, the anti-hierarchical and liberatory mingling of the masquerade participants allows Burney to comment on the changes affecting English society at this time. Structurally, the deployment of disguises and performances at the masquerade clarifies how artifice and fictitiousness construct the spectacular in accordance with the novel's underlying isotopy of inversion.

The vogue for masquerades reached England in the early eighteenth century, when aristocratic travelers returning from the Grand Tour brought back with them their newly acquired taste for the luxurious masked fêtes they had enjoyed in the capitals of Europe.[72] In England's flourishing capitalist society of the first two decades of the century, masquerades became an extremely popular form of commercial public entertainment, quickly associated with sexual and social promiscuity and morbid excitement. Participants needed to be masked to be admitted, a condition that allowed for a degree of freedom unavailable at other kinds of social gatherings. High-ranking women mixed with ordinary prostitutes, and aristocrats and the wealthy mixed with the poor, in an irreverent overturning of all distinctions of rank and gender. Their anonymity protected by enveloping dominoes, their faces concealed by vizards, participants could mingle, accost each other, even engage in sexual activity with complete freedom and in secret. Like all those whose sexuality was heavily repressed or regulated by the strict social and gender codes of the eighteenth century, women could act and express themselves untrammeled by the usual constraints, and custom dictated that they not be escorted by a male chaperon. As an institutionalized form of disorder, carnival, and inversion, the masquerade "served both as a voluptuous release from ordinary cultural prescriptions and as a stylized comment on them."[73] Masks and costumes allowed women (and any other gendered-constrained individual) to adopt a different public persona, engaging in an act of self-reappropriation within an alternative reality that Terry Castle has called "a theatre of female power."[74]

The erotic *frisson* of such entertainments was enhanced by the fantastic costumes, often inspired by historical, mythological, or folkloric characters. The variety of masks Cecilia sees at the Harrels' is representative of the wide range and originality of costumes at any masquerade: "Dominos of no character, and fancy-dresses of no meaning, made, as usual at such meetings, the general herd of the company: for the rest, the men were Spaniards, chimney-sweepers, Turks, watchmen, conjurers and old women; and the ladies, shepherdesses, orange girls, Circassians, gipseys, haymakers, and sultanas" (*Cecilia,* 106–107).[75] The narrator does not need to mention that it was common to speak and act in character, a custom that made for a significant degree of continuity between social actor and masked actor. This continuity was achieved through language, gestures, and expressions and would even extend to moral attitudes, making the disguise an ideal platform for the display of repressed fantasies.[76]

The masquerade's domestic setting is worth noting, since the Harrels' entertainment involves a perverse spectacularization of domestic privacy that makes it worthy of the epithet "the Temple of Luxury, the Theatre of Madness, the Habitation of Folly," used at the time to stigmatize the public venues where commercial masquerades were held.[77] Already firmly established as a narrative topos in eighteenth-century literature,[78] the masquerade in *Cecilia* therefore functions as a moral trope, revealing the fictitiousness, deception, and artifice of the London world Burney describes. Rather than being merely another example of the amusements the capital has to offer, it resonates metatextually throughout the novel, bringing to the surface elements that remain covert or undeveloped elsewhere. On the level of the plot, it marks a turning point, since the expenses incurred by the Harrels for this display of lavish ostentation significantly worsen their financial situation. Only a few days later, Harrel will ask Cecilia for a loan, the first in an escalating series of demands that will exhaust her inheritance—and ultimately drive him to suicide. The masquerade thus sets up a fundamental inversion of genre in the novel between the brilliant comedy of manners of the first section and the darker, dramatic tones of the subsequent books.

The characters at the masquerade include not only Miss Larolles, Mr. Gosport, or Mr. Morrice—who, as we have seen, pertain to the novel's comedy of manners—but also those characters who have a more strictly causal relationship to Cecilia's story, such as Mr. Monckton and Mortimer Delvile. Figure 20 lists the most important characters at the masquerade, together with their disguises. Cecilia is the only character who does not wear a costume, a choice that paradoxically makes her the center of attention: "Before nine, there were so many masks that Cecilia wished she had herself made one of the number, as she was far more conspicuous in being almost the only female in a common dress, than any masquerade habit could have made her" (*Cecilia,* 106). She is therefore an easy target for the devil, Mr. Monckton, who quickly stations himself beside her, blocking her movements with increasing determination: "When the room was filled, and the general

FIGURE 20. Characters' masquerade costumes in *Cecilia*

Character	Costume
Mr. Monckton	Devil
Mr. Belfield	Don Quixote
Mr. Morrice	Harlequin
Mortimer Delvile	White Domino
Mr. Briggs	Chimneysweep
Mr. Gosport	Schoolmaster
Sir Robert Floyer	Turk
[Miss Larolles	Minerva]

crowd gave general courage, she was attacked in a manner more pointed and singular" (*Cecilia,* 107). Just like the "homespun gown" and "plain muslin tucker" Pamela dons to present herself to Mr. B,[79] or the French milliner disguise that turns Juliet into a seductive object of male voyeurism in *The Wanderer,* Cecilia's dress ultimately functions as a captivating costume, evoking innocence and artlessness and forcing her into an unwilling "masquerade of femininity."[80]

As shown in figure 20, the costumes reveal the true nature of the characters who attend the masquerade. Their performance "in character" creates a double of their ordinary social behavior, stylized and de-familiarized in such a way as to cast a fresh light on them and provide the reader with a new moral perspective. The only exception to this rule is the frivolous socialite, Miss Larolles (hence the brackets in the table). Her antiphrastic disguise as Minerva, the Roman goddess of wisdom, reflects another widespread custom: that of impersonating a character whose qualities are the opposite of one's own.

Mr. Morrice, whose constant acrobatic feats and boundless physicality associate him with pantomime, is dressed as Harlequin, and his restlessness is put to good use as he wields his wooden sword in an attempt to protect Cecilia from the devil's bullying. His well-intentioned swordplay ends in farce, of course: "The consequence was such as might naturally be expected; he could not accomplish his purpose, but, finding himself falling, imprudently caught hold of the lately erected Awning, and pulled it entirely upon his own head, and with it the new contrived lights, which in various forms were fixed to it, and which all came down together" (*Cecilia,* 124).

Assisting Morrice in his defense of Cecilia is Delvile, who from the outset is designated as her protector against Monckton's threatening behavior. Doody interprets Delvile's white domino as signifying his desire "to remain innocent, uncommitted, incontaminated,"[81] particularly in regard to the difficult choice between his love for Cecilia and his respect of his father's will. As Doody's point suggests, Delvile is an atypical hero. His jealousy, his moral dilemma, and the psychological pressure he places on Cecilia to agree to a secret marriage to protect his relationship with his father all cast doubt on his attitude toward Cecilia, who will be driven to madness by his hesitations and uncertainty. His white cloak is an undecipherable costume that should therefore be read as an allegory of his divided nature: although he obviously loves Cecilia and wants to protect her, he proves incapable of doing so adequately.[82]

The analogy between character and costume applies to major and minor characters alike. In accordance with his role as *didascalus* (or director of the chorus in classical drama), who instructs Cecilia about the fashionable world, Gosport is disguised as a schoolmaster, while Floyer's dazzling Turk costume reflects not only the Orientalizing taste of the time, but also his great wealth and pride—the baronet, as Compton Delvile admiringly notes, "has a noble estate" (*Cecilia,* 157).[83]

Cecilia's guardian, Mr. Briggs, is dressed as a chimneysweep, a grotesque costume suited to his miserly and coarse character. He circulates among the astonished crowd dragging a shabby sack in which he jocosely threatens to put Cecilia. Having spotted her, closely confined by the devil, Briggs approaches, exclaiming: "'Ah ha . . . found at last;' then, throwing down the shovel, he opened the mouth of his bag, and pointing waggishly to her head, said 'Come, shall I pop you?—A good place for naughty girls; in, I say, poke in!—cram you up the chimney" (*Cecilia,* 117). Considered in light of the episode as a whole, this apparently humorous invitation is ominous. In the rhetorical economy of the masquerade, the participants "mask the face, t'unmask the mind."[84]

The Harrels' masquerade seems to suggest a grotesque and frightening allegory of Cecilia's situation—or, rather, a complex spectacular meta-representation of it. The ontological confusion produced by the disguises entails a doubling or overlapping of reality and fiction, breaking down the distinction between them. Victimized, blackmailed, and betrayed, her friendships and movements limited, Cecilia now finds herself surrounded by disturbing masked characters whose gestures and behavior ritually stage the psychological pressures and physical violence she experiences in reality. The themes of women's independence and men's protection, often stressed in the course of the novel, are here staged in a dreamlike "mummery"—as the narrator describes the devil's movements (*Cecilia,* 107)—in which the male protagonists contend for physical (and therefore psychological) control over Cecilia. Briggs's threatening sack therefore can be read as a ridiculous—but no less sinister—representation of the financial trap set by Harrel, while Monckton's imperious magic wand is a visual counterpart to the highly effective and highly interested advice with which he manipulates Cecilia. Cecilia herself remarks explicitly on the double significance of the men's behavior as soon as she has regained her freedom of movement and her status as a "free agent": "I was so tired of confinement, that my mind seemed almost as little at liberty as my person" (*Cecilia,* 100, 112).

The desire to manipulate, control, and limit Cecilia's actions is most apparent in Monckton's case. His devil's wand "obstruct[s] her passage" (*Cecilia,* 107); he wields it with such "ferocity" (*Cecilia,* 108) that no one can approach, making it impossible for her "[to] speak [and] to be spoken to" (*Cecilia,* 111). Monckton's patently phallic wand represents his sexual aggressiveness both metonymically and metaphorically, and the omniscient narrator explicitly informs the reader of the purpose of his "persecuting" attentions: "He had intended, in the character of a tormentor, not only to pursue and hover around her himself, but he had also hoped, in the same character, to have kept at a distance all other admirers" (*Cecilia,* 123). Monckton's aggressive mummery is a direct representation of his secret designs, and it hardly seems coincidental that when Cecilia discovers his scheming she should compare his behavior to that of a demon: "a design black, horrible, diabolical! a design which must be formed by a Daemon, but which even a Daemon could never, I think execute!" (*Cecilia,* 765).[85] The devil's wand is also significant from an intertextual standpoint, since magic wands were a standby of Georgian spectacular theater. Also known as a "bat," the wand was the instrument Harlequin employed to activate the wonderful set changes of pantomime, where the scene-changing machinery gave full scope, according to John O'Brien, to the morphic possibilities of the stage.[86] We can further note that in harlequinades based on the Faustus myth, it was Mephistopheles who gave Harlequin the magic wand with which he could bend the real world and human beings to his will.

According to O'Brien, the spectacular scene effects of the Georgian stage "mirror[ed] the transformation of the British theatre itself from a morally uplifting medium that understood language to be its most important component to a profit-hungry institution devoted to spectacle."[87] Where *Cecilia* is concerned, it seems possible to apply O'Brien's point not only to the London social scene—always concealed, as Henry Fielding put it, "under false Vizors and Habits"[88]—but also to the genre of the novel. Through a complex allegorical and ostensive mechanism, the Harrels' "meta-masquerade" reveals the epistemological fissures within Georgian society whereby artifice and deception can expose, amplified, the true nature of the characters in Burney's novel.

The paradoxical principle of inversion that underlies *Cecilia* therefore becomes fully explicit at the masquerade. The fantastic costumes that conceal the identities of those who wear them simultaneously bring to the surface their hidden moral qualities or defects and their secret desires. If, as Castle suggests, the masquerade embodies "a world of metamorphosis and fluidity" reflecting the phenomenological duplicity inherent in the protean social and civic transformations of the eighteenth century,[89] then the episode of the masquerade cannot be considered a mere digression in Cecilia's history but must be read as paradigmatic. In a novel dominated by the textual isotopies of artifice and disguise, this apparent digression performs a paradoxical fiction "degree zero."[90] It is perhaps the only place in the novel where imposture is licensed to display itself openly, claiming a role for itself, and in so doing it is neutralized and made transparent, innocent, and even truthful.

FIVE

Texts, Bodies, Performance

Staging Madness in *Cecilia* and *The Wanderer*

From earliest childhood [a woman] has been taught and persuaded to survey herself continually. And so she comes to consider the *surveyor* and the *surveyed* within her as the two constituent yet always distinct elements of her identity as a woman.

—John Berger, *Ways of Seeing* (1972)

In the best places, where straitjackets are abolished, doors are unlocked, leucotomies largely forgotten, these can be replaced by more subtle lobotomies and tranquillizers that place the bars of Bedlam and the locked doors *inside* the patient.

—R. D. Laing, *The Divided Self* (1960)

Although Frances Burney's journals, novels, and plays are chronologically distinct works written over many years, they share a number of recurring themes, among them that of a female protagonist who undergoes an experience of alienation that can broadly be termed an episode of "madness." The importance of such episodes in the novels *Cecilia* and *The Wanderer,* and their presence in Burney's letters and journals, as well as in her tragedies, suggests that an isotopy of madness runs through Burney's macro-text.

In this chapter, I examine the episodes of madness in *Cecilia* and *The Wanderer* through a semiotic analysis of their underlying dramatic structure. What emerges from my analysis is that these episodes function as nodes within the narrative, immediately preceding—and precipitating—the plot's resolution. To fully account for their narrative function, however, I have found it necessary to supplement close reading with dramatic analysis, treating these episodes as a sequence of scenes, or acts, in a play. I contend that the limit experiences they describe disrupt narrative norms. If, from an epistemic standpoint, such limit experiences involve instances of a repressed marginality erupting to the surface, and creating a fissure within eighteenth-century monological discourse, from a literary standpoint they can be associated with the strong anti-realist currents that emerged at the end of the century. Their effect, in Burney's novels, is to dissociate narrative text from its customary function as diegetic "narrated action," bringing it closer to the mimetic "spoken action" typical of the drama.[1]

Burney relied heavily on the theatrical conventions of her time in portraying her mad heroines. Their expressions, movements, mode of articulation, rhetoric—all appear indebted to the drama. As a result, in these novels the traditional narrative syntagm, or sequence, is reconceived as a macro-structure whose kinesic, proxemic, paralinguistic, and sartorial codes, among others, can be analyzed in relation to both of the representational modes Burney experimented with throughout her life.[2] We have already seen how Burney's contemporaries were quick to remark on the theatrical quality of a number of episodes in her novels—Richard Sheridan and Arthur Murphy were particularly struck by this in *Evelina* (see chapter 2). Although repressed in public, Burney's enduring interest in playwriting went hand in hand with the novel writing that brought her fame and seems to require a macro-textual analysis that can encompass both genres.

It is worth stressing that the eighteenth-century novel already harbored within it the "three-dimensionality" typical of the drama: the written, narrated text of eighteenth-century novels is always potentially a text that can be acted.[3] Marcello Pagnini rightly observes that "texts suitable for performance," or what he calls "performable texts," differ from "texts that are teleologically intended for reading, since for its full realization the reading experience requires particular gestures and spaces, quite distinct from the requirement—crucial to the theater—that the performance be a *socially . . . meaningful* event."[4] Because it was consumed communally, the eighteenth-century novel should therefore be considered a hybrid text. This is exemplified by the practice of reading aloud, which, as we have seen when looking at the Burney family's reading of *The Witlings,* is a para-theatrical experience that highlights the creative and participatory—one might even say *performative*—role played by the eighteenth-century reader. Furthermore, the novel's mode of reception was closely linked to its mode of production. Richardson's novels are an excellent example. Their production was inextricably tied to the communications network initiated, or maintained, by Richardson's correspondents, whose contributions as literary advisers was so extensive as to turn them into virtual coauthors of the novels.[5]

On the reception end, the eighteenth-century custom of reading novels aloud in the family circle shows how the communal consumption of novels fulfilled a "sociopetal" function, providing a moment of "social attraction" much like that offered by any other informal performance.[6] The pragmatic, rhetorical, and paralinguistic conventions for reading aloud were not far removed from those regulating theatrical communication, and the interaction between audience and actor, or among audience members, were likewise similar. The reader's intensity and emotional involvement had a direct impact on the family audience, who could represent what they were hearing in their own "theater of the mind," or through their mind's eye, in a process that activated (or "staged") the author-character-audience empathy latent in the text.

Susanna Burney's account of overhearing Dr. Burney reading *Evelina* to his wife, dated 5 July 1778, is illuminating in this context: "This morning between seven and eight I was woke by a noise in the next room—upon listening a minute or two I found it was my father and mother laughing in a most extraordinary manner—presently I heard by the voice of the former that he was reading . . . they were in the midst of the Ridotto scene—P. 64—and the eclats of Laughter that accompanied it—did my heart good" (*ED*, 2:238–39). Some days later, on 16 July, Susanna reports overhearing Dr. Burney reading a more sober passage from the novel and comments on her own reactions to his performance: "The conclusion of [Mr. Villars'] Letter, P. 130, lost nothing of its pathos *by the manner in which it was read.* The subsequent epistle of Lady Belmont's affected him very much—and me, by the *nervous, energetic manner* in which he read it, *much more than when I read it myself.* Indeed I have found this to be the case frequently in listening to my father, tho' it has been impossible for me to hear him always distinctly. *He stopt several times in the course of this letter—nor was his handkerchief useless*" (*ED*, 2:243; emphasis added). The reading in effect produces a second text whose reader merges with the figure of the narrator (and, by extension with that of the author, according to the self-authoring conventions of epistolary fiction). Susanna reports on the cathartic climax of the reading:

> But the Scene between her and her father . . . *you* would have cried had you heard him [Dr. Burney] read it, and stop as he did to cry himself—I declare I could scarce prevent myself from *making a noise*—his [Belmont's] being unable to open Lady Belmont's letter and agonies at reading it—his [Belmont's] sudden transitions from tenderness to fury and despair—his [Belmont's] returns again to Eve-

> lina, he [Dr. Burney] mark'd so well that no one could I am sure have heard him [Dr. Burney, and Belmont!] without tears—and his own [Dr. Burney's] flowed plentifully—When he had done he shut up the book for a while and said—" 'twas an *amazing scene*." (*ED*, 2:246)

Because of the merging of reader, narrator, and author functions in Susanna's account of Charles Burney's performance, her letter becomes enmeshed in a syntactical tangle, producing a "nice derangement of personal pronouns" all the more confused by being the effect of projection.[7]

Madness already featured prominently on the seventeenth-century stage. By the eighteenth century, the figure of the madman, and especially of the madwoman, had become a fixture both in the drama and in literature.[8] From the deranged heroines of she-tragedy and the "splenetic humour" of the Augustans to the excessive nervous sensibility of William Cowper's Crazy Jane or Henry Mackenzie's unnamed madwoman in *The Man of Feeling*, in poetry, in the theater, and in the visual arts, the madwoman had become a cultural icon. In discussing the simultaneously mimetic and reformative function of these figures, Kathryn Tucker notes how the aesthetic theories of the time dictated that "audiences should see themselves in the characters portrayed and learn from the characters' moral failings."[9] And, I would add, they should acquire a broader moral education by witnessing the characters' behavior to each other, allowing them to gain a new awareness, through their own cathartic experience of it, of the injustice and abuse—moral, legal, and social—to which the characters were often subjected.

Madwomen had appeared successfully on stage ever since the reopening of the theaters during the Restoration and had continued to be very popular in the Augustan period. The female protagonists of Thomas Otway, Thomas Southerne, and Nicholas Rowe (respectively, Belvidera in *Venice Preserv'd*, Isabella in *The Fatal Marriage*, and the eponymous heroine of *Jane Shore*) represent the archetypical passive heroine who is betrayed, ensnared by political plots, and generally prevented from taking action or expressing her own desire. She can escape her situation only through madness or death, and suicide is often her only option for asserting her independence. These victimized women constitute what I would call a paradigm of "passive, or contained, madness." But gradually another type of heroine emerged whose violence and lack of restraint represent the opposite of this paradigm of passivity; I would call it a paradigm of "vindictive, or uncontainable, madness."[10] Nicholas Rowe's tragedy *Jane Shore* is particularly interesting in this respect because it includes both types of women's insanity and pits one against the other. Jane Shore embodies the passive, contained paradigm of madness while her rival, Alicia, represents the vindictive, uncontrollable madwoman.

Having left her husband for love of Edward IV, Jane Shore finds herself in a vulnerable position after the king's death and the rise to power of Gloucester—the future Richard III and brother of the dead king. In act 5, exhausted by the physical and psychological suffering she has endured, she seeks refuge with her friend Alicia, who, however, considers her a rival for Hastings's affections and whose passion for him has already led her to the brink of insanity. Once the two women are under the same roof, the tension between them comes to a head in a famous "theatrical *tour de force*."[11] The audience has been informed of Jane's pitiable state even before she appears on stage, and Bellmour's description of her early in the last act emphasizes her passivity and weakness at a moment when political machinations have deprived her of the ability to assert, or even express, her will:

> Submissive, sad, and lowly was her look;
> A burning taper in her hand she bore,
> And on her shoulders, carelessly confus'd,
> With loose neglect her lovely tresses hung.
> Upon her cheek a faintish flush was spread;
> Feeble she seem'd, and sorely smit with pain,
> While barefoot as she trod the flinty pavement,
> Her footsteps all along were marked with blood.
> Yet silent still she pass'd and unrepining;
> Her streaming eyes bent ever on the earth,
> Except when in some bitter pang of sorrow,
> To heav'n she seemed in fervent zeal to raise,
> And beg that mercy deny'd her here. (*Jane Shore*, 5.1)[12]

Bellmour's lines synthesize the text's dramatic potential, operating on several levels at once. They describe Jane's attitude (her "look"), the prop she carries in her hand (the "burning taper"), her complexion ("a faintest flush"), her costume ("barefoot"), her deportment ("feeble" and "silent"), her expression ("sorely smit with pain"), the movements of her head and eyes ("bent ever on the earth," except when raised "in fervent zeal" to heaven), and her disheveled hair ("carelessly confused,/With loose neglect"). Rowe uses these coded signs to evoke the image of a woman worn out by the suffering caused by an impure passion. When Jane actually appears on-stage in the fifth act, the audience's expectations are fully met as she enters with *"her hair hanging loose on her shoulders, and barefooted"*[13] (see gallery). Women's loose, tousled hair was a familiar iconographic and cosmetic sign in the eighteenth-century theatrical tradition. It was associated with lust and, after the 1780s, particularly with Ophelia (see gallery). As Jane E. Kromm has shown, representations of the mad Ophelia on stage placed a special emphasis "on her hair as the crowning mark of her derangement."[14]

In Rowe's tragedy, Jane's physical passivity is contrasted with Alicia's verbal violence. Alicia's rage against Hastings, for example, is expressed in the agitated, impassioned tones of a rant, represented textually through a liberal use of exclamation marks and thematically through a profusion of appalling images:

> Insatiate, savage, monster! Is a moment
> So tedious to thy malice? Oh, repay him,
> Thou great Avenger; give him blood for blood!
> Guilt haunt him! Fiends pursue him! Lightnings blast him!
> Some horrid, cursed kind of death o'ertake him,
> Sudden, and in the fullness of his sins!
> That he may know how terrible it is
> To want that moment he denies thee now. (*Jane Shore,* 4)[15]

The difference between the two women, and their opposite psychological states, is especially apparent in Alicia's final lines, marked by a suicidal frenzy that has none of Jane's sad resignation. Whereas Jane will die on-stage after a cathartic reunion with her husband, Alicia asserts she will not, like Jane, be a "wretch," and then rushes off-stage to kill herself:

> Let her take my counsel!
> Why shouldst thou be a wretch? Stab, tear thy heart,
> And rid thyself of this detested being;
> I wo'not linger long behind thee here. (*Jane Shore,* 5)[16]

Like the drama, eighteenth-century fiction exploited this conventional contrast between passive and violent madness, often adding further nuances to it, especially toward the end of the century. In Richardson's *The History of Sir Charles Grandison* (1751), the contrast between Clementina della Porretta and the Countess Olivia does not stray significantly from Rowe's model, except that Olivia's Italian origins are stressed to increase her exoticism, and she perhaps anticipates those more properly Romantic female characters whose passionate love is expressed through their homicidal tendencies—she goes as far as to attempt to stab Grandison with a dagger.[17] But already in Charlotte Lennox's *The Female Quixote* (1752), Arabella's madness takes a new form: her peculiarly literary derangement involves a fantasy of absolute domination over the men in her life, whose actions she seeks to control through the rhetoric of romance. It is no accident that her relinquishment of the fantasy coincides with a return not only to reality but also to impotence.

The midcentury vogue for pathetic sensibility added its own sexual and gender connotations to the depiction of women's madness. When Laurence Sterne's Yorick encounters Maria in *A Sentimental Journey* (1768), he beholds a perfect example of the beautiful and utterly passive madwoman. Maria is an extreme instance of the ideal of submissive, artless, inarticulate femininity promoted by the conduct books of the time. Far from repelling him, therefore, her madness awakens the most exquisite sensations in Yorick, inspiring a feeling of noble altruism certainly not unmixed with erotic stimulation. Maria can thus be said to represent a typical pathetic *spectacle:* a woman (mute, mad, or witless as the case may be, but always defenseless) placed at the center of the man's voyeuristic gaze, her imperfectly dressed body patently a "site of sexual display."[18]

Nor should we forget that until 1770, London's Bethlem Hospital for the insane, commonly known as Bedlam, was virtually an entertainment venue for Londoners keen to gratify their craving for curious spectacles. Robert Altick notes that when the hospital was finally closed to the public, "One venerable source of merriment was deleted from London's list." The ghastliness of the place, famously illustrated by William Hogarth in the last plate of *A Rake's Progress* (ca. 1735), "The Rake in Bedlam" (also known simply as "The Madhouse"), was precisely what drew visitors, who had no qualms about inciting the inmates to spectacular displays of deranged behavior: "The cells were arranged in galleries, in the manner of cages in a menagerie or booths at a fair, and in each one was a chained lunatic, whose behaviour, if it were not sufficiently entertaining to begin with, was made so by the spectators' prodding him or her with their sticks or encouraging further wildness by ridicule, gestures, and imitation." Altick also points out that visitors could enjoy similar amenities to those provided at nearby Bartholomew Fair, "with nuts, fruit . . . beer brought in from nearby taverns."[19]

A sinister house of detention inhabited by grotesque beings, the madhouse represents the containment and repression of heterodoxy, and as the eighteenth century wore on it took on the status of a trope for the female condition. Whereas in Smollett's *The Adventures of Sir Launcelot Greaves*

(1760–61) the heroine is briefly confined in an asylum before the hero comes to her rescue, Mary Wollstonecraft's Maria (in *Maria; or, The Wrongs of Woman* [1798]) is "buried alive" in an asylum by her brutal husband even though she is sane.[20] Plunged into the Gothic nightmare environment of the asylum, subjected to constant, claustrophobic surveillance, and unable to communicate with the external world and assert her rights, Maria becomes convinced of the injustice and inequality of the condition of women. "Was not the world a vast prison, and women born slaves?" she asks.[21] As Kromm notes, the French Revolution played a significant role in politicizing madness at the end of the century, contributing greatly to the nineteenth-century construction of women's mental illness in particular:

> The shift from male dominant to female dominant constructions of madness was thus accomplished in discreet stages from the 1780s through the first half of the nineteenth century. . . . The gender shift achieved further credibility through a change in representational context following the revolutionary decade when the female stereotype was transposed from a primarily poetic visual and literary field to an increasingly contemporary, politicised position. This transposition from gender poetics to gender politics supports the multiple nineteenth-century ideologies that function to control or contain women's sexuality and to constrain or thwart their public ambitions.[22]

Two more female characters should be mentioned in this overview of the cultural context for Burney's representations of madness: Ellinor, in Sophia Lee's *The Recess; or, A Tale of Other Times* (1785)—perhaps the first serious attempt to write an English historical novel—and Lucy Ashton, in Walter Scott's *The Bride of Lammermoor* (1819). Ellinor's fate in *The Recess* is doubly tragic. The secret daughter of Mary Queen of Scots, she vainly seeks to save both her mother's life and that of her beloved Lord Essex by accepting to marry Lord Arlington; when she learns that both have been executed, she becomes insane. Furthermore, Arlington has arranged, after his death, for Ellinor to be immured in a remote section of the abbey where she had been brought up. Ellinor's madness is clearly her only way to overcome the pain she has endured. But her insanity is not only a defense mechanism; it also frees her from conventional restraints, as she tells her sister Matilda: "The season of dissimulation is past, and my tortured heart will utter nothing but the truth." Paradoxically, her loss of reason allows her to assert her right to her own, independent judgment and to express truths that can no longer be contained: "I perceive I have in the wild colourings of a disordered imagination, unfolded a truth my heart almost burst with."[23] Losing one's sanity is thus equivalent to gaining access to the truth, and to the words to utter it. The verbal intrusiveness of the deranged woman coincides, metaphorically, with the power she gains to assert her own female voice. We might add that in the same way that madness allows Ellinor to say what she wants to say, it also grants her author the freedom to voice a kind of social criticism that the dominant discourse otherwise would have disallowed.

The trope of women's madness reaches its fullest spectacular potential with Walter Scott's Lucy Ashton. Scott's detailed account of Lucy's story seems to capture perfectly the moment of transition from the earlier paradigm of "passive, or contained, madness" to the hyperbolic "vindictive, or uncontainable, madness" best suited to the early Romantic taste for *coups de théâtre.* Lucy, an "exquisitely beautiful" young woman with "somewhat girlish features . . . soft, timid, and feminine,"[24] is forced by her mother to marry Bucklaw despite her love for the absent Ravenswood. On Ravenswood's return immediately after the marriage, Lucy's reason gives way and she stabs her husband on their wedding night. The commotion alerts the household, but when help arrives, Lucy at first cannot be found:

> There was no private passage from the room, and they began to think that she must have thrown herself from the window, when one of the company . . . discovered something white in the corner of the great old-fashioned chimney of the apartment. Here they found the unfortunate girl, seated, or rather couched like a hare upon its form—her head-gear dishevelled; her night-clothes torn and dabbled with blood,—her eyes glazed, and her features convulsed into a paroxysm of insanity. When she saw herself discovered, she gibbered, made mouths, and pointed at them with her bloody fingers, with the frantic gestures of an exulting demoniac.[25]

As Helen Small has pointed out, the murder perpetrated by Lucy Ashton symbolizes the breakdown of the passive, vulnerable role traditionally assigned to women. It was to set an important precedent and became a recurrent theme in nineteenth-century opera.[26] When Gaetano Donizetti adapted Scott's novel for his opera *Lucia di Lammermoor* (first performed in Naples in 1835 with a libretto by Salvatore Cammarano), he fully exploited the dramatic potential of the episode, turning it into a virtuosic double aria, undoubtedly the climactic attraction of the whole entertainment. In the scene, the soprano's vocal and gestural virtuosity are employed to express the spectacular violence of a mad woman's ravings, and the stage directions carefully set out how she is to appear, and act, on-stage:[27]

> *Lucia è in succinta e bianca veste; ha le chiome scarmigliate ed il suo volto, coperto da uno squallore di morte, la rende simile ad uno spettro, anziché ad una creatura vivente. Il di lei sguardo impietrito, i moti convulsi, e fino un sorriso malagurato manifestano non solo una spaventevole demenza, ma ben anco i segni di una vita che già volge al suo termine.* (*Lucia di Lammermoor,* 2.5)[28]
>
> [*Lucia is lightly clad in a white gown; her hair is disheveled and her face, pale as death, resembles that of a ghost rather than a living being. Her stony gaze, her convulsive movements, and her ghastly smile reveal not only a frightful derangement but also the ebbing away of life itself.*]

Clearly, as Small states, "Stories about women who go mad when they lose their lovers were extraordinarily popular during the late eighteenth and early nineteenth centuries."[29] I would argue, however, that toward the end of the eighteenth century something else also happens: the idea of madness becomes so polysemic and polymorphous a concept as to take on the status of a sign of the times and of a radical questioning of Enlightenment values. It is no accident that this should happen just a few years after the French Revolution, which was widely perceived in England as a phenomenon of mass insanity that could well overflow across the Channel onto English shores. The most eloquent voice of anti-Jacobin sentiment in England, Edmund Burke, conceived of the French Revolution as a malady affecting the intellect and shattering the natural order, and his portrayal of the revolutionaries is thoroughly theatrical: "The Assembly, their organ, acts before them the farce of deliberation with as little decency as liberty. They act like the comedians of a fair before a riotous audience; they act amidst the tumultuous cries of a mixed mob of ferocious men, and of women lost to shame, who, according to their insolent fancies, direct, control, applaud, explode them."[30] Burke's evocation of this hideous spectacle of disorder sounds more like an attempt at exorcism than political analysis, however hostile. But British readers of the 1790s must have been thoroughly accustomed to drawing links between collective madness and revolution, loss of reason and the overthrowing of governments, mental and social disease. It is hardly coincidental that the Gothic dramas performed on the British stage in this period frequently portrayed representatives of constituted authority who lost their reason—scenes that regularly migrated into the novels of the time, where they became powerful illustrations of collective upheaval, such as that closing M. G. Lewis's *The Monk* (1796).[31] In 1788–89, Britain had undergone its most dangerous constitutional crisis of the century due to the mysterious malady of George III. Modern scholars have diagnosed the illness as a violent attack of porphyria, which prevented the king from governing for several months and placed William Pitt's government in jeopardy, precipitating the first regency crisis in 1789.[32] As keeper of the robes to Queen Charlotte since 1786, Frances Burney found herself at the center of this crisis and became a chronicler of it.

Burney wrote at length in her journals about the situation at Court during the king's illness, describing her encounters with the mad king in the hallways at Windsor. Her pages evoke the same sense of fear and impending disaster expressed by Burke. In her description, dated 5 November 1788, anxiety and paralysis have gripped the now hushed castle, where all of the usual activities have been suspended. Only the voice of the king is heard, babbling incessantly:

> A stillness the most uncommon reigned over the whole house. Nobody stirred; not a voice was heard; not a step; not a motion. I could do nothing but watch, without knowing for what: there seemed a strangeness in the house most extraordinary . . .
>
> The King, at dinner, had broken forth into positive delirium, which long had been menacing all who saw him most closely . . . No one knew what was to follow—no one could conjecture of the event. (*DL,* 4:129, 131)[33]

In Burney's account of the king's madness, metaphor and synecdoche build a complex code derived from the rhetoric of sensibility and replacing ordinary referential language. The mad king is described as the "Royal sufferer" (*DL,* 4:135), a formula that acknowledges the threat to his power while stressing his royal status; the unnamed and strange illness becomes the "high fever" responsible for the torrent of words he discharges onto the silenced courtiers. The king seems driven by an excess of energy that prevents him from checking the words issuing from somewhere deep within: "I had a sort of conference with his Majesty, or rather I was the object to whom he spoke, with a manner so uncommon, that a high fever alone could account for it; a rapidity, a hoarseness of voice, a volubility, an earnestness—a vehemence, rather—it startled me inexpressibly" (*DL,* 4:120). And a few days later, on 6 November 1788, she wrote: "The King . . . kept talking unceasingly; his voice was so lost in hoarseness and weakness, it was rendered almost inarticulate" (*DL,* 4:135).[34]

Two decades later, in 1811, George III suffered another attack of porphyria that did not respond to treatment. The king's throne, it seemed, was to be permanently replaced by the chair to which he was bound in a straitjacket, the tenuous difference between the two virtually disappearing. Shortly before his son took over as regent, George III ordered that a concert be held in honor of the Duke of Cambridge. Only works by Handel, the king's favorite composer, were to be performed, and all of the selections related to insanity and blindness. By organizing this literally melodramatic public staging of his own condition, the king was deliberately spectacularizing his mental illness, as Helen Small remarks: "There was, in the proper sense of the hyperbole, something 'overreaching' about the king's engagement with his own madness on the Duke of Cambridge's night. Through the concert, George III made his insanity the occasion for an artistic display at which he, along with his court, was one of the audience. . . . [H]e evidently found consolation in this hyperbolic displacement of his suffering into the register of the stage."[35]

Perhaps the best modern exploration of this threefold symbiotic connection of royal madness, theater, and revolution is Alan Bennett's play *The Madness of George III* (1991). The action takes place in the king's state rooms at Windsor, surrounded on all sides by hallways vanishing into the distance, the perspective emphasizing the smallness of the courtiers' living quarters and the endless corridors.[36] Bennett's text explores the incessant refractive play between performance and sincerity, seeming and being, expression and repression that the king's madness sets in motion.

The dangerous political consequences of the king's illness are obvious to those who have witnessed his behavior. As Captain Fitzroy cynically asks, using a well-worn metaphor linking the body of the king to the state: "If His Majesty cannot regulate himself how should he regulate the country?"[37] But if the political situation is still, for the moment, under control, at Court a radical revolution has thoroughly disrupted the complex set of conventions and rules of etiquette regulating daily life.[38] A powerful inner force is compelling the king to throw off all formal constraints in an irrepressible, liberating assertion of self ("I am the King. I say what I want"):

Dundas. What is it [madness] like?
Thurlow. Like taking off one's braces.
Dundas. There is consolation in it, you mean?

Thurlow. For some. Were the king not in pain one might envy him. Saying what he likes.[39]

By contrast, when the king returns to his senses, he also returns to a regime of dissimulation and appearances but with a new awareness of the rules governing "make-believe":

Thurlow. Your Majesty seems more yourself.
King. Do I? Yes, I do. I have always been myself even when I was ill. Only now I seem myself. That's the important thing. I have remembered how to seem.[40]

Bennett's refractive approach to madness ultimately collapses the distinction between real madness and literary madness, producing an inextricable ontological overlap between reality and verisimilitude that verges on the postmodern. Had the king been deemed unfit to govern, he would have been in the same position as Wollstonecraft's Maria, subjected to the same mechanism of coercive power that reduced her from subject to object. Bennett makes the point explicitly in an exchange added for the screenplay but absent from the play text:

Dundas. But he will recover in time . . . surely?
Pitt. What good is that? Once he's made Regent the Prince will have him locked away in some Windsor hellhole and mad or sane no one will ever know.
Thurlow. You have been reading too many novels.[41]

It is hardly accidental therefore that when George III slowly regains his reason (and his power), he also regains full command over the linguistic and psychological potential inherent in the word and expresses an indisputable verbal assertiveness: "I am the King. I tell. I am not told. I am the verb, sir. I am not the object."[42] His language echoes that of his unconstrained mad self but with a crucial new awareness that his status raises him above the level both of object and subject.

Madness and reason, freedom and constraint, but also madness and disintegration—these are the end-century polarities we have been exploring. On one hand, madness is a symptom of the inability to communicate or to find expression in the context of marital, familial, or social oppression. On the other hand, madness brings enfranchisement, liberation, and an uncontainable assertive urge expressed through hyperphasia—a breakthrough to incessant speech following aphasic tremors and a fragmented, elliptic kind of speech that disrupts the linear progression of narrative and is based on free association and metaphor. This opposition coincides with that between two contrasting approaches to psychiatry: a modern approach that considers insanity the symptom of a self so unable to cope with social pressures that it disintegrates, and an older conception of madness, current in the eighteenth century, that considers the insane to have overstepped all boundaries and that represents them as hyperbole incarnate.

In the early 1970s, another approach emerged: the anti-psychiatric school of thought associated with Ronald D. Laing, which has contributed to defining schizophrenia, and mental illness in general, as a symptom of a social process that often involves a desperate attempt to communicate and protest, particularly by women.[43] Because of its emphasis both on social factors and on gender, this approach is especially useful in considering the epistemic dimensions of Burney's representations of madness. My analysis of the "mad" episodes in Burney's work will therefore explore how their latent social and gender significance situates them at an epistemic crossroads.

Between 1782 (the year of *Cecilia*'s publication) and 1814 (that of *The Wanderer*), the presence of madwomen in Burney's writings becomes so frequent that we can consider it an isotopy connecting the generically diverse works she produced in this period. It is to be expected that we should find it in her tragedies, given the conventions of the genre at the time, and characters such as Cerulia in *Hubert de Vere* (1790) and the unidentified "female . . . wild and unknown" in a fragment usually considered part of *Elberta* (begun in 1790) are fairly representative types.[44] Burney also reported on her encounters with deranged women in her journals. As we shall see, one particular instance of a woman exhibiting irrational and apparently inexplicable behavior is especially significant. But it is Burney's treatment of madness in her novels that functions most clearly as a semantic core, or hypogram, in Burney's work and that generates the most suggestive intertextual possibilities.

It is worth stressing at the outset that in Burney's tragedies, as in most early eighteenth-century she-tragedies, madness immediately precedes the heroine's death. Otway's Belvidera, for example, dies on-stage after seeing the ghosts of her husband and of Pierre. In Burney's novels, however, madness is distinct from the plot's resolution; it intervenes before the resolution but does not lead into it directly. This fits well with an interpretation of Burney's novels as inversions of the feminine bildungsroman: the mad episodes in the novels are part of a teleological process of (dis)education whereby the heroine is waylaid on her path to education.[45] In this sense, madness is a crucial stage in the process of anti-formation to which Burney's *Bildungsheldin* is subjected.[46] At the same time, it is also true that Burney's heroines develop according to what Susan Fraiman has called a "logic of impediment," so that we must consider their madness as an escape from enforced passivity, a physical and verbal display of rebellion in the face of the growing psychological pressures placed on them.[47]

As discussed earlier, this means that from a literary standpoint the mad episode sheds its characteristics as "narrated action" to take on the quality of a theatrical scene that can operate on several communicative levels at once. The heroine's words are endowed with paralinguistic connotations; the action takes place in locations that function like stage sets; and proxemic relations become especially important. Viola Papetti has noted how characters in eighteenth-century novels tend to be "no longer eye, but voice."[48] But a semiotic analysis of narrative episodes of insanity suggests that these episodes constitute a hybrid narrative syntagm in which the absence of the eye is counterbalanced by a strong emphasis on staging and proxemics. As a result, different levels of non-verbal communication are activated simultaneously, and are complementary to each other, while "dialogue . . . functions as one level among other, non-verbal, levels."[49]

Dialogue and dramatic monologue do, of course, feature prominently in the staging of these episodes. In the throes of madness, heroines obey a logic of non-reason that allows them to express verbally (in Cecilia's case) or oneirically (in Cerulia's case and, later, in Camilla's in the eponymous novel) the fear and rage building up within them. But they can only express what is otherwise repressed or suppressed by throwing off their social mask and entering the anti-realist realm of nightmare or of an attack of insanity. I therefore cannot fully agree with Margaret Anne Doody's view that Burney's mad episodes "stand out a trifle oddly in the novels in which they occur." In my reading, the Gothic nightmare is less that evoked by Cecilia's madness or Camilla's terrifying dream than the daily life from which they have suddenly awoken.[50]

Cecilia's episode of madness is a good example of this. After marrying Delvile without his father's consent, Cecilia is driven out of her home by the Egglestons, who have inherited her property. She travels to London, planning to follow her husband and mother-in-law abroad, and seeks advice about the journey from young Mr. Belfield. While she is discussing the matter with him, Delvile suddenly enters the room, is clearly very disturbed at the sight of them alone, and after a few hurried words leaves without explanation. Terrified that he may challenge Belfield to a duel, Cecilia frantically rushes out in search of him. She goes first to his London home, but he is not there, and the obdurate Compton Delvile refuses to admit her or even speak to her. At a loss as to where to find her husband, and having no friend to turn to, she begins her headlong rush from one end of town to the other. As Erik Bond points out, Cecilia's anguished search is a carefully planned strategy on Burney's part, emphasized in the title of the chapter, "A Pursuit": Cecilia's urban disorientation externalizes her psychological disorientation, transposing it into a plastic dimension. "Lacking a Freudian vocabulary for talking about the interior," Bond explains, "Burney places Cecilia on the streets alone (that is, Burney makes Cecilia exhibit improper conduct) to express Cecilia's interior breakdown."[51] Isolated, rejected, convinced that a catastrophe is imminent, and for the first time in her life deprived of any close social or familial ties, Cecilia leaps out of the carriage to continue her pursuit on foot, only to be stopped by the coachman who demands payment and by a stranger who grasps her hand, offering his services: "This moment, for the unhappy Cecilia, teemed with calamity; she was wholly overpowered; terror for Delvile, horror for herself, hurry, confusion, heat and fatigue, all assailing her at once, while all means of repelling them were denied her, the attack was too strong for her fears, feelings and faculties, and her reason suddenly, yet totally failing her, she madly called out, 'He will be gone!'" (*Cecilia,* 897).

As her "rising frenzy" drives her forward, Cecilia, "with a strength wholly unknown to her . . . forcibly disengaged herself from her persecutors" (*Cecilia,* 896) and, breaking through the crowd, runs on until she reaches a pawnbroker's shop, where she collapses in exhaustion. Her temporary insanity reduces Cecilia to a sign, a social and narratological construct governed first by the irrepressible language of the body and then by violent delirium: "She forced herself along by her own vehement rapidity, not hearing what was said, not heeding what was thought. . . . She scarce touched the ground; she scarce felt her own motion; she seemed as if endued with supernatural speed, gliding from place to place, from street to street; with no consciousness of any plan, and following no other direction than that of darting forward where-ever there was most room, and turning back when there was an obstruction" (*Cecilia,* 897). The shop owners mistake her for a madwoman "escaped from her keepers" (*Cecilia,* 898) and carry her upstairs, locking her in a small attic, a part of the house whose manifold connotations have been made familiar to modern readers by Gilbert and Gubar. Here, Cecilia becomes delirious, her insanity expressed through a flood of words that seem to gush forth from a "tap" that cannot be turned off:[52]

> In this miserable condition, alone and raving, she was left to pass the night! in the early part of it, she called upon Delvile without intermission . . . but afterwards, her strength being wholly exhausted by these various exertions and fatigues, she threw herself upon the floor, and lay for some minutes quite still. . . . She still, however, tried to get away; talked of Delvile without cessation, said she should be too late to serve him, told the woman she desired but to prevent murder, and repeatedly called out, "Oh! beloved of my heart! wait but a moment, and I will snatch thee from destruction!" . . . Cecilia grew worse every moment, called out twenty times in a breath, "Where is he? which way is he gone?" and implored the woman by the most pathetic remonstrances . . . At other times she talked of her marriage, of the displeasure of his family, and of her own remorse. . . . And thus, *though naturally and commonly of a silent and quiet disposition,* she was now not a moment still, for the irregular starts of a terrified and disordered imagination, were changed into the constant ravings of morbid delirium. (*Cecilia,* 898–901; emphasis added)

Cecilia's madness can clearly be read as a trope. Her frenzied rush through the streets of London is a dramatic metaphor for her constantly interrupted and diverted course of formation, and her convulsive movements and relentless onrush of words ("ravings" and "vehement cries") show that only her derangement allows her finally to express the anguish and alienation that otherwise would have no vent.[53] Cecilia's speech is no longer linear, and what surfaces through her otherwise conventional expressions of grief over her husband's fate is her own anxiety over her status as an unacknowledged wife.

Cecilia is still delirious when Delvile finds her after reading an advertisement inviting "whoever she belongs to" (*Cecilia,* 901) to call at the shop. In their first encounter, her most deep-seated fears rise to the surface. Her desperate anxiety about his fate (she has not yet recognized him and still imagines him wounded in a duel) can be read as terror about her own fate; likewise, the mourning she foresees so vividly might not be for Delvile's death but for her own: "'Ah,' cried she, more wildly, 'no one will save me now! I am married and no one will listen to me! ill were the auspices under which I gave my hand! Oh it was a work of darkness, unacceptable and offensive! it has been sealed, therefore with blood, and tomorrow it will be signed with murder! . . . I must go to St. James's Square,—if I stay an instant longer, the passing-bell will toll, and then how shall I be in time for the funeral?'" (*Cecilia,* 903–904). The double meaning of Cecilia's anguished pleas becomes even more significant in her exchange with Delvile, who remorsefully berates himself for having abandoned her. She demands that he leave her immediately—not, perhaps, because she has failed to recognize him and fears him as a stranger, but because she has indeed recognized him and fears him precisely because she knows who he is:

> Cecilia now, half rising, and regarding him with mingled terror and anger, eagerly exclaimed, "If you do not mean to mangle and destroy me, begone this instant. . . ."
>
> "Too cruel, yet justly cruel Cecilia!—is, then Delvile utterly renounced? . . ."
>
> "Is your name, then, Delvile? . . ."
>
> "'Tis a name," cried she, sitting up, "I well remember to have heard, and once I loved it . . . and when I was abandoned and left alone, I repeated it and *sung* to it." (*Cecilia,* 906–907; emphasis added).

Cecilia's mention of singing evokes the image of Ophelia, in an intertextual reference that, like others in the scene, relies on the reader's cultural competence and inter-media skills. Thus, Delvile's first sight of her immediately calls up the customary appearance of mad heroines: as she enters the room assisted by the maid, "her changed complection, and the wildness of her eyes and air . . . made him start" (*Cecilia,* 905). Cecilia's helplessness is conveyed semiotically through her need for support to walk: "Cecilia . . . was again dressed in her riding habit. This operation over, she moved towards the door, the temporary strength of her delirium giving her a hardiness that combated fever, illness, fatigue, and feebleness. Mary, however averse, assisted her. . . . Cecilia, however, felt her weakness when she attempted to move down stairs; her feet tottered, and her head became dizzy; she leaned it against Mary, who called aloud for more help, and made her sit down till it came" (*Cecilia,* 904). Cecilia's tottering steps suggest a regression to childishness. In difficult situations, or when subjected to psychological pressure, all of Burney's heroines are described as "tottering."[54]

Burney's stress on the non-verbal elements of her characters' interactions is especially evident in an encounter between Cecilia and Albany, who is in the neighborhood and has heard a "mad woman" is in the shop:

> When he entered the room, she was sitting upon her bed, her eyes earnestly fixed upon the window, from which she was privately indulging a wish to make her escape. Her dress was in much disorder, her fine hair was dishevelled, and the feathers of her riding hat were broken and half falling down, some shading her face, others reaching to her shoulder. . . .
>
> She started at the sound of a new voice, she looked round,—but what was the astonishment of Albany to see who it was!—He stept back,—he came forward,—he doubted his own senses,—he looked at her earnestly,—he turned from her to look at the woman of the house,—he cast his eyes round the room itself, and then, lifting up his hands, "O sight of woe!" he cried . . . "is *This* Cecilia!" (*Cecilia,* 902)

Burney's careful description of dress, gestures, expressions, and tone of voice closely approximates stage directions and is clearly intended to aid in visualizing the scene and mentally dramatizing the interaction between the characters.

Cecilia's hallucinations and delirium eventually give way to stupor and an utter indifference to her situation that lasts many hours. In this state, she "appeared unconscious even of her existence; and but that she breathed, she might already have passed for being dead" (*Cecilia,* 911). Her lethargy is followed by a deep sleep, a necessary formal transition that makes way for her return to reason and sober acceptance of her marriage to Delvile—that is, her acceptance of her new status as a wife. But given the way it is constructed, Cecilia's episode of madness casts a sinister light on the novel's dénouement and calls into question the customary, negative view of Cecilia's insanity. Burney herself suggests this interpretation by her refusal to alter the unusual ending of the novel, in which the couple relinquish Cecilia's inheritance and instead retain the Delvile name. Burney's decision to work against the conventions of romance in the conclusion—and hence, to give such prominence to the madness episode—was due to her insistence on the importance of verisimilitude. She argued strongly "in defence of following nature as much in the conclusion as in the progress of the tale" (*DL,* 2:80–81), considering verisimilitude absolutely essential to fiction. Cecilia's madness, and Burney's defense of it, are both the result of the desire to assert one's voice over that of external authority: the creator of the narrative, and its protagonist, speak the same language, demanding that we uncover the ideological crypto-discourse concealed in the text and that we disentangle the intertextual web in which it is enmeshed.

The coupling of madness and spectacle that we have seen in Donizetti's *Lucia di Lammermoor* and in the self-referential performance of madness set up by George III becomes all the more significant when the person who goes mad (or feigns to do so) is an actress. In her journal to her sister Susanna of June 1792, Frances Burney writes about an odd encounter at the Shakespeare Gallery. In this pseudo-theatrical setting, among paintings by Henry Fuseli depicting Shakespearean subjects such as the ghost in *Hamlet* and King Lear in the storm, Burney and her friends see a woman "dressed rather singularly, quite alone, & extremely handsome," who wanders from room to room ostentatiously sniffing the flowers in her hand and obviously aiming to attract the attention of the other visitors (*JL,* 1:207–12). The woman fixes her gaze on Burney's group, staring particularly at her friend Mrs. Crewe while softly humming "various quick passages, without words or connection." "I saw Mrs. Crewe much alarmed, & advanced to stand by her, meaning to whisper her that we had better leave the Room; & this idea was not checked by seeing that her *Flowers* were artificial. By the looks that we inter-changed, we soon mutually said, This is a Mad woman! We . . . gently retreated . . . when she bounced up with a great noise, & throwing the veil of her Bonnet violently back, as if fighting it, she looked after us, pointing at Mrs. Crewe" (*JL,* 1:208). Like a stage curtain, the woman's veil is suddenly lifted to reveal her face. Burney and the others immediately recognize her as Mary Wells, an actress well known for her eccentric behavior.[55] Mrs. Crewe becomes alarmed at the woman's insistent stare, "But before Mrs. Crewe's astonishment & resentment found words, Mrs. Wells, singing, & throwing herself into extravagant attitudes, again rushed down the steps, & fixed her Eyes on Mrs. Crewe" (*JL,* 1:209). One of the gentlemen of the group is then sent to inform an attendant that someone is creating a disturbance. It seems clear that Mrs. Wells is here treating the gallery's visitors as an improvised audience before which she can test the effect of her bizarre behavior or "vagaries," as Burney puts it (*JL,* 1:209).

Performing madness in this way involves flouting the conventions of feminine behavior (Burney stresses that unlike Mrs. Crewe and herself, who are visiting the gallery in company, Mrs. Wells wanders about the rooms "quite alone"), but it also involves doing away with the class distinctions separating members of the upper classes from the demonized category of actors. At the same time, Mary Wells's performance of madness appropriates the spectators' gaze—instead of being the consumers of spectacle, they are forced into the position of being themselves a spectacle for the actress, who observes their reactions with scornful amusement. As in the confrontation in Bennett's play between the mad king and his doctor, to gain mastery over the gaze is equivalent to grasping power, an act that entails crossing a boundary:

> *King.* Do you look at me, sir?
> *Willis.* I do, sir.
> *King.* I have you in my eye.
> *Willis.* No. I have you in my eye.
> *King.* You are bold, but by God I am bolder.[56]

In the medieval feast of fools, the carnivalesque performance of madness abolishes hierarchies and restraints, staging a revolutionary process that subverts class distinctions. It is in this spirit that Mrs. Wells asserts that "one person is as good as another in a public place" (*JL,* 1:211). But what is more significant for our purposes is that Mrs. Wells subverts gender constructions by deliberately performing madness before an unwitting audience. As we shall see, Elinor Joddrel's relationship with Albert Harleigh in *The Wanderer* is characterized by precisely this sort of subversive behavior.

The Wanderer was published in 1814, after Burney had spent eleven years in France with her husband, Alexandre d'Arblay, unable to return to England due to the Napoleonic Wars. In the novel, Burney offers a mature appraisal of the social and cultural issues raised in her previous novels and plays. She addresses the rights of women and the need for their economic emancipation; her treatment of the inadequacy of female education is a direct attack against conduct book literature and the false expectations raised by romance novels. But *The Wanderer* also bitingly satirizes the narrow-mindedness of English society, offering a disenchanted historical perspective on England in the 1790s, "during the dire reign of the terrific Robespierre" (*The Wanderer,* 11). Because of its historical setting, the novel can be considered a female version of Walter Scott's *Waverley,* published the same year. Looking backward, Burney addresses the traditional debate about the eighteenth-century man of feeling, but she also tackles modern issues linked to race, ethnicity, nationality, gender, and class. These are crucial to the plot, which revolves around the violence and ill-treatment meted out to a poor and friendless French woman who has sought refuge in the supposedly enlightened and humanitarian England of the end of the century, where she attempts to support herself through her own work. Extraordinarily rich and complex, the novel was harshly criticized when it came out and has been strangely overlooked until very recently even by Burney scholars.[57]

Burney admits to the complexity of her narrative structure in the preface, where despite stating that she is not "venturing upon the stormy sea of politics" (*The Wanderer,* 4), she does suggest that the French Revolution will loom large: "To attempt to delineate, in whatever form, any picture of actual human life, without reference to the French Revolution, would be as little possible, as to give an idea of the English government, without reference to our own: for not more unavoidably is the last blended with the history of our nation, than the first, with every intellectual survey of the present times" (*The Wanderer,* 6). The French Revolution is, in fact, so important in the novel that Burney embodies it in the figure of the deuteragonist, the apparently mad Elinor Joddrel, for whom the political has merged into the personal. Elinor's presence in France at the start of the revolution has transformed her: she has internalized the new ideology, particularly where gender is concerned, and her transformation is reflected in her behavior, her deportment, even her clothes. But in Burney's portrayal of Elinor's madness, personal transformation is inextricably linked to its public performance, or staging, to such an extent that the two can be considered a main theme, or isotopy, running through the novel.

Elinor's story begins when the wealthy Dennis Harleigh proposes marriage to her. Just before her departure for France, however, she falls in love with his brother, Albert, and defying convention she declares her love to him. Burney ironically implies that Elinor's provocative and unconventional act is more apparent than real, given her readiness to defy the dictates of education, conventional morality, and feminine conduct only to subject herself completely to Albert Harleigh's will: "I have conquered the tyrant false pride; I have mocked the puerilities of education; I have set at nought and defeated even the monster custom; but you, Oh Harleigh! you I obey, without waiting for a command; you, I seek to humour, without aspiring to please! To you, my free soul, my liberated mind, my new-born ideas, all yield, slaves, willing slaves, to what I only conceive to be your counsel" (*The Wanderer,* 189–90). This split in Elinor's personality is expressed somatically. While her words assert her freedom to judge and act independently, and so to declare her love openly, the equally expressive language of her body reveals by its color coding (she blushes, goes pale) and involuntary movements that the social construction of femininity has so deeply penetrated her consciousness as to have become inseparable from her physical being:

"She stopt, and the deepest vermillion overspread her face; her effort was made; she had boasted of her new doctrine" (*The Wanderer,* 154).

Elinor does not know whether Albert Harleigh returns her feelings, and when they are joined by a female stranger on their escape from France during the Terror, she is stung by jealousy, and her doubts become obsessive. The stranger is taken in by Elinor's aunt, Mrs. Maple, but refuses to disclose her true identity and eventually becomes known as "Ellis." In the course of their stay with Mrs. Maple, Ellis reluctantly agrees to participate in a private theatrical performance, and when Elinor witnesses her interaction with Harleigh during rehearsals, she becomes convinced that his obvious admiration for the stranger must mean he is in love with her. The situation is brought to a head by the arrival of Elinor's betrothed, who is unsure whether they are in fact engaged. Setting aside all false delicacy, Elinor categorically refuses to marry him and decides the time has come to stage a confrontation with Albert Harleigh to finally ascertain his feelings for her. Burney sets up the scene in which Elinor makes this decision in a thoroughly theatrical way. As the excerpt in figure 21 shows, the language describing Elinor's behavior and movements departs from standard narrative in order to take on the "square" characteristics of a playtext, relying heavily on kinesic, proxemic, and paralinguistic dramatic conventions.[58] As a result, the reader is brought so close to the action as to virtually become an interlocutor on stage.

Just as the actress Mary Wells had feigned madness to "try effect" (*JL,* 1:209), Elinor plans to enact a hyperbolic and spectacular display of her own mental disorder, using as her main prop the dagger ("something in a shagrin case") that is here introduced for the first time.

The encounter between Elinor and Harleigh takes place in the presence of Ellis. Having set the stage in a summer-house, Burney describes the interaction between the characters in great detail, noting the paralinguistic connotations of their speeches as well as their mode of delivery; she reports their gestures and attitudes, and her descriptions of their facial expressions, tone of voice, and inflection fulfill all the requirements of stage directions as prescribed by the acting theories of the time. That Burney is here "theatricalizing" narrative is apparent from the way the episode defines "the relationships between the characters on stage" in accordance with the characteristics Serpieri attributes to theatrical narrative.[59]

Burney deploys a range of communication codes, both linguistic and paralinguistic, in her description of Elinor's declaration of love: she enters the room "precipitately," "extremely pale" and agitated; she shuts the door, and sits down, "assuming a mien of austerity, though her voice betrayed

FIGURE 21. Dramatic conventions in *The Wanderer* vol. 1, chap. 17

She *paced* hastily up and down the room;	Movement (the scene is indoors)
sat, in turn, upon a chair, a window seat,	
and the bed; *talked* to herself, sometimes	Utterance
with a *vehemence* that made several	Tone
detached words, though no sentences,	
intelligible; sometimes in softer accents,	
and with *eyes* and gestures of exultation;	Expression/Gesture
and, frequently, she *went* into a corner by	Movement
the side of the window, where she looked,	
in secret, at something in a *shagrin case*	Prop
that she held in her hand, and had brought	
out of her chamber; and to which she	
occasionally addressed herself, with a	
fervency that shook her whole frame, and	Utterance
with *expressions* which, though broken, and	Tone
half pronounced, denoted that she	
considered it as something sacred. At	
length, with an air of transport, she	Expression
exclaimed, "Yes! That will produce the	Dramatic monologue
best effect! What an ideot have I been to	
hesitate!" . . . She *reddened*; passion	Expression
took possession of every feature, and for	
a moment nearly choaked her *voice*: she	Tone
again *walked*, with rapid motion, about the	Movement
room, and then *ejaculated*, "Let me be	Rant
patient! Let me not take away all grandeur	
from my despair, and reduce it to mere	
common madness!—Let me wait the fated	
moment, and then—let the truth burst,	
blaze, and flame, till it devour me!" (*The*	
Wanderer, 168–69; emphasis added)	

internal tremour" (*The Wanderer*, 172–73). As the following passages demonstrate, Burney makes explicit every nuance of the movements, gestures, and expressions accompanying Elinor's words as she attempts to declare her love:

> She stopt, confused, rose, and again seated herself, before she could go on. (173)
>
> She arose, and, clasping her hands, with strong, yet tender, emotion, exclaimed, "That I should love you—" She stopt. Shame crimsoned

her skin. She covered her face with both her hands, and sunk again upon a chair. (174)

She breathed hard, and spoke with difficulty. . . . sunk gently upon her chair, yet left him full possession of her hand . . . "Dear, dear delicious poison! thrill, thrill through my veins! throb at my heart! new string every fibre of my frame! Is it, then, granted me, at last, to see thee thus." (175–76)

Elinor became but more urgent, and more disordered. . . . "Speak!—if you would not devote me to distraction! Speak!—if you would not consign me to immediate delirium!" . . .

"Elinor, are you mad?"

"No, Harleigh, no!—but I am wild with anguish." (179)

As Elinor's suicidal frenzy gradually builds, her speech becomes halting. On the textual level, the urgency of her utterances is indicated typographically through the increased use of dashes; on the dramatic level implicit in the text, it is signaled by the many exclamation marks and by the use of semicolons rather than commas, simplifying elocution. This is apparent in Elinor's quasi-heroic dramatic monologue just before she unsheathes the dagger: "Looking at him, then, with uncontrolled emotion . . . 'For me,—my glass is run,—my cup is full,—I die! . . . Die, yes! . . . or sleep! call it which you will! so animation be over, so feeling be past, so my soul no longer linger under the leaden oppression of disappointment; under sickness of all mortal existence; under incurable, universal disgust . . . Harleigh! dearest Harleigh, Adieu!'" (*The Wanderer,* 181–82). At this point, Elinor grasps the dagger hidden in her breast and attempts to stab herself before Harleigh, but is stopped by Ellis.[60] Figure 22 notes the theatrical conventions Burney employs in the scene.

In planning her declaration, Elinor had conceived of the scene in theatrical terms from the start, describing it as the third act "of the comedy, tragedy, or farce, of my existence" (*The Wanderer,* 161), and Burney takes the theatrical structure of the episode through to the end of the chapter, which concludes with Ellis and Elinor leaving the scene together, the latter leaning on her rival's arm, and moving with the "tottering steps" (*The Wanderer,* 185) typical of tragic heroines.

Elinor's suicide attempt is clearly inspired by the taste for *coups de théâtre* associated with the new Romantic aesthetics. Her act is meant to shock Harleigh, to electrify him with its sublimity, and to move him by display-

FIGURE 22. Dramatic conventions in *The Wanderer* vol. 1, chap. 18

Her *voice* now faultered, and she shook so	Tone
violently that she could not *support*	Movement
herself. She *put her hand* gently upon the	Gesture (hand)
arm of Harleigh, and gliding nearly behind	
him, *leant* upon his shoulder. He would	Movement/Attitude
have spoken words of comfort, but she	
seemed incapable of hearing him.	Expression
"Farewell!" she *cried*, "Harleigh! Never	Utterance
will I live to see Ellis your's!	
Farewell!—a long farewell!" Precipitately	
she then *opened* the shagrin case, and was	Gesture (prop)
drawing out its contents, when Ellis,	
darting forward, caught her arm, and	Movement
screamed, rather than articulated, "Ellis	Tone
will never be his! Forbear! Forbear! Ellis	
will never be his!" . . . And, from a	
change of emotion, too sudden and too	
mighty for the shattered state of her	
nerves, [Elinor] *sunk* senseless upon the	Movement (swoon)
floor. The motive to the strange	
protestation of Ellis was now apparent: a	
poniard *dropt* from the hand of Elinor as	Gesture (prop)
she fell, of which, while she spoke her	
farewell, Ellis had caught a glance. (*The*	
Wanderer, 183; emphasis added)	

ing the intensity of her feelings. Like one of the special effects that were becoming ever more popular in performances during the Romantic period, Elinor's act of love is intended, "like an explosion of thunder, [to] burst upon his head at once" (*The Wanderer,* 157).[61] It is hardly surprising therefore that when Elinor again tries to kill herself, she should do so almost literally at center stage during a concert held for Ellis's benefit. Convinced that Ellis and Harleigh are in love, Elinor has left her aunt's house and has disappeared without a trace. She returns disguised as a man on the night of the performance, with the intention of stabbing herself in front of Harleigh and the rest of the audience. Unlike Ellis, who has been forced to perform in public because of her straitened circumstances, and who is unable to overcome her shame at being thus exposed, Elinor's constant quest for "Effect, public Effect" (*The Wanderer,* 365) leads her to turn her pain into public spectacle.

Elinor's decision to appear on the scene dressed as a man is significant. Aside from intensifying the spectacular effect of her love-induced madness, it calls up a number of intertextual relations.[62] Female characters disguised as men were a fixture of Shakespearean and Jacobean drama; we need think only of Julia in *The Two Gentlemen of Verona* or Viola in *Twelfth Night,* or Portia disguised as a lawyer in *The Merchant of Venice,* and, above all, Rosalind in *As You Like It,* whose strategic use of disguise seems ideologically closest to Elinor's in *The Wanderer.* According to Terry Castle, cross-dressing (whether by men or women) was a form of cross-gender imitation that became increasingly popular in the course of the eighteenth century. She suggests that cross-dressers, or "sexual shape shifters," enacted a parody of the "hieratic fixities of gender" that enabled eighteenth-century society to begin exploring its "secular and artifactual nature."[63] On-stage, the figure of the disguised heroine appeared with ever greater frequency at this time: introduced by Restoration writers and Italian Commedia dell'arte, the figure recurs again and again throughout the period, from George Farquhar's *The Constant Couple* (Drury Lane, 1699), with its famous "breeches part" of Sir Harry Wildair, to Catherine Trotter's *The Revolution of Sweden* (Queen's Theatre in the Hay-Market, 1706) and to Sheridan's *The Duenna* and *St. Patrick's Day* (Drury Lane, 1775). But in the late eighteenth century, theatrical cross-dressing became an "increasingly disturbing spectacle" for many critics, and female actresses' impersonations of men, instead of being perceived as playful masquerade, were met with serious opposition.[64] The actress in breeches was not a passive object of masculine visual pleasure but, rather, a subject who appropriated gender-determined behavior that would otherwise have been off-limits to her, since they contravened the dominant gender-approved codes of conduct. The risk, critics thought, was that the gender subversion would spill off the stage into real life. Taking our cue from a point made by Celestine Woo, we might say that the problem lay in the potential that a titillating breeches part intended solely to give the audience pleasure would turn into a "cross-gendered role," all the more dangerous because it might be irreversible.[65] This concern would explain why criticism of the breeches-wearing actress Dorothy Jordan was particularly harsh (see gallery). Jordan was one of the most successful Sir Harry Wildairs of the century, and yet, as Leigh Hunt asserted with reference to Jordan in particular: "The male attirement of actresses is one of the most barbarous, injurious, and unnatural customs of the stage. . . . In all cases it is injurious to the probability of the author and to the proper style of the actress, for if she succeeds in her study of male representation she will never entirely get rid of her manhood with its attire; she is like the Iphis of Ovid, and *changes her sex unalterably*."[66] Hunt's view leads us back to the theme of the *prodigium* that we encountered in discussing the gender–intellect connection staged by the bluestockings. The cross-dressing actress, Hunt decrees, goes not only against culture, but also against nature; she, too, is a hermaphrodite, the symptom of an inversion leading to a disorder.

Burney knew the part of Sir Harry Wildair well and had seen the play in 1788 at Cheltenham, with Dorothy Jordan in the lead role, although she did not much enjoy the performance (*DL,* 4:54). Burney's decision to have Elinor disguise herself as a man therefore seems intended to mobilize the intertextual competence of her readers, who would easily be able to situate the scene in its proper theatrical and cultural context.

Elinor's disguise is described in detail. Aiming to pass as a "deaf and dumb stranger," she wears a hat and a mask that conceal her face and is completely enveloped in "a large scarlet coat," except where a showy embroidered waistcoat can be glimpsed, above which "a cravat of enormous bulk" (*The Wanderer,* 356–57) reaches up to her nose. Walking into the concert hall, the stranger takes his place among the audience, directly in front of Ellis's harp. When Ellis comes on-stage, she suddenly intuits that the disguised foreigner must be Elinor, and having seen the dagger, she faints in terror. The ensuing commotion puts an end to the concert, creating an opening for Elinor's own tragic performance. In terms of performance history, Burney's ingenious spatial and visual juxtaposition of her characters in this scene encapsulates the moral and gender antinomies that had arisen by the turn of the century over the sexuality of the actress: whereas Ellis is unwillingly forced to perform a masquerade of femininity, her purity emphasized by her white satin gown, Elinor instead has chosen to play a role in a disguise whose ambiguity destabilizes the feminine.

Aside from preserving Ellis from the shame of performing for a paying audience, her providential recognition of Elinor renders the latter's disguise useless. She removes her outer layer of men's clothes, and appears in the tragic stage costume of a madwoman:

> The large wrapping coat, the half mask, the slouched hat, and embroidered waistcoat, had rapidly been thrown aside, and Elinor appeared in deep mourning; *her long hair; wholly unornamented, hanging loosely down her shoulders.* Her complexion was wan, her eyes were fierce rather than bright, and her air was wild and menacing. "Oh Harleigh!—adored Harleigh!—" she cried, as he flew to catch her des-

> perate hand;—but he was not in time; for, in uttering his name, she plunged a dagger into her breast. The blood gushed out in torrents, while, with a smile of triumph, and eyes of idolizing love, she dropped into his arms, and *clinging round him,* feebly articulated, "here let me end!" (*The Wanderer,* 359; emphasis added)

Burney's repeated emphasis on the masculine disguise is not accidental.[67] Elinor's public attempt to commit suicide for love of Harleigh reflects her rejection of conventional codes of feminine conduct. The revolutionary doctrines she has been exposed to in France have taught her that nothing should prevent women from expressing their love for a man even before he has declared his own feelings. In a brief but suggestive synopsis of the events leading up to the concert scene, the narrator explains that on arriving at the Isle of Wight, Elinor had engaged "a foreign servant" to procure "some clothes of an indigent emigrant" (*The Wanderer,* 395). The nationality of this emigrant is not specified, but we can hypothesize from macro-textual evidence,[68] as well as from the location of the Isle of Wight, that he could have been one of the many French exiles fleeing the Terror (Burney herself had married one of them). If this is the case, then in choosing to wear the garb of a French refugee for her performance of mad passion, Elinor would be, metaphorically, wearing the revolutionary ideals of France.

But the ambiguities in Elinor's disguise are not only political. They extend to its gender connotations as well, anticipating a double reversal of gender roles in the course of the scene. Although she is disguised as a man, the apparent masculine assertiveness of her costume is undercut by the fact that she is impersonating a disabled man who can neither speak nor hear. When, instead, she spectacularly asserts her desire for Harleigh, she does so as a woman, who is traditionally barred from any such self-expression. Given this context, Elinor's dagger should be seen less as a stage prop than as an objective correlative for her insane passion. Burney appears to be drawing on Otway's *Venice Preserv'd* for this scene, a tragedy she had seen with Sarah Siddons in the role of Belvidera (*DL,* 1:351), and in which a dagger features prominently. Like the dagger itself, Elinor's desperate clinging to Harleigh recalls the dramatic climax in the fourth act of Otway's tragedy, when Jaffeir threatens to stab his wife because she has induced him to betray the rebels' cause. In the scene, famously illustrated in a painting by Johann Zoffany (1763; see gallery), Belvidera asks her husband to kill her while she clings to him:

Jaffeir. Know, Belvidera, when we parted last,
I gave this dagger with thee, as in trust,
To be thy portion, if I e'er proved false,
On such condition was my truth believ'd:
But now 'tis forfeited, and must be paid for.
Offers to stab her again.
Belvidera. (*Kneeling*) Oh! mercy!
Jaffeir. Nay, no struggling.
Belvidera. Now, then, kill me.
Leaps upon his neck and kisses him.
Belvidera. While thus I cling about thy cruel neck,
Kiss thy revengeful lips, and die in joys
Greater than any I can guess hereafter. (*Venice Preserv'd,* 4.2.517–27)[69]

Belvidera's influence on her husband has led him to betray his closest friend, Pierre, undermining his masculinity. Similarly, the effect of Elinor's display of mad passion on Harleigh is to emasculate him. In fact, Harleigh's name should itself suffice to make readers question his manliness, given its perfect homophony with that of Henry Mackenzie's "man of feeling," Harley. Harleigh weeps, blushes, and faints and is ultimately subjected to the same erotic rhetoric usually employed to ensnare women. Elinor's intentional staging of her passion turns Harleigh into a victim of her assertive will, putting him in the awkward position of having to accept the love of a woman he does not love or see her die for love of him—an intentional reversal of a narrative convention Burney had already employed in an earlier novel. In *Camilla,* Eugenia finds herself forced to accept Bellamy's marriage proposal when he threatens to commit suicide: "Instantly he lifted up his pistol, and calling out; 'Forgive, then, O hard-hearted Eugenia, my uncontrollable passion, and shed a tear over the corpse I am going to prostrate at your feet!' was pointing it to his temple, when, overcome with horror, she caught his arm exclaiming; 'Ah! stop! I consent to what you please!' It was in vain she strove afterwards to retract; one scene followed another, till he had bound her by all she herself held sacred, to rescue him from suicide, by consenting to the union" (*Camilla,* 806). Harleigh is enmeshed in the same amorous discourse that traps Eugenia, and the theatrical setting adds a further dimension to his discomfort by making him an unwilling participant in Elinor's performance: "Ashamed, in the midst of his concern, at his own situation, thus publicly avowed as the object of this desperate act; [he] earnestly wished to retreat from the gazers and the remarkers, with whom he shared the notice and the wonder excited by Elinor. . . . *He severely felt the part he seemed called upon to act*" (*The Wanderer,* 361–62; emphasis added). Elinor's mad passion turns him from spectator into spectacle, from subject into object, from man of feeling into a victim of the sexual ideology of sensibility.

A final spectacular display of Elinor's madness takes place in a cemetery, where she has contrived to appear, ghostlike, before Harleigh and Ellis. The situation Burney sets up here has lost all of its referentiality and can be considered a straightforward application of well-worn literary conventions: the early hour, the eerie setting, the shadow gliding among the tombs "with arms uplifted" (*The Wanderer,* 575)—all of these Gothic trappings would have been familiar to readers equipped with a modicum of intertextual literary competence. Although Elinor's final suicide attempt involves pistols, the description of her shroud-like costume recalls the Romantic iconography of madwomen in white who, driven by homicidal mania, brandish daggers: "Startled, [Ellis] looked more earnestly, and then clearly perceived, though half-hidden behind a monument, a form in white; whose dress appeared to be made in the shape, and of the materials, used for our last mortal covering, a shroud. A veil of the same stuff fell over the face of the figure, of which the hands hung down strait at each lank side. . . . [S]he now, slowly raising her right hand, waved to them to follow; while, with her left, she pointed to the church, and uttering a wild shriek, flitted out of sight" (*The Wanderer,* 579). Elinor's gesture, the color of her dress, and her deranged appearance immediately recall the characters played by Sarah Siddons (from Euphrasia in Arthur Murphy's *The Grecian Daughter* to Lady Macbeth [see gallery]),[70] but the texture of the white, flowing folds of her dress and veil recalls more closely the costume worn by Evelina's ghost in M. G. Lewis's *The Castle Spectre* (Drury Lane, 1797), described in the list of costumes for the staged play as a "plain, white muslin dress, white head dress, or binding under the chin, light loose gauze drapery."[71] A consolidated theatrical tradition, the white gown of madwomen—whether of muslin, satin, or linen—was such a fixture by the mid-eighteenth century that it had become the subject of satire. It is here amusingly mocked by Puff in Richard Sheridan's *The Critic:*

Puff. . . . Now enter Tilburina!—
Sneer. Egad, the business comes on quick here.
Puff. Yes, Sir—now she comes in stark mad in white satin.
Sneer. Why in white satin?
Puff. O Lord, Sir—when a heroine goes mad, she always goes into white satin—don't she, Dangle?

Dangle. Always—it's a rule.
Puff. Yes—here it is—[*looking at the book*] "Enter Tilburina stark mad in white satin, and her confidant stark mad in white linen." (*The Critic,* 3.1)

But Elinor's final appearance as a madwoman is directly indebted, I think, less to literary precedent than to the visual arts, and in particular to Fuseli's sketch "Woman with a Stiletto; Man's Head with a Startled Expression" (ca. 1810). The sketch has often been considered, perhaps mistakenly, a portrait of the matricide Mary Ann Lamb.[72] It shows a deranged woman after her thirst for vengeance has been satisfied: in her right hand she grasps a stiletto that she has just used to sever the leg of an animal, perhaps a deer or a sheep, which she holds uplifted in her left hand. Behind her is the frightened face of a man witnessing the spectacle. Philip Martin has described this sketch as conveying the repressed nightmare of Romanticism, while Adriana Craciun has interpreted Mary Ann Lamb's homicidal mania as exposing a subversive nexus of violence, madness, and femininity.[73] In Burney's agenda, which situates Elinor's mad fury in the rich and recognizable context of contemporary theater and the visual arts, Elinor's madness has succeeded in recoding social deviance as social revenge. All a terrified man can do, like the spectator we can see behind Mary Ann Lamb, is look on in shock and horror.

An Index to Frances Burney's *Theatralia*, 1768–1804

This appendix lists the plays, operas, musical performances, and other productions that Frances Burney attended, read, performed in, or referred to in writing between 1768 and 1804, the period covering the correspondence, novels, and plays discussed in this book. Each section of the appendix was produced by collating and cross-referencing Burney's letters and journals with her novels and with her biography of her father, published in 1832.

In the first four sections of the appendix, each entry lists the author's name and the title of the work, followed by parentheses containing the abbreviation for the work's genre and the year in which it was first published or performed. Where possible, I have also given the original venue of the performance and, for operas, the name of the librettist. Below each entry, in square brackets, is the year in which Burney refers to a work and, when reported, the names of the principal performers. At the end of each entry is the source for Burney's reference. The sources by Burney are given in the following sequence: novels (listed in order of date of publication); the biography of Charles Burney; and the letters and journals. Novels are cited by volume, book, and chapter number, except for *Evelina,* which is cited by volume and chapter only.

Where Shakespeare's plays are concerned, it is worth bearing in mind that Burney often refers to one of the many adaptations commonly staged in the second half of the eighteenth century. When Burney mentions a specific adaptation, its author is listed together with the year in which it was adapted.

The final section of the appendix lists the actors, musicians, and playwrights mentioned in Burney's writings during the same period. It was compiled by collating her letters and journals with the *Memoirs of Doctor Burney.* For authors or performers Burney mentions very frequently (e.g., David Garrick or Richard B. Sheridan), I have selected only the most significant references.

The bio-bibliographical information in the appendix is derived from Burney's primary texts as listed in the bibliography and from cross-referencing and collating, among other sources, the *Oxford Dictionary of National Biography* (available online at http://www.oxforddnb.com) and the *Catalogue of the John Larpent Plays* (processed by Professor Donald MacMillan and Brooke Dykman Dockter and available online at http://www.oac.cdlib.org). A comparable attempt to catalog the theatrical and opera references in Burney's work is in the appendix to Tara Ghoshal Wallace's edition of Burney's *A Busy Day* (1984). Since its publication, however, additional scholarly editions of Burney's letters and journals have been published. In addition to benefiting from this new material, which has helped expand the list by more than one hundred items, this appendix has been supplemented by historical and biographical information not included in Wallace's appendix.

Furthermore, Wallace's edition did not draw on Burney's novels, which are crucial not only to identifying her dramatic models, but also to recovering the metatextual web in which the novels are embedded and to reconstructing the "pervasive theatricality" in Burney's texts that I examine in this volume.

ABBREVIATIONS FOR GENRES OF WORKS

[C]	Comedy
[T]	Tragedy
[TC]	Tragicomedy
[D]	Drama
[O]	Opera (comic and dramatic)
[V]	Various (farce, musical farce, prelude, pantomime, afterpiece)

PLAYS, OPERAS, AND OTHER PERFORMANCES ATTENDED BY FRANCES BURNEY

Andrews, Miles Peter

Dissipation; or, Seduction ([C] 1781, Drury Lane)
[1787] *DL*, 3:285

Anfossi, Pasquale

La marchesa giardiniera ([O] 1774, also known as *La finta giardiniera,* dramma giocoso; libretto by Giuseppe Petrosellini?)
[1775; with Giovanna Sestini as prima buffa; Giovanni Lovattini as primo buffo] *EJL*, 2:67

Il trionfo della costanza ([V] 1782, King's Theatre; libretto by Carlo Francesco Badini)
[1782] *DL*, 2:148

Arne, Thomas

Artaxerxes ([O] 1762, opera based on Metastasio's *Artaserse;* libretto by Thomas Arne)
[1773] *EJL*, 1:244

The Masque of Alfred ([O] 1740, first performed at Clivedon House, Maidenhead; libretto by James Thomson and David Mallet)
[1773] *EJL*, 1:312

Bertoni, Ferdinando Giuseppe
Cimene ([O] 1783, King's Theatre; libretto by Benedetto Pasqualigo)
[1783] *DL*, 2:170–71

Orfeo e Euridice ([O] 1776; libretto by Ranieri de' Calzabigi)
[1778; with Gasparo Pacchierotti] *EJL*, 3:184

Bickerstaffe, Isaac
The Padlock ([O] 1768, Drury Lane)
[1780] *DL*, 1:328

Bottarelli, Giovanni Gualberto
Armida ([O] 1774; music by Antonio Sacchini)
[1774] *EJL*, 2:54

Burney, Charles
Queen Mab ([V] 1750, Drury Lane; pantomime with music by Charles Burney)
Memoirs of Doctor Burney, 1:20

Cobb, James
Doctor and Apothecary ([V] 1788, Drury Lane)
[1792] *JL*, 1:113

The Humourist ([O] 1785, Drury Lane)
[1788] *DL*, 3:401

Coffey, Charles
The Devil to Pay; or, The Wives Metamorphos'd ([V] 1731, Drury Lane)
[1789] *DL*, 4:302

Colman, George, the Elder
The Deuce Is in Him ([V] 1763, Drury Lane)
[1771] *EJL*, 1:170, 269

Elfrida ([T] 1772, Covent Garden; adapted from the dramatic poem by William Mason; music by Thomas Arne)
[1773] *EJL*, 1:232

The Jealous Wife ([C] 1761, Drury Lane)
[1789; with Sarah Siddons as Mrs. Oakley] *DL*, 4:308

The Musical Lady ([V] 1762, Drury Lane)
[1773; with Jenny Barsanti as Sophy] *EJL*, 1:261

An Occasional Prelude for the Opening of the Theatre Royal in Covent Garden ([V] 1772; dramatic prelude composed for Jenny Barsanti's first appearance as an actress)
[1773] *EJL*, 1:232
ED, 1:191

The Suicide ([C] 1778, Haymarket)
[1779] *EJL*, 3:388

Colman, George, the Elder, and David Garrick
The Clandestine Marriage ([C] 1766, Drury Lane)
[1769; with David Garrick as Lord Ogleby] *EJL*, 1:94

Colman, George, the Younger
Heir at Law ([C] 1796, Haymarket)
[1798] *JL*, 4:90

Cowley, Hannah
The Belle's Stratagem ([C] 1780, Covent Garden)
[1798] *JL*, 4:129

Cumberland, Richard
The West Indian ([C] 1771, Drury Lane)
[1773; with Jenny Barsanti as Charlotte Rusport] *EJL*, 1:314

Dryden, John, and William Davenant
The Tempest; or, The Enchanted Island ([C] 1667, Duke of York's Theatre, Lincoln's Inn Fields)
[1779] *EJL*, 3:393
DL, 1:288

Foote, Samuel
The Commissary ([V] 1765, Haymarket)
[1789] *DL*, 5:302

Garrick, David
The Alchymist ([C] 1747; adapted from Ben Jonson's *The Alchemist*)
[1777; with David Garrick as Abel Drugger] *EJL*, 1:313–14

The Country Girl ([C] 1766; adapted from *The Country Wife* by William Wycherley)
[1788] *DL*, 4:47
[1801; with Dorothy Jordan as the Country Girl] *JL*, 4:494

The Irish Widow ([V] 1772, Drury Lane; based on *Le mariage forcé* by Molière)
[1789] *DL*, 4:302

Gay, John
The Beggar's Opera ([O] 1728, Lincoln's Inn Fields)
Memoirs of Doctor Burney, 1:21
[1775] *EJL*, 2:189

Gluck, Christoph Willibald
Orfeo ed Euridice ([O] 1762; libretto by Ranieri de' Calzabigi)
[1773; with Giuseppe Millico as Orfeo] *EJL*, 1:264

Goldsmith, Oliver

The Novel; or, Mistakes of a Night ([C] 1773, Covent Garden; produced as *She Stoops to Conquer*)

[1773] *EJL*, 1:254

[1778] *EJL*, 3:41

Hasse, Johann Adolph

Artaserse ([O] 1730; libretto by Metastasio)

[1773] *EJL*, 1:268

Holcroft, Thomas

He's Much to Blame ([C] 1798)

[1798?] *JL*, 4:79

Home, John

Douglas. A Tragedy ([T] 1756, Edinburgh)

[1780; with John Lee as Old Norval] *DL*, 1:409

Inchbald, Elizabeth

The Midnight Hour ([C] 1787, Covent Garden; adapted from the French)

[1789] *DL*, 4:216

Such Things Are ([C] 1787, Covent Garden)

[1787] *DL*, 3:302

Jonson, Ben

The Alchemist ([C] 1611. *See* David Garrick, *The Alchymist*)

Lewis, Matthew Gregory

The Castle Spectre ([D] 1797, Drury Lane)

[1798] *JL*, 4:129

Lloyd, T. A.

The Romp ([V] 1778, Covent Garden)

[1788; with Dorothy Jordan as Priscilla Tomboy] *DL*, 3:368

Madden, Samuel Molyneux

Themistocles, the Lover of His Country ([T] 1729, Theatre Royal, Lincoln's Inn Fields)

[1770] *EJL*, 1:118

Mason, William

Elfrida, a Dramatic Poem, Written on the Model of the Ancient Greek Poetry ([V] 1752. *See* George Colman, the Elder, *Elfrida*)

Metastasio (pseudonym of Pietro Antonio Domenico Trapassi)

Artaserse ([O] 1730)

[1778; music by Ferdinando Bertoni; with Gasparo Pacchierotti] *EJL*, 3:184

Didone abbandonata ([O] 1724)

[1775; music by Giuseppe Colla; with Lucrezia Agujari] *EJL*, 2:155

Didone abbandonata ([O] 1724)
[1775; mezzo pasticcio. Recitativi by Antonio Sacchini; cantabili by Venanzio Rauzzini; with Caterina Gabrielli] *EJL,* 2:160, 165

Morton, Thomas
Secrets Worth Knowing ([C] 1798, Covent Garden)
[1798] *JL,* 4:101–102

O'Brien, William
Cross Purposes ([V] 1772, Covent Garden)
[1773] *EJL,* 1:232

O'Hara, Kane
The Two Misers: A Musical Farce ([V] 1775, Covent Garden)
[1780] *DL,* 1:333

Otway, Thomas
Venice Preserv'd; or, A Plot Discovered ([T] 1682, Duke's Theatre)
[1780; also referred to as *Belvidera;* with John Lee as Pierre, and Sarah Siddons as Belvidera] *DL,* 1:351

Rauzzini, Venanzio
Piramo e Tisbe ([O] 1769, King's Theatre; libretto by Ranieri de' Calzabigi)
[1775] *EJL,* 2:133, 176, 262

L'eroe cinese ([O] 1782, King's Theatre; based on Metastasio's text)
[1782] *DL,* 2:77

Reynolds, Frederick
Cheap Living ([C] 1797, Drury Lane)
[1797] *JL,* 4:29

Rowe, Nicholas
Tamerlane ([T] 1701, New Theatre, Little Lincoln's Inn Fields)
[1768] *EJL,* 1:42–43

Sacchini, Antonio
Il Gran Cid ([O] 1773; libretto by Giovan Gualberto Bottarelli)
[1773] *EJL,* 1:234–38, 257

Montezuma ([O] 1775)
[1775] *EJL,* 2:78
[1779] *EJL,* 3:309

Tamerlano ([O] 1773)
[1773] *EJL,* 1:256–58, 271

Sauvé, dit De La Noue, Jean-Baptiste
La coquette corrigée ([C] 1756, Théâtre de la Comédie Française)
[1787] *DL,* 3:224

Shakespeare, William

As You Like It ([C] ca. 1599)

[1789; with Sarah Siddons as Rosalind] *DL,* 4:303

King Lear ([T] ca. 1605)

[1773; adaptation by Nahum Tate and David Garrick; with David Garrick as King Lear] *EJL,* 1:242, 265

Macbeth ([T] ca. 1605)

[1773; with David Garrick as Macbeth] *EJL,* 1:167

[1773; with Jenny Barsanti as Lady Macbeth] *EJL,* 1:261

The Merchant of Venice ([C] ca. 1597)

[1788; with Sarah Siddons as Portia] *DL,* 3:401

[1797] *JL,* 4:23

Much Ado About Nothing ([C] ca.1598)

[1771, David Garrick as Benedick] *EJL,* 1:153

Richard III ([T] ca. 1598)

[1772; Drury Lane; adapted by Colley Cibber with the title *The Tragical History of Richard III* (ca. 1700), with David Garrick as Richard III] *EJL,* 1:224–25

Sheridan, Richard B.

The Critic; or, A Tragedy Rehearsed ([V] 1779, Drury Lane)

[1780] *DL,* 1:330

The Duenna ([O] 1774, Drury Lane)

[1775] *Memoirs of Doctor Burney,* 1:21

The School for Scandal ([C] 1777, Drury Lane)

[1780] *DL,* 1:330

Thomson, James, and David Mallet

Alfred ([V] ca. 1744–45, private production; a masque, with music by Charles Burney]

Memoirs of Doctor Burney, 1:16–17

Tancred and Sigismunda ([T] 1745?)

[1786] *DL,* 3:139

Vanbrugh, John

The Provok'd Husband; or, A Journey to London ([C]; unfinished work, completed by Colley Cibber in 1728]

[1787] *DL,* 4:305–306

Villiers, George, Second Duke of Buckingham

The Rehearsal ([C] 1671)

[1772; with David Garrick as Bayes] *EJL,* 1:200, 273

Yarrow, Joseph
The Country Farmer Deceived; or, Harlequin Statue ([V] 1739?)
[1770] *EJL,* 1:118

PLAYS READ BY FRANCES BURNEY

Colman, George, the Elder
The English Merchant ([C] 1767, Drury Lane; adapted from *L'Écossaise* by Voltaire)
[1790] *DL,* 5:361

The Man of Business ([C] 1774, Covent Garden)
[1790] *DL,* 4:362–63

Polly Honeycombe ([V] 1760, Drury Lane)
[1790] *DL,* 4:359

Corneille, Pierre
Rodogune ([T] 1644–45)
[1791] *JL,* 1:95

Polyeucte martyr ([D] 1643)
[1791] *JL,* 1:96

Cumberland, Richard
The West Indian ([C] 1771, Drury Lane)
[1775] *EJL,* 2:161
[1779] *EJL,* 3:400

Fielding, Henry
Pasquin. A Dramatick Satire on the Times ([V] 1736, Little Theatre in the Haymarket)
[1783] *DL,* 2:226

Goldoni, Carlo
Tutto il teatro [Complete Works]
[1800] *JL,* 4:399, 443, 504–505

Jerningham, Edward
The Siege of Berwick ([T] 1793, Covent Garden)
[1794] *JL,* 3:79

Johnson, Samuel
Irene ([T] composed 1737; 1749, Drury Lane)
[1778] *EJL,* 3:130

Molière
Les femmes savantes ([C] 1672, Théâtre du Palais-Royal, Paris)
[1797] *JL,* 4:2

Murphy, Arthur
The Way to Keep Him ([C] 1760, Drury Lane)

[1768] *EJL*, 1:24
[1775] *EJL*, 2:198

Reynolds, Frederick
The Dramatist; or, Stop Him Who Can ([C] 1789, Covent Garden)
[1789] *DL*, 4:339

Shakespeare, William
A Comedy of Errors ([C] 1594; perhaps Thomas Hull's adaptation of 1762, also known as *The Twins; or, Comedy of Errors*)
[1785] *DL*, 2:312

Hamlet ([T] ca. 1600)
[1768] *EJL*, 1:5
[1786] *DL*, 3:124

Plays and Poems (also referred to as "Edmond Malone's Shakespeare" [1790])
[1791] *JL* 1:26

Sheridan, Richard B.
The Critic; or, A Tragedy Rehearsed ([V] 1779, Drury Lane)
[1779] *EJL*, 3:444
[1780] *DL*, 1:450

The Rivals ([C] 1775, Drury Lane)
[1790] *DL*, 4:382

Voltaire
Tancrède ([T] 1760)
[1793] *JL*, 2:15

Walpole, Horace
The Mysterious Mother ([T] 1768)
[1786] *DL*, 3:119

PLAYS PERFORMED BY FRANCES BURNEY

Addison, Joseph
The Drummer; or, The Haunted House ([C] 1716, Drury Lane)
[1771; with Frances Burney as Lady Truman; Maria Allen as Sir George Truman] *EJL*, 1:171–72

Cibber, Colley
The Careless Husband ([C] 1704, Drury Lane)
[30 June 1771; with Jenny Barsanti as Edging; Frances Burney as Lady Easy and Lady Graveairs; Maria Allen as Sir Charles Easy] *EJL*, 1:159–63

Colman, George, the Elder
The Deuce Is in Him ([V] 1763, Drury Lane)
[1777] *EJL*, 2:248

Fielding, Henry

The Tragedy of Tragedies; or, The Life and Death of Tom Thumb the Great ([V] 1730, Little Theatre in the Haymarket)
[1777] *EJL*, 2:236, 244–51, 262–63

Garrick, David

Miss in Her Teens; or, The Medley of Lovers ([V] 1747, Covent Garden)
[1770; with Frances Burney as the maid Tag; Dr. Burney as Will Fribble] *Memoirs of Doctor Burney*, 1:60
EJL 1:116

Murphy, Arthur

The Way to Keep Him ([C] 1760, Drury Lane)
[April 1777; with Frances Burney as Mrs. Lovemore] *EJL*, 2:237–44, 252–53

PLAYS, OPERAS, AND OTHER PERFORMANCES MENTIONED IN FRANCES BURNEY'S WRITINGS

Addison, Joseph

Cato ([T] 1713, Drury Lane)
[1781] *The Wanderer*, II (iv, 40), V (ix, 85)
DL, 1:467

The Drummer; or, The Haunted House ([C] 1716, Drury Lane)
Evelina, III (15)

Rosamond: An Opera ([O] 1707, Drury Lane; set by Thomas Clayton)
Cecilia, III (v, 7)
The Wanderer, III (v, 50)

Baillie, Joanna

De Monfort ([T] 1800, Drury Lane; written ca. 1798)
[1800] *JL*, 4:417

Beaumont, Francis and John Fletcher

Laws of Candy ([TC] ca. 1619; published 1647)
The Wanderer, IV (vii, 68)

Bickerstaffe, Isaac

The Hypocrite ([O] 1768, Covent Garden; adaptation of *The Non-Juror* by Colley Cibber, itself an adaptation of Molière's *Tartuffe*]
EJL, 1:49

The Doctor Last in His Chariot ([V] 1769, Haymarket; sequel to Samuel Foote's *The Devil upon Two Sticks*)
[1769] *EJL*, 1:81

The Padlock ([O] 1768, Drury Lane)
The Wanderer, III (vi, 51)

Boaden, James
Ozmyn and Daraxia ([V] 1793, Drury Lane)
Camilla, II (iv, 8)

Burney, Charles
The Cunning Man. A Musical Entertainment ([V] 1766, Drury Lane; musical adaptation of *Le divin du village* by Jean-Jacques Rousseau [1752])
Memoirs of Doctor Burney, 1:165
DL, 6:22

Butt, George
Timoleon ([T] 1777)
[1780] *DL,* 1:361

Centlivre, Susannah
A Bold Stroke for a Wife ([C] 1718, Lincoln's Inn Fields Theatre)
Cecilia, III (v, 7)

Cibber, Colley
The Careless Husband ([C] 1704, Drury Lane)
[1777] *EJL,* 2:241

The Lady's Last Stake; or, The Wife's Resentment ([C] 1707, Queen's Theatre)
Cecilia, IV (vii, 9)

The Refusal; or, The Ladies' Philosophy ([C] 1721, Drury Lane)
[1775; with Jenny Barsanti as Lady Dainty] *EJL,* 2:162

Colman, George, the Elder
Bonduca ([T] 1778; adapted from Francis Beaumont and John Fletcher; music by Henry Purcell; prologue by David Garrick)
[1778] *EJL,* 3:75

The Deuce Is in Him ([V] 1763, Drury Lane)
Evelina, I (20)
[1773] *EJL,* 1:269

The Jealous Wife ([C] 1761, Drury Lane)
[1789] *DL,* 4:421

The Man of Business ([C] 1774)
Cecilia, III (v, 12)

Colman, George, the Elder, and David Garrick
The Clandestine Marriage ([C] 1766, Drury Lane)
[1775] *EJL,* 2:137
[1778] *EJL,* 3:13, 49, 116
[1778] *DL,* 1:96
[1798] *DL,* 3:463

Congreve, William
Love for Love ([C] 1695, Lincoln's Inn Theatre)
Evelina, I (20)

Crisp, Samuel
Virginia ([T] 1754, Drury Lane; with prologue and epilogue by David Garrick)
Memoirs of Doctor Burney, 1:176–78
[1785] *DL,* 2:298–99

Delap, John
The Royal Suppliants; or, Macaria ([T] 1781, Drury Lane)
[1779] *EJL,* 3:276, 280

Demoustier, Charles Albert
Les femmes ([C] 1793, Théâtre de la Nation, Paris)
[1797] *JL,* 3:308

Dryden, John
All for Love; or, The World Well Lost ([T], Theatre Royal; staged December 1677, printed 1678)
[1778] *EJL,* 3:89

Etherege, George
The Man of Mode; or, Sir Fopling Flutter ([C] 1676, Dorset Gardens Theatre)
[1779] *EJL,* 3:283

Farquhar, George
The Constant Couple; or, A Trip to the Jubilee ([C] 1699, Drury Lane)
[1788; with Dorothy Jordan as Sir Harry Wildair] *DL,* 4:54

Fielding, Henry
The Tragedy of Tragedies; or, The Life and Death of Tom Thumb the Great ([V] 1730, Little Theatre in the Haymarket)
[1779] *JL,* 4:319

Foote, Samuel
The Commissary ([V] 1765, Haymarket)
Evelina, II (13)

The Minor ([C] 1760, Drury Lane)
Evelina, II (13)

The Devil upon Two Sticks ([C] 1768, Haymarket)
[1769] *EJL,* 1:76

The Mayor of Garratt ([C] 1763, Haymarket)
[1774] *EJL,* 2:57

Garrick, David
Cymon ([O] 1767, Drury Lane; music by Michael Arne; adaptation of John Dryden's *Cymon and Iphigenia*)
[1792] *JL,* 1:113

Lethe; or, Aesop in the Shades ([V] 1740, Drury Lane)
[1775; a reading performed for King George III] *EJL*, 3:227
[1790] *DL*, 4:361

Isabella; or, The Fatal Marriage ([T] 1757, Drury Lane; altered from Thomas Southerne)
[1774] *EJL*, 2:59

An Occasional Prelude on Quitting the Theatre ([V] 1776, Drury Lane; also known as *An Occasional Prologue Spoken by Mr Garrick, 10 June 1710.*)
The Wanderer, IV (vii, 70)

A Peep behind the Curtain ([V] 1767, Drury Lane; also known as *A Peep behind the Curtain; or, The New Rehearsal*)
[1798] *JL*, 4:221

Goldsmith, Oliver
The Good-Natur'd Man ([C] 1768, Covent Garden)
[1768] *EJL*, 1:12
[1778] *EJL*, 3:95

Heywood, Thomas
The Fair Maid of the West ([C] printed 1631)
The Wanderer, I (i, 20)

Hoadley, Benjamin
The Suspicious Husband ([C] 1747, Covent Garden)
[with David Garrick as Ranger] *Evelina*, I (10)
[1775; with Jenny Barsanti as Clarinda] *EJL*, 2:114

Johnson, Samuel
Irene ([T] composed 1737; 1749, Drury Lane)
[1778] *EJL*, 3:110

Jonson, Ben
The Alchemist ([C] 1611)
[1775; as altered from Ben Jonson by David Garrick; with Garrick as Abel Drugger] *EJL*, 2:95

Every Man in His Humour ([C] 1598, Curtain Theatre, Shoreditch)
[1775] *EJL*, 2:143
Camilla, III (vi, 4)

Every Man in His Humour ([C] 1598, Curtain Theatre, Shoreditch; altered by David Garrick in 1751)
Memoirs of Doctor Burney, 1:347
[1771] *EJL*, 1:172

Kelly, Hugh
False Delicacy ([C] 1768, Drury Lane)
Evelina, II (28)

Kyd, Thomas
The Spanish Tragedy ([T] ca. 1582–92)
Cecilia, III (v, 8)
Camilla, II (iv, 8)

Lally-Tolendal, Trophime-Gérard
Le Comte de Strafford ([T] 1795)
[read in manuscript in 1792] *JL,* 1:127

Tuathal-Tearmour, ou, la restauration de la monarchie en Irlande ([T] 1797; completed 1824)
[1797] *JL,* 4:53

Lee, Nathaniel
The Rival Queens; or, The Death of Alexander the Great ([T] 1677, Theatre Royal)
[1770] *The Wanderer,* III (v, 46)
EJL, 1:115

Lessing, Gotthold Ephraim
Emilia Galotti ([T] 1772)
[1794] *JL,* 3:88

Mason, William
Elfrida, A Dramatic Poem, Written on the Model of the Ancient Greek Poetry ([V] 1752; adapted by George Colman, the Elder, 1772, Covent Garden)
Cecilia, II (iv, 5)

Merry, Robert
Lorenzo ([T] 1791, Covent Garden)
[1791] *JL,* 1:85

Metastasio (pseudonym of Pietro Antonio Domenico Trapassi)
Artaserse ([O] 1730) [1778; music by F. Bertoni]
Cecilia, I (i, 8)

Molière
Les précieuses ridicules ([C] 1659, Théâtre du Petit-Bourbon, Paris)
[1775] *EJL,* 2:121

More, Hannah
Percy ([T] 1777, Covent Garden)
[1778] *EJL,* 3:133

Murphy, Arthur
All in the Wrong ([C] 1761, Drury Lane)
[1802] *JL,* 5:210

The Citizen ([V] 1761, Drury Lane)
[1802] *JL,* 5:211

The Grecian Daughter ([T] 1772, Drury Lane)
[1802] *JL,* 5:210

Know Your Own Mind ([C] 1777, Covent Garden)
[1778] *EJL*, 3:110
[1802] *JL*, 5:210

The Way to Keep Him ([C] 1760, Drury Lane)
[1802] *JL*, 5:210

O'Keeffe, John
The Agreeable Surprise ([V] 1781, Haymarket)
[1788] *DL*, 4:88

Otway, Thomas
Venice Preserv'd; or, A Plot Discovered ([T] 1682, Duke's Theatre)
Cecilia, V (x, 2)

Piccinni, Niccolò
La Cecchina, ossia la buona figliuola ([O] 1760; libretto by Carlo Goldoni)
[1769] *EJL*, 1:56
[1777] *EJL*, 2:263

Pope, Alexander
"Prologue to Mr. Addison's Cato" (published 1736)
The Wanderer, V (ix, 82)

Richardson, Elizabeth
The Double Deception; or, Lovers Perplex'd ([C] 1779, Drury Lane)
[1779] *EJL*, 3:264

Rowe, Nicholas
Tamerlane ([T] 1701, New Theatre, Little Lincoln's Inn Fields)
[1792] *JL*, 1:121

Shakespeare, William
As You Like It ([C] ca. 1599)
Cecilia, IV (viii, 5)

Hamlet ([T] ca. 1600)
Cecilia, I (i, 2), II (iv, 6), III (v, 5), IV (vii, 3), V (ix, 10)
Camilla, II (iv, 8), V (x, 4), V (x, 6) [twice], V (x, 9)
The Wanderer, I (ii, 12), II (iv, 36), II (iv, 40), IV (vii, 68), V (ix, 85) [twice]
[with David Garrick as Hamlet] *Memoirs of Doctor Burney*, 1:358
[1768] *EJL*, 1:5
[1775] *EJL*, 2:189
[1778] *EJL*, 3:59, 81
[1779] *EJL*, 3:349
[1786] *DL*, 3:72
[1801] *JL*, 4:503

1 Henry IV ([T] 1597)
Cecilia, I (ii, 3)

The Wanderer, IV (vii, 61), IV (viii, 74)
[1779] *EJL,* 3:407

2 Henry IV ([T] 1600)
Cecilia, I (ii, 4)

Julius Caesar ([T] 1599)
[1775] *EJL,* 2:123
[1791] *JL,* 1:95

King Lear ([T] ca. 1605)
Evelina, I (12)
Cecilia, I (ii, 3)
[1783] *DL,* 2:228

Macbeth ([T] 1606)
Evelina, prefatory letter
Cecilia, III (vi, 3)
Camilla, II (iv, 8)
[1779] *EJL,* 3:345
[1802] *JL,* 5:167

Measure for Measure ([C] ca. 1605)
[1788] *DL,* 3:468

The Merchant of Venice ([C] ca. 1596)
Evelina, prefatory letter (twice)
Cecilia, I (ii, 3), IV (vii, 9), IV (viii, 1)
Camilla, II (iv, 8)
The Wanderer, III (vi, 53), III (vi, 56)
[1797] *JL,* 3:296

The Merry Wives of Windsor ([C] ca. 1604)
[1769] *EJL,* 1:81
[1778] *EJL,* 3:130, 178
[1779] *EJL,* 4:312

A Midsummer Night's Dream ([C] ca. 1595)
[1792] *JL,* 1:205

Much Ado about Nothing ([C] 1600)
[1775] *EJL,* 2:164
[1778] *EJL,* 3:35
[1790] *DL,* 4:348
[1797] *JL,* 3:297

Othello ([T] ca. 1604)
Camilla, II (iv, 8), V (x, 4)
The Wanderer, II (iv, 38), IV (vii, 70), V (ix, 83)
Memoirs of Doctor Burney, 2:158

[1775] *EJL,* 2:113
[1778] *EJL,* 3:42, 74, 154
[1779] *EJL,* 3:349, 416
[1791] *DL,* 4:449
[1795] *JL,* 3:112
[1799] *JL,* 4:311

Richard III ([T] ca. 1598)
Evelina, I (12)

Romeo and Juliet ([T] ca. 1599)
Cecilia, I (i, 9), III (vi, 9) [twice]
The Wanderer, IV (vii, 68)

The Tempest ([C] ca. 1610)
[1798; probably David Garrick's version, 1756] *The Wanderer,* III (vi, 54), IV (vii, 68), V (x, 89)
JL, 4:233

Twelfth Night; or, What You Will ([C] 1623 folio)
Evelina, I (17)

Sheridan, Frances
The Discovery ([C] 1763, Drury Lane)
ED, 2:290

Sheridan, Richard B.
The Critic; or, A Tragedy Rehearsed ([V] 1779, Drury Lane)
[1795] *JL,* 3:107

The School for Scandal ([C] 1777, Drury Lane)
[1779] *EJL,* 3:234

Smart, Christopher
An Epilogue, Spoken by Mrs. Midnight's Daughter (1753)
Cecilia, II (iv, 6)

Vanbrugh, John, and Colley Cibber
The Provok'd Husband; or, A Journey to London ([C]; unfinished work, completed by Colley Cibber in 1728)
Cecilia, II (iv, 6)
Camilla, II (iii, 13)
The Wanderer, I (x, 1)
[1787; reading by Sarah Siddons] *DL,* 4:307

Villiers, George, Second Duke of Buckingham
The Rehearsal ([C] 1671)
[1778] *Memoirs of Doctor Burney,* 1:350
EJL, 3:50, 72

Walpole, Horace
The Mysterious Mother ([T] 1768)
[1768] *DL,* 3:254

ACTORS, SINGERS, AND PLAYWRIGHTS MENTIONED IN FRANCES BURNEY'S BIOGRAPHICAL AND AUTOBIOGRAPHICAL WRITINGS

Abington, Frances (1737–1815)
EJL, 2:94
DL, 2:143, 146

Aickin, James (ca. 1736–1803)
JL, 1:85

Barsanti, [Jane], known as Jenny (d. 1795)
EJL, 1:73, 159–64, 172, 177, 197, 261, 314, 323, 2:81, 94, 114, 135, 150, 161–62, 198–99, 3:337

Bensley, Robert (ca. 1741–1817)
JL, 3:100

Betterton (or Butterton), Julia (1779–1850)
JL, 4:23, 79

Brunton, Anne (1769–1808)
JL, 1:85

Burgoyne, John (1723–92)
DL, 1:317

Butt, George (1741–95)
DL, 1:361

Cibber (neé Arne), Susannah Maria (1714–66)
Memoirs of Doctor Burney, 1:14, 17

Colman, George, the Elder (bapt. 1732–94)
Memoirs of Doctor Burney, 1:204

Colman, George, the Younger (1762–1836)
Memoirs of Doctor Burney, 1:204

Cumberland, Richard (1732–1811)
EJL, 3:87–88, 227, 386–78, 398–400, 410
DL, 3:71
JL, 3:101, 105, 108–10

Delap, John (1725–1812)
EJL, 3:276, 280, 283–96, 311–20, 389–90, 395–96, 402–404, 414–15, 418, 441–43

Dodd, James William (ca. 1740–96)
JL, 1:85

Elliot (or Elliott), Ann (1743–1769)
JL, 5:209–11

Farren, Elizabeth (*married name,* Elizabeth Smith Stanley, countess of Derby] (1759–1829)
DL, 3:239
JL, 3:295, 4:23

Foote, Samuel (ca. 1720–77)
EJL, 3:378

Ford, Harriet Ann (1754–1825)
EJL, 1:40, 144–46, 2:75

Garrick, David (1717–79)
Memoirs of Doctor Burney, 1:15, 165–72, 344–60, 2:99–100, 201–304
EJL, 1:147–51, 167, 183–84, 215, 225, 242, 265, 271–73, 311–14, 322, 2:40, 80, 94–97, 100, 227–29, 3:75, 137–38, 228, 417
DL, 1:346, 351, 409, 2:343

Goldoni, Carlo (1707–93)
JL, 4:369, 399, 504–505

Goldsmith, Oliver (ca. 1728–1774)
EJL, 3:95, 251

Jerningham, Edward (1737–1812)
JL, 3:79, 83–84

Jordan, Dorothy (also known as Dorothy Bland and Dorothy Phillips) (1761–1816)
DL, 3:385–86, 4:47, 54, 59
JL, 4:25, 494

Kemble, John Philip (1757–1823)
JL, 3:79, 88, 98–100, 4:47

Lalauze, Charles (ca. 1729–1775)
EJL, 1:97–98, 2:16, 127

Lalauze, Miss (1754–ca. 1809)
EJL, 1:118–19, 2:153

Lee, John (1725–1781)
DL, 1:351, 376

Mills, Theodosia (fl. 1748–94)
EJL, 1:314–15

More, Hannah (1745–1833)
EJL, 3:119–20, 227–28

Murphy, Arthur (1727–1805)
Memoirs of Doctor Burney, 2:174–76

EJL, 3:111, 138, 207, 243–47, 250–52, 278–79, 283–97, 347, 353–54
DL, 1:318–9, 323, 449–50, 2:75, 3:505
JL, 5:209–12

Murray, Clemens (1754–1821)
JL, 4:79

Palmer, John (1744–98)
JL, 1:85, 3:100

Parson, William (1736–95)
JL, 1:85

Pope, Jane (1744–1818)
EJL, 1:177

Pope (*née* Campion), Maria Ann (performed under the name Mrs. Spencer) (1775–1803)
JL, 4:79

Quick, John (1748–1831)
DL, 4:301

Quin, James (1693–1766)
EJL, 3:82
DL, 1:409

Reddish, Samuel (1735–85)
EJL, 2:135

Richardson, Elizabeth (dates unknown)
EJL, 3:263–64

Sheridan, Richard B. (1751–1816)
Memoirs of Doctor Burney, 3:136–39
EJL, 1:249, 3:229–36, 342, 418
DL, 1:315–16, 347, 361, 2:54, 3:411, 479
JL, 1:117, 2:4, 3:98–100, 120, 334–55, 4:134, 5:106

Siddons (*née* Kemble), Sarah (1755–1831)
DL, 1:351, 2:141–43, 146, 175, 343, 3:305–307, 385, 401, 4:150, 303, 305, 308
JL, 3:99–100

Thomson, James (1700–48)
Memoirs of Doctor Burney, 1:204

Wallis (*married name,* Campbell), Tryphosa Jane (1774–1848)
JL, 4:24

Wells, Mary Anne (1762–1829)
DL, 4:302
JL, 1:207–212

Yates, Mary Ann (1728–87)
EJL, 2:56, 160–61, 172, 250

Young, Elizabeth (known as Mrs. Dorman) (d. 1773)
EJL, 2:161

Notes

INTRODUCTION

1. For the discourse of hauntology, see Derrida, *Specters of Marx.* Recent studies on the relation between eighteenth-century theater and the novel are Anderson, *Eighteenth-Century Authorship and the Play of Fiction;* Nachumi, *Acting Like a Lady.* Among the most helpful introductions to the eighteenth-century stage are Bevis, *English Drama;* Boas, *An Introduction to Eighteenth-Century Drama;* Craik et al., *The Revels History of Drama in English,* vols. 5–6; Donohue, *The Cambridge History of British Theatre,* vol. 2; Nicoll, *A History of English Drama,* vols. 1–3. The introduction to *The London Stage, 1660–1800* is also very useful.

2. Colman, "Advertisement" to *The Jealous Wife:* see Loftis, *Sheridan and the Drama of Georgian England,* 28.

3. As James Edward Austen-Leigh recalled of his aunt, "Every circumstance narrated in Sir Charles Grandison, all that was ever said or done in the cedar parlour, was familiar to her; and the wedding days of Lady L. and Lady G. were as well remembered as if they had been living friends": Austen-Leigh, *A Memoir of Jane Austen,* 331. Austen's works lend themselves very well to the sort of metaliterary analysis that allows characters to display their moral characteristics. In *Sense and Sensibility* (chap. 10), the romantic lovers Marianne and Willoughby appreciate Cowper and Scott while admiring Pope "no more than is proper." In *Northanger Abbey* (chap. 7), the boorish John Thorpe dismisses Frances Burney's *Camilla,* one of Austen's favorite novels. And in *Persuasion,* Captain Benwick praises the exaggerated sensibility of the romantic poets to such an extent that Anne "recommend[ed] a larger allowance of prose in his daily study": Austen, *Persuasion,* 122. Austen's own affective responsiveness as a reader is of course fully in line with eighteenth-century aesthetics, and particularly with Adam Smith's theory of the sympathizing imagination. For a recent discussion, see Bray, *The Female Reader in the English Novel,* chap. 1.

4. Susan Staves uses the term "embedding" in an illuminating essay on eighteenth-century novelists' appropriation of Restoration drama. She acutely observes that "the embedding of the Restoration play-texts in the eighteenth-century novels

reveals an appropriation by bourgeois women of sentiments and entitlements that had formerly been the property of the aristocracy. . . . Sometimes the words of the earlier drama allow later hearers, speakers or readers to possess intensities and kinds of feelings which the polite world stipulated they could not own more directly": Staves, "Fatal Marriages?" 96.

5. Fielding, *The History of Tom Jones, a Foundling,* 566.

6. Noyes, *The Neglected Muse,* 5.

7. See Ricoeur, *Memory, History, Forgetting.*

8. My analysis of transtextuality in Burney's macro-text is deeply indebted to Genette, *Palimpsests.*

9. Colman, *Polly Honeycombe,* vii.

10. Among many descriptions of such readings, particularly suggestive are those that relate to Sarah Siddons's dramatic readings at the Argyle Rooms, in Boaden, *Memoirs of Mrs. Siddons,* 457–62.

11. After great difficulty, Johnson's tragedy *Irene* (written ca. 1737) was finally performed at the Drury Lane Theatre in 1749 but met with little success. Smollett's tragedy *The Regicide* was written circa 1738 and was never performed. He later fictionalized his endeavors to stage the play in chapters 62 and 63 of *Roderick Random* (1748).

12. It is thanks to feminist criticism that Behn's role as the first female novelist, if not the first novelist, has been reassessed: see the classic Spencer, *The Rise of the Woman Novelist.* For further details, see Spengemann, "The Earliest American Novel." In relation to the theater, see Zimbardo, "Aphra Behn." Attesting to a longstanding inter-artistic dialogue, Behn's *Oroonoko* was first dramatized by Thomas Southerne in *Oroonoko: A Tragedy* (Theatre Royal, 1696) and later by John Hawkesworth (Drury Lane, 1759).

13. Pagnini, *Pragmatica della letteratura,* 89. Translations from Italian in this volume are by Laura Kopp.

14. Barthes, *S/Z,* 15.

15. On the figure of the writerly reader, see ibid., 4.

16. De Marinis, "Dramaturgy of the Spectator," 102.

17. This paradoxical classification of Burney's writings was a late-Romantic invention, but its longevity was confirmed by the surprising discussion over the wording to be used for the memorial window to Burney in Poets' Corner, Westminster Abbey. Paula Stepankowski, president of the Burney Society, remarked that "the listing of Fanny's accomplishments" (as "novelist," "diarist," "playwright," and "Daughter of Charles Burney, Mus. D.") gave rise to a lively debate. "The problem, of course, is due to everyone's own particular interest. The historians and biographers amongst us naturally thought Fanny's diaries to be of supreme importance, whilst those involved in English literature thought she was far better known for her novels": Stepankowski, "Plaque Wording Proposed." After a first phase, in which all members of the society seemed to agree that Burney's role as playwright should be listed before her role as daughter—but not before any other label on the list—the formula "Novelist, Playwright, Diarist" was finally chosen, illustrating both the

recent drive to include all of Burney's writings in the canon of her works and the altered critical assessment of her dramatic writings. The formula was ultimately not used due to space constraints.

18. Tara Ghoshal Wallace, "Burney as Dramatist," in Sabor, *The Cambridge Companion to Frances Burney,* 55–74. The first book length study of the dramatic works of Burney was Darby, *Frances Burney Dramatist.*

19. No analysis of the novel's emergence out of the drama would be complete without referring, albeit in passing, to the most important histories of the novel, starting with Watt, *The Rise of the Novel* (1957). Although this classic study is often criticized as limited and outdated, it remains an essential starting point. Other influential analyses offering innovative interpretations combined with methodological rigor—while also participating in an ongoing dialogue with Watt's work—are Davies, *Factual Fictions;* Hunter, *Before Novels;* McKeon, *The Origins of the English Novel;* Rivero and Justice, *The Eighteenth-Century Novel;* Spacks, *Novel Beginnings;* Warner, *Licensing Entertainment,* esp. chaps. 1–2. Also useful is the issue of *Eighteenth-Century Fiction* devoted to "Reconsidering the Rise of the Novel" (January–April 2000), with contributions by most of the literary historians listed earlier. For an excellent and clear summary, see esp. Folkenflik, "The New Model Eighteenth-Century Novel." The most recent work on the intersections between the novel and the theater is Anderson, *Eighteenth-Century Authorship and the Play of Fiction.* The volume unfortunately appeared too late for me to make full use of it in this study.

20. I have intentionally omitted from my analysis a full discussion of the economic, social, historical, and philosophical factors that contributed to the novel's rise and the theater's relative decline. They are discussed at length in the works cited in n. 19, to which I would add an essential reference to Brewer, *The Pleasures of the Imagination.* I shall, however, offer a brief summary of those factors: (1) the withdrawal of royal patronage from the theater after the death of Charles II in 1685; (2) the long-standing bias against the theater that originated with the Puritans, combined with new attacks associated with the moral campaigns of the societies for the reformation of manners; (3) the Stage Licensing Act of 1737, entailing preventive censorship, the license system, and the creation of what would become the double monopoly of the Drury Lane and Covent Garden theaters; (4) the consolidation of entrepreneurial power; (5) the moralizing influence exercised by the female public; and (6) the lack of financial security inherent in the system of benefit performances. As regards, instead, the circulation of print culture, scholars agree on the importance of the following: (1) changes in the composition and structure of the reading public; (2) the expansion of the publishing market (and the consequent end of the booksellers' domination of the market, the growth of provincial publishing, the development of periodical literature, the lower price of novels, and the emergence of lending libraries); (3) the professionalization of writing (with increased financial security for novelists and their emancipation from aristocratic patronage and commission work); and, finally, (4) the emergence of new social classes and the increase in leisure (particularly for women). The consensus among scholars, as both of these lists show,

is that the main cause of the novel's emergence was the ascendance of bourgeois ideology and the resulting inclusion of the middle classes in the new culture of leisure of the eighteenth century.

21. Barthes, *Writing Degree Zero.*

22. For a discussion of the hybrid theatrical productions of the time, see Saggini, "A Stage of Tears and Terror."

23. Epstein, *The Iron Pen,* 3; emphasis added.

24. *EJL,* 3:238.

ONE. IN THE BEGINNING

1. "The very next reflection that I made was this, That an Heroick Play ought to be an imitation, in little of an Heroick Poem: and, consequently, that Love and Valour ought to be the Subject of it": Dryden, *Of Heroique Playes,* 10. The first line of Ludovico Ariosto's *Orlando Furioso* in Sir John Harington's translation of 1591 is, "Of Dames, of Knights, of armes, of loves delight."

2. Bertinetti, *Storia della letteratura inglese,* 1:293.

3. Brown, *English Dramatic Form,* 17.

4. Johnson, *Lives of the English Poets,* 1:360–61.

5. *The Correspondents,* 25–26. See Noyes, *The Neglected Muse,* 42–43.

6. Watt, *The Rise of the Novel,* 202.

7. See the seminal Roach, *The Player's Passion.* See also Billi, "La recita delle passioni."

8. Billi, "Dal teatro al romanzo," 41.

9. See Saggini, "Radcliffe's Novels and Boaden's Dramas."

10. Dryden, *All for Love,* preface, 217–18. The many productions of Dryden's tragedy throughout the eighteenth century suggest how well it suited the aesthetic tastes of the new century's audiences. "[Dryden's] version of the immortal story of Antony and Cleopatra attained 110 presentations during the years from 1702 to 1776, with occasional lapses . . . whereas Shakespeare's tragedy, in the version of Edward Capell (1758), was revived only once in the century, unsuccessfully": Noyes, *The Neglected Muse,* 21.

11. Brown, *English Dramatic Form,* 85.

12. Fielding, *The History and Adventures of Joseph Andrews and His Friend Mr. Abraham Adams,* 143.

13. In Aristotle's ethics, virtue is the prerogative of the upper classes. Although *Poetics* states that the playwright can portray individual goodness "in every class of persons," the statement is highly qualified. "A woman may be good and a slave may be good, though perhaps as a class women are inferior and slaves utterly base": Aristotle, *Poetics,* 60. Late-seventeenth-century tragedy had clearly distanced itself from Aristotle's position, especially where women's roles were concerned.

14. Lillo, *The London Merchant,* dedication, 228.

15. Rowe, *The Fair Penitent,* 3.

16. Richardson, *Clarissa,* preface, 36.

17. *The Friends,* 2:95–96. See Noyes, *The Neglected Muse,* 11.

18. Christopher J. Wheatley, "Tragedy," in Fisk, *The Cambridge Companion to English Restoration Theatre,* 72.

19. Gentleman, *The Dramatic Censor,* 2:462. See Noyes, *The Neglected Muse,* 49.

20. Joseph Addison, "English Tragedy: Poetic Justice, Tragic-Comedy, Double Plots, Rants," *Spectator* 40 (1711), in Steele and Addison, *Selections from the "Tatler" and the "Spectator,"* 322–23. Addison's point about the drama was taken up by Richardson in his postscript to *Clarissa,* where he quotes Addison's essay at length in order to justify the novel's tragic conclusion: see Richardson, *Clarissa,* 1495–97.

21. Johnson, *Johnson on Shakespeare,* 161. Dennis had written: "'Tis true, indeed, upon the stage of the world the wicked sometimes prosper, and the guiltless suffer. But that is permitted by the Governor of the world to shew, from the attribute of his infinite justice, that there is compensation in futurity. . . . But the poetical persons in tragedy exist no longer than the reading or the representation . . . and therefore, during that reading or representation, according to their merits or demerits, they must be punished or rewarded." Johnson comments on the passage in "Life of Addison," *Lives of the English Poets,* 2:135. See also Wilkins, "John Dennis and Poetic Justice."

22. Fielding, *The Life of Mr. Jonathan Wild, the Great,* 163.

23. The other model can be traced back to Restoration comedy and its sentimental obsession with sexual relations and the gender of its heroines. On Richardson's dramatic models, see Konigsberg, "The Dramatic Background of Richardson's Novels." Konigsberg concludes, "It is difficult not to suspect that Richardson was directly influenced by *Caelia* when writing *Clarissa.* The two works resemble one another not only in theme, plot, and major characters, but both also possess such similar details as the presentation by each heroine of a ring to one of her jailers, such similar lines as those uttered by the dying villains, and such similar secondary figures as the villains' morally converted friends": Konigsberg, "The Dramatic Background of Richardson's Novels," 52.

24. *Theatrical Review,* 1:71–72, quoted in Noyes, *The Neglected Muse,* 50.

25. Richardson, *Clarissa,* 620.

26. Brown, *English Dramatic Form,* 180.

27. Charles Gildon, *The Lives and Characters of the English Dramatick Poets* (1699), 111, quoted in Jean Marsden, "Spectacle, Horror, and Pathos," in Fisk, *The Cambridge Companion to English Restoration Theatre,* 182.

28. Mackenzie, *The Man of Feeling,* chap. 28.

29. Brown, *English Dramatic Form,* 86.

30. Konigsberg, "The Dramatic Background of Richardson's Novels," 47–48.

31. Lillo, *The London Merchant,* prologue, 290.

32. Noyes, *The Neglected Muse,* 51. "*Arpasia.* Oh! dismal! 'tis not to be born. Ye Moralists, Ye Talkers, what are all your Precepts now? Patience? Distraction? blast the Tyrant, blast him. Avenging Lightnings, snatch him hence, ye Fiends! Love! Death! *Moneses!* Nature can no more, Ruin is on her, and she sinks at once. [*She sinks down*]": Rowe, *Tamerlane,* 5.1.

33. For example, through the influence exercised on Frances Burney's work by Rowe's poetics, as expressed in the prologue to *The Fair Penitent* (see chapter 4 in this volume).

34. Theophilus Cibber, prologue to Johnson, *Caelia.*

35. I use the term "formal realism" in Watt's classic sense to describe narrative directed "towards the delineation of the domestic life and the private experience of the characters who belong to it: the two go together—we get inside their minds as well as inside their houses": Watt, *The Rise of the Novel,* 175. It is worth noting that already in *Venice Preserv'd,* Pierre, Jaffeir, and Belvidera speak in blank verse, whereas the "low" and mercenary relationship of the prostitute Aquilina and Antonio is rendered in prose.

36. Watt, *The Rise of the Novel,* 176.

37. Lillo, *The London Merchant,* preface, 290–91. A few years later (and after the novel had already come into its own), another middle-class playwright, Edward Moore, used similar terms in his preface to *The Gamester* (1753) to justify his use of the middle style: "The play of the *Gamester* was intended to be a natural picture of that kind of life, of which all men are judges; and as it struck at a vice so universally prevailing, it was thought proper to adapt its language to the capacities and feelings of every part of the audience."

38. There are three moments of resolution in the play: at the end of act 3 (Barnwell's crime is discovered and he is thrown into prison), of act 4 (Marwood's connivance is revealed and she is arrested), and of act 5 (Barnwell and Marwood are hanged). The explanatory meeting of Barnwell, Maria, and Trueman serves only to juxtapose the guilty apprentice with characters who embody Pure Love and Disinterested Friendship. It departs from Aristotle by being connected to the *fabula* neither by necessity nor by verisimilitude and is warranted only by the new pathetic requirements of eighteenth-century tragedy.

39. Lillo, *The London Merchant,* dedication, 288. The use of the lexeme "force" here does not seem accidental; Samuel Johnson uses its variant, "power," in his famous essay on the novel in *Rambler* No. 4. "But if the power of example is so great, as to take possession of the memory by a kind of violence, and produce effects almost without the intervention of the will, care ought to be taken that, when the choice is unrestrained, the best examples only should be exhibited": Johnson, *The Rambler* No. 4, 22. For Johnson, the danger of the novel lies precisely in its "low" language and subject matter. As we have seen, these also feature in pathetic and bourgeois tragedy.

40. Lillo, *The London Merchant,* dedication, 287.

41. Richardson, preface to *Pamela,* 31. Cf. "Advertisement to the Reader," in Johnson, *Caelia:* "If these Scenes shall have any Effect on the Morals of our Youth, and prove a Caution to the Young and Innocent of the Fair Sex, I shall think my self well rewarded."

42. Richardson, preface to *Clarissa,* 36.

43. Brown, *English Dramatic Form,* 146.

44. Johnson, "Life of Nicholas Rowe," *Lives of the English Poets,* 2:67.

45. See Barker-Benfield, *The Culture of Sensibility.*

46. The term was used for a type of comedy set in Spain that was characterized by intricate plots, mistaken identities, and an elevated moral tone. The English model for this short-lived genre is Samuel Tuke's *The Adventures of Five Hours* (Lincoln's Inn Fields, 1661), a well-crafted adaptation of a Spanish play, *Los empeños de seis horas,* attributed to Calderón.

47. Wycherley, *The Plain Dealer,* 13, lines 24–27.

48. Congreve, *Congreve's Amendments of Mr. Collier's False and Imperfect Citations,* 12–13.

49. See Tave, *The Amiable Humorist.*

50. Steele, *The Lying Lover,* epilogue. Steele's use of the verb "chastise" here is suggestive: derived from "chaste," it adds distinct moral connotations to his aesthetic point. A similar effect is achieved by Addison's allegory in *Spectator* No. 35, which associates true humor with truth and good sense and false humor with falsehood, nonsense, and laughter. In *Spectator* No. 47, he uses Hobbes's *Discourse of Human Nature* (1650) to attack the farcical aspects of comedy. "Every one laughs at some Body that is in an inferior State of Folly to himself": Joseph Addison, "Laughter," in Steele and Addison, *Selections from the "Tatler" and the "Spectator,"* 337–38.

51. See also the dialogue between Sir Friendly Moral and the scarcely repentant gambler, Lord Wronglove, in act 3 of Colley Cibber's *The Lady's Last Stake* (1707). When Wronglove tells Sir Friendly, "O dear Sir, I'm grown a Fellow of the most retir'd Conversation in the World," Sir Friendly replies, "Your Reformation is not of a very long Date, I'm afraid; for if I don't mistake, I saw you but yesterday at the Thatch't-house, with a Napkin upon your Head, at the Window in very hopeless Company."

52. Richardson, *The History of Sir Charles Grandison,* vol. 4, letter 27.

53. Ibid., vol. 3, letter 3.

54. One may think here of Austen's Mary Crawford and Emma Woodhouse, characters who display their author's Johnsonian uneasiness with amoral and irreverent wit, or of Elizabeth Bennett, who at first admits, "I dearly love a laugh," only to be reproved by Darcy ("The wisest and best of men—nay, the wisest and best of their actions—may be rendered ridiculous by a person whose first object in life is a joke") and is thus prompted to rectify: "I hope I never ridicule what is wise or good": Austen, *Pride and Prejudice,* 47.

55. Carchia, *Retorica del sublime,* 147.

56. See Stone, *The Family, Sex, and Marriage in England.*

57. Bertinetti, *Storia del teatro inglese dalla Restaurazione all'Ottocento,* 45. The best-known contemporary criticism of the libertine is William Hogarth's sequence *The Rake's Progress* (1733–35), which illustrates eight scenes in the life of Tom Rakewell, who ends his debauched career first in prison and then in Bedlam.

Polydore's monologue in *The Orphan* is a paean to animal instincts.

Who'd be that sordid foolish thing called man,
To cringe thus, faun, and flatter for a pleasure,

Which beasts enjoy so very much above him?
The lusty bull ranges through all the field,
And, from the herd singling his female out,
Enjoys her, and abandons her at will.
It shall be so; I'll yet possess my love. (Otway, *The Orphan,* 1.1.363–69)

See also the many metaphors involving animals and the hunt employed by Lovelace and Belford, clearly intended to add a culturally defined, as well as a pathological, subtext to Lovelace's views on sex and predatory human nature.

58. Shadwell, *The Squire of Alsatia.* The quotations are drawn from the descriptive—arguably, "para-novelistic"—list of dramatis personae.

59. Bertinetti, *Storia della letteratura inglese,* 1:313.

60. Watt, *The Rise of the Novel,* 199.

61. Bertinetti, *Storia della letteratura inglese,* 1:303.

62. Watt associates this phenomenon specifically with Pamela, who overthrows class distinctions by marrying a man who is not only above her in station but is also her master: Watt, *The Rise of the Novel,* 154.

63. The narrative structure of the Gothic, whether in plays or novels, is based on the distinction between the main plot (with its hero, heroine, and villain) and the comic subplot, often instrumental to the main plot, which serves to contain the Gothic's ontological uncertainty. In the theater especially, "Gothic strategies [could be trusted] to deliver thrills and yet contain and dissolve the fear": Backscheider, *Spectacular Politics,* 187. Among the few analyses of the figure of the servant in Gothic narrative is an essay by Janet Todd, who describes Paolo in Ann Radcliffe's *The Italian* as a "foil to the sentimental Gothic hero." "For this, his humor is indispensable, for sentiment and humor in the heroic lover do not mingle. . . . Paolo is foil too in his down-to-earthness which contrasts with his master's romantic sensitivity. While his master is mind, Paolo can be body": Todd, "Posture and Imposture," 33.

64. See Loftis, *Comedy and Society from Congreve to Fielding.* Corroborating Loftis's argument is the fact that following the Glorious Revolution of 1688, the aristocracy began to rely on the same sources of income that had enriched the merchant class. Manufacturing and commerce thus joined agriculture as a source of income, producing first an economic, then also a social and ideological, rapprochement between the classes.

65. Watt, *The Rise of the Novel,* 166.

66. Congreve, *The Way of the World,* dedication, 489.

67. Ibid., 490.

68. See, among others, the famous essay in *Tatler* No. 271, in which Steele relinquishes his alter ego, Isaac Bickerstaff, and openly avows the didactic purpose of the entire project, which aimed to balance "the Weight of Reason with the Agreeableness of Wit." "The general Purpose of the whole has been to recommend Truth, Innocence, Honour, and Virtue, as the Chief Ornaments of Life": Steele and Addison, *Selections from the "Tatler" and the "Spectator,"* 189.

69. Billi, "Il Settecento," 348.

70. Aristotle, *Poetics,* 46.

71. Richardson, *The History of Sir Charles Grandison,* preface, 4. Grandison's character is based on a number of literary models, among them—in the drama—Colley Cibber's Sir Friendly Moral (in *The Lady's Last Stake* [Haymarket, 1707]) and Bevil Junior in Steele's *The Conscious Lovers,* who is hailed at one point as "our general benefactor! Excellent young man, that could be at once lover to her beauty and a parent to her virtue" (5.3): in Steele, *The Conscious Lovers,* 175.

72. Brown, *English Dramatic Form,* 170.

73. Steele, *The Conscious Lovers,* preface, 108.

74. Ibid., prologue, 112.

75. Ibid., preface 110.

76. Barker-Benfield, *The Culture of Sensibility,* 80–81.

77. Richardson, *The History of Sir Charles Grandison*, 207.

78. Steele, *The Conscious Lovers,* preface, 111.

79. Watt, *The Rise of the Novel,* 13.

80. Brown, *English Dramatic Form,* 183.

TWO. "IN THE NOVEL WAY, THERE IS NO DANGER"

1. Burney, *Memoirs of Doctor Burney,* 1:26. My account of Charles Burney's biography is indebted to Doody, *Frances Burney;* Hemlow, *The History of Frances Burney.*

2. Johnson considered Charles Burney "*one of the first writers of the age* for travels": Hemlow, *The History of Frances Burney,* 48. For the major works by Charles Burney, all of which were reprinted in the twentieth century, see the bibliography.

3. Doody, *Frances Burney,* 10.

4. "To Doctor Burney," in Burney, *The Wanderer,* 3–10.

5. Burney, *Memoirs of Doctor Burney,* 2:124.

6. See the allusion to Evelina's "nobodiness" in Zunshine, *Bastards and Foundlings,* 131.

7. Shelley, *Frankenstein,* 10. For a definition of abjection in relation to oppression and the maternal body, see Kristeva, *Powers of Horror.*

8. The dedicatory poem, "To ———," is at Burney, *Evelina,* 4; the prefatory letter "To the Authors of the 'Monthly' and 'Critical Reviews'" is at ibid., 4–6; and the preface is at ibid., 7–9.

9. See Gilbert and Gubar, *The Madwoman in the Attic.*

10. On the construction of women's identity in relation to their emergence as professional writers in the eighteenth century, see Poovey, *The Proper Lady and the Woman Writer.* The ideological construction of the eighteenth-century feminine paradigm was the work of a wide range of authors, from anonymous contributors to widely circulated journals, poets such as John Duncombe, and compilers of women's conduct books such as Dr. John Gregory: see Jones, *Women in the Eighteenth Century.* Also useful are Jones, *Women and Literature;* Kowaleski-Wallace, *Their Fathers' Daughters.*

11. Although Burney disavowed her professional status publicly, referring to her novel as the diversion of a "few idle hours," a letter to Lowndes reveals how she

privately recodified the manuscript as a manufactured product, a piece of literary merchandise deserving of fair remuneration. To Lowndes's offer of 20 guineas for her manuscript, Burney responded curtly: "Sir, I am very much gratified by your good opinion of the M.S. with which I have troubled you; but I must acknowledge that, though it was originally written merely for amusement, I should have not taken the pains to Copy & Correct it for the Press, had I imagined that 10 Guineas a volume would have been more than its worth": *EJL*, 2:288.

12. This interpretation concurs with Barbara Zonitch's analysis of Burney's novels. On Burney's appeal to the critics, she notes, "The male critic . . . is expected to shield her literary, social, and sexual reputation": Zonitch, *Familiar Violence,* 58.

13. On the period's taste for exhibitions of natural monstrosities, see "Monster-Mongers and Other Retailers of Strange Sights," in Altick, *The Shows of London,* 34–49. The use of the term "monstrum" to signify "divine omen" is in Virgil's *Aeneid* (3:26), where Aeneas describes his reaction to a branch oozing blood: "Horrendum et dictu video mirabile monstrum." In the gendered scientific discourse of the time, intellectual independence and ratiocination in women were categorized taxonomically as monstrous and unnatural. "A woman without religion, is raging and monstrous. A woman with a beard is not so disgusting as a woman who acts the free-thinker": Lavater, *Physiognomy,* 200. For the actress as a prodigy, see my discussion of Rousseau's letter to M. d'Alembert in chapter 3 in this volume.

14. Burney repeatedly stressed how crucial anonymity was to her social autonomy. See her retrospective description of *Evelina* in the prefatory advertisement to the 1782 edition of *Cecilia* and the letter "To Doctor Burney," in Burney, *The Wanderer,* 3–10 .

15. Evelina's full name, derived from the surname Evelyn, is a double assertion of the only lineage she can claim: her mother's. On the semantic connotations of Evelina's name, Margaret Anne Doody concludes, "The hint or clue of an anagram is inviting. 'Evelina Anville' is 'Eve in A Veil'—Woman not known, woman obscured. But her name is also 'Elle is Alive'—Woman persisting in living. 'Evelina struggled herself into life'": Doody, *Frances Burney,* 40. On Evelina's illegitimacy, see Greenfield, *Mothering Daughters,* 35–56; Zunshine, *Bastards and Foundlings.*

16. For the use of the adjective "natural" to mean "consistent with nature; normal, expected," see *Oxford English Dictionary,* 2d ed. (1989), def. 2. The meaning of the noun "the natural" as something probable or likely is explained in ibid., def. 9.b: "That which belongs to the natural world or occurs in the ordinary course of things." The dictionary quotes Horace Walpole's correspondence as a source for 1765: "An attempt to blend the marvellous of old story with the natural of modern novels."

17. George Colman, prologue to Garrick, *Bon Ton; or, High Life below Stairs* (Drury Lane, 1775), 254–55.

18. The natural environment of Evelina's childhood is conveyed by the name of Berry Hill, the home of Reverend Villars, where Evelina spent her first seventeen years. A semantic reading of the characters' names in *Evelina* suggests a homophonic association between the surname Anville and the French "*en ville* (in town),"

the site where Evelina's desire to establish her social position can be fulfilled. Conversely, Orville's near-homophone, "*hors ville* (out of town)," anticipates the interruption of Evelina's *Bildung* after her marriage. "Her marriage then would seem semantically at odds with her desire for knowledge and her impulse to enter a less sheltered space": Fraiman, *Unbecoming Women,* 46.

19. The centrality of city life to Restoration comedy is nicely summed up in an exchange between Dorimant and Harriet in George Etherege's *The Man of Mode* (Duke's Theatre, 1676), one of very few seventeenth-century comedies of manners Burney refers to directly: *EJL,* 3:89. "*Dorimant.* To be with you I could live there [in the country], and never shed one thought to London. *Harriet.* Whate'er you say, I know all beyond Hyde Park's a desert to you, and that no gallantry can draw you farther": Etherege, *The Man of Mode,* 5.2.162–65.

20. I use the term "theatrical site" to refer to any public space or gathering place where the social and cultural life of the eighteenth century was dominated by regulation, observation, ritualistic performance, and reciprocal gazing. Thus, in addition to theaters, theatrical sites are structures whose urban and social functions are primarily spectacular and performative, such as gardens and walks, ballrooms, military encampments, and even the courtrooms and squares where justice was administered.

21. The comment, by Henry Angelo, is in Donohue, "The London Theatre at the End of the Eighteenth Century," 353.

22. Townley, *High Life below Stairs,* I.2. Joseph Donohue organizes Georgian London's theatrical sites ("spas, pleasure gardens, taverns, circus rings, exhibition halls, and other pleasure resorts") into three categories: "resorts, such as Vauxhall, Ranelagh and Marylebone Gardens, that offered evening concerts and in some cases fireworks, as well as facilities for eating and drinking; gardens or spas connected with mineral springs, such as Bagnigge Wells, Sadler's Wells (the most famous and important), and the Dog and Duck in St. George's Fields; and tea gardens, found as far north as Highbury Barn and in almost every other district of London as well": Donohue, "The London Theatre at the End of the Eighteenth Century," 346. On Burney's use of Vauxhall Gardens in *Cecilia,* see chapter 4 in this volume.

23. Varey, *Space and the Eighteenth-Century English Novel,* 102. For a cultural history of Bath's spaces in the eighteenth century, see Davis and Bonsall, *A History of Bath,* chaps. 7–11.

24. McIntyre, *Garrick,* 300. On Methodism and the culture of sensibility, see Barker-Benfield, *The Culture of Sensibility,* 266–79.

25. Among the many letters about the topic is one dated 11 June 1777 from the Reverend Henry Bate to Garrick. "Poor Foote sighs his soul out for the loss of his *dramatic diadem:* is the man mad? Or does he think that mankind will be apt to make a distinction between the two theatrical abdications of 1776 . . . ?": Garrick, *The Private Correspondence of David Garrick,* 2:226. It is no accident that in the "Occasional Prelude" that Garrick wrote when he left the stage, the list of his career milestones includes all of his greatest tragic roles but none of his comic roles: Garrick, *The Poetical Works of David Garrick,* 2:325–27. On Burney and the "Occasional Prelude," see the appendix.

26. Benedetti, *David Garrick and the Birth of the Modern Theatre,* 72.

27. Shakespeare's influence on the eighteenth-century novel was immense, so it is hardly surprising that most of the theatrical citations in Burney's writings are from Shakespeare or from the adaptations by Rowe and Tate. See the appendix for a list of all theatrical citations, including Shakespeare, in Burney's novels and journals (1768–1804). On eighteenth-century adaptations of Shakespeare, see Dobson, *The Making of the National Poet;* Innocenti, *La scena trasformata;* Marsden, *The Re-Imagined Text.* On Shakespeare's influence on the eighteenth-century novel, see Noyes, *The Thespian Mirror.*

28. "The shift toward a different sensibility by the end of the eighteenth century leads to privileging simple, ordinary language . . . as a reaction against the artificiality of neoclassical poetic diction. . . . A distinction between the *general* and the *universal* marks the difference between neoclassical and pre-Romantic sensibilities: the general is associated with the contingent and the ordinary; the universal is shared by all and endures through time. From Johnson onward, interpretations of Shakespeare stress his universal qualities": Innocenti, *La scena trasformata,* 122–23.

29. As explained in the introduction to this volume, descriptions of theatrical performances within novels were fairly common in the eighteenth century. In his exhaustive compendium of theatrical references, Robert Noyes finds at least five novels of the 1760s to 1780 whose characters comment on or describe tragedies. They are Maria Susannah Cooper's *Masquerades; or, What You Will* (1780), the anonymous *The Exemplary Mother; or, Letters between Mrs. Villars and Her Family* (1769), Henry Higgs's *High Life: A Novel; or, The History of Miss Faulkland* (1768); Mary Walker's *Memoirs of the Marchioness De Louvoi* (1777); and the anonymous *Altamont in the Capital to His Friends in the Country* (1767): Noyes, *The Neglected Muse,* 39, 88, 126, 134, 161. In these works, however, the relation between novel and play is not properly inter-textual or metatextual because the performances remain isolated episodes, the subject of commentary only.

30. The physical violence typical of the exchanges between Captain Mirvan and Madame Duval begins in earnest in another incident in book 1, when Madame Duval, coming out of Ranelagh "entirely covered in mud, and in so great a rage," furiously accuses Mirvan of having caused her mishap. In turn, the captain "put his hands upon her shoulders, and gave her so violent a shake, that she screamed out for help": Burney, *Evelina,* 73. Mirvan is something of a stock character and his bravado parodically hints at the stage. Heroic, patriotic English sailors and their cowardly French counterparts wrangled on-stage throughout the Seven Years' War (1756–63). Among the many plays that exploited such characters was Tobias Smollett's farce *The Reprisal; or, The Tars of Old England* (Drury Lane, 1757).

31. The cosmetic tribulations suffered by Madame Duval bring the farcical episode to a head. Doody notes the resemblance between the grotesque, carnivalesque image of the disheveled Madame Duval and the "dames" of modern British pantomime, suggesting that "[Burney's] family certainly saw the transvestite role that is Madame Duval's part in the novel": Doody, *Frances Burney,* 50–51. This is confirmed by Susanna Burney, who in her diary describes Samuel Crisp dressing up as

Madame Duval. "Monday night after supper we were all made very merry by Mr. Crisp suffering his wig to be turn'd the hind part before, and my cap put over it—Hetty's cloak—and Mrs Gast's apron and ruffles—in this ridiculous trim he danced a minuet with Hetty, personifying *Madam Duval,* while she acted *Mr Smith* at the Long Room, Hampstead": *ED,* 1:lviii.

32. *London Chronicle,* 3–5 March 1757, cited in Benedetti, *David Garrick and the Birth of the Modern Theatre,* 136; see McIntyre, *Garrick,* 96–97. Another model one could suggest is Polly Peachum, in John Gay's *The Beggar's Opera.* Charles Bannister's famous interpretation of the role was depicted in widely circulated prints.

33. Frye, *Anatomy of Criticism,* 163.

34. The recommendation was, in fact, that of the *Critical Review* (cited in Gonda, *Reading Daughters' Fictions,* 110).

35. For a detailed discussion of the link between journal writing and fiction, see Spacks, *Imagining a Self,* esp. 158–92.

36. Samuel Crisp urged Burney to write freely. "Dash away, whatever comes uppermost; & believe me, You'll succeed better, than by leaning on your Elbows, & studying what to say. . . . You Young Devil You, You know in your Conscience I devour greedily your Journalizing letters": EJL, 1:108.

37. Devlin, *The Novels and Journals of Fanny Burney,* 22.

38. On "voice" in narrative, see Genette, *Narrative Discourse.*

39. Epstein, *The Iron Pen,* 51. On the epistolary style in *Evelina,* see the careful analysis in ibid., 97–102.

40. Richardson, *Clarissa,* 915. Richardson also states his poetics in the preface. "[The letters] abound not only with critical Situations, but with what may be called *instantaneous* Descriptions and Reflections (proper to be brought home to the breast of the youthful Reader): as also with affecting Conversations: many of them written in the dialogue or dramatic way": ibid., 35. Of course, as Julia Epstein reminds us, the apparently simple and spontaneous discourse of epistolary fiction "camouflage[s] a sophisticated rhetoric of disguise": Epstein, "Fanny Burney's Epistolary Voices," 176.

41. Letter dated 3 January 1801, in Austen, *Selected Letters,* 45. On Austen's shift from the epistolary style to third-person narrative in composing *Sense and Sensibility* and *Pride and Prejudice,* see Southam, *Jane Austen's Literary Manuscripts.* Southam's remains the fullest analysis of the early versions of Austen's novels.

42. Pamela's sexual integrity is reflected symbolically in the privacy that preserves her letters from Mr. B.'s gaze: the violation of the latter (the letters' penetration by the gaze) cannot but entail the loss of the former. As Mr. B. archly puts it, "'Now . . . it is my opinion that [the letters] are about you; and I never undressed a girl in my life; but I now will begin to strip my pretty Pamela; and I hope I shall not go very far before I find them.' And he began to unpin my handkerchief": Richardson, *Pamela,* 271.

43. It is Lovelace, of course, who defines what he is doing as "writing to the moment": Richardson, *Clarissa,* 721. Typical examples of Richardson's parenthetical "stage directions" in *Clarissa* are: "(*heroically stalking about*)" (ibid., 686); "(looking as if she was afraid to hear what)" and "(angrily, and drawing back her face)" (ibid.,

626, 628); and "(tears in her eyes)" (ibid., 933). Of the many studies that address the dramatic background to Richardson's novels, the two most important are Kinkead-Weekes, *Samuel Richardson Dramatic Novelist* and Konigsberg, *Narrative Techniques in the English Novel.* Essential essays on Richardson's narrative technique are Hughes, "Theatrical Convention in Richardson"; Sherburn, "Samuel Richardson's Novel and the Theatre"; Sherburn, "Writing to the Moment." On theatrical representations of Lord Rochester, one of the literary and cultural models for Lovelace, see Harris, "Protean Lovelace."

44. Richardson, *Clarissa,* 900. Lovelace himself compares the novel's events to those of a play, in which the climax (Clarissa's seduction) must be reached no sooner than dramatic tradition demands. "Sally, a little devil, often reproaches me with the slowness of my proceedings. But in a play, does not the principal entertainment lie in the *first four acts*? Is not all in a manner over when you come to the *fifth*?": Lovelace to Bedford, letter 175, in ibid., 574. On Richardson's influences (especially Fielding), see, in addition to the works mentioned in n. 43, Park, "Clarissa as Tragedy."

45. As George Sherburn notes, "[Richardson] had a naturally strong visual imagination: small details show that in his mind he actually *saw* the episodes that he depicted": Sherburn, "Writing to the Moment," 201. Similarly, Ira Konigsberg considers the ability to visualize a key feature of Richardson's novel, emphasizing how previous novels "did not . . . depict events and characters with sufficient specificity to allow the reader an internal visual experience": Konigsberg, *Samuel Richardson and the Dramatic Novel,* 4.

46. See Roach's authoritative *The Player's Passion* and, more recently, Paul Goring, "The Art of Acting," *The Rhetoric of Sensibility in Eighteenth-Century Culture,* 114–41. See also Saggini, "Identità a soggetto."

47. Billi, "Dal teatro al romanzo," 37.

48. Hill, *An Essay on the Art of Acting,* 10. See Howells, *Love, Mystery, and Misery,* 21–22. Richardson's famous letter to Hill on testing Hill's acting techniques ("I endeavoured to follow you in your wonderful Description of the Force of Acting, in the Passion of Joy, Sorrow, Fear, Anger &c. And my whole Frame, so nervously affected before, was shaken by it") is discussed in Goring, *The Rhetoric of Sensibility in Eighteenth-Century Culture,* 1–2.

49. Sherburn, "Samuel Richardson's Novels and the Theatre," 325; emphasis added.

50. As R. C. Alston notes, "The interest in pronunciation which was so characteristic of writers on English in the second half of the eighteenth century . . . can be traced back to sixteenth-century manuals of pulpit oratory, but the movement . . . has its origins in a complex coincidence of interests: among which are the improvement of dramatic speech . . . and parliamentary debate": quoted in Woods, *Garrick Claims the Stage,* 31. It is worth recalling that such acting conventions were also influenced by French theater, where "formal declamation" predominated over more natural speech. On Betterton and the actor's rhetoric, see Goring, *The Rhetoric of Sensibility in Eighteenth-Century Culture;* Roach, *The Player's Passion.*

51. On the dramatic sources for the duel scene in *The Conscious Lovers,* and on

Colley Cibber's contribution, see Parnell, "A Source for the Duel Scene in 'The Conscious Lovers,'" 13–15.

52. Richardson, *The History of Sir Charles Grandison,* 6:55.

53. Konigsberg, *Samuel Richardson and the Dramatic Novel,* 2.

54. Richardson, *Clarissa,* 42; emphasis added.

55. Konigsberg, *Samuel Richardson and the Dramatic Novel,* 12.

56. Ibid.

57. Ibid., 90.

58. Burney perfected her external descriptions of characters in her journals, where she created portraits that, in Samuel Crisp's words, display "such strong marks of Nature that one instantly pronounces them like, without ever having seen the originals": *EJL,* 1:178. A good example is her account of meeting a Miss Reid (ibid., 2:70–71), in which a mixture of diegetic commentary and mimetic notation works both on external and internal levels. Burney's use of *is* (emphases added throughout) assumes an internal perspective on the character: "She *is* a very clever woman . . . but her turn of mind *is* naturally melancholy." She then switches to an external viewpoint ("[She] *has* a Countenance the most haggard and wretched I ever saw, added to which, she *Dresses* in a style the most strange") before reverting to an internal viewpoint again ("The unhappiness of her *mind,* I have heard attributed to so great & extraordinary an unsteadiness, not only of Conduct, but of principle. . . . Her *mind* is thus in a state of perpetual agitation"). Further outward characteristics are given in detail: "We found her *Trying on* a Coat she was altering. . . . It was curious to see the ill managed contrivance of poor Miss Reid, who . . . *was piecing* a blue & white tissue with a large Patch of black silk. She *had on* a large dirty wing Cap . . . & a shawl, that had been a very fine spotted one, but which was more soiled than if she had been embraced by a chimney sweeper." Burney's careful selection of external details (the dirty shawl, the mismatched fabrics) is a diegetic technique whose strong visual impact provides an iconic counterpart to the various idiolects used by characters in her novels.

59. On Burney's epistolary technique, see Lars Troide's introduction to *EJL,* esp. xviii; Joyce Hemlow's introduction to *JL,* 1:xxxi–ii.

60. My analysis of transtextuality in *Evelina* is informed by Genette, *Palimpsests.*

61. Ibid., 280. For ostension as the occurrence of "a given object or event produced by nature or human action . . . 'picked up' by someone and *shown* as the expression of the class of which it is member," see Eco, *A Theory of Semiotics,* 224–25.

62. The number is in Pedicord, *The Theatrical Public in the Time of Garrick,* 198–99.

63. See Donohue, "The London Theatre at the End of the Eighteenth Century."

64. See the appendix in this volume.

65. The fops appear in George Etherege's *The Man of Mode; or, Sir Fopling Flutter* (1676), John Crowne's *Sir Courtly Nice; or, It Cannot Be* (1685), William Congreve's *The Double Dealer* (1693), and John Vanbrugh's *The Relapse* (1696).

66. The expression "mollifying elegance," easily associated with "molly," the slang term for male homosexuals, of course implies effeminacy. The disparagement

of Frenchified foppish characters in the theater is only one aspect of the xenophobia and homophobia rampant in eighteenth-century English society, as Kristina Straub shows in *Sexual Suspects.* Straub provides a thorough historical account of the social and gender construction of the figure of the fop. For a recent discussion of the fop's sexuality, see also Pat Gill, "Gender, Sexuality, and Marriage," in Fisk, *The Cambridge Companion to English Restoration Theatre,* esp. 202–207; Williams, *The Restoration Fop.* The fop–rake contrast is discussed in McGirr, *Eighteenth-Century Characters.*

67. Staves, "A Few Kind Words for the Fop," 426–27.

68. Burney was to have played the part of Tag in *Miss in Her Teens* but balked at the "shocking" role: *EJL,* 1:116. Pedicord notes that *The Careless Husband* was one of the favorite comedies of the mid-Georgian period; it was performed fifty-eight times between 1747 and 1776: Pedicord, *The Theatrical Public in the Time of Garrick,* 200–201. The equally successful *Miss in Her Teens* was performed 125 times in the middle decades of the century: Pedicord, *The Theatrical Public in the Time of Garrick,* 198–99.

69. On the metatextual relation involving hypotext and hypertext, see Genette, *Palimpsests,* 4. On the model reader, see Eco, *The Role of the Reader.*

70. Oliver Goldsmith, "An Essay on the Theatre; or, a Comparison between Laughing and Sentimental Comedy," *The Collected Works of Oliver Goldsmith,* 3:213. The same point is made by David Garrick in his famous prologue to Goldsmith's *She Stoops to Conquer* (Covent Garden, 1773).

> Excuse me, Sirs, I pray—I can't yet speak—
> I'm crying now—and have been all the week!
> 'Tis not alone this mourning suit, good masters;
> I've that within—for which there are no plaisters!
> Pray wou'd you know the reason why I'm crying?
> The Comic muse, long sick, is now a dying! (in Goldsmith, *The Collected Works of Oliver Goldsmith,* 5:102)

Given the popularity of both texts, it is very likely that Burney is alluding to them directly in *Evelina.*

71. Goldsmith, "An Essay on the Theatre," *The Collected Works of Oliver Goldsmith,* 3:211, 213.

72. Johnson's stricture is in "Life of Congreve," *Lives of the English Poets,* 2:222. See Markley, "The Canon and Its Critics," 230–31.

73. See also Burney's criticisms of George Farquhar's *The Constant Couple* and of *The Country Girl* (Garrick's adaptation of William Wycherley's *The Country Wife*) in *DL,* 4:47, 54.

74. The parallel applies not only to *Love for Love* but also to *The Minor.* In both cases, criticism of the play is based on the moral evaluation of its characters, thus activating a metatextual relation on more than one level.

75. Bertinetti, *Storia del teatro inglese dalla Restaurazione all'Ottocento,* 96–97.

76. Nahum Tate's adaptation, *The History of King Lear: Revived with Alterations,*

has been reprinted in the modern edition *The History of King Lear,* edited by James Black. Garrick's version was published as *King Lear, a Tragedy, Altered from Shakspeare by D. Garrick,* in 1786. The works are listed in the bibliography under Tate and Shakespeare, respectively. Pedicord has calculated that in the course of his career, Garrick performed Lear (as he did Hamlet) fifty-six times: Pedicord, *The Theatrical Public in the Time of Garrick,* 198–99.

77. The passage is quoted in Downer, "Nature to Advantage Dressed," 1015. On "functional signs," see Billi, "Dal teatro al romanzo," 40.

78. Garrick, *The Private Correspondence of David Garrick,* 1:158.

79. Thrale, *Thraliana,* 1:110.

80. "'He the best player!' cries Partridge, with a contemptuous sneer, 'why, I could act as well as he himself. I am sure *if I had seen a ghost,* I should have looked in the very same manner, and done just as he did'": Fielding, *The History of Tom Jones, a Foundling,* 613; emphasis added.

81. Quoted in Downer, "Nature to Advantage Dressed," 1015.

82. Aristotle, *Poetics,* 56.

83. Ibid., 61.

84. Ibid.

85. Burney's *Diaries and Letters* presents a vivid account of the emotion aroused in two young female spectators by the death of Douglas in John Home's eponymous tragedy (1756). "Two young ladies, who seemed about eighteen, and sat above us, were so much shocked by the death of Douglas, that they both burst into a loud fit of roaring, like little children,—and sobbed on, afterwards, for almost half the farce! I was quite astonished; and Miss Weston complained that they really disturbed her sorrows; but Captain Bouchier was highly diverted, and went to give them comfort, as if they had been babies, telling them it was all over, and that they need not cry any more": *DL,* 1:409.

THREE. CALIBAN'S MIRROR

1. Greenfield, "Oh Dear Resemblance of Thy Murdered Mother," 320. Beth Kowaleski-Wallace even suggests that "Burney wrote the novel to 'seduce' her father and . . . she succeeded": Kowaleski-Wallace, "Milton's Daughters," 276.

2. Kowaleski-Wallace, "Milton's Daughters," 276–77.

3. Doody, *Frances Burney,* 66–68.

4. Prose, *The Lives of the Muses.*

5. It is interesting to compare Burney's account of life at Streatham in 1778–82 with Hester Thrale's, whose private views on the Burneys are sometimes surprisingly at odds with those she professed openly. A typical example is the discrepancy between her public praise and private criticism of *Evelina.* According to Burney's journals, "Mrs. Thrale . . . likes it VASTLY—is EXTREMELY pleased with it. . . . It's writ by somebody that knows *the top & the bottom—the highest & the lowest* of Mankind"" *EJL,* 3:35n.12. Hester Thrale's diary utterly subverts this view. "I was shewed a little Novel t'other Day which I thought pretty enough. . . . it was written by his [Dr. Burney's] second Daughter Fanny, who must certainly be a Girl of

good Parts & some Knowledge of the World too, or She could not be the Author of Evelina—flimzy as it is, compar'd with the Books I've just mentioned [Richardson, Lennox, Smollett, and Fielding]": Thrale, *Thraliana,* 1:328–29.

6. On Johnson's friendship with the women of his circle, see Dussinger, "Hester Piozzi, Italy, and the Johnsonian Aether"; Hain and McAllister, "James Boswell's Ms. Perceptions and Samuel Johnson's Ms. Placed Friends." On Johnson's relationship with Hester Thrale and Frances Burney in particular, see also Clarke, *Dr. Johnson's Women.*

7. In her journals, Burney often reports conversations as theatrical dialogue, sometimes announcing her shift from narrative to dramatization explicitly ("I think I shall, occasionally *Theatricalise* my Dialogues" or "I must now write in dialogue fashion," as she notes a few days before she meets Sheridan: *EJL*, 3:146, 216), and sometimes implicitly, as in a conversation introduced by, "Just then the door opened, and Mr. Sheridan entered," a sentence that operates much like a stage direction. Other examples are in ibid., 2:170, 186.

8. Besides the injunction against cross-dressing in the Bible (Deuteronomy), the main sources for the patristic tradition are Tertullian (*De Spectaculis* and *De cultu feminarum*), John Chrysostom, and Saint Augustine. Particularly influential Puritan anti-theatrical texts were William Prynne's *Histrio-mastix, The Players' Scourge* (1633) and Jeremy Collier's *A Short View of the Immorality and Profaneness of the English Stage* (1698). In his *Lettre à M. d'Alembert sur les spectacles* (1758), Rousseau states: "How is it possible for a profession, whose only aim is to appear in public, and what is worse, to appear for money, how is it possible, I say, for such a profession to suit virtuous women, and be consistent with modesty and good manners?": Rousseau, *A Letter from M. Rousseau,* 119. See the discussion of Rousseau in Nicholson, "The Theater," 299. An early overview of the debate is in Barish, *The Antitheatrical Prejudice.* For a more recent survey of views on the issue, see *The Restoration Stage Controversy,* which includes Collier's classic attack as well as a number of reactions to it, among them Vanbrugh's *A Short Vindication of "The Relapse" and "The Provok'd Wife"* and Congreve's *Amendments of Mr. Collier's False and Imperfect Citations,* both published the same year as Collier's piece.

9. Burney, of course, had applied the phrase "frivolous amusement" to *Evelina* in her dedication "To the Authors of the Monthly and Critical Reviews." On the opposition between the closet and the stage, see Saggini, "Memories beyond the Pale."

10. Quoted in Cotton, *Women Playwrights in England,* 182. The anonymous seventeenth-century coinage "great Apollo's Salic law" is discussed fully in Gadeken, "Sarah Fielding and the Salic Law of Wit."

11. Rousseau, *A Letter from M. Rousseau,* 120. On female playwrights in the early eighteenth century, see Donkin, *Getting into the Act;* Pearson, *The Prostituted Muse.*

12. Excellent examples of what Genette (*Palimpsests,* 277–92) calls "intramodal transmodalizations" are Garrick's *The Country Girl* (Drury Lane, 1766), a rewriting of Wycherley's *The Country Wife,* and Sheridan's bowdlerization of Congreve's comedies during the 1776–77 season. To these can be added *A Trip to Scarborough* (Drury Lane, 1777), Sheridan's rewriting of Vanbrugh's *The Relapse,* where Loveless

explains that the comedy has been adapted to the changed tastes of spectators by "a little wholesome pruning" (2.1). In Sheridan's version of *The Critic* (*The Critic; or, A Comedy Rehearsed* [Drury Lane, 1779]), Mr. Dangle comments, "Now, egad, I think the worst alteration is in the nicety of the audience. No double-entendre; no smart innuendo admitted, even Vanbrugh and Congreve obliged to undergo a bungling reformation!" (1.1.19–21).

13. See Straub, *Sexual Suspects.*

14. Colley Cibber is a case in point. His image was so closely linked to the effeminate fops he played (from Sir Novelty Fashion in *Love's Last Shift* to Lord Foppington in *The Relapse* and Sir George Brilliant in *The Lady's Last Stake*) that he was never taken seriously in tragic roles: ibid., 48–61.

15. Duncombe, *The Feminiad,* line 140.

16. A close friend of Samuel Johnson, Arthur Murphy was a regular guest at Streatham. Burney may have known his Shakespeare criticism published in *Gray's-Inn Journal* in 1754 and 1756 (on which see Aycock, "Shakespearian Criticism in the 'Gray's-Inn Journal'"). In her diaries, she mentions Murphy's comedies *All in the Wrong* (1761) and *The Citizen* (1763), as well as *The Grecian Daughter* (1772), his most famous tragedy. In 1761, he managed the Haymarket Theatre together with Samuel Foote. He was to remain one of Burney's favorite playwrights. As late as 1802, she reported to her husband, Alexandre d'Arblay, that some sad news about Murphy had affected her deeply: *JL,* 5:210–11. In her account of her family's performance of Murphy's *The Way to Keep Him* (followed by Fielding's *Tom Thumb* as an afterpiece), Burney's attention to the costumes and hairstyles is remarkable. Her interest in the iconic register shows her awareness of the importance of non-verbal signs in a theatrical performance.

17. The comedy was first edited by C. J. Delery as a Ph.D. thesis in 1989. In 1994, it was included in *The Meridian Anthology of Restoration and Eighteenth-Century Plays by Women,* and one year later, a new edition was published in the *Complete Plays* edited by Sabor and Sill, who also published a 1997 edition of *"The Witlings"; and, "The Woman-Hater."* The edition used here is *CP.* Parenthetical references in the text are to act and line numbers; the edition does not use scene numbers.

18. Lynch, "Counter Publics," 226.

19. Because Mrs. Voluble belongs to the comedy's subplot, it is fitting that her sympathy for the unfortunate Cecilia should be restricted to mundane concerns, while the purer expressions of sentiment are reserved for the higher plot level involving Cecilia and Beaufort.

20. H. Kelly, *The School for Wives,* ii. See Ellis, *Sentimental Comedy,* 10. For Northrop Frye's definition of classical comedy, see *Anatomy of Criticism,* 163–86. On the structure of classical drama, the definitions of "*katastrophe*" and "*peripeteia*" in Pavis, *Dictionary of the Theatre,* 44, 262, are useful: "[The catastrophe] designates the moment at which the action comes to an end . . . [it] is not necessarily related to the notion of a disastrous event, but may sometimes entail a logical conclusion of the action"; *peripeteia,* on the other hand, is a "Sudden and unforseen change, *turning point* or 'reversal in the action.'"

21. Lynch, "Counter Publics," 226.

22. Among comedies of the time that featured exclusively indoor settings, two of the most popular were Oliver Goldsmith's *The Good-Natur'd Man* (1768) and Richard Cumberland's *The West Indian* (1771). For a full description of the theaters and stage production practice at the time of the composition of *The Witlings,* see Charles Beecher Hogan's introduction to *The London Stage,* pt. 5. For contemporary documents, see the section on "Stage Presentation" edited by Victor Emeljanow, in Roy, *Romantic and Revolutionary Theatre,* 221–58.

23. The Minories were an eastern ward of the City of London: see Tomlinson, *A History of the Minories.* The name Burney chooses for Mrs. Wheedle's client clearly suggests a desire to "ape" the lifestyle and habits of the aristocracy and a criticism of merchants' unwillingness to identify with their own group. Her portrait of Belfield in *Cecilia* is even more critical of the shame felt by merchants about their connection with the world of business.

24. Lynch, "Counter Publics," 226.

25. Aside from revealing his own bias, Crisp's point seems to ignore the effect of the Licensing Act of 1737 on Fielding's theatrical career. By granting patents only to the Covent Garden and Drury Lane theaters and establishing the Lord Chamberlain as censor, the law severely curtailed theatrical production. The effects were felt strongly among women playwrights, as theater managers sought to avoid the financial risk of staging plays by authors who were not yet established. The Licensing Act thus contributed to channeling women's literary efforts toward the new genre of the novel, as was the case for Eliza Haywood. In Fielding's case, censorship was enforced all the more strongly because his farces had targeted Prime Minister Robert Walpole. On Fielding and the playwrights of the 1730s, see Hunter, *Occasional Form.* See also Hume, *Henry Fielding and the London Theatre;* Lewis, *Fielding's Burlesque Drama.* The first volume of the essential Wesleyan Edition of the Works of Henry Fielding has a very useful general introduction (Lockwood, *Plays,* xix–xxviii); the individual introductions to each play also give information essential to reconstructing the stage history and contemporary reception of Fielding's plays.

26. For an introduction to the debate between "theatricalists" and "textualist" among scholars of "dramatic literature"—a genre that, as Marcello Pagnini (*Semiosi,* 125) reminds us, is "completely invented" —see de Marinis, *The Semiotics of Performance.* See also Serpieri, "Ipotesi teorica di segmentazione di un testo teatrale." In English, see Serpieri et al., "Towards a Segmentation of the Dramatic Text."

27. Serpieri, "Ipotesi teorica di segmentazione di un testo teatrale," 20.

28. Serpieri, Introduction to *Amleto,* 11–12.

29. Pagnini, *Pragmatica della letteratura,* 90.

30. Adams, "The Text of Sheridan's *The Rivals,*" 90. Adams quotes the criticism of the comedy in the *Morning Chronicle* of 20 January 1775. "The play itself is a *full hour* longer in representation than any piece on the stage. This last circumstance is an error of such a nature as shows either great obstinacy in the Author, or excessive ignorance in the managers": ibid., 171. Adams even suggests that Sheridan reacted

to the failure of the first performance by cutting two whole scenes and curtailing the text by a third.

31. We can get a sense of the theatrical potential of Burney's comedy from Ian Kelly's reflections on the two productions of *A Busy Day* in which he played Frank (Bristol, 1993, and London, 2000). Kelly, a star actor and multi-awarded biographer, recalls, "Some problems with the play began to surface; the meandering length of the third act, set in Hyde Park, which feels even longer to a modern audience waiting for their one interval (Fanny was presumably planning several). More importantly, the production highlighted problems with the final act; a problem Fanny shares with all comic writers; making the 'pay-off' . . . and thus keeping the energy going to the end of the play. . . . Characters tended to drift in and out for no discernible reason, or stay in fixed relation when their dramatic imperative would be to move. . . . The play ran nearly three hours long at the read-through. In the end, only Act 4 survived uncut into the West End, and Act 5 was shaved down to about its original length": I. Kelly, "A Busy Day," 24, 31–32. The firsthand view of an actor, rather than of a critic or a well-intentioned adviser, confirms that Burney did indeed have a gift for comedy. The fact that she was not able to benefit from the suggestions of actors or from a first performance (as was the case for Sheridan's *The Rivals*) means that we can analyze her comedy only as a *virtual* theatrical text.

32. The comedy was first read in public only in the 1990s. Selections were read at the general meeting of the Burney Society on 11 October 1996: Burney Society, "Annual General Meeting Minutes." Two years later, in *Burney Letter* 4, no. 1 (1998), Kate Chisholm reported that on 28–29 November 1997, the Bare Boards Company directed by Chris Board had organized a staged reading at London's Covent Garden Theatre. "The hope is to encourage sponsorship for a full dramatized production of the comedy": Chisholm, "'Witlings' Takes a London Bow." In the same issue of the *Burney Letter,* Chisholm then reports that "in early February [1998], The Main Street Theatre in Houston mounted a full-dress, full-length production of the play . . . directed by Rebecca Greene Udden." That performance, in effect the comedy's premiere after 219 years, is especially significant. Although the comedy was still more than three hours long, the director had perceptibly shortened it. The review notes the success of the production, which "ran through March 15." After these pioneering experiments, several others followed, showing the potential success of Burney as a dramatist. One of the most recent was the New York production organized by the Magis Theater Company from 18 May to 1 June 2008 at the West End Theater, which revealed that the play could be staged and audiences could still enjoy it. As Odai Johnson enthusiastically commented about that production, "What makes the Main Street Theatre company's recovery project so remarkable is not that they have discovered a new eighteenth-century playwright whose work—as it turns out—can stand up with the best of Goldsmith and Sheridan. . . . This brilliant and brittle comedy of manners launches both play and playwright back into the circulation she deserves and proves itself every bit as playable as Burney's better known contemporaries": Johnson, "Review of *The Witlings,*" 543–44.

33. Doody was the first to note the novelty of the setting. "It is hard to convey to the reader unversed in the late eighteenth-century comedy the freshness of the surprise at coming upon an opening like this—the setting is so entirely different from the usual sort": Doody, *Frances Burney,* 77. Lynch agrees and notes that the shop performs two functions. On one hand, it serves as an alternative center of women's sociability; on the other, it is a "news room . . . at the nexus of news culture," to which "almost all the important pieces of intelligence that move Burney's plot find their way": Lynch, "Counter Publics," 225–26.

34. Alessandro Serpieri and his colleagues further stress that "theatrical language is permeated by deictic expressions to a degree quite unknown to other literary genres, above all because the theatre exists *on the axis of the present* in a specific spatial situation": Serpieri et al., "Towards a Segmentation of the Dramatic Text," 167.

35. See Burney's later disclaimer of Molière's influence in *EJL,* 3:345. Although Burney never discusses Molière in her letters and diaries, she probably knew about plays that drew directly on *Les femmes savantes* (1672), whose subject most closely resembles that of *The Witlings.* A popular ten-volume English edition of Molière's plays was published in London in 1739 and reprinted several times in the following decades. An anthology of Molière's stock characters was published by Lewis Chambaud in London in 1761 (*Dialogues in French and English, upon the most entertaining and humorous subjects extracted out of the comedies of Molière and containing the idiom of the conversation of courtiers, citizens, merchants, tradesmen, and almost all states and professions in life*). On Molière's influence on Restoration and early eighteenth-century playwrights (including Colley Cibber, who was well known to Burney and who adapted a number of Molière's texts, including *The Refusal, or The Ladies' Philosophy,* Theatre Royal, 1721, based on *Les femmes savantes*), see Miles, *The Influence of Molière on Restoration Comedy;* Wilcox, *The Relation of Molière to Restoration Comedy.* On the relationship between Burney and Molière, see in Peter Sabor and Geoffrey Sill, "Burney and Molière," in Burney, *"The Witlings"; and, "The Woman-Hater,"* app. C.

36. Sheridan's Mr. Dangle states, "You will not easily persuade me that there is no credit or importance in being at the head of a band of critics, who take upon them to decide for the whole town, whose opinion and patronage all writers solicit, and whose recommendation no manager dares refuse!": Sheridan, *The Critic,* 1.1.20–24.

37. For an analysis of Burney as conduct-book writer, see Hemlow, "Fanny Burney and the Courtesy Books." See also Barney, *Plots of Enlightenment.*

38. Wollstonecraft, *A Vindication of the Rights of Woman,* esp. chap. 2. The conservative Hannah More's *Strictures on the Modern System of Female Education* (1799) takes the opposite stance to *A Vindication of the Rights of Woman* (1792), although they paradoxically agree in recommending that women's education be based on reason.

39. The advice is in Gregory's influential tract, *A Father's Legacy to His Daughters,* 37–38.

40. More, *Strictures on the Modern System of Female Education,* 211, advised women to not chafe "with an impious discontent" at "the post which God has assigned them in this world." See Spencer, *The Rise of the Woman Novelist,* 168.

41. Seward's poem was published in the anthology *A Collection of Poems in Six Volumes,* 2:299, lines 137–39; emphasis added. See the discussion of the poem in Myers, *The Bluestocking Circle,* 126. The model of women's education provided by the bluestockings was sanctioned in Richardson, *The History of Sir Charles Grandison,* a novel that exerted a deep influence throughout the eighteenth century. Richardson's description of Harriet Byron's education shows that women's virtue can coexist with a (limited) education. This change in perspective is all the more striking when compared with the attack on women's erudition only a few decades earlier in Jonathan Swift's "Of the Education of Ladies," *The Works of Jonathan Swift,* 9:175–79, on which see Gubar, "The Female Monster in Augustan Satire."

42. The quotation from Cumberland's article is in Heller, "Bluestocking Salons and the Public Sphere," 69. On the bluestockings and their public image, see most recently Eger and Peltz, *Brilliant Women* (the catalogue of the exhibition held at the National Portrait Gallery in London, 13 March–15 June, 2008).

43. Pearson, *The Prostituted Muse,* 83.

44. Burney, *The Complete Plays of Frances Burney,* 1:13n.201.

45. Pope, "An Essay on Criticism," 145.

46. Doody, *Frances Burney,* 84 and 86.

47. Locke, *An Essay Concerning Human Understanding,* 163.

48. The parallel between Lady Smatter's literary gathering and Mrs. Voluble's supper—a comparison clearly intended to belittle the cultural importance of the Esprit Party—is emphasized by the repeated substitution of food for pen and paper, the traditional tools of knowledge. Cecilia's request for pen and paper is ignored by Mrs. Voluble, who instead invites her to partake of her supper.

> *Cecilia.* If you will be so good as to lend me your Pen and Ink once more, I will send another man after [my messenger]. . . .
> *Miss Jenny.* I believe she's talking to herself.
> *Mrs. Voluble.* Yes, she has a mighty way of Musing. I have a good mind to ask her to Eat a bit, for, poor Soul, I dare say she's hungry enough. . . .
> *Cecilia.* Mrs. Voluble, is your Pen and Ink here?
> *Mrs. Voluble.* You shall have it directly; but pray, ma'am, let me persuade you to Eat a morsel first. (*CP,* 5:86–115)

49. Lady Smatter's malapropisms and inaccurate quotations offer a good illustration of the many transmutations undergone by comic characters in this period, in both high and low comedy. Burney was probably influenced most directly by the character Mrs. Heidelberg in the immensely successful *The Clandestine Marriage* by George Colman and David Garrick (Drury Lane, 1766), on which see Pedicord, *The Theatrical Public in the Time of Garrick,* 193–99. Burney certainly knew the play well (see the appendix in this volume). James Townley's farce *High Life below Stairs* provides an amusing "low" example of bardolatry to set beside Lady Smatter's.

> *Lady Bab.* I never read but one Book.
> *Kitty.* What is your Ladyship so fond of?

Lady Bab. Shikspur. Do you never read Shikspur?
Kitty. Shikspur? Who wrote it? (*High Life below Stairs,* 2.1.)

And, as I suggested in the text, Bickerstaffe's *The Doctor Last in His Chariot* also abounds in examples of cultural malapropism, including that in which the Medicean Venus is famously rebaptized as "Venus the Methodist." Once again, we can see how the intertextual web works across genres to reposition Burney's comedic models: multiple transmutations and variations in inflection create a theatrical spectrum that has at its seemingly opposite poles the theater of Molière, and that of Samuel Foote.

50. Delightfully nonsensical as they may be, it might be possible to trace specific "sentimental" sources for Dabler's poems. For instance, his "An Epitaph on a Fly Killed by a Spider" (*CP,* 3.391) could be drawn from the well-known episode in Laurence Sterne's *Tristram Shandy* in which Uncle Toby frees a fly caught in a web or from an episode in James Thomson's poem "Summer." But beyond potential specific references, it is his poems' aesthetic affinities to a whole cultural system that define Dabler's *poiesis.*

51. Manuscript letter from Susanna Burney to Frances Burney, quoted in Doody, *Frances Burney,* 92; emphasis added.

52. On reading aloud, aside from David Hume's *A Treatise on Human Nature* (1739–40) and Adam Smith's *The Theory of Moral Sentiments* (1759), see Thomas Sheridan's *Lectures on the Art of Reading* (1775). That Burney was fully aware of the semiotics of reading aloud is clear from, among others, the episode of Melmond, the histrionic reader par excellence, in *Camilla,* bk. 2, chap. 5, 99–103.

53. Oliver Goldsmith, "Essay on the Theatre," *The Collected Works of Oliver Goldsmith,* 3:213.

54. It seems clear that Burney intentionally censored these letters because of what I would call a "dynamics of self-restraint," following Spacks's theory of fear-induced self-censorship: Spacks, *Imagining a Self,* 158–92. The fact appears to be confirmed by the suppression of the entire episode in the *Memoirs of Doctor Burney,* in which Frances Burney reconstructs much of her own literary career. Of her four comedies and three tragedies, Burney briefly mentions only one "pastoral tragedy, of which his daughter [Frances] had shown him the manuscript before her marriage": Burney, *Memoirs of Doctor Burney,* 3:284. The tragedy was probably *Hubert de Vere.* Thus, she disowned the sizable quantity of her work that her father never accepted.

55. "To the Authors of the 'Monthly' and 'Critical Reviews,'" in *Evelina,* 4.

56. Johnson's views on women's writing perfectly agreed with Crisp's. "Miss Burney is a real wonder. What she is, she is intuitively": *ED,* 1:228.

57. Doody supports this hypothesis, quoting a letter in which Charles Burney reminds Frances that his only disagreement with her in many years has been over "the Blue Stocking-Club-Party" and then urges her to permanently suppress "the whole piece": Doody, *Frances Burney,* 95. Sylvia Myers instead maintains that in *The Witlings,* "Fanny Burney's responses to the bluestocking ladies show a positive feeling and even a sense of solidarity with women who had been singled out for their abilities": Myers, *The Bluestocking Circle,* 257. Doody's view seems to have become

the standard one, however. Lynch, for example, agrees that the comedy's suppression was mainly due to Charles Burney and Samuel Crisp, who "were convinced that the blue-stocking circle headed by Elizabeth Montagu would see themselves as the originals for [the play's] characters": Lynch, "Counter Publics," 229.

58. Thrale, *Thraliana,* 1:381, 1:381n.3.

59. This is the view held by Tara Ghoshal Wallace in her edition of Burney's *A Busy Day* (160).

60. The social subordination of a music master to those who hire him is apparent in the episode of Richard Steele's *The Conscious Lovers* in which the virtuous Bevil engages Carbonelli to entertain his beloved Indiana:

> *After the sonata is played,* BEVIL *waits on the Master to the door.*
>
> *Bevil.* You smile, Madam, to see me so complaisant to one whom I pay for his visit. Now I own I think it is not enough barely to pay those whose talents are superior to our own (I mean such talents as would become our condition, if we had them). Methinks we ought to do something more, than barely gratify them, for what they do at our command, only because their fortune is below us.
>
> *Indiana.* You say I smile: I assure you it was a smile of approbation; for indeed, I cannot but think it is the distinguishing part of a gentleman to make his superiority of fortune as easy to his inferiors as he can. (*The Conscious Lovers,* 2.2)

The exceptional nature of Bevil's attitude towards the music master is emphasized by the repeated references to the latter's financial dependence—a condition effectually shared by all artists. Bevil's status as a gentleman makes him different, and inescapably superior, to the man he employs. On Charles Burney's social background, see Chisholm, *Fanny Burney.* James Macburney, Charles's father, had erased his Scottish origins by Anglicizing his name to Burney. Chisholm briefly describes his career. "James junior was lured away from such a respectable career [the legal profession] by his dream of becoming famous as an actor. Before he was nineteen, he eloped with a fifteen-year-old actress. . . . He spent the rest of his life struggling to make enough money as an itinerant actor, musician and portrait painter": Chisholm, *Fanny Burney,* 3.

61. One of many anecdotes is that of Elizabeth Inchbald, who was invited by Thomas Harris, the manager of Covent Garden, to come to see him to make changes to one of her comedies. When he suddenly assaulted her, she quickly reacted to his passionate advances by violently pulling his hair. "Oh! if he had wo-wo-worn a wig, I had been ru-ruined," she is reported to have stuttered to a friend immediately after the incident: quoted in Donkin, *Getting into the Act,* 112. See also the interesting reconstruction of the theatrical world at the end of the century in Tomalin, *Mrs. Jordan's Profession.*

FOUR. THE THEATER AND THE CITY

1. Manuscript letter transcribed in Doody, *Frances Burney,* 96.

2. Hemlow, *The History of Frances Burney,* 139.

3. Doody notes Hester Thrale's significant contribution to the novel's composition. "[Thrale] was privileged to participate in the novel's creation as a reader . . . who offered instant impressions before the novel was finished": Doody, *Frances Burney,* 108. Her affectionate enthusiasm was especially necessary to Burney after the debacle of *The Witlings.* "Care, concern, mutual support, the lightening of burdens—these were involved in a friendship that had gone far beyond the polite entertainments of Streatham's witty drawing-room. . . . Frances Burney's trust in the love afforded by her family (and by her adoptive elder, Samuel Crisp) had presumably been shaken by the treatment of *The Witlings;* the new warm friendship outside the family would appear to have become increasingly important": ibid., 103.

4. The theatrical can be considered a subset of the spectacular. On the spectacular quality of London's many theatrical sites, see n. 20 in chapter 2 of this volume.

5. "Burney's Draft Introduction to *Cecilia,*" in *Cecilia,* 945.

6. Doody, *Frances Burney,* 101.

7. See her complaints in her letters to Susanna. "O that I could defer the publication & relieve my Mind from this vile solicitude which does but shackle it, & disturb my rest so abominably, that I cannot sleep half the Night for planning what to write next Day,—& am next Day half dead for want of rest": quoted in Chisholm, *Fanny Burney,* 107.

8. Employing the same mirror metaphor I used for the chapter on *The Witlings,* the anonymous reviewer for the *Gentleman's Magazine* concluded that "the novel holds up a mirror to the gay and dissipated of both sexes in which they may see themselves and their deformities at full length": *Gentleman's Magazine,* vol. 52, 1782, 485, quoted in Doody, *Frances Burney,* 143.

9. Samuel Crisp to Sophia Gast, quoted in Hemlow, *The History of Fanny Burney,* 148.

10. Austen continues, "From pride, ignorance, or fashion our foes are almost as many as our readers. . . . there seems almost a general wish of decrying the capacity and undervaluing the labour of the novelist, and of slighting the performances which have only genius, wit, and taste to recommend them": Austen, *Northanger Abbey,* 58.

11. This anticipates the structural importance of tragedy in *Cecilia.* According to Aristotle's *Poetics,* tragedy employs causal necessity to link the parts of the *fabula.* Burney's novel adheres rigorously to Aristotle's poetics. The sequence of episodes builds logically according to tragic rules of cause and effect, and even incidental episodes are causally connected to the main plot through necessity and verisimilitude.

12. Zonitch calls this a strategy of "patrilinear repair" and explains that it had become common practice in periods of demographic crisis such as the end of the seventeenth century: Zonitch, *Familiar Violence,* 19.

13. In order, "Rich," "wealth," "store," "inherited," "bequeathed," "£10,000," "accumulated possessions," "prosperous," "heiress," "estate of £3,000 per annum," "riches."

14. Craft-Fairchild, *Masquerade and Gender,* 131.

15. See Tessari, *Teatro e spettacolo nel Settecento,* 53–106.

16. Cf. Markley, "Sentimentality as Performance." See also Craft-Fairchild, *Masquerade and Gender.*

17. Cecilia realizes she is the object of Sir Robert Floyer's gaze in an earlier passage, as well. "Cecilia, offended by [Sir Robert's] boldness, looked a thousand ways to avoid him; but her embarrassment, by giving greater play to her features, served only to keep awake an attention which might otherwise have wearied": *Cecilia,* 36.

18. I am much indebted to Ludovico Zorzi's excellent *Il teatro e la città* for my observations on the spectacular dimension of urban civic and social life.

19. Jill Campbell has called auctions a "kind of theatrical event" in which the auctioneer talks up the merchandise and triggers a mechanism of "audience interaction": Campbell, "When Men Women Turn," 73. A clear instance is in Sheridan's *School for Scandal* (3.3, 4.1), which fully exploits the theatrical potential of an auction.

20. Burke, *Reflections on the Revolution of France.* Cf. John Bender's interesting *Imagining the Penitentiary,* esp. 231–48. See also the analysis of the ideological and didactic-admonitory functions of public executions in Foucault, *Discipline and Punish.*

21. Wordsworth, "Residence in London," *The Prelude,* bk. 7, lines 228–39.

22. *Knight's Cyclopaedia of London,* 766.

23. See Hartpole-Lecky, *A History of London in the Eighteenth Century,* 3:137.

24. In order, these are Cecilia's letter to Floyer of 11 May 1779 (*Cecilia,* 312); the letter from Mrs. Delvile to Cecilia of 12 June 1779 and that from Mortimer Delvile to Cecilia of 20 September 1779 (ibid., 379, 561); the message Mrs. Delvile sends Cecilia from Bristol on 21 October 1779 (ibid., 700); the note from Briggs of 8 November 1779 (ibid., 721); the letter from Mortimer of 2 April 1780 (ibid., 814); and the exchange with Compton Delvile of 29 April and 1 May 1780 (ibid., 863, 867).

25. Although it seems to have been overlooked by critics, these phrases are employed so frequently in the novel that their recurrence hardly seems accidental. See the start of chapters 6, 8, 9, and 10 in book 1; chapters 4, 6, and 8 in book 2; chapter 6 in book 3; chapters 2, 3, 4, 7, and 9 in book 4; chapters 2, 3, 6, and 11 in book 5; chapters 2, 8, and 10 in book 6; and chapter 4 in book 7, where Cecilia attains her majority.

26. Cf. the following expressions in vols. 3–5: "Three days passed thus" (*Cecilia,* 634); "During the following week" and "When this week was expired" (ibid., 695); and "Another week passed" (ibid., 815).

27. Only characters who have a causal connection to the plot or who are directly linked to the themes of love and independence that drive the plot are reported in figure 16.

28. Doody, "Introduction," in *Cecilia,* xvi. Cecilia's gender reversal is paralleled by Mortimer's situation should he marry Cecilia and take on her name, thus becom-

ing what Zonitch calls a "fictive male tail" to the Beverley lineage: Zonitch, *Familiar Violence,* 19. The adjective "fictive" here evokes the legal fictions inherent in the legal terminology in the Dean's will and is therefore related to the theme of artifice that runs through the novel. Mrs. Delvile expresses her disapproval of her son's marriage under the conditions stipulated by the Dean. "How will the blood of your wronged ancestors rise into your guilty cheeks, and how will your heart throb with secret shame and reproach, when wished joy upon your marriage by the name of *Mr. Beverley!*": *Cecilia,* 677.

29. The word recurs frequently in the novel, independently of Briggs. It also appears on pp. 199, 295, 370, 744, 750, 752.

30. Davies, *Factual Fictions,* 183.

31. Konigsberg, *Samuel Richardson and the Dramatic Novel,* 102.

32. Oliver Goldsmith, *She Stoops to Conquer,* 5.3. Goldsmith's disparaging phrase should be read in light of his criticism of the mixture of comic and pathetic elements in contemporary comedies. Burney's dissatisfaction with the mechanical contrivance of Censor's gift at the end of *The Witlings* led her to consider an alternative ending to the play. As she wrote to Samuel Crisp, her plan was "to restore to Censor his £5,000 and not trouble him even to offer it;—To give a new friend to Cecilia, by whom her affairs shall be retrieved, and through whose means the catastrophe shall be brought to be happy": *DL,* 1:316.

33. The review appeared in January 1783 in the *English Review* and is quoted in Doody, *Frances Burney,* 144.

34. Hybrid stage productions such as "entertainments," comic operas, and pantomimes were extraordinary successful in the second half of the eighteenth century. H. W. Pedicord's appendix to *The Theatrical Public in the Time of Garrick,* 220–23, notes that the most frequently performed work at Covent Garden between 1747 and 1776 was the hybrid, and anonymous, *The Coronation,* which was performed 180 times. Shakespeare's tragedies, such as *Romeo and Juliet, Richard III,* and *Hamlet,* came next in frequency of performance, followed by comedies, with *The Provok'd Husband* heading the list (fifty-one performances). The situation at Garrick's Drury Lane was slightly different because Garrick himself performed in so many productions. Benjamin Hoadley's *The Suspicious Husband* was performed 126 times, 109 of these with Garrick in the role of Ranger; the greatest tragic playwrights of the Restoration were also well represented, with Otway's *The Orphan* receiving seventy-seven performances and Rowe's *The Fair Penitent,* seventy-four : Pedicord, *The Theatrical Public in the Time of Garrick,* 198–201.

35. Tessari, *Teatro e spettacolo nel Settecento,* 82.

36. Loftis, *Comedy and Society from Congreve to Fielding,* 1–5.

37. Colman and Garrick, *The Clandestine Marriage,* 275–76. The comedy was one of the most popular works of the time: see Pedicord, *The Theatrical Public in the Time of Garrick,* 198–99. It was also one of Burney's favorites, cited more often than any other in her journals and letters: see the appendix in this volume.

38. It is also worth recalling that reprints of Henry Fielding's comedy *The*

Miser (1741) remained very popular throughout the century. A skillful adaptation of Molière's *L'Avare,* it had already gone through six editions by 1775.

39. On the influence of *The Conscious Lovers* on *Evelina,* see chapter 2 in this volume.

40. Steele, *The Conscious Lovers,* 158.

41. Bevis, *English Drama,* 182. Among the major historians of the English stage who have written specifically about early eighteenth-century harlequinades are Hughes, *A Century of English Farce;* Nicoll, *The World of Harlequin.*

42. Tessari, *Teatro e spettacolo nel Settecento,* 58.

43. "Annually from 1750 to 1756 Woodward produced a new pantomime and each met with overwhelming success. That his *Queen Mab, Harlequin Ranger, The Genii, Fortunatus, Proteus, or Harlequin in China,* and *Mercury Harlequin* proved popular enough to satisfy the desires of the managers and entertaining enough to draw crowds of people is indicated by the box receipts, by the long runs they enjoyed at Drury Lane, and by the fact that they were kept in the repertoire of the theatre for years afterwards": Stone, "*A Midsummer Night's Dream* in the Hands of Garrick and Colman," 468. Pedicord has calculated that the four most frequently performed works at Drury Lane between 1747 and 1776 were Woodward's harlequinades (*Queen Mab* [1750], 259 performances; *The Genii* [1752], 207 performances; *Fortunatus* [1753], 158 performances). Garrick's own critical response to the immense success of the harlequinade was *Harlequin's Invasion* (1759). Paradoxically, it became his repertory's greatest success. According to Denise Sechelski's careful reconstruction, Garrick's debut was in the pantomime *Harlequin Student; or, The Fate of Pantomime,* even before he famously appeared as Richard III. Garrick appears symbolically to have repressed this experience in later years, both culturally and psychologically: see Sechelski, "Garrick's Body and the Labor of Art in Eighteenth-Century Theater."

44. Frye, *Anatomy of Criticism,* 218.

45. Blank verse was commonly used for tragedies throughout the eighteenth century. As Richard Bevis explains, "[Although] something in the age again lusted after heroics . . . blank verse remained the norm": Bevis, *English Drama,* 201. Shakespeare was still the model. Playwrights had been adapting his tragedies since the Restoration, and Dryden's *All for Love* had ensured his canonical status. Shakespeare's reputation was further consolidated in the eighteenth century due to Nicholas Rowe's critical edition of his plays (1709). All major tragedies of the century were composed in blank verse, from Addison's *Cato* (1713) to Murphy's *The Grecian Daughter* (1772) and Hannah More's highly successful *Percy* (1777). Burney herself used blank verse in the four historical tragedies she composed in the last decades of the century. The exception to the dominant tendency of the age was domestic tragedy. In accordance with their bourgeois, antiheroic subjects, George Lillo and Edward Moore used prose in tragedies such as *The London Merchant* (1730) and *The Gamester* (1753).

46. These binary oppositions are discussed by the characters themselves. Mortimer Delvile chooses to follow his heart rather than yield to his father's will: "The die is finally cast, and the conflict between bosom felicity and family pride is deliberately

over" (*Cecilia,* 563). In her first meeting with Cecilia, Mrs. Delvile accuses the young woman of wanting to marry Delvile out of a selfish desire to gratify her passion: "'Hear me then, I beg of you, with no pre-determination to disregard me. . . . Not easy indeed is such a task, to a mind pre-occupied with the intention to be guided by the dictates of inclination,—' 'You wrong me, indeed, madam!' interrupted Cecilia, greatly hurt, 'my mind harbours no such intention, it has no desire but to be guided by duty, it is wretched with the consciousness of having failed in it!'" (ibid., 637). Compton Delvile, furthermore, justifies his opposition to the marriage by pitting wealth against lineage: "Where the birth is such as Mortimer Delvile may claim, the fortune generally fails; and where the fortune is adequate to his expectations, the birth yet more frequently would disgrace us" (ibid., 500).

47. Rowe, prologue to *The Fair Penitent,* lines 1–30; emphasis added.

48. See Frye, *Anatomy of Criticism,* 206–23.

49. Brown, *Ends of Empire,* 65.

50. Repentant gamblers also feature most notably in Susanna Centlivre's *The Basset Table* and *The Gamester* (1705) and in John Vanbrugh's *The Confederacy* (1705). Later in the century, they are featured in Thomas Holcroft's *Duplicity* (1781 [the year before the publication of *Cecilia*]), and, beyond the confines of the period covered by this chapter, in his greatest success, *The Road to Ruin* (1792).

51. See the appendix in this volume.

52. For a detailed discussion of women's consumerism in the eighteenth century, see Barker-Benfield, *The Culture of Sensibility.*

53. D. Grant Campbell explains: "As denizens of fashionable society and conspicuous consumption founded upon credit, the Harrels in *Cecilia* reflect both their [*sic*] economic climate in England and a complex of prevalent ideological responses to that climate. . . . Their lavish expenditure epitomizes an explosion in consumer spending which occurred in England in the late eighteenth century": Campbell, "Fashionable Suicide," 133. See also Copeland, "Money and the Novels of Fanny Burney," 29, which discusses the "plot of hard cash" in *Cecilia.*

54. On the complex socioeconomic relations Burney describes in *Cecilia* and her other works, see Zonitch, *Familiar Violence.*

55. The etymology of "asylum" from the Latin for "sanctuary" (from the Greek *asylon* [refuge]) shifts by the eighteenth century to encompass the notion of a place of confinement. As Foucault's *Madness and Civilization* eloquently shows, the institutional function of the asylum dates to the second half of the eighteenth century. The *Oxford English Dictionary* (2nd ed., 1989) confirms this, giving 1776 as the first use of the term to signify "a benevolent institution affording shelter and support to some class of the afflicted, the unfortunate, or destitute; *e.g.* a 'lunatic asylum,' to which the term is sometimes popularly restricted."

56. Hence Evelina's reply to Orville's question "whether she depends wholly on herself, or whether there is any other person for whose interest I must solicit?" is "I hardly know myself to whom I most belong" (*Evelina,* 392). The meaning of "owning" as both "acknowledging" and "possessing" is made very clear in Evelina's second

meeting with her father. Her melodramatic appeal exposes the possessive violence concealed by the rhetoric of sensibility: "'Yes, Sir,' cried I, springing forward, and kneeling at his feet, 'it is your child, if you will *own* her!'" (ibid., 425; emphasis added).

57. Burney draws on established convention for this characterization, as well. City bankers were commonly portrayed as miserly, as in Pope's "Epistle III: To Allen, Lord Bathurst" (*Epistles to Several Persons*) of 1732, also known as "Of the Use of Riches." See note 38 in this chapter on theatrical representations of misers.

58. Likewise, in noting the similarities among Juliet's suitors in *The Wanderer*, Catherine Craft-Fairchild rightly observes that "woman's lack is the guarantee of man's possession, placing her as the other of and mirror for the masculine subject. . . . The virtual sameness of many men in the text is yet another of Burney's 'excesses'": Craft-Fairchild, *Masquerade and Gender*, 139–40.

59. On Gothic stage scenery, see Ranger, *"Terror and Pity Reign in Every Breast."*

60. A semiotic analysis of the characters' names in *Cecilia* is revealing. The Eglestons swoop down on Cecilia like eagles, keen to claim their inheritance and to put an end to the charity she had extended to her poorest tenants. "Compton" (Delvile) suggests assonance with "contempt," fitting his arrogance and pride, whereas his son Mortimer seems to bear in his name the potential extinction, or mortality, of his lineage, should he marry Cecilia and take on the Beverley name. Besides having proto-Gothic overtones (its homophony with "monk" brings to mind the classic antagonist of the Gothic tradition, later canonized by the figure of the Armenian monk in Schiller's *Der Geisterseeher* [1786], translated as *The Ghost-Seer; or, Apparitionist* in 1795), Monckton's name suggests the way he makes a mockery of Cecilia's friendship—and of marriage, given his eagerness to be rid of his tyrannical wife. Once again, Burney is drawing on the conventions of seventeenth-century drama, as adapted through the eighteenth-century *lectiones* provided by Fielding, Richardson, and contemporary playwrights such as Sheridan.

61. Donna Andrew notes that the *Daily Advertiser* was "wildly successful, it continued to be London's first and chief advertiser until its demise in 1795": Andrew, "The Press and Public Apologies in Eighteenth-Century London," 209.

62. Ibid.

63. Crisp is referring to Edward Francesco Burney, Frances's cousin and a talented painter who had created three illustrations for *Evelina* in 1780: see Chisholm, *Fanny Burney*, 122. Edward Francesco did in fact draw some illustrations for *Cecilia*. One of them (the original is at the Berg Collection of the New York Public Library) shows Cecilia offering financial assistance to Mrs. Hill. It is reproduced as illustration no. 15 in Doody, *Frances Burney*.

64. Altick, *The Shows of London*, 94.

65. "[Ranelagh Gardens] were a vast *amphitheatre*, finely gilt, painted and illuminated, into which everybody that loves eating, drinking, *staring*, or crowding, is admitted for a twelvepence": Horace Walpole to Sir Horace Mann, letter, 26 May 1742, in Walpole, *Horace Walpole's Correspondence with Sir Horace Mann*, 434.

66. Altick, *The Shows of London,* 95.

67. Hayman's paintings are analyzed in detail in Edelstein, "Vauxhall Gardens." See also Merchant, "Francis Hayman's Illustrations of Shakespeare."

68. Altick, *The Shows of London,* 95.

69. See Archer, *"Rus in Urbe."* It is important to note that in this respect, *Cecilia* distances itself from the traditional city–country dichotomy. Not only is the evil, Machiavellian Mr. Monckton based in the country, but rural areas and nature more generally are themselves conceived of as an extension of the city, as the *natura naturata* of Vauxhall Gardens suggests.

70. Frye, *Anatomy of Criticism,* 182ff.

71. Lovelace's death also takes place "off-stage" and is announced by a servant. This convention originated with Greek tragedy, in which violent actions taking place off-stage were communicated by strangers or messengers. See Aristotle, *Poetics,* 56n.6.

72. I am indebted to Terry Castle's studies for this historical background on the masquerade. See her "The Carnivalization of Eighteenth-Century English Narrative" and "Eros and Liberty at the English Masquerade" (both slightly revised in *The Female Thermometer,* 82–100, 101–19). On Burney's *Cecilia,* see esp. her *Masquerade and Civilization.* Castle's approach in these essays is influenced by Bakhtin, *Rabelais and His World.*

73. Castle, "Eros and Liberty at the English Masquerade," 159.

74. Castle, "The Carnivalization of Eighteenth-Century English Narrative," 909. Taking her cue from plate 2 of Hogarth's *The Harlot's Progress,* Elizabeth Hunt has written that "the masquerade became an intensely charged erotic arena, in which participants were thought to endanger their virtue": Hunt, "A Carnival of Mirrors," 91. For a homoerotic—and exotic—perspective on this form of entertainment, see Williams, "Horace in Italy."

75. In her description of the Harrels' masquerade, Burney refers twice to men disguised as women. Aside from the brief reference cited above, the narrator also mentions "an apparent old woman, who was a young man in disguise" (*Cecilia,* 114). The fondness for cross-dressing typical of the eighteenth century (one need think only of the actress Charlotte Charke, or of Fielding's Mary Hamilton, or of the Chevalier d'Eon's martial disguises later in the century) was one of the most frequently cited reasons for objecting to masquerades. Relying on the scriptural condemnation of the practice in Deuteronomy, puritanical critics of masked entertainments charged that the anonymity granted by the disguise encouraged homosexuality. The period's partiality for this form of transgressive behavior was much discussed at the time in periodicals such as the *Spectator,* as well as in literature, where the most famous instance is perhaps in John Cleland's *Memoirs of a Woman of Pleasure* (1749). But the reference to carnivalesque cross-dressing also recalls the portrayal of Madame Duval as a character "in drag" (see chapter 2, n. 31), as well as the various theatrical models Burney adapted to her own ends.

76. Castle ("The Carnivalization of Eighteenth-Century English Narrative," 905) agrees to some extent with this analysis. I should perhaps clarify that although

my own analysis is indebted to Castle's in several ways, her brief discussion of the masquerade in *Cecilia* is concerned primarily with relating it to the dominant social and literary paradigms of the time, whereas I seek to explore the episode's relation to the novel as a whole, and especially to the textual isotopy of the fictitious. The practice of acting "in character" at a masquerade is also mentioned in Burney's diaries. In her only reference to a masquerade in her journals, Burney relates how she avoided dressing up as a nun or a Quaker because it would have been difficult "to keep character with those personages" (*EJL*, 1:98). Lars Troide remarks on Burney's unwillingness to let it be known that she attended public masked entertainments (see *DL*, 2:16n.37). Her reluctance is consistent with the traditional disapproval of masquerades, as expressed, for example, in Fielding's *Amelia* and *Tom Jones.* "Nancy is, I am certain, too good a girl to desire to go; for she must remember when you carried her hither last year, it almost turned her head, and she did not return to herself or to her needle in a month afterwards": Fielding, *The History of Tom Jones,* 500–501. A detailed description of how to behave at a masquerade is in chapter 2 of Maria Edgeworth's *Belinda* (1801), in which Belinda and Lady Delacour dress, respectively, as the muse of tragedy and the muse of comedy. "Lady Delacour opened her dressing-room door, and pointed to her as she stood with the dress of the comic muse on one arm, and the tragic muse on the other. 'I am afraid I have not spirits enough to undertake the comic muse,' said Miss Portman. . . . 'Your ladyship's taller than Miss Portman by half a head,' said Marriott, 'and to be sure will best become tragedy, with this long train. . . . ' [A]fter the muses had performed their parts to the satisfaction of the audience, and their own, the conversation ceased to be supported in masquerade character; muses and harlequins, gipsies and Cleopatras, began to talk of their private affairs, and of news and the scandal of the day": Edgeworth, *Belinda,* 19, 23. For a discussion of masquerade costumes, see Ribeiro, *The Dress Worn at Masquerades in England.*

77. The quote is in Hunt, "A Carnival of Mirrors," 94.

78. Castle lists many novels, plays, and essays that discuss the masquerade. A comprehensive list, covering the period from the first performance of *Masquerade; or, an Evening's Intrigue* by Benjamin Griffin (1717) to Edgeworth's *Belinda,* is in Castle, "Eros and Liberty at the English Masquerade," 158n.5, This was further expanded in "The Carnivalization of Eighteenth-Century English Narrative," 915n.2.

79. "As soon as Mr. B saw me, 'Come in,' said he . . . 'who is it you put your *tricks* upon? I was resolved never again to honour you with my notice; and so you must *disguise* yourself, to attract me, and yet pretend, like an hypocrite as you are—' 'I beseech you, sir,' said I, 'do not impute *disguise* and hypocrisy to me. I have put on no *disguise*'": Richardson, *Pamela,* letter 24, 90; emphasis added.

80. Craft-Fairchild, *Masquerade and Gender,* 142. On the language of fashion in the eighteenth century, see Barker-Benfield, *The Culture of Sensibility,* 82–90.

81. Doody, *Frances Burney,* 134.

82. As noted earlier, Delvile's actantial role shifts in the course of the novel.

83. See Defoe's *Roxana* (1724), in which the heroine attends a masquerade in Turkish costume. As the costume historian Aileen Ribeiro has shown, there was a

spike in the popularity of "Oriental" styles toward the end of the century: Ribeiro, "Turquerie." See also Joshua Reynolds's portrait of Nancy Parsons in Turkish dress (1767–69).

84. Fielding, "The Masquerade," 3.

85. Given Monckton's portrayal as a villainous Machiavellian character, his presence at the masquerade strongly supports the view that *Cecilia*'s structure is basically tragic. Northrop Frye notes the close affinity between the Machiavellian type and the diabolical, making it one of the recurrent types in tragedy: Frye, *Anatomy of Criticism,* 216.

86. O'Brien, *Harlequin Britain,* 108.

87. Ibid., 115.

88. Fielding, "An Essay on the Knowledge of the Characters of Men," 155.

89. Castle, "The Carnivalization of Eighteenth-Century English Narrative," 904.

90. Barthes, *Writing Degree Zero.*

FIVE. TEXTS, BODIES, PERFORMANCE

1. Serpieri, Introduction to *Amleto,* 13.

2. See the section on "Theatrical Systems and Codes" in Elam, *Semiotics of Theatre,* 43–77.

3. Serpieri, Introduction to *Amleto,* 11.

4. Pagnini, *Semiosi,* 126.

5. In addition to Konigsberg's classic *Samuel Richardson and the Dramatic Novel* and Kinkead-Weekes's essential *Samuel Richardson,* Elaine McGirr's "Why Lovelace Must Die" is very useful on the influence of the Restoration, and of Dryden in particular, on Richardson. On the role played by Richardson's readers, see Budd, "Why Clarissa Must Die."

6. Elam, *Semiotics of the Theatre,* 58. For an introduction to the practices of silent reading and reading aloud in eighteenth-century England, see the contributions in Raven et al., *The Practice and Representation of Reading in England.* The dynamics of the reading process are also explored in Alsop and Walsh, *The Practice of Reading,* esp. chaps. 1–3; Bray, *The Female Reader in the English Novel.*

7. Gonda, *Reading Daughters' Fictions,* 121.

8. On madness in late-eighteenth-century and Romantic theater, see "Acting the Part of a Madman: Insanity and the Stage," in Ingram and Faubert, *Cultural Constructions of Madness in Eighteenth-Century Writing.* On Augustan splenetic humor, see DePorte, *Nightmares and Hobbyhorses.* On the representation of madness across the arts, including nineteenth-century opera, see Clausen, *Macbeth Multiplied,* esp. 108–34. Foucault, *Madness and Civilization,* is, of course, essential reading.

9. Tucker, "Joanna Baillie's and Elizabeth Inchbald's Moral Aesthetics," 337.

10. In the Romantic period, this second category was embodied in the figure of the erotomaniac, especially after the publication of Erasmus Darwin's *Zoonomia; or, The Laws of Organic Life* in 1794. Thus, Jane Kromm's discussion of Romanticism and women's madness identifies a new medical construct at this time—that of

the "sexually provocative madwoman": Kromm, "The Feminization of Madness in Visual Representation," 507.

11. Bevis, *English Drama,* 132.

12. Rowe, *The Tragedy of Jane Shore,* 96.

13. Ibid., 99. Cf. the last scene of Thomas Southerne's *Isabella; or, The Fatal Marriage,* in which the heroine enters "distracted, held by her women, her Hair dishevelled" (5.4) and then stabs herself on stage. In William Hamilton's famous watercolor, *Sarah Siddons as Jane Shore* (1791), the bewildered heroine's hair is also disheveled. The picture's codified image of the madwoman proved very influential.

14. Kromm, "The Feminization of Madness in Visual Representation," 513. See also Showalter, "Representing Ophelia," for an analysis of representations of Ophelia in relation to feminine sexuality in nineteenth-century culture.

15. Rowe, *The Tragedy of Jane Shore,* 94.

16. Ibid., 102.

17. On the exotic dimensions of derangement, see Broome, "Her Lovely Arm a Little Bloody." Richardson's use of stage props and clothing in *Grandison* is discussed in Hughes, "Theatrical Conventions in Richardson."

18. Kromm, "The Feminization of Madness in Visual Representation," 508. See also Robert Markley, "Sentimentality as Performance," in Nussbaum and Brown, *The New Eighteenth Century.* Scientific discourse of the nineteenth century extended contemporary gender constructions into the field of mental illness. Elaine Showalter discusses the Victorian psychiatrist Henry Maudsley (the author of *The Pathology of the Mind: A Study of Its Distempers, Deformities, and Disorders* [1895]), according to whom the traits typical of "femininity" were retained even in female patients affected by the most extreme forms of insanity. "[They did not] evince such lively exultation and energy as men, and they had quieter and less assertive delusions of grandeur conformable with their gentler natures and the quieter currents and conditions of their lives": Showalter, *The Female Malady,* 8.

19. Altick, *The Shows of London,* 45.

20. Wollstonecraft, *"Mary" and "The Wrongs of Woman,"* 85. According to Jeffrey Cox, Wollstonecraft's *Maria* directly influenced Matthew Lewis's *The Captive* (1803), a monodrama about a "captive wife, imprisoned in an asylum by her cruel husband": Cox, *Seven Gothic Dramas,* 38. Furthermore, Cox has shown that the monodramatic focus on a persecuted heroine's emotions (which Matthew Lewis returned to in *Adelgitha; or, The Fruits of a Single Error* [1806]) also inspired a number of Romantic plays, such as Percy B. Shelley's *The Cenci* and Charles Maturin's *Bertram,* in which "there are many scenes depicting the movement of a distressed female through the stages of madness": ibid., 40. Romantic representations of madness often portrayed individuals who are driven beyond the normal boundaries of subjectivity, as in John Cartwright Cross's *Julia of Louvain; or, Monkish Cruelty* (1797) and Joanna Baillie's *Orra* (1812).

21. Wollstonecraft, *"Mary" and "The Wrongs of Woman,"* 79.

22. Kromm, "The Feminization of Madness in Visual Representation," 530–31.

23. Lee, *The Recess,* 161, 345.

24. Scott, *The Bride of Lammermoor,* 39–40.

25. Ibid., 323.

26. Small, *Love's Madness,* 124–25.

27. Ibid., 14. By contrast, Augustan adaptations of Shakespeare's *Hamlet* censored the lines Ophelia speaks when she is mad. Considered indecent, they were substituted by songs: Showalter, *The Female Malady,* 11.

28. Donizetti, *Lucia di Lammermoor,* 33.

29. Small, *Love's Madness,* vii.

30. Burke, *Reflections on the Revolution in France,* 161.

31. On Gothic drama, power, and madness, see Backscheider, *Spectacular Politics,* 229–30.

32. For a modern analysis of the king's illness, see the classic study by Macalpine and Hunter, *George III and the Mad-Business.*

33. Volume 4 of Burney's *Diaries and Letters* is devoted almost entirely to the king's illness. But Kate Chisholm has noted that "we have to look elsewhere—for instance to the Diaries of Colonel 'Wellbred' Greville, one of the King's equerries—for the details of how the King's illness wrought disturbing changes in his behaviour, so that he became quite violent, hitting out at his pages and swearing uncouthly at those obliged to wait on him. . . . Greville tells us what went on behind those doors closed to Fanny—that the royal pulse was measured as 140 on one occasion; that the King talked sometimes for nineteen hours without a pause and went without sleep for twenty-nine hours": Chisholm, *Fanny Burney,* 147–48.

34. On 19 October 1788, Burney briefly noted: "In mere desperation, for employment, I have just begun a tragedy. We are now in so spiritless a situation that my mind would bend to nothing less sad, even in fiction. But I am very glad something of this kind has occurred to me; it may while away the tediousness of this unsettled, unoccupied, unpleasant period" (*DL* 4:118). This is her first reference to composing a tragedy, probably *Edwy and Elgiva.*

35. Small, *Love's Madness,* 75.

36. "The Windsor Castle in which much of the action takes place is the castle before it was reconstructed in the 1820s. The 18th century wasn't all elegance and there should be a marked contrast between the state rooms, in which the King's life was largely spent, and the back parts of the building, those tiny rooms and attics, cubicles almost, where, because the court was so crowded, most of the courtiers had to lodge. . . . But scrubbed and white-painted as these quarters may have been, cramped they certainly were and often situated behind and adjacent to the state rooms and grand corridors where the ceremonial life of the court was led. Access to these back parts is through doors flush with the panelling or covered in camouflaging wallpaper; when Greville, say, comes on duty it's as if he's threading his way through a complicated backstage before coming out onto the set. . . . [W]hen [the King] periodically escapes into the back parts of the castle . . . it's comparable to his escape into the back parts of his personality, the contrast between what he seems and what he is echoed by that between the state rooms and the attics": Bennett, *The*

Madness of King George, v–vi. Cf. Burney's description of Kew: "I have two rooms there; both small, and up two pair of stairs; but tidy and comfortable enough. Indeed all the apartments but the King's and Queen's, and one of Mrs. Schwellenberg's, are small, dark, and old-fashioned. There are staircases in every passage, and passages to every closet. I lost myself continually, only in passing from my own room to the Queen's" (*DL,* 2:402).

37. Bennett, *The Madness of George III,* 41.

38. In her journals, Burney included an ironic "conduct manual" entitled "Directions for coughing, sneezing, or moving, before the King and Queen" (*DL,* 2:345–46) in which she describes how a courtier's body in the royal presence must be so regulated, repressed, and stifled that its only form of release is either a physical breakdown or an act of self-cannibalism. Burney's increasingly violent somatic description also seems to evoke the extreme discomfort experienced by the mad king himself: "In the first place, you must not cough. . . . If you find yourself choking with the forbearance, you must choke, but not cough. In the second place, you must not sneeze. If you have a vehement cold . . . you must oppose it, by keeping your teeth grinding together; if the violence of the repulse breaks some blood-vessel, you must break the blood vessel—but not sneeze. In the third place, you must not, upon any account, stir either hand or foot. If, by chance, a black pin runs into your head, you must not take it out. . . . If the agony is very great, you may, privately, bite the inside of your cheek, or of your lips, for a little relief; taking care, meanwhile, to do it so cautiously and to make no apparent dent outwardly. And, with that precaution, if you even gnaw a piece out, it will not be minded, only be sure either to swallow it, or to commit it to a corner of the inside of your mouth till they are gone—for you must not spit."

39. Bennett, *The Madness of George III,* 26, 74.

40. Ibid., 81–82. See also Bennett's remark in the screenplay that "monarchy is a performance and part of the King's illness consists in his growing inability to sustain that performance": Bennett, *The Madness of King George,* xxi.

41. Bennett, *The Madness of King George,* 42.

42. Bennett, *The Madness of George III,* 58.

43. Showalter, *The Female Malady,* 220–23. See esp. Laing, *The Divided Self;* Laing, *The Self and Others;* Laing and Esterson, *Sanity, Madness, and the Family.*

44. Aside from *Hubert de Vere* (1790–97) and the *Elberta* fragment (1791–1814), Burney's tragedies are *Edwy and Elgiva* (1788–95) and *The Siege of Pevensey* (1790–91).

45. Fraiman, *Unbecoming Women,* 37.

46. The feminine *Bildung* of Burney's heroines reveals the inadequacy and idealism of the model on which she is basing it. Goethe's classic paradigm envisages a perfect integration of the individual in society, showing how heavily late-eighteenth-century pedagogy relied on the notion of a coherent identity and on an ideology, or mythology, of individual opportunity. But Goethe's conception of *Bildung,* as described in *Wilhelm Meisters Lehrjahre* (*Wilhelm Meister's Apprenticeship* [1795–96]) and *Wilhelm Meisters theatralische Sendung* (*Wilhelm Meister's Theatrical Calling* [1776–85]) seems applicable only to men, and even then it requires that one assume a

utopian equality of opportunity for all men, independent of variables linked to class or religion. The difference between masculine and feminine *Bildung* is particularly striking in relation to the theater. Whereas Wilhelm Meister's experience of the theater is crucial to his formation, in the case of Juliet in *The Wanderer,* it can only compromise her status and reputation (*The Wanderer,* 336–40).

47. Fraiman, *Unbecoming Women,* 35.

48. Papetti, "Letteratura e arti figurative nel Settecento," 280.

49. Pagnini, *Semiosi,* 130.

50. Doody, "Deserts, Ruins, and Troubled Waters," 552. My reading is closer to Sedgwick's in *The Coherence of Gothic Conventions.*

51. Bond, "Flights of Madness."

52. Bennett (*The Madness of George III,* 68) describes it this way: "[Willis *suddenly gags the* King *in full flow*] . . . there is no more disrespect in it than turning off a tap. . . . All men . . . nurture such thoughts, but they do not infect our talk, because discretion and decorum filter them out. It is that filter His Majesty refuses to operate, must learn to operate again."

53. Julie Park offers a different interpretation. "Cecilia's reversals of fortune, and surrenders to madness serve as extremely apologetic compensation for [her] mistakes and failures. . . . Burney's fiction chillingly demonstrates the notion of 'good enough' for female subjects is, in the end, impossible to fulfill, and yet the beginning for an obsessively self-admonishing mode of behavior and consciousness. . . . Burney's novels, in consistently developing the relationship between abjection, automatism, and female conduct, represent late eighteenth-century femininity as a condition enmeshed in the compulsory aspects of female dollship, the phantasmatic properties of objectivity, and most of all, the failed vision of Enlightenment standards for individual autonomy and classical images of beauty": Park, "Pains and Pleasures of the Automaton," 39. In my reading, on the contrary, the moment of madness works to dismantle what Park calls the discourse of female mechanical, or automatized, "dollship."

54. The use of this verb in *Cecilia* is always linked to situations in which the heroine is subjected to oppression or victimization. For example, immediately after the mysterious interruption of her wedding with Delvile, "She made not any answer; but still, though tottering as much from emotion as Mrs. Charlton from infirmity, she walked on" (*Cecilia,* 626). Another example is the dramatic confrontation with Mrs. Delvile: "Mrs. Delvile now came to the parlour door, and looked aghast at the situation in which she saw [Mortimer and Cecilia]: Cecilia again moved on, and reached the stairs, but tottered, and was obliged to cling to the banister" (ibid., 679). The term is all the more significant here, given that faltering steps are also attributed to the country girl forsaken by Albany in his youth, who, in his absence, has been seduced and abandoned by another. When he returns to rescue her, "She trembled, she could scarce totter, but neither consented nor refused" (ibid., 707). In Burney's tragedy, *Hubert de Vere,* Cerulia also "totters" about the stage.

55. Mary Stephens Wells (1762–1829) made her debut as Jane Shore at Covent Garden in 1785. In his autobiography, *The Life and Times of Frederick Reynolds*

(1826), the playwright calls her the most beautiful actress of the day and describes the eccentric behavior that led to her being considered mad. Mary Wells denied the accusations of madness in her own autobiography, *Memoirs of the Life of Mrs Sumbel, Late Wells* (1811). See K. A. Crouch's article on Wells in the *Oxford Dictionary of Literary Biography,* available online at http://www.oxforddnb.com/view/article/29016. Laura Engel has written about Wells's madness in "Notorious Celebrity."

56. Bennett, *The Madness of George III,* 50.

57. Croker, "Review of *The Wanderer.*" Scholars who have written specifically on *The Wanderer* since 1996 include Allen, "Staging Identity"; Gemmeke, *Frances Burney and the Female Bildungsroman;* Henderson, "Burney's *The Wanderer* and Early-Nineteenth-Century Commodity Fetishism"; Jones, "Radical Ambivalence"; Salih, "*Camilla* and *The Wanderer*"; Thompson, "How *The Wanderer* Works."

58. In Serpieri's definition of the dramatic text, "The linear word, or typographical word . . . has a tendency to become 'square'; that is, it enters and moves through the three-dimensional space of the stage": Serpieri, Introduction to *Amleto,* 11.

59. Ibid., 17.

60. A dagger is used in a scene of attempted suicide in William Hodson's *Zoraida: A Tragedy* (Drury Lane, 1779–80). Innumerable heroines wield daggers in the iconography of Romantic theater. Among others are Henry Fuseli's *Macbeth and Lady Macbeth after the Murder of Duncan* (c. 1760–66), John Keyse Sherwin's *Sarah Siddons in "The Grecian Daughter"* (1784), Thomas Beach's *Sarah Siddons and John Philip Kemble in "Macbeth"* (1786), Henry Fuseli's *Lady Macbeth Seizing the Daggers* (1812), Johann Zoffany's *David Garrick as Macbeth and Hannah Pritchard as Lady Macbeth* (n.d.), and Robert Edge Pine's *Sarah Siddons as Euphrasia* (n.d.). On the portraits of Siddons, in particular, see Asleson et al., *A Passion for Performance.*

61. See Ranger, *"Terror and Pity Reign in Every Breast."*

62. The contextual significance of Elinor's disguise is analyzed in detail in Craft-Fairchild, *Masquerade and Gender,* 123–62.

63. Castle, *The Female Thermometer,* 83.

64. Marsden, "Modesty Unshackled," 21.

65. Woo, "Sarah Siddons's Performances as Hamlet," 575–76.

66. Hunt, *Dramatic Essays,* 1:83; emphasis added.

67. My interpretation differs from Debra Silverman's feminist reading. She quotes the same passage of the novel primarily to stress Elinor's "Medusa-like appearance": Silverman, "Reading Frances Burney's *The Wanderer,*" 73.

68. See, e.g., Burney, *Brief Reflections Relative to the Emigrant French Clergy.*

69. Otway, *Venice Preserv'd,* 376.

70. The influence on Burney of *The Grecian Daughter* seems extremely likely here, not only because she knew Arthur Murphy, who had offered his assistance with *The Witlings,* but also because she refers to the play directly in her 1802 journals (*JL,* 5:210). Burney also knew Shakespeare's *Macbeth* very well. In addition to frequent references to the play (e.g., in *JL,* 3:345, 5:167), she reports attending a performance of it in 1773, with Jenny Barsanti in the role of Lady Macbeth (*EJL,* 1:261).

71. Lewis, *The Castle Spectre,* 11. Burney attended a performance of the play in 1798 (see the appendix).

72. On the attribution of the sketch (no. 45 in the catalog), see Schiff, *Zeichnungen von Johann Heinrich Füssli.*

73. Martin, *Mad Women and Romantic Writing,* 89. See Craciun, *Fatal Women of Romanticism,* 21–46.

Bibliography

A Collection of Poems in Six Volumes. By Several Hands. London: Printed by J. Hughs for R. and J. Dodsley, 1763.

Adams, Joseph Quincy, Jr. "The Text of Sheridan's *The Rivals.*" *Modern Language Notes* 25, no.6 (1910): 171–73.

Allen, Emily. "Staging Identity: Frances Burney's Allegory of Genre." *Eighteenth-Century Studies* 31 (1998): 433–51.

Alsop, Derek, and Chris Walsh. *The Practice of Reading: Interpreting the Novel.* Basingstoke: Macmillan, 1999.

Altick, Richard D. *The Shows of London.* Cambridge, Mass.: Harvard University Press, 1978.

Anderson, Emily Hodgson. *Eighteenth-Century Authorship and the Play of Fiction: Novels and the Theater, Haywood to Austen.* New York: Routledge, 2009.

Andrew, Donna T. "The Press and Public Apologies in Eighteenth-Century London." In *Law, Crime, and English Society, 1660–1830,* ed. Norma Landau, 208–30. Cambridge: Cambridge University Press, 2002.

Archer, John. "*Rus in Urbe:* Classical Ideals of Country and City in British Town Planning." *Studies in Eighteenth-Century Culture* 12 (1983): 159–86.

Aristotle. *Poetics.* Trans. James Hutton. New York: Norton, 1982.

Asleson, Robyn, Shelley Bennett, Mark Leonard, and Shearer West, eds. *A Passion for Performance: Sarah Siddons and Her Portraitists.* Los Angeles: J. Paul Getty Museum, 1999.

Austen, Jane. *Northanger Abbey.* Ed. Anne Ehrenpreis. Harmondsworth: Penguin, 1985.

———. *Persuasion.* Ed. Gillian Beer. New York: Penguin, 1998.

———. *Pride and Prejudice.* Ed. Margaret Drabble. London: Virago, 1989.

———. *Selected Letters.* Ed. R. W. Chapman. Oxford: Oxford University Press, 1985.

———. *Sense and Sensibility.* Ed. James Kinsley. Oxford: Oxford University Press, 2004.

Austen-Leigh, James Edward. *A Memoir of Jane Austen.* In *"Persuasion" with "A Memoir of Jane Austen."* Ed. D. W. Harding. Harmondsworth: Penguin, 1985.

Aycock, Roy E. "Shakespearian Criticism in the 'Gray's-Inn Journal.'" *Yearbook of English Studies* 2 (1972): 68–72.

Backscheider, Paula. *Spectacular Politics: Theatrical Power and Mass Culture in Early Modern England.* Baltimore: Johns Hopkins University Press, 1993.

Bakhtin, Mikhail. *Rabelais and His World.* Trans. Hélène Iswolsky. Bloomington: Indiana University Press, 1993.

Barish, Jonas. *The Antitheatrical Prejudice.* Berkeley: University of California Press, 1981.

Barker-Benfield, G. J. *The Culture of Sensibility: Sex and Society in Eighteenth-Century Britain.* Chicago: University of Chicago Press, 1996.

Barney, Richard E. *Plots of Enlightenment: Education and the Novel in Eighteenth-Century England.* Stanford, Calif.: Stanford University Press, 1999.

Barthes, Roland. *S/Z.* Trans. Richard Miller. London: Jonathan Cape, 1975.

———. *Writing Degree Zero.* Trans. Annette Lavers and Colin Smith. New York: Hill and Wang, 1968.

Bender, John. *Imagining the Penitentiary: Fiction and the Architecture of the Mind in Eighteenth-Century England.* Chicago: University of Chicago Press, 1987.

Benedetti, Jean. *David Garrick and the Birth of the Modern Theatre.* London: Methuen, 2002.

Bennett, Alan. *The Madness of George III.* London: Faber and Faber, 1992.

———. *The Madness of King George.* London: Faber and Faber, 1995.

Bertinetti, Paolo. *Storia del teatro inglese dalla Restaurazione all'Ottocento, 1660–1895.* Turin: Einaudi, 1997.

———, ed. *Storia della letteratura inglese,* 2 vols. Turin: Einaudi, 2000.

Bevis, Richard W. *English Drama: Restoration and Eighteenth Century, 1660–1789.* London: Longman, 1988.

Billi, Mirella. "Dal teatro al romanzo: Trasformazioni e transmodalizzazioni del dramma elisabettiano nella narrativa gotica inglese." *Anglistica* 28, no. 2 (1985): 7–46.

———. "Il Settecento." In *Storia della letteratura inglese*, vol. 1: *Dalle origini al Settecento,* ed. Paolo Bertinetti, 316–83. Turin: Einaudi, 2000.

———. "La recita delle passioni." In *Le passioni tra ostensione e riserbo,* ed. Romana Rutelli and Luisa Villa, 99–116. Pisa: Edizioni ETS, 2000.

Boaden, James. *Memoirs of Mrs. Siddons, Interspersed with Anecdotes of Authors and Actors.* London: Gibbings, 1893.

Boas, Frederick S. *An Introduction to Eighteenth-Century Drama.* Oxford: Oxford University Press, 1953.

Bond, Erik. "Flights of Madness: Self-Knowledge and Topography in the Cities of Burney and Dickens." *Literary London* 1, no. 1 (2003). Available online at http://www.literarylondon.org/london-journal/march2003/bond.html (accessed 27 May 2010).

Bray, Joe. *The Female Reader in the English Novel: From Burney to Austen.* New York: Routledge, 2009.

Brewer, John. *The Pleasures of the Imagination: English Culture in the Eighteenth Century.* London: HarperCollins, 1997.

Broome, Judith. "'Her Lovely Arm a Little Bloody': Richardson's Gothic Bodies." *Gothic Studies* 8 (2006): 9–21.

Brown, Laura. *Ends of Empire: Women and Ideology in Early Eighteenth-century English Literature.* Ithaca, N.Y.: Cornell University Press, 1993.

———. *English Dramatic Form, 1660–1760: An Essay in Generic History.* New Haven, Conn.: Yale University Press, 1981.

Budd, Adam. "Why Clarissa Must Die: Richardson's Tragedy and Editorial Heroism." *Eighteenth-Century Life* 31, no. 3 (2007): 1–28.

Burke, Edmund. *Reflections on the Revolution in France.* Ed. Conor Cruise O'Brien. Harmondsworth: Penguin, 1986.

Burney, Charles. *A General History of Music from the Earliest Ages to the Present Period* (1935), 2 vols., repr. ed. Ed. Frank Mercer. New York: Dover, 1957.

———. *Dr. Burney's Continental Travels, 1770–1772* (1927), repr. ed. Ed. Cedric Howard Glover. New York: AMS Press, 1978.

———. *Dr. Burney's Musical Tours in Europe,* 2 vols. Ed. Percy A. Scholes. London: Oxford University Press, 1959.

———. *The Present State of Music in France and Italy* (1771). London: Travis and Emery Music Bookshop, 2002.

———. *The Present State of Music in Germany, the Netherlands, and the United Provinces,* 2 vols. London: T. Becket, 1773.

Burney, Frances. *A Busy Day.* Ed. Tara Ghoshal Wallace. New Brunswick, N.J.: Rutgers University Press, 1984.

———. *Brief Reflections Relative to the Emigrant French Clergy.* London: T. Cadell, 1793.

———. *Camilla; or, A Picture of Youth.* Ed. Edward A. Bloom and Lillian D. Bloom. Oxford: Oxford University Press, 1983.

———. *Cecilia; or, Memoirs of an Heiress.* Ed. Peter Sabor and Margaret Anne Doody. Oxford: Oxford University Press, 1988.

———. *The Complete Plays of Frances Burney,* 2 vols. Ed. Peter Sabor. London: Pickering and Chatto, 1995.

———. *Diaries and Letters of Madame D'Arblay,* 6 vols. Ed. Austin Dobson. Basingstoke: Macmillan, 1904–1905.

———. *The Early Diary of Frances Burney, 1768–78,* 2 vols. Ed. Annie Raine Ellis. London: George Bell, 1889.

———. *The Early Journals and Letters of Fanny Burney,* 5 vols. Ed. Lars Troide, Stewart J. Cooke, and Betty Rizzo. Oxford: Oxford University Press, 1988–2012.

———. *Evelina; or, The History of a Young Lady's Entrance into the World.* Ed. Margaret Anne Doody. Harmondsworth: Penguin, 1994.

———. *The Journals and Letters of Fanny Burney (Madame D'Arblay), 1791–1840,* 12 vols. Ed. Joyce Hemlow, Curtis D. Cecil and Althea Douglas. Oxford: Oxford University Press, 1972–84.

———. *Memoirs of Doctor Burney, Arranged from His Own Manuscripts, from Family Papers, and Personal Recollections by His Daughter, Madame d'Arblay* (1832), 3 vols., repr. ed. New York: AMS Press, 1975.

———. *The Wanderer; or, Female Difficulties.* Ed. Margaret Anne Doody, Robert Mack, and Peter Sabor. Oxford: Oxford University Press, 1991.

———. "*The Witlings;* A Comedy by Frances Burney, A Sister of the Order: An Edition, with Supplementary Material." Ed. Clayton G. Delery. Ph.D. thesis, City University of New York, 1989.

———. *The Witlings.* In *The Meridian Anthology of Restoration and Eighteenth-Century Plays by Women,* ed. Katharine Rogers. New York: Meridian, 1994.

———. *"The Witlings"; and, "The Woman-Hater."* Ed. Peter Sabor and Geoffrey Sill. Peterborough, Ont.: Broadview, 2002.

Burney Society. "Annual General Meeting Minutes, 11 October 1996." *Burney Letter* 2, no. 2 (1996).

Campbell, D. Grant. "Fashionable Suicide: Conspicuous Consumption, and the Collapse of Credit in Frances Burney's *Cecilia.*" *Studies in Eighteenth-Century Culture* 20 (1989): 131–45.

Campbell, Jill. "'When Men to Women Turn': Gender Reversal in Fielding's Plays." In *The New Eighteenth Century: Theory, Politics, English Literature,* ed. Felicity Nussbaum and Laura Brown, 62–83. New York: Methuen, 1987.

Carchia, Gianni. *Retorica del sublime.* Bari: Laterza, 1990.

Castle, Terry. "The Carnivalization of Eighteenth-Century English Narrative." *PMLA* 99 (1984): 903–16.

———. "Eros and Liberty at the English Masquerade, 1710–1790." *Eighteenth-Century Studies* 17 (1983–84): 155–76.

———. *The Female Thermometer: Eighteenth-century Culture and the Invention of the Uncanny.* Oxford: Oxford University Press, 1995.

———. *Masquerade and Civilization: The Carnivalesque in Eighteenth-century English Culture and Fiction.* Stanford, Calif.: Stanford University Press, 1986.

Chisholm, Kate. *Fanny Burney: Her Life, 1752–1840.* London: Chatto and Windus, 1998.

———. "'Witlings' Takes a London Bow." *Burney Letter* 4, no. 1 (Spring 1998): 4.

Cibber, Colley. *The Careless Husband.* In *Three Sentimental Comedies,* ed. Maureen Sullivan, 85–174. New Haven, Conn.: Yale University Press, 1973.

———. *The Lady's Last Stake.* London: Bernard Lintott, 1707.

———. *Love's Last Shift; or, The Fool in Fashion.* In *Three Sentimental Comedies,* ed. Maureen Sullivan, 1–84. New Haven, Conn.: Yale University Press, 1973.

Clarke, Norma. *Dr. Johnson's Women.* London: Hambledon and London, 2000.

Clausen, Christoph. *Macbeth Multiplied: Negotiating Historical and Medial Difference between Shakespeare and Verdi.* Amsterdam: Rodopi, 2006.

Colman, George. *The Jealous Wife: A Comedy, as It Is Acted at the Theatre-Royal in Drury-Lane.* London: J. Newbery, 1761.

———. *Polly Honeycombe: A Dramatick Novel of One Act, as It Is Now Acted at the Theatre-Royal in Drury-Lane.* London: T. Becket and T. Davies, 1760.

Colman, George, and David Garrick. *The Clandestine Marriage.* In *Eighteenth-Century Plays,* ed. J. Hampden, 163–235. London: Dent, 1928.

Congreve, William. *Congreve's Amendments of Mr. Collier's False and Imperfect Citations.* London: J. Tonson, 1698.

———. *The Way of the World.* In *Restoration Plays,* ed. Robert Lawrence, 481–570. London: Everyman, 1994.

Copeland, Edward W. "Money in the Novels of Fanny Burney." *Studies in the Novel* 8 (1976): 24–37.

The Correspondents, an Original Novel; in a Series of Letters. London: T. Becket, 1775.

Cotton, Nancy. *Women Playwrights in England, c. 1363–1750.* Lewisburg, Penn.: Bucknell University Press, 1980.

Cox, Jeffrey N., ed. *Seven Gothic Dramas, 1789–1825.* Athens: Ohio University Press, 1992.

Craciun, Adriana. *Fatal Women of Romanticism.* Cambridge: Cambridge University Press, 2003.

Croker, John Wilson. "Review of *The Wanderer; or Female Difficulties,* by Madame D'Arblay." *Quarterly Review* 11 (April 1814): 123–30.

Craft-Fairchild, Catherine. *Masquerade and Gender: Disguise and Female Identity in Eighteenth-century Fictions by Women.* University Park: Pennsylvania State University Press, 1993.

Craik, T. W., Clifford Leech, and Lois Potter, eds. *The Revels History of Drama in English,* 8 vols. London: Methuen, 1975–83.

Crouch, K. A. "Mary Stephens Wells." *Oxford Dictionary of Literary Biography.* Available online at http://www.oxforddnb.com/view/article/29016 (accessed 8 October 2011).

Darby, Barbara. *Frances Burney Dramatist: Gender, Performance, and the Late Eighteenth-Century Stage.* Lexington: University Press of Kentucky, 1997.

Davies, Lennard. *Factual Fictions: The Origins of the English Novel.* New York: Columbia University Press, 1983.

Davis, Graham, and Penny Bonsall. *A History of Bath: Image and Reality.* Lancaster: Carnegie, 2006.

De Marinis, Marco. "Dramaturgy of the Spectator." *Drama Review* 31, no. 2 (1987): 100–14.

———. *The Semiotics of Performance.* Trans. Aine O'Healy. Bloomington: Indiana University Press, 1993.

DePorte, Michael V. *Nightmares and Hobbyhorses: Swift, Sterne, and Augustan Ideas of Madness.* San Marino, Calif.: Huntington Library, 1974.

Derrida, Jacques. *Specters of Marx: The State of the Debt, the Work of Mourning, and the New International.* Trans. Peggy Kamuf. London: Routledge, 1994.

Devlin, David D. *The Novels and Journals of Fanny Burney.* London: Macmillan, 1987.

Dobson, Michael. *The Making of the National Poet: Shakespeare, Adaptation and Authorship, 1660–1769.* Oxford: Clarendon, 1994.

Donizetti, Gaetano. *Lucia di Lammermoor.* Libretto by Salvatore Cammarano. Naples: Tipografia Flautina, 1935.

Donkin, Ellen. *Getting into the Act: Women Playwrights in London, 1776–1829.* London: Routledge, 1995.

Donohue, Joseph, ed. *The Cambridge History of British Theatre.* Cambridge: Cambridge University Press, 2004.

———. "The London Theatre at the End of the Eighteenth Century." In *The London Theatre World, 1660–1800,* ed. Robert Hume, 337–72. Carbondale: Southern Illinois University Press, 1980.

Doody, Margaret Anne. "Deserts, Ruins, and Troubled Waters: Female Dreams in Fiction and the Development of the Gothic Novel." *Genre* 10 (Winter 1977): 529–72.

———. *Frances Burney: The Life in the Works.* New Brunswick, N.J.: Rutgers University Press, 1988.

Downer, Alan S. "Nature to Advantage Dressed: Eighteenth-Century Acting." *PMLA* 58 (1943): 1002–37.

Dryden, John. *All for Love; or, the World Well Lost.* In *Restoration Plays,* ed. Robert Lawrence, 203–306. London: Everyman, 1994.

———. *Of Heroique Playes. An Essay.* In *The Works of John Dryden,* vol. 11, ed. E. N. Hooker, H. T. Swedenberg, and V. A. Dearing, 8–18. Berkeley: University of California Press, 1956–2000.

Duncombe, John. *The Feminiad. A Poem.* London: M. Cooper, 1754.

Dussinger, John A. "Hester Piozzi, Italy, and the Johnsonian Aether." *South Central Review* 9 (1992): 46–58.

Eco, Umberto. *The Role of the Reader: Explorations in the Semiotics of Texts.* London: Hutchinson, 1981.

———. *A Theory of Semiotics.* Bloomington: Indiana University Press, 1976.

Edelstein, T. J. "Vauxhall Gardens." In *Eighteenth-Century Britain,* vol. 5 of *The Cambridge Cultural History of Britain,* ed. Boris Ford, 203–15. Cambridge: Cambridge University Press, 1991.

Edgeworth, Maria. *Belinda.* Oxford: Oxford University Press, 1999.

Eger, Elizabeth, and Lucy Peltz, eds. *Brilliant Women: Eighteenth-Century Bluestockings.* London: National Portrait Gallery, 2008.

Elam, Keir. *The Semiotics of Theatre and Drama,* 2nd ed. New York: Routledge, 2002.

Ellis, Frank. *Sentimental Comedy: Theory and Practice.* Cambridge: Cambridge University Press, 1991.

Engel, Laura. "Notorious Celebrity: Mary Wells, Madness, and Theatricality." *Eighteenth-Century Women* 5 (2008): 181–205.

Epstein, Julia. "Fanny Burney's Epistolary Voices." *Eighteenth-Century* 27 (1986): 162–79.

———. *The Iron Pen: Frances Burney and the Politics of Women's Writing.* Madison: University of Wisconsin Press, 1989.

Etherege, George. *The Man of Mode; or, Sir Fopling Flutter, a Comedy: Acted at the Duke's Theatre.* London: J. Macock, 1676.

Fielding, Henry. "An Essay on the Knowledge of the Characters of Men." In *Miscellanies by Henry Fielding, Esq.*, vol. 1, ed. Henry Knight Miller. Oxford: Oxford University Press, 1972.

———. *The History and Adventures of Joseph Andrews and His Friend Mr. Abraham Adams.* In "*The History and Adventures of Joseph Andrews and His Friend Mr. Abraham Adams*" and "*An Apology for the Life of Mrs. Shamela Andrews,*" ed. Douglas Brooks Davies, 1–303. Oxford: Oxford University Press, 1990.

———. *The History of Tom Jones, a Foundling.* Ed. Doreen Roberts. Ware, UK: Wordsworth Editions, 1999.

———. *The Life of Mr. Jonathan Wild, the Great.* Ed. Hugh Amory, Linda Bree, and Claude Rawson. Oxford: Oxford University Press, 1999.

———. "The Masquerade." In *The Grub-Street Opera. As It Is Acted at the Theatre in the Hay-Market. By Scriblerus Secundus. To Which Is Added, The Masquerade, a Poem.* London: J. Roberts, 1731.

Fisk, Deborah Payne, ed. *The Cambridge Companion to English Restoration Theatre.* Cambridge: Cambridge University Press, 2000.

Folkenflik, Robert. "The New Model Eighteenth-Century Novel." *Eighteenth-Century Fiction* 12, no. 23 (January–April 2000): 459–78.

Foucault, Michel. *Discipline and Punish: The Birth of the Prison.* Trans. Alan Sheridan. Harmondsworth: Penguin, 1977.

———. *Madness and Civilization: A History of Insanity in the Age of Reason.* Trans. Richard Howard. London: Tavistock Publications, 1971.

Fraiman, Susan. *Unbecoming Women: British Women Writers and the Novels of Development.* New York: Columbia University Press, 1993.

The Friends; or, Original Letters of a Person Deceased, 2 vols. London: J. Bell, 1773.

Frye, Northrop. *Anatomy of Criticism: Four Essays.* Princeton, N.J.: Princeton University Press, 1957.

Gadeken, Sara. "Sarah Fielding and the Salic Law of Wit." *Studies in English Literature* 42 (2002): 541–57.

Garrick, David. *Bon Ton; or, High Life below Stairs.* In *Garrick's Own Plays, 1767–1775,* vol. 2 of *The Plays of David Garrick,* ed. Harry Pedicord and Frederick Bergan, 251–82. Carbondale-Edwardsville: Southern Illinois University Press, 1980.

———. *The Poetical Works of David Garrick, Esq.,* 2 vols. London: Printed for George Kearsley at Johnson's Head, Fleet-Street, 1785.

———. *The Private Correspondence of David Garrick,* 2 vols. Ed. James Boaden. London: H. Colburn and R. Bentley, 1831.

Gemmeke, Mascha. *Frances Burney and the Female Bildungsroman: An Interpretation of The Wanderer: or, Female Difficulties.* Frankfurt: Peter Lang, 2004.

Genette, Gérard. *Narrative Discourse: An Essay in Method.* Trans. Jane E. Lewin. Ithaca, N.Y.: Cornell University Press, 1980.

———. *Palimpsests: Literature in the Second Degree.* Trans. Channa Newman and Claude Doubinsky. Lincoln: University of Nebraska Press, 1997.

Gentleman, Francis. *The Dramatic Censor,* 2 vols. London: J. Bell, 1770.

Gilbert, Sandra, and Susan Gubar. *The Madwoman in the Attic: The Woman Writer and the Nineteenth-Century Literary Imagination.* New Haven, Conn.: Yale University Press, 1979.

Gill, Pat. "Gender, Sexuality, and Marriage." In *The Cambridge Companion to English Restoration Theatre,* ed. Deborah Payne Fisk, 191–208. Cambridge: Cambridge University Press, 2000.

Goldsmith, Oliver. *The Collected Works of Oliver Goldsmith,* 5 vols. Ed. Arthur Friedman. Oxford: Clarendon, 1966.

Gonda, Caroline. *Reading Daughters' Fictions, 1709–1834: Novels and Society from Manley to Edgeworth.* Cambridge: Cambridge University Press, 1996.

Goring, Paul. *The Rhetoric of Sensibility in Eighteenth-Century Culture.* Cambridge: Cambridge University Press, 2005.

Greenfield, Susan C. *Mothering Daughters: Novels and the Politics of Family Romance, Frances Burney to Jane Austen.* Detroit: Wayne State University Press, 2002.

———. "'Oh Dear Resemblance of Thy Murdered Mother': Female Authorship in *Evelina.*" *Eighteenth-Century Fiction* 3 (1991): 301–20.

Gregory, John. *A Father's Legacy to His Daughters.* London: Cadell, 1814.

Gubar, Susan. "The Female Monster in Augustan Satire." *Signs* 3 (1997): 380–94.

Hain, Bonnie, and Carole McAllister. "James Boswell's Ms. Perceptions and Samuel Johnson's Ms. Placed Friends." *South Central Review* 9 (1992): 59–70.

Harris, Jocelyn. "Protean Lovelace." In *Passion and Virtue: Essays on the Novels of Samuel Richardson,* ed. David Blewett, 92–113. Toronto: University of Toronto Press, 2001.

Hartpole-Lecky, William. *A History of London in the Eighteenth Century.* London: Longmans, Green, 1890.

Heller, Deborah. "Bluestocking Salons and the Public Sphere." *Eighteenth-Century Life* 22, no. 2 (1998): 59–82.

Hemlow, Joyce. "Fanny Burney and the Courtesy Books." *PMLA* 65 (1950): 732–61.

———. *The History of Fanny Burney.* Oxford: Clarendon Press, 1958.

Henderson, Andrea. "Burney's *The Wanderer* and Early-Nineteenth-Century Commodity Fetishism." *Nineteenth-Century Literature* 57 (2002): 1–30.

Hill, Aaron. *An Essay on the Art of Acting; in Which, the Dramatic Passions Are Properly Defined and Described.* London: J. Dixwell, 1779.

Howells, Coral Ann. *Love, Mystery, and Misery: Feeling in Gothic Fiction.* London: Athlone, 1978.

Hughes, Leo. *A Century of English Farce.* Princeton, N.J.: Princeton University Press, 1956.

———. "Theatrical Conventions in Richardson: Some Observations on a Novelist's Technique." In *Restoration and Eighteenth-Century Literary Essays in Honor of Alan Dougald McKillop,* ed. Carroll Camden, 239–50. Chicago: University of Chicago Press, 1963.

Hume, Robert D. *Henry Fielding and the London Theatre, 1728–1737.* Oxford: Oxford University Press, 1988.

Hunt, Elizabeth. "A Carnival of Mirrors: The Grotesque Body of the Eighteenth-Century English Masquerade." In *Lewd and Notorious: Female Transgression in the Eighteenth Century,* ed. Katharine Kittredge, 91–111. Ann Arbor: University of Michigan Press, 2003.

Hunt, Leigh. *Dramatic Essays,* 3 vols. Ed. William Archer and Robert W. Lowe. London: Walter Scott, 1894.

Hunter, J. Paul. *Before Novels: The Cultural Contexts of Eighteenth-Century English Fictions.* New York: Norton, 1990.

———. *Occasional Form: Henry Fielding and the Chains of Circumstance.* Baltimore: Johns Hopkins University Press, 1975.

Ingram, Allan, and Michelle Faubert. *Cultural Constructions of Madness in Eighteenth-Century Writing: Representing the Insane.* Basingstoke: Palgrave Macmillan, 2005.

Innocenti, Loretta. *La scena trasformata. Adattamenti neoclassici di Shakespeare.* Florence: Sansoni, 1995.

Johnson, Charles. *Caelia.* London: J. Watts, 1733.

Johnson, Odai. "Review of *The Witlings,* by Frances Burney." *Theatre Journal* 50 (1998): 543–44.

Johnson, Samuel. *Johnson on Shakespeare.* Ed. Walter Raleigh. Oxford: Clarendon, 1929.

———. *Lives of the English Poets,* 3 vols. Ed. G. B. Hill. Oxford: Clarendon, 1905.

———. *The Rambler* No. 4 (31 March 1750). In *The Yale Edition of the Works of Samuel Johnson,* vol. 3, ed. W. J. Bate and Albrecht B. Strauss, 19–25. New Haven, Conn.: Yale University Press, 1969.

Jones, Darryl. "Radical Ambivalence: Frances Burney, Jacobinism, and the Politics of Romantic Fiction." *Women's Writing* 10 (2003): 3–25.

Jones, Vivien, ed. *Women and Literature, 1700–1800.* Cambridge: Cambridge University Press, 2000.

———, ed. *Women in the Eighteenth Century: Constructions of Femininity.* London: Routledge, 1990.

Kaneko, Yuji, ed. *The Restoration Stage Controversy.* London: Routledge, 1996.

Kelly, Hugh. *The School for Wives: A Comedy.* London: T. Becket, 1774.

Kelly, Ian. "'A Busy Day' in the West End." *Burney Journal* 5 (2002): 18–42.

Kinkead-Weekes, Mark. *Samuel Richardson: Dramatic Novelist.* London: Methuen, 1973.

Knight's Cyclopaedia of London. London: Charles Knight, 1851.

Konigsberg, Ira. "The Dramatic Background of Richardson's Novels." *PMLA* 83 (1968): 43–53.

———. *Narrative Techniques in the English Novel: Defoe to Austen.* Hamden: Archon, 1985.

———. *Samuel Richardson and the Dramatic Novel.* Lexington: University of Kentucky Press, 1968.

Kowaleski-Wallace, Beth. *Their Fathers' Daughters: Hannah More, Maria Edgeworth and Patriarchal Complicity.* Oxford: Oxford University Press, 1991.

———. "Milton's Daughters: The Education of Eighteenth-Century Women Writers." *Feminist Studies* 12 (1986): 275–93.

Kristeva, Julia. *Powers of Horror: An Essay on Abjection.* Trans. Leon S. Roudiez. New York: Columbia University Press, 1982.

Kromm, Jane E. "The Feminization of Madness in Visual Representation." *Feminist Studies* 20 (1994): 507–35.

Laing, Ronald D. *The Divided Self.* London: Tavistock, 1960.

———. *The Self and Others.* London: Tavistock, 1961.

Laing, Ronald D., and Aaron Esterson. *Sanity, Madness, and the Family.* London: Tavistock, 1964.

Lavater, Johann Caspar. *Physiognomy; or, The Corresponding Analogy between the Conformation of the Features and the Ruling Passions of the Mind.* London: Cowie, Low, 1826.

Lee, Sophia. *The Recess; or, A Tale of Other Times.* London: T. Cadell, 1785.

Lewis, Matthew G. *The Castle Spectre.* In *The Hour of One: Six Gothic Melodramas,* ed. Stephen Wischhusen. London: Gordon Fraser, 1975.

Lewis, Peter. *Fielding's Burlesque Drama: Its Place in the Tradition.* Edinburgh: Edinburgh University Press, 1987.

Lillo, George. *The London Merchant.* In *Eighteenth-Century Plays,* ed. Ricardo Quintana, 287–342. New York: Random House, 1952.

Locke, John. *An Essay Concerning Human Understanding.* Ed. Peter H. Nidditch. Oxford: Oxford University Press, 1975.

Lockwood, Thomas, ed. *Plays. Volume 1: 1728–1731.* Wesleyan Edition of the Works of Henry Fielding. Oxford: Clarendon, 2004.

Loftis, John. *Comedy and Society from Congreve to Fielding.* Stanford, Calif.: Stanford University Press, 1959.

———. *Sheridan and the Drama of Georgian England.* Oxford: Blackwell, 1976.

The London Stage, 1660–1800. Carbondale: Southern Illinois University Press, 1960–68.

Lynch, Deidre Shauna. "Counter Publics: Shopping and Women's Sociability." In *Romantic Sociability: Social Networks and Literary Culture in Britain, 1770–1840,* ed. Gillian Russell and Clara Tuite, 211–36. Cambridge: Cambridge University Press, 2002.

Macalpine, Ida, and Richard Hunter. *George III and the Mad-Business.* London: Allen Lane, 1969.

Mackenzie, Henry. *The Man of Feeling.* London: T. Cadell, 1771.

Markley, Robert. "The Canon and Its Critics." In *The Cambridge Companion to English Restoration Theatre,* ed. Deborah Payne Fisk, 226–41. Cambridge: Cambridge University Press, 2000.

———. "Sentimentality as a Performance: Shafesbury, Sterne, and the Theatrics of Virtue." In *The New Eighteenth Century: Theory, Politics, English Literature,* ed. Felicity Nussbaum and Laura Brown, 210–30. New York: Methuen, 1987.

Marsden, Jean. "Modesty Unshackled: Dorothy Jordan and the Dangers of Cross-Dressing." *Studies in Eighteenth-Century Culture* 22 (1992): 21–35.

———. *The Re-Imagined Text: Shakespeare, Adaptation, and Eighteenth-Century Literary Theory.* Lexington: University Press of Kentucky, 1995.

———. "Spectacle, Horror and Pathos." In *The Cambridge Companion to English Restoration Theatre,* ed. Deborah Payne Fisk, 174–90. Cambridge: Cambridge University Press, 2000.

Martin, Philip. *Mad Women and Romantic Writing.* Sussex: Harvester, 1987.

McGirr, Elaine. *Eighteenth-Century Characters: A Guide to the Literature of the Age.* Basingstoke: Palgrave Macmillan, 2007.

———. "Why Lovelace Must Die." *Novel: A Forum on Fiction* 37 (2003–2004): 1–22.

McIntyre, Ian. *Garrick.* Harmondsworth: Penguin, 1999.

McKeon, Michael. *The Origins of the English Novel, 1660–1740.* Baltimore: Johns Hopkins University Press, 1987.

Merchant, William Moelwyn. "Francis Hayman's Illustrations of Shakespeare." *Shakespeare Quarterly* 9, no. 2 (1958): 141–47.

Miles, Dudley H. *The Influence of Molière on Restoration Comedy.* New York: Columbia University Press, 1910.

Moore, Edward. *The Gamester.* Augustan Reprint Society no. 14. New York: Kraus Reprint, 1967.

More, Hannah. *Strictures on the Modern System of Female Education. With a View of the Principles and Conduct Prevalent among Women of Rank and Fortune.* Dublin: William Porter, 1799.

Myers, Sylvia Harcstark. *The Bluestocking Circle: Women, Friendship, and the Life of the Mind in Eighteenth-Century England.* Oxford: Clarendon, 1990.

Nachumi, Nora. *Acting like a Lady: British Women Novelists and the Eighteenth-Century Theater.* New York: AMS Press, 2008.

Nicholson, Eric. "The Theater." In *Renaissance and Enlightenment Paradoxes,* vol. 3 of *A History of Women in the West,* ed. Natalie Zemon Davis and Arlette Farge, 295–314. Cambridge, Mass.: Harvard University Press, 1994.

Nicoll, Allardyce. *A History of English Drama, 1660–1900,* 6 vols. Cambridge: University Press, 1952–59.

———. *The World of Harlequin.* Cambridge: Cambridge University Press, 1963.

Noyes, Robert G. *The Neglected Muse: Restoration and Eighteenth-Century Tragedy in the Novel, 1740–1780.* Providence, R.I.: Brown University Press, 1958.

———. *The Thespian Mirror: Shakespeare in the Eighteenth-Century Novel.* Providence, R.I.: Brown University Press, 1953.

Nussbaum, Felicity, and Laura Brown, eds. *The New Eighteenth Century: Theory, Politics, English Literature.* New York: Methuen, 1987.

O'Brien, John. *Harlequin Britain: Pantomime and Entertainment, 1690–1760.* Baltimore: Johns Hopkins University Press, 2004.

Otway, Thomas. *The Orphan.* London: R. Bentley and M. Magnes, 1680.

———. *Venice Preserv'd; or, A Plot Discovered.* In *Restoration Plays,* ed. Robert Lawrence, 307–94. London: Dent, 1994.

Pagnini, Marcello. *Pragmatica della letteratura.* Palermo: Sellerio, 1980.

———. *Semiosi. Teoria ed ermeneutica del testo letterario.* Bologna: Il Mulino, 1988.

Papetti, Viola. "Letteratura e arti figurative nel Settecento." In *Il Settecento. Il Romanticismo. Il Vittorianesimo,* vol. 2 of *Storia della civiltà letteraria inglese,* ed. Franco Marenco, 276–96. Turin: Utet, 1996.

Park, Julie. "Pains and Pleasures of the Automaton: Frances Burney's Mechanics of Coming Out." *Eighteenth-Century Studies* 40 (2006): 23–49.

Park, William. "Clarissa as Tragedy." *Studies in English Literature* 16, no. 3 (1976): 461–71.

Parnell, Paul E. "A Source for the Duel Scene in 'The Conscious Lovers.'" *Notes and Queries* 9 (1962): 13–15.

Pavis, Patrice. *Dictionary of the Theatre: Terms, Concepts, and Analysis.* Trans. Christine Shantz. Toronto: University of Toronto Press, 1998.

Pearson, Jacqueline. *The Prostituted Muse: Images of Women and Women Dramatists, 1642–1737.* Hemel Hempstead: Harvester Wheatsheaf, 1988.

Pedicord, Harry William. *The Theatrical Public in the Time of Garrick.* Carbondale: Southern Illinois University Press, 1954.

Poovey, Mary. *The Proper Lady and the Woman Writer: Ideology as Style in the Works of Mary Wollstonecraft, Mary Shelley, Jane Austen.* Chicago: University of Chicago Press, 1984.

Pope, Alexander. "An Essay on Criticism." In *The Poems of Alexander Pope,* ed. John Butt, 143–68. London: Methuen, 1980.

Prose, Francine. *The Lives of the Muses: Nine Women and the Artists They Inspired.* New York: Harper Perennial, 2003.

Ranger, Paul. *"Terror and Pity Reign in Every Breast": Gothic Drama in the London Patent Theatres, 1750–1820.* London: Society for Theatre Research, 1991.

Raven, James, Helen Small, and Naomi Tadmor, eds. *The Practice and Representation of Reading in England.* Cambridge: Cambridge University Press, 1996.

"Reconsidering the Rise of the Novel." *Eighteenth-Century Fiction* 12, nos. 2–3 (January–April 2000).

Ribeiro, Aileen. *The Dress Worn at Masquerades in England, 1730 to 1790.* New York: Garland, 1984.

———. "'Turquerie': Turkish Dress and English Fashion in the Eighteenth Century." *Connoisseur* 201 (May 1979): 16–23.

Richardson, Samuel. *Clarissa; or, The History of a Young Lady.* Ed. Angus Ross. Harmondsworth: Penguin, 1985.

———. *The History of Sir Charles Grandison.* Ed. Jocelyn Harris. Oxford: Oxford University Press, 1986.

———. *Pamela; or, Virtue Rewarded.* Ed. Peter Sabor. Harmondsworth: Penguin, 1985.

Ricoeur, Paul. *Memory, History, Forgetting.* Trans. Kathleen Blamey and David Pellauer. Chicago: University of Chicago Press, 2004.

Rivero, Albert, and George Justice, eds. *The Eighteenth-Century Novel,* 8 vols. New York: AMS Press, 2001–10.

Roach, Joseph R. *The Player's Passion: Studies in the Science of Acting.* Newark: University of Delaware Press, 1985.

Rousseau, Jean-Jacques. *A Letter from M. Rousseau, of Geneva, to M. D'Alembert, of Paris, Concerning the Effects of Theatrical Entertainments on the Manners of Mankind.* London: Printed for J. Nourse, 1759.

Rowe, Nicholas. *The Fair Penitent.* Ed. Malcom Goldstein. London: Arnold, 1969.

———. *Tamerlane.* London: Tonson, 1702.

———. *The Tragedy of Jane Shore.* In *Eighteenth-Century Plays,* ed. Ricardo Quintana, 57–108. New York: Random House, 1952.

Roy, Donald, ed. *Romantic and Revolutionary Theatre, 1789–1860.* Cambridge: Cambridge University Press, 2003.

Sabor, Peter, ed. *The Cambridge Companion to Frances Burney.* Cambridge: Cambridge University Press, 2007.

Saggini, Francesca. "A Stage of Tears and Terror: Il teatro (gotico) di fine Settecento." In *Il teatro della paura: Scenari gotici del Romanticismo europeo,* ed. Diego Saglia and Giovanna Silvani, 61–76. Rome: Bulzoni, 2005.

———. "Identità a soggetto. Figurazioni dell'attore nella cultura inglese del Settecento." In *Narrare/Rappresentare. Incroci di segni tra immagine e parola,* ed. Diego Saglia and Giovanna Silvani, 33–49. Bologna: Clueb, 2003.

———. "Memories beyond the Pale: The Eighteenth-Century Actress between Stage and Closet." *Restoration and Eighteenth-Century Theatre Research* 19 (2004): 43–63.

———. "Radcliffe's Novels and Boaden's Dramas: Bringing the Configurations of the Gothic on Stage." In *Rites of Passage: Rational/Irrational, Natural/Supernatural, Local/Global,* proceedings of the 20th conference of the Italian Society for the Study of English (Catania-Ragusa, 4–6 October 2001), ed. Carmela Nocera, Gemma Persico, and Rosario Portale, 193–203. Soveria Mannelli: Rubbettino, 2003.

Salih, Sara. "*Camilla* and *The Wanderer.*" In *The Cambridge Companion to Frances Burney,* ed. Peter Sabor, 39–54. Cambridge: Cambridge University Press, 2007.

Schiff, Gert. *Zeichnungen von Johann Heinrich Füssli.* Zurich: Schweizerisches Institut für Kunstwissenschaft, 1959.

Scott, Walter. *The Bride of Lammermoor.* London: Everyman, 1988.

Sechelski, Denise. "Garrick's Body and the Labor of Art in Eighteenth-Century Theater." *Eighteenth-Century Studies* 29 (1996): 369–89.

Sedgwick, Eve Kosofsky. *The Coherence of Gothic Conventions.* London: Methuen, 1986.

Serpieri, Alessandro. Introduction to *Amleto,* by William Shakespeare. Milan: Feltrinelli, 1980.

———. "Ipotesi teorica di segmentazione di un testo teatrale." In *Come comunica il teatro. Dal testo alla scena,* ed. Alfonso Cantiani, Keir Elam, Roberto Guiducci, Paola Gullì Pugliatti, Tomaso Kemeny, Marcello Pagnini, Romana Rutelli, and Alessandro Serpieri, 11–54. Milan: Il Formichiere, 1978.

Serpieri, Alessandro, Keir Elam, Paola Gullì Pugliatti, Tomaso Kemeny, and Romana Rutelli. "Towards a Segmentation of the Dramatic Text." *Poetics Today* 2 (1981): 163–200.

Shadwell, Thomas. *The Squire of Alsatia.* London: James Knapton, 1688.

Shakespeare, William. *King Lear, a Tragedy, Altered from Shakspeare by D. Garrick, Marked with the Variations in the Manager's Book at the Theatre-Royal in Drury-Lane.* London: C. Bathurst, 1786.

Sherburn, George. "Samuel Richardson's Novels and the Theatre: A Theory Sketched." *Philological Quarterly* 41, no. 1 (January 1962): 325–29.

———. "'Writing to the Moment': One Aspect." In *Restoration and Eighteenth-Century Literary Essays in Honor of Alan Dougald McKillop,* ed. Carroll Camden, 201–209. Chicago: University of Chicago Press, 1963.

Shelley, Mary. *Frankenstein; or, The Modern Prometheus.* Ed. M. K. Joseph. Oxford: Oxford University Press, 1991.

Sheridan, Richard Brinsley. *The Critic.* In *Sheridan's Plays,* ed. Cecil Price, 331–86. Oxford: Oxford University Press, 1989.

———. *The School for Scandal.* In *Sheridan's Plays,* ed. Cecil Price, 217–300. Oxford: Oxford University Press, 1989.

Showalter, Elaine. *The Female Malady: Women, Madness and English Culture, 1830–1980.* London: Virago, 1995.

———. "Representing Ophelia: Women, Madness, and the Responsibilities of Feminist Criticism." In *Hamlet,* by William Shakespeare, ed. Susan Wofford, 220–40. Boston: St. Martin's Press, 1994.

Silverman, Debra. "Reading Frances Burney's *The Wanderer; or, Female Difficulties:* The Politics of Women's Independence." *Pacific Coast Philology* 26 (1991): 68–77.

Small, Helen. *Love's Madness: Medicine, the Novel, and Female Identity, 1800–1865.* Oxford: Clarendon, 1996.

Southam, Brian. *Jane Austen's Literary Manuscripts: A Study of the Novelist's Development through the Surviving Papers.* Oxford: Oxford University Press, 1964.

Spacks, Patricia M. *Imagining a Self: Autobiography and Novel in Eighteenth-Century England.* Cambridge, Mass.: Harvard University Press, 1976.

———. *Novel Beginnings: Experiments in Eighteenth-Century English Fiction.* New Haven, Conn.: Yale University Press, 2006.

Spencer, Jane. *The Rise of the Woman Novelist: From Aphra Behn to Jane Austen.* Oxford: Blackwell, 1986.

Spengemann, William. "The Earliest American Novel: Aphra Behn's *Oroonoko.*" *Nineteenth-Century Fiction* 38 (1984): 384–414.

Staves, Susan. "A Few Kind Words for the Fop." *Studies in English Literature* 22 (1982): 413–28.

———. "Fatal Marriages? Restoration Plays Embedded in Eighteenth-Century Novels." In *Augustan Studies: Essays in Honor of Irvin Ehrenpreis,* ed. Douglas L. Patey and Timothy Keegan, 95–107. Newark: University of Delaware Press, 1985.

Steele, Richard. *The Conscious Lovers.* In *Eighteenth-Century Plays,* ed. Ricardo Quintana, 109–178. New York: Random House, 1952.

———. *The Lying Lover: or, the Ladies Friendship.* London: Bernard Lintott, 1704.

Steele, Richard, and Joseph Addison. *Selections from the "Tatler" and the "Spectator."* Ed. Angus Ross. Harmondsworth: Penguin, 1982.

Stepankowsky, Paula. "Plaque Wording Proposed." *Burney Letter* 4, no. 2 (Fall 1998): 3.

Stone, George Winchester, Jr. "*A Midsummer Night's Dream* in the Hands of Garrick and Colman." *PMLA* 54 (1939): 467–82.

Stone, Lawrence. *The Family, Sex, and Marriage in England 1500–1800.* New York: Harper and Row, 1979.

Straub, Kristina. *Sexual Suspects: Eighteenth-Century Players and Ideology.* Princeton, N.J.: Princeton University Press, 1992.

Swift, Jonathan. *The Works of Jonathan Swift,* 19 vols. Ed. Walter Scott. Edinburgh: Constable, 1814.

Tate, Nahum. *The History of King Lear.* Ed. James Black. London: Edward Arnold, 1976.

Tave, Stuart. *The Amiable Humorist: A Study in the Comic Theory and Criticism of the Eighteenth and Early Nineteenth Century.* Chicago: University of Chicago Press, 1960.

Tessari, Roberto. *Teatro e spettacolo nel Settecento.* Rome: Laterza, 1997.

Thrale, Hester. *Thraliana: The Diary of Mrs. Hester Lynch Thrale (Later Mrs. Piozzi), 1776–1809,* 2 vols. Ed. Katharine C. Baldeston. Oxford: Clarendon, 1942.

Thompson. Helen. "How *The Wanderer* Works: Reading Burney and Bourdieu." *English Literary History* 68 (2001): 965–89.

Todd, Janet. "Posture and Imposture: The Gothic Manservant in Ann Radcliffe's *The Italian.*" *Women and Literature* 2 (1982): 25–38.

Tomalin, Claire. *Mrs. Jordan's Profession.* New York: Alfred Knopf, 1995.

Tomlinson, Edward Murray. *A History of the Minories, London.* London: Smith, Elder, 1907.

Townley, James. *High Life below Stairs.* London: J. Barker, 1803.

Tucker, Kathryn. "Joanna Baillie's and Elizabeth Inchbald's Moral Aesthetics: Humanizing Actors and Madmen." *European Romantic Review* 17 (2006): 335–40.

Varey, Simon. *Space and the Eighteenth-Century English Novel.* Cambridge: Cambridge University Press, 1990.

Wallace, Tara Ghoshal. "Frances Burney as Dramatist." In *The Cambridge Companion to Frances Burney,* ed. Peter Sabor, 55–74. Cambridge: Cambridge University Press, 2007.

Walpole, Horace. *Horace Walpole's Correspondence with Sir Horace Mann.* Ed. W. S. Lewis, W. H. Smith, and G. L. Lan. New York: Yale University Press, 1955–67.

Warner, William Beatty. *Licensing Entertainment: The Elevation of Novel Reading in England 1684–1750.* Berkeley: University of California Press, 1998.

Watt, Ian. *The Rise of the Novel: Studies in Defoe, Richardson, and Fielding.* 1957. Berkeley: University of California Press, 2000.

Wheatley, Christopher. "Tragedy." In *The Cambridge Companion to English Restora-*

tion Theatre, ed. Deborah Payne Fisk, 70–85. Cambridge: Cambridge University Press, 2000.

Wilcox, John. *The Relation of Molière to Restoration Comedy.* New York: Columbia University Press, 1938.

Wilkins, A. N. "John Dennis and Poetic Justice." *Notes and Queries* 202 (October 1957): 421–24.

Williams, Andrew P. *The Restoration Fop: Gender Boundaries and Comic Characterization in Later Seventeenth-Century Drama.* Lewiston, N.Y.: E. Mellen, 1995.

Williams, Anne. "Horace in Italy: Discovering a Gothic Imagination." *Gothic Studies* 8 (2006): 22–34.

Wollstonecraft, Mary. *A Vindication of the Rights of Woman.* In *Political Writings,* ed. Janet Todd, 63–284. Oxford: Oxford University Press, 1994.

———. *"Mary" and "The Wrongs of Woman."* Ed. Gary Kelly. Oxford University Press, 1980.

Woo, Celestine. "Sarah Siddons's Performances as Hamlet: Breaching the Breeches Part." *European Romantic Review* 18 (2007): 573–95.

Woods, Leigh. *Garrick Claims the Stage: Acting as Social Emblem in Eighteenth-Century England.* Westport, Conn.: Greenwood, 1984.

Wordsworth, William. *The Prelude; or, Growth of a Poet's Mind.* Ed. Ernest De Selincourt. Oxford: Oxford University Press, 1928.

Wycherley, William, *The Plain Dealer.* Ed. James L. Smith. New York: W. W. Norton, 1979.

Zimbardo, Rose. "Aphra Behn: A Dramatist in Search of the Novel." In *Curtain Calls: British and American Women and the Theatre, 1660–1820,* ed. Mary Anne Schofield and Cecilia Macheski, 371–82. Athens: Ohio University Press, 1991.

Zonitch, Barbara. *Familiar Violence: Gender and Social Upheaval in the Novels of Frances Burney.* Newark: University of Delaware Press, 1997.

Zorzi, Ludovico. *Il teatro e la città. Saggi sulla scena italiana.* Turin: Einaudi, 1977.

Zunshine, Liza. *Bastards and Foundlings: Illegitimacy in Eighteenth-Century England.* Columbus: Ohio State University Press, 2005.

Index

Page numbers in italics refer to figures.

WINNERS OF THE WALKER COWEN MEMORIAL PRIZE

Elizabeth Wanning Harries
The Unfinished Manner: Essays on the Fragment in the Later Eighteenth Century

Catherine Cusset
No Tomorrow: The Ethics of Pleasure in the French Enlightenment

Lisa Jane Graham
If the King Only Knew: Seditious Speech in the Reign of Louis XV

Suvir Kaul
Poems of Nation, Anthems of Empire: English Verse in the Long Eighteenth Century

Richard Nash
Wild Enlightenment: The Borders of Human Identity in the Eighteenth Century

Howard G. Brown
Ending the French Revolution: Violence, Justice, and Repression from the Terror to Napoleon

Jewel L. Spangler
Virginians Reborn: Anglican Monopoly, Evangelical Dissent, and the Rise of the Baptists in the Late Eighteenth Century

Theresa Braunschneider
Our Coquettes: Capacious Desire in the Eighteenth Century

James D. Drake
The Nation's Nature: How Continental Presumptions Gave Rise to the United States of America

Francesca Saggini
Backstage in the Novel: Frances Burney and the Theater Arts
Translated by Laura Kopp